Praise for *Intui*

MW00640624

"300 years ago Jonathan Swift warned, 'It's useless to try to reason a man out of a thing he wasn't reasoned into.' With scientifically-grounded evidence, Stephen Genco documents how traditional marketing ignores this counsel by seeking to move consumers via rational, persuasive argumentation rather than by aligning with their intuitive operating systems. Marketers would do well to take into account the considerable evidence in this book when structuring their messages."
—ROBERT CIALDINI, author of *Influence* and *Pre-Suasion*

"I recommend you buy several different packets of excitingly colored Post-It Notes to accompany this book, as you will read it once and then refer to it one hundred times more."
—RORY SUTHERLAND, Vice Chairman, *Ogilvy*, author of *Alchemy: The Surprising Power of Ideas that Don't Make Sense*

"This is a very interesting, useful, and wise book. I look forward to plundering it deeply."
—LES BINET, co-author of *The Long and the Short of It*, Head of Effectiveness, *Adam & Eve DDB*

"With his new book, Steve Genco will challenge the way you think about marketing and challenge you to be better at your craft."
—NIR EYAL, author of *Hooked* and *Indistractable*

"Intuitive Marketing is the most comprehensive marketing science book you will read. Steve Genco does an incredible job exploring both neurological and psychological sciences to give readers a well-rounded perspective on all things behavior. If you are a fan of behavioral economics, behavioral design or just science-based marketing, this book is for you. Don't "over-think" this purchase. Go with your intuition and add this book to your marketing library."
—WILL LEACH, Founder, *Triggerpoint Design*, author of *Marketing to Mindstates*

"This book is a gift of wisdom and practical help that moves the conversation, practice, and execution forward."
—PETE TRAINOR, author of *Hippo: Human-Focused Digital*

"Many of my heroes are in this book, from Antonio Damasio to Daniel Kahneman and others. Add Steve Genco to that list. It's rare in my experience to find a book that comprehensively covers a topic judiciously and with deft humor and a constant eye to what's practical. Against the usual suspects—either stubborn, old-fashioned viewpoints repainted to look fresh, or huge puffballs of hype—here's the real thing. Read to learn, enjoy, and profit."
—DAN HILL, Founder, *Sensory Logic*, author of *Emotionomics* and
First Blush: People's Intuitive Reactions to Famous Art

"In this follow-up book to *Neuromarketing for Dummies*, Steve Genco clearly presents a sophisticated and informative update of intuitive marketing tactics by boiling up a vast array of theoretical research into a compelling read that I have recommended to both my academic and commercial colleagues. Steve presents a comprehensive, concise and entertaining array of classic and current research, all meant to galvanize brand success through informed strategy."
—KIMBERLY ROSE CLARK, PhD, Lecturer & Researcher,
Dartmouth College Department of Psychological & Brain Science,
Co-Founder, Chief Research Officer of *Merchant Mechanics*

"Learning in biology, psychology and the social sciences have given us new understanding of how people behave. Far from the rational 'homo economicus' beast most marketing has been built around, people are intuitive by nature and nurture. *Intuitive Marketing* draws a better map of how marketing should work and its conclusions are far from intuitive, A provocative, and important, read to inspire us to make marketing that actually works."
—GARETH KAY, Co-founder of *Chapter*, "a new type of creative studio"

"Every marketer and aspiring marketer needs to read this book. For a select few it will confirm their current practice. For a majority it will offer new insights and a deep understanding of how consumers make purchase decisions and how marketers can shape them."
—PETER STEIDL, Founder at *Neurothinking*, author of
The Market Research Revolution and *Neurobranding*

INTUITIVE MARKETING

INTUITIVE MARKETING

What Marketers Can Learn from Brain Science

Stephen J. Genco, PhD

Published by Intuitive Consumer Insights LLC
Email: books@intuitiveconsumer.com
Website: www.intuitiveconsumer.com

For information about discounts available for bulk purchases, sales promotions, fund-raising, and educational needs, contact ICI at books@inuitiveconsumer.com

Cover design and internal formatting by Ghislain Viau
Creative Publishing Book Design

The information provided in this book is for general informational and educational purposes only. The author makes no representations or warranties, express or implied, about the completeness, accuracy, reliability, suitability or availability of any information or advice contained in this book. Any use of this information is at your own risk.

First printing, ebook, paperback, and hardback, October 2019

ISBN-13: 978-0-578-56362-6 (ebook)
ISBN-13: 978-0-578-56361-9 (paperback)
ISBN-13: 978-0-578-57696-1 (hardback)

Printed in the United States of America

Table of Contents

Acknowledgments

For the most part, this book is the product of five years of obsessive isolation and minimal collaboration. However, I did poke my head up once in a while to share a few of my ideas about the future of marketing. In that regard, I would like to thank the 200 or so students and marketers who attended my Stanford University Continuing Studies course, *Neuromarketing: How Brain Science Is Changing Marketing As We Know It*, between 2016 and 2018. You helped me work through many of the ideas that eventually turned into this book.

The following friends, colleagues, generous marketers, and brain scientists kindly read and provided feedback on parts of the book or the manuscript as a whole: Les Binet, Robert Cialdini, Kimberly Rose Clark, Nir Eyal, Dan Hill, Gareth Kay, Will Leach, Thomas Ramsøy, Byron Sharp, Richard Silberstein, Peter Steidl, Rory Sutherland, Pete Trainor, and Leon Zurawicki.

I can't thank my agent or my editor because I don't have either. I do want to thank the folks at *Kindle Direct Publishing* and *IngramSpark*, who were extremely helpful in guiding me through the preparation and publication of my manuscript for ebook and print-on-demand distribution through their channels. My marketing team consists of whomever at *Amazon* maintains and promotes my book page and whomever at *IngramSpark* makes my book accessible to booksellers and libraries around the world. My publicist team consists of all my readers who have found the book useful enough to spread the word to friends and colleagues that there is something worth reading here.

I want to thank Ghislain Viau at *Creative Publishing Book Design* for the eye-catching cover and internal formatting that make this very dense book more approachable and readable than it ever would have been in my hands alone.

Finally, a special thanks to my wife and family, who never really thought this project would come to an end. Surprise!

A Note on *Quick Read* Boxes

Throughout the book, you will find snippets of text presented in a bold, boxed format like this:

> **This is a *Quick Read* box. It pulls out and highlights important sentences in the main text that summarize key points and findings.**

Think of these boxes as "pre-highlighting" key passages that contain important ideas you don't want to miss. They are not "pull-outs" that repeat statements from elsewhere in the text (like you might find in a long magazine essay). They are parts of the text that belong right where they appear.

For the really time-pressed reader, flipping through the book and reading only these boxes will give you a basic understanding of the most important ideas in *Intuitive Marketing*. Yes, you can "consume" the essence of this book in 45 minutes or less! I do not recommend you *only* read the book this way, but I recognize there may be times when you want to "cut to the chase" and leave the details for later.

I suggest you use the *Quick Read* boxes as a series of signposts for navigating through the book's many claims and arguments, each box essentially summarizing a key takeaway from that point in the text. *Quick Read* boxes are also an excellent tool for re-reading or browsing *Intuitive Marketing*. Ideal for short attention span readers ... or busy marketing professionals.

Introduction

I n this book I introduce a different way to think about marketing. I call it *intuitive marketing*. It is built on a foundation of discoveries that have emerged across multiple scientific disciplines—in particular neuroscience, social psychology, and behavioral economics—over the last few decades.

> To date, intuitive marketing has been somewhat hidden from the marketing world and from consumers. For the most part, it has been buried within an approach to market research called *neuromarketing*.

I know something about neuromarketing, having toiled in its vineyards since 2006. Misnamed and misunderstood, neuromarketing has not achieved the uptake we all expected and hoped for in those early days, when we were sure our radical new measurement techniques would sweep away the old world of consumer surveys and self-reports, ushering in a new era of deep understanding of the real needs, motivations, and decision processes of consumers.[1] Eventually, I believe I figured out what went wrong,[2] and the result of that realization is this book.

Neuromarketing is not a form of marketing, as the name erroneously implies. If we define neuromarketing literally as "marketing to the brain," then let's be honest, all marketing is neuromarketing. Neuromarketing is simply a new set of methods and tools for measuring how people respond to marketing, advertising, products, and brands in both conscious and unconscious ways.

> Neuromarketing adds unconscious measures to the market researcher's toolkit, that is basically all it does.

But even that relatively modest contribution to research techniques and methodologies, although well-supported by decades of scientific findings, has not been received without controversy. Indeed, it has been met with resistance and skepticism by many marketers,[3] especially those who have only heard about it through popular media and press accounts. One of my goals in this book is to show that much of this skepticism is misplaced, because it is based on a serious misunderstanding of the unconscious, how it works, and how it interacts with our conscious minds. Shockingly, our popular press does not always get it right when it comes to understanding science.

But this is not the only reason neuromarketing has failed to catch on. In my 2013 book with Andrew Pohlmann and Peter Steidl, *Neuromarketing for Dummies*, we identified a new model for understanding consumers, which we called the *intuitive consumer model*. I revisit that model in Chapter 1, but the gist of it is simply this: intuitive consumers think, choose, and behave very differently from how the traditional marketing model assumes they do. The difference is so profound, as we will see, that it is not just new measures that are required to understand intuitive consumers.

> **What is required is that marketers ask *new questions*, and actually conduct marketing in *new ways*, and that is what intuitive marketing is all about.**

That's the insight that got me started writing this book. Marketers need to change how they do marketing. And this new way to do marketing, oriented around reaching and communicating to intuitive consumers, is what I call intuitive marketing.

As an initial exploration into intuitive marketing, this book is not going to be perfect. But we need to get started. I believe marketing has driven into a kind of cul-de-sac, and serious new thinking is required. In our modern, media-saturated world, marketing and advertising are everywhere.

> **Marketers cry out to be noticed, to "rise above the clutter," to achieve "stopping power," but to average consumers, it's all clutter, it's all annoying, it's all an imposition on their already overworked conscious minds, and they have no desire to stop and listen.**

For the sake of both those who sell and those who buy the goods and services that drive our modern global economy, we can do better. And I believe intuitive marketing offers a promising path forward.

Chapter 1

The Promise of Intuitive Marketing

Reaching the Intuitive Consumer

"These are not the droids you're looking for"
–Obi Wan Kenobi

There is more to consumers, and more to marketing, than meets the conscious mind.

Marketers are just beginning to appreciate the many and varied roles the unconscious plays in consumer responses, choices, and behavior. But for the most part, they are still in the mode of watching, learning, and waiting. Marketing *practice* has so far changed very little. Marketers remain concerned with the same topics they have always been concerned with: promoting (including advertising in all its forms), packaging, pricing, and placing products and brands. They also continue to maintain a fuzzy boundary with their sister discipline, *sales*.

This book is about how marketing is going to change in response to findings from the brain sciences. In the chapters that follow, I will show how a new kind of marketing is emerging, based on a scientific model of consumer choice and behavior that embraces the mechanisms and functions of both unconscious and conscious processing in the mind. I call this new approach *intuitive marketing*.

In contrast, the *persuasive marketing model* that has dominated marketing practice for decades has operated on two basic assumptions. First, consumers are essentially *rational decision makers* in the sense that they decide to buy one product rather than another based on a logical comparison of product benefits or attributes. And second, the preferences and behavior of these rational consumers can best be influenced using the following formula: first grab their *attention*, then communicate to them *persuasive arguments* that show why your product is superior to others,

1

then *repeat* those arguments until they are committed to memory, then *activate* that memory when the consumer is at a point of sale.

But as we shall see, an overwhelming body of research across several brain science disciplines tells us unequivocally that these assumptions are wrong. Human beings are seldom rational decision makers—especially when they are acting as consumers—and direct persuasion is an effective way to influence their behavior only in limited circumstances—none of which apply in the majority of marketing contexts. Instead, brain science tells us that consumers are usually *intuitive decision makers* who do not pay much attention to marketing, resist explicit persuasive messaging, seldom make product choices based on information and logic, employ processes they are not consciously aware of to make decisions, and have extremely faulty memories.

In other words, brain science tells us that traditional marketing has been looking in the wrong place.

Rational consumers are not the droids marketers should be looking for (apologies to Obi Wan Kenobi).

It is important to recognize a nuance here. Marketers today do not walk around with a little card in their pockets describing the rational consumer model for easy reference. On the contrary, most would argue that this is an archaic model that has little to do with the sophisticated approaches they deploy today. But over the years, this model has become embedded in the methods of marketing research, so it continues to influence marketing by influencing the ways in which marketers measure the effectiveness of their marketing and advertising messages. For example, marketers are obsessed with attention, and spend significant time and effort attempting to create messages that will be noticed, preferably at the expense of competing marketing messages that are clamoring to achieve the same result. They do this because they believe attention is required to deliver a persuasive message and make it memorable. Many of the variables marketers regularly measure in their survey questionnaires, such as "attitude toward the ad," "attitude toward the brand," and "purchase intent," are all measures of conscious responses to the persuasive content of the marketing message. Finally, the most prominent metric used to measure marketing success is "recall," a conscious memory measure that captures how well a message can be spontaneously remembered at a later point in time. Good recall is seen as a prerequisite for later action at a point of sale after exposure to a message. A whole industry, including some billion dollar companies, has been built up around the measurement of conscious attention, persuasion, and recall.

Eight Brain Science Findings that Change Marketing as We Know It

Traditional marketing—with its emphasis on attention, information, persuasion, and recall—is based on a set of assumptions about how consumers think, act, and respond to marketing. In *Neuromarketing for Dummies*, we called this set of assumptions the *rational consumer model*. We also could have called it the *engaged consumer model* or the *intentional consumer model*. The key idea behind this perspective is that consumers use conscious thinking and deliberation to decide what, when, and where to buy, and can be influenced by marketers who address that conscious reasoning process with persuasive marketing messages that will be committed to memory.

Intuitive marketing is also built on a set of foundational principles about how consumers think, act, and respond to marketing, which we called in *Neuromarketing for Dummies* the *intuitive consumer model*. As we have seen, the assumptions underlying intuitive marketing paint quite a different picture of the consumer than those underlying persuasive marketing. In the next sixteen chapters we will look closely at these principles, the science behind them, and the implications they hold for marketers, consumers, and the emerging practice of intuitive marketing.

Here are eight brain science findings upon which the house of intuitive marketing is built, along with a preview of when and where we will explore them in more detail in the following pages.

We sense and respond to signals around us even when we are not paying attention

Most marketers assume that attention is a required first step in any marketing communication. Under a purely conscious processing model, this seems self-evident. But conscious perception is only a subset of the ways in which our brains take in features of the world around us. As we will see in Chapter 3 and Chapter 4, intuitive marketing treats attention as a tool in the marketer's toolkit, not as a goal, and definitely not as *the* goal of marketing.

> **Sometimes intuitive marketers want to wake up attention and sometimes they want to let it sleep.**

The role of attention in marketing is closely connected to the role of *System 2* conscious processing in marketing, because attention is the gateway to conscious processing. In Chapter 3 we will see why this is the case and discuss how and when attention can be most effectively attracted—to the mutual benefit of both marketers and consumers. In Chapter 4 we will consider how marketing can operate in the absence of attention and explore ways in which intuitive marketing can be effective in both low-attention and no-attention conditions.

We infer value and meaning from ease of processing

Chapter 6 introduces the concept of *processing fluency*.

> **Brain scientists often describe the human brain as a *cognitive miser*. Given the choice, our brains prefer less conscious thinking to more.**

Attraction to processing fluency—things or situations that are easy to process mentally—is one of the key unconscious strategies our brains use to conserve cognitive energy while ascribing value and meaning to features of the world around us. But the importance of processing fluency goes well beyond this basic principle. We not only prefer fluency to disfluency, but we also unconsciously endow easy-to-process things with additional positive meaning and value. We tend to see them as more familiar, more likable, more beautiful, more true, and less risky. The implications for marketing are considerable, as we will see in Chapter 6.

Our preferences are largely constructed in the moment

Another concept explored in Chapter 6 and Chapter 7 is consumer preferences. Traditional marketing models treat preferences as logically-derived, information-based, relatively stable over time, and preceding rather than following consumer choices and actions. But brain science tells a radically different story, one that is fundamental to intuitive marketing.

> **Our belief in stable preferences is mostly an illusion.**

Brain scientists have found that people make decisions based on heuristics and cognitive shortcuts (see Chapter 15 and Chapter 16), and then infer their preferences from the decisions they've made. Researchers have found preferences to be highly malleable and sensitive to seemingly minor differences in context, such as presence of other people, cognitive distractions, time pressures, and unconscious primes.

Our behavior is heavily dependent on automatic emotional reactions that occur outside our conscious awareness

Emotions come in both conscious and unconscious flavors. Brain scientists use the term *feelings* to describe consciously experienced emotional states, and *affect* or *affective states* to describe unconscious emotional responses. Marketers have recognized that emotions are important to persuasive marketing, but their focus has been mostly on conscious feelings, measured by self-reports collected after experiencing a marketing message.

> Not only has brain science shown that after-the-fact evaluations are often unreliable, but more importantly, it has shown that most of the impact of emotions on consumer evaluations, decisions and actions accrues slowly over time, and is largely unconscious.

In Chapter 8 and Chapter 9, we will see how conscious feelings and unconscious affect function and interact in consumer responses to marketing. We will see that marketers' increasing emphasis on "big emotion" in marketing and advertising, enshrined recently in highly emotional story-telling in Super Bowl ads,[1] may be missing the mark with regard to how emotion actually contributes to the choices and behavior of intuitive consumers in the marketplace.

We pursue goals we do not know we are pursuing

One of the most fascinating and counterintuitive findings in the brain sciences is the discovery of unconscious goal pursuit. Conscious goals have always been of interest to marketers. Most traditional marketing and advertising is essentially an effort to persuade consumers to have particular goals and not have others. But social psychologists have recently learned that human beings can also have unconscious goals, and these goals can be activated, pursued, and accomplished completely outside of conscious awareness. This surprising discovery has deep implications for intuitive marketing, as we will see in Chapter 10 and Chapter 11.

Much of what we learn is acquired implicitly, effortlessly, and without conscious awareness

Memory and its relationship to learning is a deep and complex topic, and one that is terribly simplified in the traditional model of marketing. Persuasive marketing focuses on *explicit memory*—the deliberate memorization or learning of facts and logical associations—and *explicit recall*—the ability to retrieve those explicit memories unaided at a later point in time. In Chapter 12 and Chapter 13, we will see that intuitive marketing draws on a much richer and more realistic view of memory and learning, one that emphasizes the mechanisms of *conditioning* and *implicit memory*, both of which can bypass conscious recall altogether.

Overt persuasion often fails to change our behavior

This is a key theme of the book that will be introduced later in this chapter and examined in much more detail in Chapter 12, Chapter 13, and Chapter 14.

> **In contrast to overt persuasion, unconscious processes of *implicit learning, conditioning, priming*, and biased *knowledge accessibility* do much of the work that traditional marketers believe is done by persuasive messaging.**

Priming, as we will see, is the extremely important mechanism by which external cues in our environment trigger responses in our minds, largely in the absence of conscious awareness. These mechanisms produce influence, rather than persuasion, and are central to how intuitive marketing works.

Our choices are shaped by context more than we realize

This is the fundamental principle of both behavioral economics and intuitive marketing. In Chapter 15 and Chapter 16, we will see how and why context can be such a powerful influence on consumers' choices and actions, focusing on the roles of *judgment heuristics* and *behavioral designs* in consumer decision making. This is one aspect of intuitive marketing that does seem to have achieved some penetration in the thinking of traditional marketers. But the powerful effects of context are generally unknown to consumers, which creates an opportunity for *covert persuasion* in marketing. The ethics of covert persuasion and behavioral designs are discussed in Chapter 16.

Meet the Intuitive Consumer

Given this wealth of new knowledge coming from brain science, we need to reconsider the question of *who consumers really are*. When compared to the traditional model of the rational consumer, intuitive consumers are most recognizable by what they don't do, rather than what they do. As noted above, they don't pay much attention to marketing and advertising. If asked, they will say they find the clutter of advertising and marketing intrusive and annoying. They don't hold marketing in high regard. In most surveys of attitudes toward professions, they rank marketers and advertisers near the bottom, right around car salespeople and that most benighted of professions, members of Congress.[2] They don't think of themselves as "consumers"—that's a designation given to them by marketers, not themselves. They don't usually make purchase decisions based on close scrutiny of comparative

6

information. In fact, they really don't like analyzing information at all, and try to avoid it if they can. They are naturally attracted to things that are simple, familiar, and comfortable, and are naturally suspicious of things that are new and different. Their memories are constructed and embellished, not accurate representations of the past. They make decisions about products and brands using automatic processes that are inaccessible to their conscious minds, so they are often unable to tell marketers and researchers why they make the choices they make. Most worrisome for marketers, they are unaware of the extent to which they are influenced by unconscious processes outside their conscious awareness. Perhaps because of this blind spot, they tend to be over-confident about their self-knowledge. When asked about their preferences or their likely future behaviors, they express high confidence in their answers, even though research shows time and again that these self-reports are poor predictors of actual future behavior.

There is a misconception promoted by some in neuromarketing and the sensationalist wing of science journalism that the discovery of unconscious processes in the minds of consumers makes them easier targets for marketing than rational consumers would be. There is talk of unconscious *buy buttons in the brain* which, when pressed, will reliably trigger unconscious processes that make intuitive consumers unable to resist the messages of marketers and advertisers. This conception is pure "neurobollocks," as knowledgeable observers have pointed out.[3] In fact, as we shall see, unconscious processes often make consumers *more resistant* to marketing, not less.

> Consumers' aversion to persuasion runs deep, and is supported by unconscious filters and defensive mechanisms that, when understood, conspire to make marketers' jobs more challenging, not easier.[4]

The intuitive consumer is no pushover. Our unconscious perceptual, evaluative, emotional, and motivational systems have been passed down from our ancestors because they are adaptive and make us smarter in dealing with the world around us. They do not make us easy dupes for manipulation by wily marketers. On the contrary, this book tells a different story.

> If marketers want to reach intuitive consumers and build mutually beneficial relationships with them, they need to understand and respect *both* the conscious and unconscious processes that drive them.

7

Three Prerequisites for Understanding Intuitive Marketing

The research domain I call "brain science" encompasses a broad range of scientific disciplines and subdisciplines that revolve around three main fields that have contributed most to our understanding of intuitive marketing today: neuroscience, social psychology, and behavioral economics.

Neuroscience is the study of the human nervous system, including the brain, its anatomy, functions, and the peripheral nervous system the brain controls. Neuroscience provides a foundation for intuitive marketing by offering insights into how brain states and physiological reactions can be triggered by exposure to brands, products, and marketing materials, and how those reactions can be measured.

Social psychology is a branch of psychology devoted to understanding how people think and act in the real or imagined presence of other people. In recent years, social psychology researchers have led the way in studying the impact of unconscious processes on human actions. Social psychology provides a foundation for intuitive marketing through its examination of how conscious and unconscious brain processes work together to produce consumer choice and behavior.

Behavioral economics is a relatively new cross-disciplinary field that studies how people make economic and financial decisions in the real world. Behavioral economists provide a foundation for intuitive marketing by studying how situations and contexts influence consumer choice and behavior. Behavioral economics has spawned *behavioral design*, a practical discipline that revolves around designing *choice architectures* to influence consumer choice at points of sale.

For both traditionally trained marketers and most consumers, these scientific fields represent a brand new and somewhat intimidating landscape.

> **Brain science is yielding new concepts and ideas about marketing and consumer behavior that often appear counterintuitive, if not downright bizarre.**

I have struggled with many of these ideas myself. Having devoted many hours to explaining these concepts to hundreds of marketers and market researchers, I've discovered that focusing upfront on three brain science concepts can help make the process less disorienting. These three concepts are:

- Understanding dual-process models of the mind—*System 1* vs. *System 2*
- Distinguishing between content, form, and context in consumer choice
- Respecting, not fearing, the unconscious mind

Understanding System 1 and System 2 Thinking

The idea that human brains engage simultaneously in two very different kinds of thinking—so-called "dual process" brain models—has been around for a long time. Like many concepts in psychology, this one finds an early and influential formulation in the work of William James in the late 19th century. In 1890, James wrote about *associative thought* or "empirical thinking" as "trains of thought suggested one by another." He contrasted this mode of thinking with *reasoning*, which he saw as our capacity to deal with novelty, to "help us out in unprecedented situations." James' formulation captures some of the key elements of dual process models that are in use today.[5]

But the dual-process model of thinking only became something of a household idea when psychologist Daniel Kahneman placed it at the center of his Nobel Economics Prize lecture in December 2002, and then popularized it further in his best-selling book, *Thinking, Fast and Slow*, published in 2011.[6] In Kahneman's version, the two modes of thinking are dubbed *System 1* and *System 2,* and are described in a way that has become familiar not only to researchers in both psychology and economics, but also to marketers, market researchers, and—thanks to its inclusion in many popular business and science books and press accounts—members of the reading public as well.[7]

System 1 and *System 2* describe two different ways of thinking, each supported by different regions and paths in the brain. Some of the most important aspects of *System 1* thinking are that it occurs without conscious awareness, it is fast and effortless, it can handle many tasks simultaneously, and it utilizes, as James pointed out, an associative process to link our thinking from one idea to the next. Because it operates below conscious awareness, most people have no idea they are engaging in *System 1* thinking, even though *System 1* activity takes up far more of the brain's processing capacity than *System 2* activity.

System 2 thinking, in contrast, is the type of thinking we all know and love. It's that little voice in our heads we hear when we are consciously deliberating. It is slow and effortful, it can only handle one task at a time, and it utilizes logical or propositional thinking—that is, it takes us from one idea to the next using *if-then* logic and our knowledge of the world to set expectations, make predictions, and draw conclusions.

To understand how intuitive marketing works, we need to focus on the idea of associative processing in *System 1.*

> **An associative connection is established through the simplest of mechanisms—if two objects or events appear together, if they follow in sequence, and if they have occurred together recently, or are observed more than once, an association is unconsciously created in our minds.**

The more often we observe these associations, or think about them, the stronger they get. The key point is that associative connections need not have any logic and reasoning behind them. They can be, and often are, completely illogical.

System 1 does not assess observed associations, it simply records them and incorporates them into action plans that may or may not ever reach conscious awareness. Kahneman emphasizes this in one of his chapter titles in *Thinking, Fast and Slow.*

> ***System 1* is "a machine for jumping to conclusions." It ignores ambiguity and suppresses doubt.**

Why does it operate this way? *System 1* is for action, it's for *getting things done*, as quickly and efficiently as possible. *System 2*, on the other hand, is for *thinking about getting things done*. It is for drawing inferences and conclusions, as well as for planning future behavior. As such, and unlike *System 1*, it is constantly concerned about things like risk, uncertainty, and ambiguity. This also has obvious survival value, because it allows us to think outside the current moment and to act strategically, not just reactively.

Jumping to conclusions based on *System 1* associations serves us quite well as long as the conclusions are likely to be accurate and the costs of an occasional misstep are tolerable. It saves huge amounts of time and effort. However, jumping to conclusions can also be extremely risky, even life-threatening, when the situation is ambiguous, unfamiliar, or deliberately constructed to be deceptive. But that is what *System 2* is for—to pull us back from automatically jumping to conclusions so we can consider the situation coldly, rationally, and logically.

In the world of marketing, the potential costs of jumping to conclusions are relatively small, some would say miniscule compared to more dangerous contexts. Indeed, it could be argued that marketing, advertising, and shopping are all designed—both by convention and by regulatory oversight—to make jumping to conclusions safe, because this is what facilitates both the consumer's desire to fulfill wants and needs efficiently and the seller's desire to operate in an open marketplace where their product can compete against others to meet demand on a relatively even playing field.

Under the traditional model of marketing, it is assumed that jumping to conclusions in the marketplace is still a conscious and relatively information-driven

System 2 process. But brain research is proving that this view fails to appreciate the counterintuitive nature of *System 1* associative thinking. Marketers may feel compelled to put persuasive arguments, "reasons to believe," and benefit demonstrations into their advertising, but it may be the simple juxtaposition of people enjoying themselves alongside presentation of the product or brand, reinforced by repetition, that is actually establishing the connections in memory that get activated at a later time of purchase.

This is why the *System 1* vs. *System 2* distinction is an important foundation for understanding intuitive marketing.

> **All marketing operates at both *System 1* and *System 2* levels. Intuitive marketing differs from traditional persuasive marketing in that it is aware of this fact, and is planned and executed to connect with consumers' wants and needs in the most efficient and least intrusive way.**

Often this means relying on unconscious *System 1* associative processing instead of conscious *System 2* logical *if-then* thinking. We will cover this topic in more detail in Chapter 12 and Chapter 13.

Distinguishing Between Content, Form, and Context

A second idea that is important to understanding how intuitive marketing differs from traditional marketing is the insight that consumers often mistakenly believe they are responding to the *content* of a marketing or advertising message, when in fact they are responding to the *form* or the *context* of that message.

As depicted in Figure 1, it is useful to think of content, form, and context in marketing as three concentric circles that are perceived and reacted to, consciously or unconsciously, by the intuitive consumer.

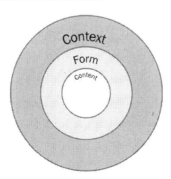

Figure 1. Marketing as Seen by the Intuitive Consumer

By *content*, I'm referring to the explicit meaning or message that is deliberately conveyed by the marketing material. Messages are meticulously crafted by traditional marketers and are the central focus of almost all marketing efforts.

By *form*, I mean the way in which a message is presented. Form should not be confused with packaging, as in a product package. As we will see in Chapter 6, the most important aspect of form in marketing is the ease with which an object, message, or situation can be decoded and processed by our brains. Brain scientists call this attribute *processing fluency*, and it is a function of form, not content. For example, a message presented in an easy-to-read font can be processed more fluently than the same message presented in a hard-to-read font. Processing fluency is experienced consciously—that is, we are aware of the experience of fluency or its opposite, disfluency - but for the most part it influences our thinking unconsciously, quite independently from the meaning conveyed by the content of a marketing message.

Finally, by *context*, I mean the surrounding situation or environment within which a marketing message is embedded. Context is particularly important for understanding shopping situations and consumer choice. It has even been found to affect how people respond to TV ads when presented in the context of different programming. Understanding how context influences choice has been a major preoccupation of behavioral economics since its inception, and research in that field has found numerous ways in which our choices can be altered by behavioral designs that adjust elements of the context of choice. We will examine this research and its implications for intuitive marketing in Chapter 15 and Chapter 16.

Put simply, content is the *what* of marketing, form is the *how*, and context is the *where, when, and who*.

This distinction is important for understanding intuitive marketing not just because our minds are sensitive to all three of these aspects of marketing. It is important because form and context—which mostly influence us outside of conscious awareness—have been found in many circumstances to have a *greater* impact on our perceptions, judgments, decisions, and behaviors as consumers than the content at the center of marketing.

This is news that traditional marketing has yet to internalize. Most marketing is still based on the assumption that people derive beliefs, attitudes, and ultimately behavior about a product or brand from the content of marketing messages.

> **Traditional marketers focus most of their effort on tinkering with what their messages say, rather than on the form of how they say it or the context within which they say it.**

For intuitive marketing, every message is understood as content presented in a certain form and wrapped within a particular context—and these additional elements need to be considered as potentially *greater* influences on the consumer's response than the content itself. In addition, because the influences of form and context operate largely through *System 1*, there is no reason to expect them to be logical or even make sense. Rather, because they are based on associative connections in the unconscious mind, they may seem totally nonsensical and irrational when observed and measured by traditionally-trained marketers and market researchers, or when explained to consumers. But such results are business-as-usual for intuitive marketing, which acknowledges the importance of content, but is equally concerned with understanding and optimizing the form and context within which that content is presented.

Respecting, Not Fearing, the Unconscious Mind

This is the hardest foundation of intuitive marketing for traditional marketers and consumers to accept. Beginning with Freud's original formulation of the unconscious as a primal, unruly, dangerous cauldron of irrationality and unspeakable desires, the popular perception of the unconscious has been highly negative—an uninvited and potentially lethal invader trying to break into our happy, conscious mental homes. This sense of unease was forever married to advertising and marketing by the influential ideas in Vance Packard's *The Hidden Persuaders* and similar exposés of "subliminal persuasion" in the 1950s. Since then, popular depictions of the unconscious in films and novels like *The Manchurian Candidate*, *A Clockwork Orange*, and *Inception*, have continued to reinforce the key point: the unconscious is a scary "back door" into our minds through which we can be manipulated by evil marketers and other nefarious elites, and over which we have no control.

Not without irony, the unconscious mind has become a victim of its own processes. Decades of repeated associations between the concept of the unconscious and primal fears of powerlessness, manipulation, and mind control have left their mark. In a public opinion poll published 36 years after *The Hidden Persuaders*, 75% of Americans were familiar with the term "subliminal persuasion," and of those, 75% believed it worked.[8]

What modern brain science tells us is a completely different story. The unconscious mind is not the enemy of the conscious mind. It is not a "barbarian at the gate." It is not Freud's wild and unruly unconscious.

Brain scientists now think of our unconscious, *System 1* mental processes as a *behavioral guidance system*[9] that in fact plays a fundamental role in all of the activities we perform every day.

It operates in tandem with our conscious minds, not in opposition.

How does this unconscious behavioral guidance system work? Basically, its function is to deal automatically with the moment-to-moment sensory flow that confronts our brains continually throughout every day. It does this by engaging in a massive filtering and classifying operation. An often-quoted statistic is the calculation that our sensory systems (vision, hearing, taste, smell, touch) take in about 11 million bits of information every second. Yet our conscious minds are capable of processing at most only about 40 bits of information per second.[10] What happens to all the rest of those bits? *Every one of them* reaches our brains, and is processed in one way or another. Most are discarded by unconscious processing (see Figure 8). Some are processed and acted upon unconsciously, without engaging the conscious mind. And a small proportion of them are elevated to conscious thought, where we become aware of "thinking about something."

This filtering function is important for marketing because it allows the unconscious mind to deal with exactly the kind of clutter and distraction traditional marketing puts in front of us every day.

Especially for experienced consumers in a media-saturated environment, most marketing and advertising is simply screened out by unconscious filtering processes.

It neither reaches conscious awareness nor is it subjected to any unconscious processing that can subsequently influence immediate or delayed behavior. It just gets discarded.

Before sensory inputs can be selected for the discard pile, dealt with unconsciously by *System 1*, or passed on to *System 2* for conscious deliberation, the unconscious must perform a vast number of critical operations on the incoming information. First, it must decode the information, translating raw sensory impulses into *mental representations* of the external world. This is a perceptual function that occurs extremely rapidly and completely outside our conscious awareness. Next, both meaning and value must be attached to the mental representation. This is done by activating associations in memory to identify the representation and attach various attributes—meanings and values—to it. This turns the representation into a recognizable object of thought. Some of these attributes are physical characteristics, such as size, location, and weight. Some have to do with the *expectedness* of the object. Our unconscious minds are constantly creating and updating expectations about what will happen next. If we perceive something in our environment that creates an *expectancy violation*, this will trigger additional unconscious and possibly conscious processing. If, in contrast, we perceive something that matches expectations, it is likely to be processed with less conscious involvement. Finally, and closely associated with expectations, emotional and motivational attributes are automatically assigned to every perceived object, including *emotional valence* (liking-disliking) and *approach-withdrawal propensity* (attraction-aversion).

All of these operations occur rapidly, automatically, simultaneously, and without conscious awareness, every second of every day in every human brain. The emerging scientific consensus is that the unconscious keeps us oriented in the present, providing us with automatic behavioral guidance "nudges" that direct us toward behavior that has a high likelihood of being safe, correct, and appropriate in the current situation. That leaves the conscious brain free to do what it does best, which is to engage in what social psychologist John Bargh calls "time travel"—recollecting the past to codify what we've learned and imaginatively projecting ourselves into the future to plan and anticipate how to achieve the future states we desire for ourselves.[11]

> Unconscious *System 1* processing is not a mystery to be feared. It is an evolutionary adaptation of significant survival value that allows us to identify and act on what is important in our environment without being overwhelmed and distracted by *everything* in our environment.

Intensive preprocessing and action preparation by our unconscious minds guides all of our actions, including our actions as consumers.

The key question is: How should we adapt our thinking to what brain science has taught us about the unconscious mind and its huge role in human thought, choice, and behavior? In the world of marketing, the traditional model for understanding consumer choice do not give us a clue.

> Marketers are willy-nilly assaulting the unconscious minds of consumers without any idea of what they are doing, how consumers are responding, or what outcomes they are producing.

15

My hope is that after reading this book, both marketers and consumers will be better informed about what is really going on, so they can be better prepared to think seriously about what to do about it.

Intuitive Marketing vs. Persuasive Marketing

Intuitive marketers know that unconscious and conscious processes—*System 1* and *System 2*—are tightly linked, rely on each other, and jointly contribute to consumer choice and behavior. What does this imply for the *look and feel* of intuitive marketing? Should we be able to recognize intuitive marketing when we see it in the marketplace? Should we be able to identify a distinctive orientation or sensibility that distinguishes it from traditional marketing? Or is this concept just "old wine in new bottles"—not really new and different enough to require us to rethink our traditional marketing practices?

It should come as no surprise that I believe intuitive marketing does, in fact, imply a very different kind of marketing. The case can be made by contrasting intuitive marketing with what I consider to be the most prominent form of traditional marketing, *persuasive marketing*.

The Perils of Persuasive Marketing

Persuasive marketing is based on the assumption that marketing exists to convince people to think or act in ways they don't want to.

The notion of persuasion is deeply entrenched in marketing and advertising's roots in sales and personal selling. Most marketing models are based on some variation of the *AIDA* model popularized at the beginning of the 20th century for door-to-door sales. *AIDA* is an acronym for a sequential approach to persuasion. To best ensure a sale, marketers and sales people must first attract *Attention*, then engage *Interest*, then trigger *Desire*, and finally provide a path to *Action*. In this formulation, attention is seen as a prerequisite for delivering the persuasive message, interest and desire are the expected emotional responses to the message, and action in the form of a purchase is the hoped-for result.[12]

Persuasion is an act that must be received consciously.

It is impossible to persuade someone if they are not consciously aware of the persuasion attempt.[13]

16

So the act of persuasion and the measurement of persuasion both occur in the conscious realm. But an unintended byproduct of this conscious focus is that persuasive messaging, in order to activate conscious attention, must wrest attention away from wherever it was focused before.

> **This act of interruption is by its very nature intrusive and disruptive, and can often produce a negative emotional reaction toward the source of interruption—the message itself and the brand or product it is promoting.**

Because this reaction is predominantly unconscious, and traditional market research is only measuring conscious reactions, marketers often remain unaware of these effects.

Persuasive marketing violates the brain's processing preferences in other important ways. Not only does it demand that we shift our attention from our own priorities to those of the messenger, it also demands that we shift to an information processing perspective, because it wants us to notice and absorb *its argument*, which is delivered in a logical *if-then* format as a benefit statement, demonstration, or comparative claim. The argument may be presented in a visual form, such as a graphic demonstration of a product in action, or in a narrative form, such as a dramatized depiction of the product solving a problem, but the desired interpretation of the message is essentially cognitive and informational. To understand, store, and later retrieve the message, persuasive marketing requires that the message be consciously converted into a proposition of the form "this product can do X, therefore I should prefer it / remember it / buy it." As we have seen, such propositional logic is uniquely available only to conscious *System 2* processing. If *System 2* is not successfully activated, the message's meaning cannot be decoded by our unconscious *System 1* behavioral guidance systems. It may be *in sight*, but it is *out of mind*, and therefore unlikely to be recalled with any precision later on. Without a full conscious commitment on the part of the consumer, persuasive marketing cannot achieve its goals.

This is not to deny that there are circumstances in which both consumers and marketers can benefit from the skilled application of persuasive marketing.

> **The key criterion for effective use of persuasive marketing is that the intended target of the marketing effort must be motivated to receive and process its message.**

This idea has been embedded in the sales version of the *AIDA* model from the beginning, in the concept of *the prospect*. A prospect is a potential buyer who is known to have an existing or potential need for, or interest in, buying a product. This need or interest can be anticipated in various direct and indirect ways. When a husband and wife walk into a mattress store, for example, there is a good chance they are motivated to listen to marketing messages about mattresses, and they are likely do so with the required conscious attention. But most marketing does not have the luxury of such direct access to motivated consumers, so it casts its marketing messages widely, knowing that it will call out to many, but few will listen. It is in these latter situations that intuitive marketing becomes a viable and effective alternative to persuasive marketing.

The Promise of Intuitive Marketing

Intuitive marketing is not marketing exclusively to the unconscious. It is not "sneaky" marketing or "stealth" marketing. It is not "subliminal marketing."

It is marketing that acknowledges and addresses both conscious and unconscious processing systems in the human brain. As we will see, it is built on very different assumptions than persuasive marketing, assumptions that are deeply grounded in recent brain science. It could be called "anti-persuasive" marketing, because in many ways it turns traditional persuasive marketing on its head. Some might even say it represents a kind of *Copernican Revolution* in marketing, recognizing that influencing consumers does not need to revolve around attention, rational benefits, persuasive messaging, and conscious recall. Instead, intuitive marketing aims to influence indirectly, by stimulating and entertaining consumers both consciously and unconsciously, thereby building positive connections with products and brands that can then be automatically activated later at a point of sale.

Intuitive marketing is *promising* in the sense that it provides a way to achieve the traditional goals of marketing while avoiding many of the most irritating and objectionable features of persuasive marketing.

Intuitive marketing does not rely on persuasion

Persuasion attempts carry a lot of baggage. They must be paid attention to, they demand logical processing, they require memory encoding and storage, and they must overcome our natural resistance to effortful thinking. Such expenditures of mental effort are appropriate and necessary in many circumstances, such as when educating ourselves and our children, or when pursuing information for a desired purchase, but they become onerous and invasive when demanded of us in the absence of any motivational interest—for example, when disrupting our favorite TV show to persuade us to buy a new car we have no interest in purchasing.

> **Intuitive marketing does not deny that influencing consumers is the purpose of marketing, it just goes about achieving that goal in a different way than persuasive marketing.**

As we will see in detail in later chapters, intuitive marketing does not try to persuade, but it does try to influence. It operates primarily—but not exclusively—through *System 1* processes, relying on *repetition, conditioning, priming,* and other unconscious mental processes to create and activate positive *associative connections* with products and brands in the minds of consumers. Later, it activates related unconscious processes at a point of sale to do the work of converting associations into immediate expectations, motivations, and behavior.

Intuitive marketing may earn attention, but does not demand it

Attention is a scarce resource in our modern world. An important principle of intuitive marketing is that direct attention is optional, not required, to achieve marketing goals.

> **In many circumstances, attention is actually counter-productive to marketing purposes.**

Many studies have shown that when we focus attention on a marketing message, we can activate conscious thinking that is devoted to counter-arguing the claims of the message, thus defeating the persuasive intent.[14] The mechanisms underlying intuitive marketing, in contrast, work well under conditions of low attention processing, and even work when no attention at all is being paid to the marketing effort. This means that intuitive marketing can avoid many of the negative consequences of persuasive marketing because it does not require interrupting a consumer's train of conscious thought with annoying and disruptive appeals in order to achieve its goals. When it does attract attention, it does so by providing a more enjoyable or intriguing experience that the consumer voluntarily attends to—it earns the consumer's attention rather than demands it.

Intuitive marketing does not need to make sense

This may be the most distinctive feature of intuitive marketing—and the one that traditional approaches to marketing find hardest to explain and understand. Because intuitive marketing recognizes and leverages *System 1* associative connectivity between ideas, it does not need to operate within the logical *if-then* processing boundaries of conscious *System 2* reasoning and deliberation.

> **Associative connections do not need to be logical, rational, or even reasonable. They simply get established in memory whenever two stimuli are repeatedly observed in physical or temporal proximity to each other, whatever the reason.**

That is how *System 1* makes connections that later get activated when either stimulus is encountered on its own. The observation or mental activation of one triggers thoughts of the other. And the more frequently and recently the association is observed, the stronger and more accessible the connection becomes.

Intuitive marketing uses this feature of unconscious processing to create successful marketing messages that make little or no logical sense. In 2007, TV viewers found themselves watching an ad that opened with a purple title screen reading "A Glass and a Half Full Production." Slowly the camera pans to an extreme close-up of a very realistic-looking gorilla's face. The gorilla seems to be deeply concentrating. Or is he meditating? Playing in the background is the Phil Collins hit, *In the Air Tonight.* The camera gradually pans back, revealing that the gorilla is sitting behind a set of drums, holding a pair of drumsticks, stretching his muscles and breathing deeply in anticipation of the iconic Phil Collins drum solo. When the moment arrives, the gorilla launches into the solo with complete abandon and exuberance. The camera continues to pan back, revealing the gorilla to be playing in a recording studio. The scene transitions to another purple screen with an image of a *Cadbury Dairy Milk* chocolate bar and the tagline "A glass and a half full of joy." The music ends and so does the ad.

This ad broke almost every rule of persuasive marketing. It contained no persuasive argument or appeal. It contained no voice track at all. It had absolutely nothing to do with chocolate. It did not even reveal the product being advertised until the last 6 seconds of the 90 second ad. It did attract attention, but it earned that attention by providing a unique visual-musical experience, it did not demand attention as persuasive marketing does. It was entertaining and memorable, won numerous creative awards, and was one of the first viral ads on the Internet. But most importantly, it delivered an ROI of 4.88 times its cost and helped produce an immediate bump in the company's lagging chocolate snack business.[15] How did it work? It associated *Cadbury* with an engaging and enjoyable experience that people wanted to watch over and over again, even though (or perhaps because?) it did not make any sense as a chocolate commercial. The *Cadbury* "Gorilla" ad was one of the first and best examples of intuitive marketing on television.

Mechanisms of Intuitive Marketing

Marketing does not need to be disruptive and annoying. Excessive reliance on persuasion is risky for marketers and exhausting for consumers. In contrast to persuasive marketing, intuitive marketing is first and foremost aligned with the purposes and needs of the consumer, and only through meeting those purposes and needs does it serve the needs of the marketer.

Achieving Influence without Persuasion

Persuasion is about getting people to do what you want them to do. Influence is about enabling people do what they want to do.

Persuasion is a transactional experience. It is fundamentally about whether I, the persuader, can get you, the target, to do what I want you to do, right now or as soon as you possibly can. Influence, in contrast, does not require an explicit transaction to operate, and it can be achieved at a distance and over time. As I write these words today, I am still being influenced by the fifth-grade teacher who 50 years ago instilled in me a life-long love of learning. Every time you make a moral or ethical choice, you are being influenced by a parent, teacher, or friend who taught you about the difference between right and wrong. These may seem lofty examples to compare to the mundane world of marketing and advertising, but the mechanisms of influence operate similarly across even these vastly different domains of experience.

Intuitive marketing works by tapping into the legitimate sources of influence that cause consumers to allow themselves to be influenced. It does not work by trickery or manipulation.

Such deceptive efforts may work one time, but once actual consumer experience fails to align with the marketing message, they will not work again. Consumers learn and remember. Deceptive influence attempts are wasted effort and wasted marketing dollars.

Five Paths to Intuitive Marketing Influence

As we delve into the workings of intuitive marketing in the following chapters, we will find ourselves returning to five sources of influence that make intuitive marketing operate differently than persuasive marketing:

- Aligned-intent (earned attention) marketing
- Low-attention marketing
- Consistency, reliability, and trust
- Small emotional rewards
- Connecting with aspirations and identity

Aligned-intent (earned attention) marketing

When intuitive marketing commands attention, it does so because it has *earned* that attention, either by aligning with the intentions, motivations, goals, and purposes of the person to whom it is directed, or by becoming a rewarding experience itself that people want to be a part of.[16] While persuasive marketing is usually oblivious to the consumer's needs and interests in comparison to its own, relegating to itself the right to interrupt and disrupt the consumer whenever and wherever it chooses, intuitive marketing recognizes the importance of anticipating and reacting to the consumer's current mental state and situation. As we shall see, this is the case in both the passive state of mind most consumers enjoy when watching TV or movies, and the much more active and goal-directed state of mind that accompanies activities like web browsing and video gaming. Intuitive marketing does not assume it has an inherent right to any consumers' attention. Rather, it recognizes that attention only helps marketing if it is voluntarily surrendered, not taken by force.

Low-attention marketing

As described earlier, intuitive marketing can operate under conditions of low attention, or even no attention. It does this by taking advantage of several unconscious mechanisms, including positive emotional markers, conditioning, and implicit memory activation (via *priming* and selective *knowledge activation*) at a point of sale. The result is marketing that does not intrude or disrupt. Low-attention marketing achieves influence without persuasion because it does not make excessive demands on consumers' attention or cognitive resources. It does not trigger defensive reactions and conscious resistance because there is nothing to resist. It provides a positive emotional experience, tightly or loosely associated with a product or brand, repeated over time.

Consistency, reliability, and trust

Intuitive marketing is consistent and therefore communicates reliability. *Expectancy violations* can be very disruptive of the mental associations laboriously built by marketers. Changing messages and themes in mid-stream to attract attention or resuscitate a tired brand is a classic error of persuasive marketing, and one that intuitive marketing avoids if at all possible. Consistency in marketing is also critical because it builds trust. Trust is largely a function of reputation, and building and reinforcing brand reputation is a critical function of marketing. As advertising executive Rory Sutherland points out, brand reputation is costly to acquire and extremely costly to lose. The trust engendered by reputation allows brands to command a price premium, but only as long as the product experiences sold under that brand live up to the brand's promises.[17]

Small emotional rewards

Intuitive marketing recognizes and leverages the power of small emotional rewards, which often provide an excellent substitute for persuasion. This source of influence is closely related to another idea introduced above: that intuitive marketing does not need to make sense. As Les Binet and Susan Carter observe in a WARC blog post entitled "*Mythbusters: The idea that marketing always needs to make sense*":

> ... it doesn't make 'sense' for Coke to sell cans with people's names on them. It didn't make much sense for Cadbury to sell chocolate with a gorilla. And it doesn't make sense for Innocent Smoothies to amuse people on its packaging. But when you do things that make people smile, they tend to buy your product.
>
> There's a generosity of spirit about a lot of this stuff—the brand is giving us an emotional freebie.[21]

We will learn more about how emotion influences consumer behavior in Chapter 8. In Chapter 9, we will explore how intuitive marketing can deploy emotion effectively in advertising and marketing messages without resorting to heavy-handed emotional manipulation. We will also see how providing small emotional rewards can positively dispose consumers toward a product or brand in the absence of traditional persuasive messaging techniques.

Connecting with aspirations and identity

At the opposite end of the spectrum from small emotional rewards is the lofty realm of human aspirations and identity needs. Human beings are hard-wired to be aspirational. We always want to achieve more, to be part of something greater than ourselves. Our aspirational nature has some downsides, such as our propensity to think way too highly of ourselves and our capabilities. But it also has significant upsides, in that it provides much of our motivation and drive to succeed. Similarly, we have a deep need to maintain an identity that bolsters our feelings of self-worth. We are constantly on the lookout for self-affirmation and evidence of our "specialness" in the world. As we will see in Chapter 11, intuitive marketing can leverage aspiration and identity needs in place of persuasion. Brands that celebrate aspirational goals and connect with the identities of their consumers—Nike and achievement, Apple and creativity, Disney and shared family experiences—are seldom found resorting to the mundane mechanics of persuasive marketing.

Turning Down the Noise:
Making Marketing Less Disruptive

In a special issue celebrating the 50th anniversary of *Admap Magazine* in October 2014, San Francisco advertising executive Gareth Kay wrote an article titled "*The post-disruptive advertising era*" in which he argues that "advertising needs to change—from a model based on introspection and disruption to one based on empathy and increasing invisibility." Kay is one of the first marketing practitioners to publicly acknowledge that the disruptive model of advertising (and, by extension, other forms of marketing) may be its own worst enemy. Using the example of elegant product design that "wins customers' trust by disappearing," Kay speculates that:

> *Maybe advertising is finally catching up with industrial design. But if it is, we are going to need to think about our models and measurement. Intrusion and noticeability (the AIDA model we tend to default to and most research companies measure by) are rather at odds with ideas that feel a little more invisible in nature.*[22]

A major rationale for intuitive marketing is to provide a path, paved by brain science, that can lead marketing out of its longstanding fixation on disruption, intrusion, and attention at all costs.

Marketing can embrace a more human-friendly orientation and, in Kay's words, by providing brand and product messages that:

> *... understand what people are interested in and work back from there. Great communication ideas act as a bridge. A bridge between what people are interested in and what you make/sell. A bridge between your world and theirs; real life and culture and commerce.*[23]

This key theme—that marketing can focus on responding to consumer's interests, not changing their minds, and can do so, paradoxically, by being less visible, not more—will be revisited throughout the following chapters. Our conclusions will be summarized in Chapter 17.

Chapter 2

Intuitive Marketing in Perspective

How It Works, Where It Works, When It Works

"They're digging in the wrong place!"
–Henry "Indiana" Jones

This chapter provides a high-level "backgrounder" on the science behind intuitive marketing and the areas of marketing where it is most likely to impact, and ultimately transform, traditional marketing practices.

First, we explore several important elements of the current scientific consensus regarding the operation of human cognition, both conscious and unconscious. The model we will use to navigate through this huge body of research is called the *cognitive timeline*. It summarizes how brain scientists view the mental processes through which humans take in, interpret, and respond to changes in the world around them, modeled as a cognitive sequence over time.

Embedded in this model is another foundational idea: that our unconscious mind provides a highly sophisticated *unconscious behavioral guidance system* that gets activated within the cognitive timeline as we interact with the world around us. This unconscious guidance system plays a large role in the choices and actions we take every day, freeing up our conscious mind for what it does best—drawing lessons from the past and anticipating and planning actions for the future. We will discuss four unconscious guidance "subsystems" that have been identified by brain scientists.

In the second half of the chapter, we shift our focus from brain science to marketing and provide an overview of where and how intuitive marketing operates in the modern marketplace. These ideas will probably be more familiar to traditional marketers, but they are worth reviewing here for the context they provide for better understanding intuitive marketing.

First is the idea of the *consumer cycle*, which reminds us that marketing does not exist, and cannot be evaluated, in a vacuum.

> **Marketing needs to be viewed as one part of a continuous, repeating cycle of consumer interaction with products and brands, from exposure to marketing messages to shopping and buying experiences to consumption and product experiences.**

Second, we will discuss an important distinction in the practice of marketing that helps demarcate where and when intuitive marketing is most likely to be effective. This is the difference between marketing that focuses on *short-term activation* (like encouraging and closing a sale, or getting a user to click on an online button to visit a website) and marketing that focuses on *long-term brand-building and relationship development*. As we will see, intuitive marketing is most appropriate for long-term brand-building, while persuasive marketing remains the dominant approach for short-term activation. We will explore why this demarcation exists and what it means for both marketers and consumers.

How Consumers Think: The Cognitive Timeline

The cognitive timeline is a simple model describing how cognitive processes are triggered in the human mind and interact over time. It was first introduced in *Neuromarketing for Dummies* and has been modified and updated based on reader feedback and additional research. The updated version is presented in Figure 2.

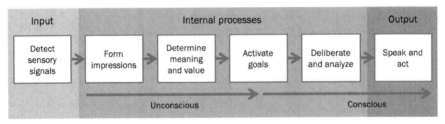

Figure 2. The Cognitive Timeline[1]

At every waking moment of every day of our lives, our brains take in a huge amount of information through our sensory systems—vision, hearing, smell, taste, touch, and body sense.[2] According to brain scientists:

- All of this information gets processed unconsciously.
- Most of it gets discarded as irrelevant to our current purposes.
- Some of it gets processed further but only unconsciously.
- A very small portion of it gets elevated to conscious processing, where we become aware of "thinking about" it.

As Figure 2 illustrates, these intensive computations begin with the *input* of sensory information through the sensory organs, proceed through *internal mental processes* of perceptual decoding, conceptual interpretation, goal activation, and optional conscious deliberation, and result in *output behavior* such as physical movement and verbal communication. The sequential nature of the stages is not absolute. Impression formation and determining meaning and value often appear to occur simultaneously, goals may be activated as part of either conscious or unconscious processing, and deliberation is often skipped when we react to sensory input or activate goals without conscious awareness.

Unconscious and Conscious Steps Along the Cognitive Timeline

Here are some important points about each step in the cognitive timeline that are relevant to understanding intuitive marketing.

Forming impressions

Sensory inputs come is "raw," so to speak, and the first task for our brains is to turn those raw signals into recognizable impressions of "scenes" and "events" and "things." This is the primary job of our perceptual systems, which perform this function incredibly rapidly and in a completely unconscious way.

> **We have no conscious access to the computations our brains use to take in sensory information and create perceptions of sight, sound, smell, taste, and texture, nor how those separate sensory streams are integrated into coherent impressions of the world around us.**

The "common sense" view most of us have about impression formation is that our brains are like a video camera, passively recording everything around us so we can play it back later, accurately, through memory recall. But in reality, the impressions we see through our eyes and experience through our other senses are highly pre-processed and quite literally created, not viewed passively, by our brains. Perhaps the best example of this is the way visual images pass through our irises to arrive at the light-sensitive back of our eyes upside down, just like images passing through a camera lens. Yet we see the world right-side up, because the vision

27

processing centers of our brains flip these images over before we "see" them. Another example that marketers often discover when they see an eye-tracking result for the first time is the extent to which our eye gaze jumps around when we are looking at something. Yet we experience none of this rapid eye movement—called *saccades* by vision researchers—because our brains grab the jittery movements before we "see" them and assemble them all into a smooth, non-jittery visual experience for our viewing convenience.

But the brain processing that contributes to impression formation goes beyond even this impressive feat.

> **In addition to constructing a coherent external reality for us to experience, our brains also replace many gaps in our sensory experience with "plausible" fillers based on prior experience and probable expectations.**

Leonard Mlodinow describes this process eloquently in his excellent book, *Subliminal*:

> *The world we perceive is an artificially constructed environment whose character and properties are as much a result of unconscious mental processing as they are a product of real data. Nature helps us overcome gaps in information by supplying a brain that smoothes over the imperfections, at an unconscious level, before we are even aware of any perception. Our brains do all of this without conscious effort, as we sit in a high chair enjoying a jar of strained peas or, later in life, on a couch, sipping a beer. We accept the visions concocted by our unconscious minds without question, and without realizing that they are only an interpretation, one constructed to maximize our overall chances of survival, but not one that is in all cases the most accurate picture possible.[3]*

As we will see in later chapters, one of the places where intuitive marketing achieves influence is in these gaps in the impression formation process. What people notice, how they interpret elements in the world around them, how they "fill in" the gaps in their perceptual intake—all of these processes can impact the associations and expectations we all develop about the products and brands that surround us in the marketplace.

Determining meaning and value

Once we have formed an impression from sensory inputs, or perhaps as we are forming those impressions, our brains are querying our memory networks to answer two key questions: *what is this thing* and *what value does it have for me?*

28

Determining *meaning* is a *classification* task. It answers the question: In what category do I place this thing I'm seeing/hearing/tasting or otherwise experiencing? Determining *value* is an *evaluation* task. It answers the question: Is this thing good or bad for me? This allows us to know whether we should move toward it or away from it. It helps us create an initial emotional response of liking or disliking (also called *emotional valence*). Determining meaning and value occurs, like impression formation, extremely rapidly and precedes conscious awareness.[4] When an impression is connected to a meaning and value, we turn that impression into a *concept*, which is why this process is sometimes called *conceptualization*. A concept, in turn, is something we can think about. It is the raw material of both conscious and unconscious thinking.

> **An important cognitive mechanism that underlies meaning and value determination is *associative activation*, also called *spreading activation* or *facilitation*.**

This is the mechanism by which one idea in our mind triggers associated ideas in memory. Those connected ideas are not brought directly into conscious awareness, because that would overwhelm our limited conscious processing capabilities. Rather, related ideas become what might be called *preconsciously prepared* for later conscious access if needed. These activated ideas are much more likely than non-activated ideas to "come to mind" in subsequent moments. That is how we get from thinking about monkeys to thinking about Charles Darwin, or vice versa. It is also how we get from seeing an exotic automobile pass us on the road to imbuing that image with an identity and a sense of how much we would like to own it. Associative activation is the central mechanism of *priming*, which we will revisit at several points in later chapters, including a detailed look in Chapter 14.

> **Determining meaning and value, or conceptualization, is an extremely important process for marketers to understand, because it is where brands and products live in the minds of consumers.**

Do you dislike the taste of spinach? Immediately when you recognize a package of spinach in the frozen food aisle, the negative value you associate with it is automatically activated and beginning to guide your next behavior—which is probably to move away from the spinach. What's the first thing that comes to mind when you think of a thirst-quenching beverage? Whether it's *Coca-Cola* or *Budweiser* or lemonade, those elements of meaning and value are part of your concept of that beverage, and they are activated every time it is triggered in your mind. That's the power of concepts that sit at the top of a category, are easily activated by associated ideas, and have natural connections with deep positive values. Determining meaning and value has direct consequences for our behavior that seldom reach our conscious awareness.

Activating goals

Goal activation sits in the middle of our cognitive timeline because it can be either conscious or unconscious, depending on circumstances. We generally think of goal activation as something we do consciously, as when we decide to go to the gas station to fill up the car. But recent research in social psychology has revealed another side of goal activation, one that is counterintuitive but central to how intuitive marketing works.

We activate goals consciously, but we also do so unconsciously.

Unconscious goal pursuit has become one of the most actively researched areas in social psychology. What scientists are finding is that we activate and pursue unconscious goals all the time, using the same cognitive mechanisms to "keep ourselves on track" that we use when pursuing conscious goals. Not only can goals be activated, pursued, and even achieved completely outside our conscious awareness, but researchers have found that automatic and unconscious goal pursuit can have significant impacts beyond achieving the goal itself, invisibly influencing our moods, judgments, and later behaviors.

Whether consciously or unconsciously activated and pursued, goals are *motivational* thoughts.

They consist of mental models of some future state plus a plan to get there. They are central to how we fulfill our needs, satisfy our wants, and improve our physical and mental well-being. They may also cause us to pursue destructive outcomes, as when the needs and wants that drive us are actually damaging to our well-being, a problem we will discuss in Chapter 10.

Goals are obviously central to marketing. Traditional marketing has always been concerned with goals and goal activation, but mostly of the conscious variety. This is because traditional marketing's understanding of the cognitive timeline has for the most part been restricted to the conscious stages of cognition. Intuitive marketing, in contrast, also recognizes and builds upon the unconscious stages in the cognitive timeline, including the activation and pursuit of unconscious goals. We will dig more deeply into the topic of goal activation and its relation to intuitive marketing in Chapter 10 and Chapter 11.

Deliberating and analyzing

Deliberation, also called *introspection* is a conscious mental process. We are all familiar with it—it is the experience of "listening to that voice in your head." It includes a wide variety of thinking activities we are directly aware of, such as remembering an event from the past, consciously memorizing new information, performing arithmetic calculations, imagining possible future scenarios, forming intentions and goals, evaluating and analyzing situations, planning future actions, and of course, deciding to act in one way rather than another.

Before knowledge of unconscious processes became commonplace, people naturally assumed that thinking began with deliberation. And they also naturally assumed that the best way to determine what was going on in someone's mind was to ask them. How could they think otherwise? This was certainly the starting point for every marketing research technique that preceded the earliest efforts to measure unconscious reactions to media and advertising in the 1970s. Today, despite knowing much more about the unconscious processes that precede deliberation, most of the major marketing research methodologies in use, some of them supporting billion dollar research companies, rely solely or predominantly on measures of deliberation, using the three traditional techniques of *self-reporting*—interviews, surveys, and focus groups.

One of the most consistent findings of modern brain science is that this most reasonable of assumptions is seriously flawed. Although humans are pretty good at remembering the broad outlines of episodes and incidents from their past—the more recent and the more emotionally relevant the better—our introspective abilities fall down considerably when we attempt two deliberative tasks that are extremely important to marketers and market researchers—remembering the details of our past behavior, and imagining what we are likely to do or think in the future.

> **Recent research tells us that our memories, like our perceptions, are largely constructed and subject to significant "drift" over time.**

It has been found that every time we retrieve a memory, we change it. Over time, in a process similar to copying a copy of a copy of an image, an episodic memory can become a very inaccurate record of its original experience. And, most damaging to self-reporting methodologies that rely on consciously accessing memories, we are completely oblivious to this transformation. To our conscious deliberating minds, our memories feel as real and accurate as our experiences in real time, even when they are not.

Like memories, our predictions of future behavior and attitudes are often expressed with high levels of confidence but end up achieving low levels of predictive accuracy.

This effect is documented especially well in recent research on happiness—in particular, people's ability to predict how happy they will be in the future if certain things happen or don't happen. As summarized by Daniel Gilbert in his entertaining book, *Stumbling on Happiness*, copious research reveals that we are consistently bad at estimating how happy some future course of action will make us.[5] Just as research shows that we significantly misremember how happy we were in the past, it also shows that we consistently fail to predict how happy we will be in the future. Given that consumers tend to buy products and brands, at least in part, in order to fulfill expectations about how those items will make them feel, this weakness in our deliberative capabilities should be of concern to marketers who base *their* predictions on these faulty consumer predictions.

Speaking and acting

Finally, the mental processes in our cognitive timeline produce observable and reportable outcomes. Speaking and acting are behaviors, consciously performed and often the result of deliberation, but sometimes triggered directly by unconscious processes as well.

Given that our memories are faulty and our self-predictive capabilities are limited, it should come as no surprise that the main examples of "speaking" of interest to marketers—self-reports expressed in interviews, surveys, and focus groups—sometimes steer marketing decisions in disastrously wrong directions.

This is why intuitive marketing does not rely exclusively, or even predominantly, on verbal expressions as indicators and predictors of consumer behavior, but rather tries to incorporate speaking and acting into a broader explanatory framework that includes the unconscious processes of impression formation, determining meaning and value, and unconscious goal activation as well, in the hopes of shedding the brightest possible light on why consumers choose what they choose, do what they do, and say what they say.

A Quick Trip Through the Human Nervous System

The *physical* nature of this cascade of processes in the cognitive timeline can be appreciated when we view these cognitive steps within the framework of the human nervous system. Our nervous system has two main parts—the *peripheral nervous system* (*PNS*), consisting of the web of nerves and pathways throughout the body, and the *central nervous system* (*CNS*) consisting of the brain and the spinal cord. The *PNS* provides the input and output functions in the cognitive timeline and the *CNS* provides the internal processing. The overall flow is illustrated in Figure 3 as a sequential process in four steps: detecting, analyzing, deciding, and executing.

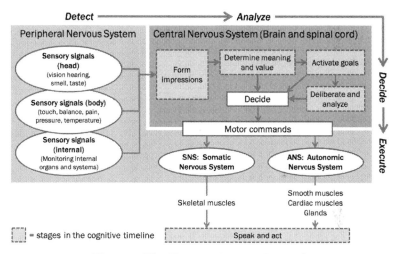

Figure 3. The Human Nervous System[6]

Sensory inputs enter the human body through the *PNS* in the form of waves and pressures of various sorts. Electromagnetic waves enter our eyes, sound waves enter our ears, physical forces press against our skin, molecules wash over the taste buds in our tongues and the chemoreceptors in our noses. The *PNS* also monitors our internal bodily states, including physical and chemical signals from our internal organs and muscles.

These raw signals are then relayed to the *CNS* where they get converted into perceptions with meanings and associated positive or negative values. Within the brain, these value-encoded and meaning-laden impressions become the cognitive inputs into goal activation, conscious deliberation, and decision-making.

When we (that is, our brains) conclude that some action or behavior is required to deal with the situation identified by all this cognitive processing, the *PNS* comes back into play in the form of two subsystems, the *somatic nervous system* (*SNS*) and the *autonomic nervous system* (*ANS*), both of which receive signals from the *CNS* in the form of *motor commands*, which direct bodily actions. The *SNS* controls our skeletal muscles for actions like walking, running, eye-blinking, smiling, speaking and other outward-oriented behaviors, while the *ANS* controls our internal organs to prepare us for action—altering our respiration, heart rate, perspiration, blood flow, pupil dilation, and other physical states according to the need at hand.

Out of this intricate dance of physical waves and pressures, massive decoding and interpretation processes, conscious and unconscious goal activation, decision-making, and orchestrated body movements that range from the twitch of an eyelid to a verbal quip to a full-body fight or flight response, we human beings sense, construct, and change the world around us, every moment of every day, from birth until death. It is an impressive system that is far more complex than the simple models of traditional marketing would allow. If nothing else, the complexity of consumers' mental lives as revealed by brain science should cause marketers to be more humble in their aspirations.

> **Influencing the intuitive consumer is a far more demanding task than anyone could have imagined even as recently as 20 years ago.**

The physiological interplay of the human body with cognitive activity is also extremely relevant to marketing and market research because each of these processes in the body and brain produces physical traces that can be measured while they are occurring, often in units of time as short as thousandths of a second (milliseconds). These physiological measurements provide the raw material for the many of the metrics that can be used to test the effects of intuitive and traditional marketing efforts, as we will illustrate throughout the following chapters.[7]

Unconscious Behavioral Guidance and Consumer Behavior

The cognitive timeline just scratches the surface of the unconscious processing that precedes our conscious thinking and acting. Social psychologists and neuroscientists have dug deeper into the functioning and origins the unconscious mind to determine how and why it operates the way it does. One approach that has gained in popularity among researchers in recent years is the *unconscious behavioral guidance* model introduced by John Bargh and Ezequiel Morsella in 2010.[8]

Unlike the old Freudian model of the unconscious as a "lockbox" for animalistic instincts and primitive sexual urges, this new model emphasizes hidden processes, not hidden desires.

Our unconscious brain processes are hidden not because they are disturbing or dangerous, but because they have been honed by evolution to guide many aspects of our behavior quickly and efficiently.

They operate unconsciously to free up our limited conscious thinking capacity for more important duties, like problem-solving and planning.

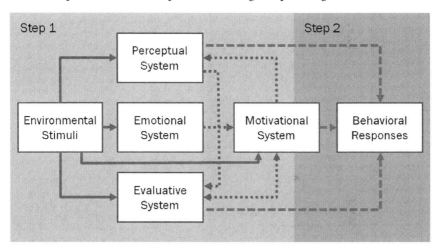

Figure 4. Four Unconscious Behavioral Guidance Systems[9]

The unconscious behavioral guidance model operates in two steps. In Step 1, external stimuli activate four consciously inaccessible behavioral guidance systems—*perceptual, emotional, evaluative* and *motivational* (solid lines in Figure 4). Also as part of Step 1, these guidance systems interact with each other (dotted lines). In Step 2, the *combined* outputs of the four behavioral guidance systems produce observable behavioral responses (dashed lines). The point of the model is that all of these activations, interactions, and impacts occur outside of conscious awareness. This, in a nutshell, is what our unconscious minds "do" when they contribute to our behavior. Let's take a look at each of these functions in turn.

What We See: Unconscious Perceptual Guidance

In most academic discussions of unconscious behavioral guidance, perceptual guidance is defined as a combination of *impression formation* and *determining meaning and value*. Impression formation comes first, operating unconsciously to both interpret and "fill in" the sensory signals that enter our bodies and brains. Impressions are then connected to meanings and values via *associative activation*, and it is this fully-loaded *perception* that guides our behavior.

> **One of the ways in which perceptions unconsciously guide us is through the processes of *priming* and *associative activation*, through which we automatically classify and make sense of the events and people in our immediate vicinity and adjust our behavior accordingly.**

Research has shown, for example, that the mere presence of events or people automatically activates internal models or *representations* of them, which in turn trigger associated knowledge structures, emotions, and goals, which then automatically influence our behavior both directly and indirectly through connections with the unconscious evaluation and motivation systems.

Unconscious perceptual guidance plays an important role in intuitive marketing, particularly in how it impacts attention and selection. Our visual systems are hard-wired to seek out certain features in visual scenes as candidate locations for focusing attention—features such as areas of high contrast, distinct borders, the center of a viewing area, tight groupings of objects, and movement. Our scanning and mapping of these features—called *bottom-up attention* by brain scientists—occurs extremely rapidly and can continue to have a significant impact on what we see and do next, even after our goal-driven attention processes—called *top-down attention*—kick in.

How We Feel: Unconscious Emotional Guidance

> **Emotions can be triggered by environmental events and in turn can trigger automatic motivational responses, which in turn can trigger behavior.**

There are two important points about emotions that need to be emphasized. First, we cannot consciously control the onset of an emotion. We might be able to consciously regulate an emotion, once we recognize we are in an emotional state, but we cannot voluntarily make ourselves "have" an emotion.

> **Emotions control us, we do not control them.**

Second, unconscious emotions do not trigger behavior directly. They only do so indirectly, through the activation of motivations and goals that then activate behavior. Both these points will prove to be critical to understanding how emotions and goals impact marketing, our topics in Chapter 8 through Chapter 11.

Leading theories of emotion posit that we cannot control emotional responses because the purpose of emotions is to provide signals of significant events or situations in our external environment—that is, things we should pay attention to and learn from because they may be potentially dangerous or beneficial to us. These signals would be compromised if we could create internal emotional states in the absence of external stimulation.[10]

Emotional states have unconscious effects when they trigger goals and motivations outside our conscious awareness and intention. For example, *anger* can unconsciously induce approach motivation with associated feelings of confidence, *disgust* can unconsciously induce a strong withdrawal motivation, not just to the source of disgust but to the surrounding context as a whole, and *sadness* can unconsciously induce a strong motivation to "change state," that is, to change one's circumstances to counteract the feeling of sadness.[11] These motivations, in turn, can trigger behavior, as is illustrated by the *emotion-motivation-action* path in Figure 4.

How We Judge: Unconscious Evaluative Guidance

Perceptions can influence behavior directly. They can also influence unconscious evaluations, which in turn can influence motivations and through those paths influence behavior—all without conscious awareness. Evaluation, as we have seen, can occur both unconsciously, as part of *determining meaning and value*, and consciously, as part of *deliberation*. As an unconscious behavioral guidance system, evaluation plays an important role in constructing preferences, activating attitudes, and triggering approach-withdrawal action tendencies.

Of particular importance for marketing, studies have confirmed that evaluations (as good or bad, positive or negative) are activated automatically—a process Daniel Kahneman calls *natural assessment*—every time we think about an object or recognize it in our environment.[12] The point is worth emphasizing.

> **Evaluations and judgments are automatic parts of the unconscious process of determining meaning and value, which means *our brains are literally incapable of recognizing something without assigning a value to it.***

This is true whether that "something" is a can of soup, a mortgage, or the family dog. This has been found to be true even for objects that are novel and unfamiliar to us. Despite the fact that an object may be completely new and unfamiliar, it is automatically evaluated by our unconscious evaluative guidance system just like a more familiar object.[13]

As a source of behavior, automatic evaluation can directly impact approach or withdrawal behavioral tendencies. Experiments that couple pushing (withdrawal) or pulling (approach) behaviors with exposure to attitude objects, for example, have consistently found that we pull faster and harder in the presence of positive objects and push faster and harder in the presence of negative objects. This is true even when the conscious task being performed has nothing to do with evaluation, for example, when it is simply to sweep objects off a computer screen with a joystick movement.[14]

Researchers have also found that this *evaluation-motivation-action* effect appears to operate in both directions. Not only do automatic evaluations trigger approach-withdrawal reactions and behaviors, but the effect can work in the opposite direction as well. In experiments where people make evaluations while engaging in approach or withdrawal behaviors (like pushing or pulling a lever), they tend to evaluate objects more positively when performing an approach movement, and more negatively when performing a withdrawal movement.[15] As with many other examples of *embodied cognition*, we see here a close two-way connection between what happens in the body and what happens in the brain.[16]

What We Want: Unconscious Motivational Guidance

As we saw in our discussion of the cognitive timeline, unconscious goals can motivate us to act, without conscious awareness that they are doing so. This is the primary mechanism of the unconscious motivational guidance system—it initiates and manages unconscious goal activation and pursuit.

> **Unconscious goal activation begins with a prime—specifically a *motivational prime*—which activates a goal and a process to pursue it.**

The motivational prime may be any sensory input—a sight, a sound, a smell, etc.—but it does more than simply trigger associative connections to other thoughts. It also triggers unconscious goal pursuit, which can be recognized by several process features shared with conscious goal pursuit that we will discuss in Chapter 11.

In contrast, a *nonmotivational prime*—also called a *perceptual prime*—tends to have a relatively short-term effect on behavior, and also tends to decrease, not increase, in intensity over time.[17]

Studies of unconscious goal priming have identified many examples of goals being activated by motivational primes without conscious awareness or intention, and then having significant impacts on later evaluations, emotional states, and behaviors. Although there has recently been controversy around this literature, due to failures to replicate some reported findings (a topic we take up in more detail in the *Addendum* to Chapter 11),[18] motivational priming with brands and other marketing-related stimuli have been found to be quite robust and reproducible. This should not come as a great surprise, given that goal activation is precisely the function marketers design these stimuli to produce.

We will explore the implications for intuitive marketing of unconscious motivational guidance in Chapter 10 and Chapter 11.

Unconscious Guidance and the Puzzles of Consumer Behavior

When combined, the cognitive timeline and unconscious behavioral guidance models paint an intricate but realistic picture of the intuitive consumer. Through these models, we see how unconscious thoughts precede and shape conscious thoughts. We also see how unconscious thoughts are made up of several interacting processes, each hidden from conscious view.

> **Perception, evaluation, motivation, and emotion all operate below the surface of conscious scrutiny to *construct*, not passively observe, the world we see and feel. They also play crucial roles in helping us identify and trigger the wants and needs that guide our expectations, plans, and actions.**

All of these systems of unconscious behavioral guidance contribute to solving many puzzles of consumer behavior that face marketers: What do consumers notice? What do they like? How do they choose? What do they gain from our products and brands? As we will see in the following chapters, both conscious and unconscious cognitive processes are highly relevant to understanding how intuitive marketing operates in the consumer's mind and in the marketplace.

The Scope of Intuitive Marketing

So far this discussion of human thought processes has been pretty abstract and general. I've described the machinery of cognition which operates in every human mind, in every context. Now we need to ground these concepts in a more specific context that is directly relevant to marketing and consumer behavior. Our framework for this purpose—called *the consumer cycle*—is illustrated in Figure 5.

The flow of expectations and associations is critical to understanding how the consumer cycle relates to intuitive marketing and the mental processes presented in this chapter.

Figure 5. The Consumer Cycle[19]

> **Each experience at each stage in the consumer cycle updates the consumer's mental associations with the product or brand experienced.**

This update may result in a more positive or more negative picture, and it may change prior associations subtly or profoundly, according to the intensity, emotional direction, and outcome of the experience. Following the experience, those freshly updated associations become part of the consumer's *expectations* when entering the next stage of the cycle. So experiencing a marketing message changes—subtly or significantly—a consumer's associations with the marketed product or brand. The next time that consumer goes shopping, those associations influence what they decide and what they do at the point of sale. *That* experience, in turn, updates their associations yet again. For products acquired, those updated associations shape the consumer's expectations for consuming or using the product, and that consumption experience again updates their associations, which alters the expectations they bring to the next marketing message they encounter, and so on, around and around the consumer cycle. For frequently purchased goods, a consumer may pass through thousands of cycles in a lifetime. This is essentially how we learn about the products and goods available to us, determining what we like, what we want, and how to get it.

The consumer cycle model emphasizes the interrelated nature of the three primary ways consumers interact with products and brands: through exposure to marketing messages, through shopping and acquisition experiences, and through product consumption and use. Each of these consumer touchpoints represents a stage in the cycle. Each stage is "pre-loaded" with expectations shaped by the mental associations formed in previously experienced stages. This continuous cycle of experiences, updated associations, and updated expectations provides the rich and complex landscape that marketers must navigate if they want to influence consumer attitudes and behavior.

> **The consumer cycle model emphasizes that no stage in the cycle can be evaluated and optimized in isolation from the others.**

Mental associations laboriously forged in the marketing stage must impact choices made in shopping and consuming stages if they are to be judged successful. Products purchased in the shopping stage must pass the test of consumption if they are ever to get past initial trial. And marketing messages must be responsive to the existing expectations of living, breathing consumers if they are to build and strengthen associations in the direction that marketers hope to achieve.

Timing and Intuitive Marketing

In Chapter 1, I mentioned that there are circumstances in which both consumers and marketers can benefit from the skilled application of persuasive marketing. I noted that persuasion can be helpful rather than annoying and disruptive if the intended target of the marketing effort is motivated to receive and process the persuasive message. I want to close this chapter with a look at when and where such motivation is likely to occur.

Short-Term Activation vs. Long-Term Brand-Building

In 2013, advertising researchers Les Binet and Peter Field published an influential study of advertising effectiveness titled *The Long and the Short of It*. The study reported on an analysis of data from the Institute of Practitioners in Advertising (IPA), a British ad industry organization. The IPA database, called *Databank*, contains information on over 1,400 award-winning ad campaigns, including details on the campaigns' objectives, duration, media coverage, and results. The purpose of the study was to find out how advertising effectiveness is influenced by campaign purpose and duration.

Binet and Field's results were surprising to many in the marketing field, because they showed a significant effect of timing—persuasive messaging campaigns that used rational arguments to encourage immediate or near-term consumer actions were more likely than non-persuasive campaigns to produce positive effects, including "very large profit growth" after one year. In contrast, advertising that featured more of an intuitive marketing approach—making emotional connections, delivering minimal or no arguments, sometimes not making sense at all—was found to generate slightly less profit growth after one year, but over longer periods significantly outperformed the "rational" campaigns. For campaign durations of three-plus years, 43% of emotional campaigns achieved very large profit growth, as compared to only 23% of rational campaigns.[20]

Digging down into these results, Binet and Field concluded that short-term and long-term impacts of advertising were in fact quite different:

The way in which long-term effects are generated is fundamentally different from how most short-term effects are produced. Although long-term effects always produce some short-term effects, the reverse is not true and long-term effects are not simply an accumulation of short-term effects.[21]

These results ran counter to a basic premise of persuasive marketing: that consumers need to be confronted with persuasive reasons to buy—that is, rational arguments—or they will not buy. A rational argument that is logically sound and drives marketplace success at one point in time should be equally sound at a later point in time, other circumstances remaining constant. But this is not what Binet and Field found. Their analysis revealed that sustained business benefits do not emerge from the simple application of rational messaging over and over again, but rather are generated by a different kind of advertising altogether. They called this different approach *emotional advertising*, but we could just as easily call it *intuitive advertising*. Applying the lens of brain science to Binet and Field's findings, it is clear that the successful ad campaign results they highlight in *The Long and the Short of It* do indeed utilize emotion, but they also apply other intuitive mechanisms such as low attention processing, conditioning, priming, and implicit learning, to produce the long-term performance advantages found in the study.

The connection between persuasion and short-term acquisition can be traced to traditional marketing's origins in door-to-door sales. In a real-time sales situation, there is always some presumption that the potential buyer is motivated to make a purchase. Persuasion is usually applied to "close the deal," that is, to overcome any resistance by the prospect to finalize the purchase, or perhaps to expand the purchase by upgrading or bundling. The immediacy of the sales context is critically important, because brain science research has found that our brains process immediate choice opportunities quite differently than choice prospects in the future.[22]

> **As Binet and Field correctly point out, *rational* (or persuasive) advertising is about overcoming resistance to buying in the short-term, while *emotional* (or intuitive) advertising is about building brand associations in order to shape expectations for the long-term.**

Given that some consumers will be in a motivated state at any point in time, while others will not, Binet and Field recommend a mixed approach, with a ratio of about 60:40 between advertising focused on long-term brand-building vs. advertising focused on short-term activation.

Another important implication from Binet and Field's study is that persuasive marketing works better in some media and channels than in others. They found, for example, that emotional advertising was most effective when presented on TV. Despite the rapid and relentless growth of digital advertising and marketing platforms, their analysis showed that TV remains the best medium for making and building emotional connections with brands—a conclusion that has been replicated by many other studies.[23] In contrast, digital channels like website stores, search advertising, and mobile apps are more often designed for short-term activation, and often excel at this purpose.

Just as Binet and Field recommend that advertisers split their ad campaigns between short-term activation and long-term brand-building, they also recommend a mix between different media and channels to fulfill those short-term and long-term objectives. But they note an important asymmetry between the two types of advertising:

> *the use of digital channels, in concert with traditional ones, serves to amplify their efficiency and represents the most effective pattern of media investment. It also appears to be the case that, in an increasingly highly cluttered online environment, campaigns that benefit from extensive offline priming in traditional media are able to succeed better.*

> **Translated into our terminology, Binet and Field are saying that intuitive marketing in traditional channels can help boost persuasive marketing in digital channels, but not the other way around.**

Intuitive Marketing Supports Persuasion, But Not Vice Versa

Intuitive marketing can reinforce and support targeted persuasive marketing, but persuasive marketing generally does nothing to enhance intuitive marketing.

Binet and Field reference Daniel Kahneman's *System 1–System 2* model to explain this asymmetry. They note that persuasion is a *System 2* process that requires attention and motivation at the moment of exposure. Presenting a rational argument, as close to the moment of purchase as possible, preferably accompanied with an easy mechanism for closing the sale, is going to be the best path to activation. And their research showed this approach to produce the strongest short-term sales response. But rational messages are quickly forgotten and persuasive effects decay very rapidly. Because persuasive arguments do not strengthen positive associations with brands, the brand itself does not benefit significantly from the transaction, and long-term effects are minimal.

In contrast, long-term brand-building is driven by *System 1* processing, which does not require high attention nor *System 2* deliberation. Binet and Field call the mechanism for this kind of influence *emotional priming*. They do not go into much detail as to how this mechanism works, but we will remedy that oversight in later chapters. They note that emotional priming delivers more modest short-term sales responses, but has stronger longer-term effects because feelings are remembered longer than messages, and learned associations can impact not just imminent purchasers, but future and potential buyers as well. Repeated exposures cause positive associations to strengthen, effortlessly and without conscious oversight, and this accumulation of mental associations over time produces the long-term effects observed in their study.[24]

Intuitive marketing can support persuasive marketing because the associations it builds can *prime* persuasive messages, making them more salient and more likely to be noticed in a cluttered environment of competing demands for the consumer's attention. But persuasive messaging cannot return the favor and contribute to strengthening intuitive marketing, because it does not build positive brand associations on its own. The missing ingredient in persuasive marketing is *learning*. Persuasive marketing is designed to get a consumer to act—ideally, to get them to buy—either immediately or at the next available opportunity. But the consumer is not expected to learn much from the persuasive message. Rather, learning is postponed until the product is experienced later in the consumer cycle, in the consuming stage. The model is "buy, then learn." The logic of intuitive marketing is precisely the opposite. The marketing is designed first and foremost to enable learning—to associate the brand with positive outcomes—and later to activate that learning through priming and other intuitive mechanisms. The model is "learn, then buy."

Persuasion, Influence, and the Future of Marketing

Our trip through the cognitive timeline, the unconscious behavioral guidance systems, the consumer cycle, and short-term activation vs. long-term brand-building has led us to the same conclusion reached by Binet and Field.

> **Persuasion has its place, but it is not the core purpose of marketing, nor is it a guaranteed route to marketing success.**

On the contrary, we have seen that persuasion is a powerful and appropriate tool when the marketing goal is to overcome buyer resistance and close a sale, but it is a poor tool for building long-term relationships with consumers and customers.

Binet and Field emphasize that persuasion operates consciously on the consumer, via *System 2*. Persuasion builds on the marketer's belief that consumers don't want to do what marketers want them to do, so they need to be persuaded to do it.

It is no coincidence that Robert Cialdini, in the introduction to his classic study *Influence: The Psychology of Persuasion*, calls his six principles of persuasion "*weapons* of influence," and confesses that he began studying the topic because he was tired of being a "patsy" for "the pitches of peddlers, fund-raisers, and operators of one sort or another."[25] All of Cialdini's principles can be seen as ways to overcome the resistance of the "patsy":

- *Reciprocity.* I did something for you, now you need to do something for me.
- *Commitment and Consistency.* You already agreed to do something like this, so you should be consistent and do this next thing for me.
- *Social proof.* Other people are doing it, so you should do it too.
- *Authority.* People who know best are saying you should do it, so do it.
- *Liking.* You like me, so you should do this for me.
- *Scarcity.* You'd better do this now, because the opportunity may be gone soon.

> **What if consumers weren't treated as "patsies"?**

What if marketing didn't operate on the presumption of resistance to any marketing message? What if people bought products and services not because they were "talked into" doing so, but because, at a given time and place, those products or services helped them achieve the goals they were already pursuing? The brain science that underlies intuitive marketing tells us that these are not unreasonable questions to ask, nor unreasonable objectives to pursue.

If marketing can be aligned with consumers' goals and intentions, if it can deliver its messages without disruption and annoyance, and if it can build trust, provide small emotional rewards, and connect to people's aspirations and identities, then perhaps it does not need to hold a black belt in arm-twisting to achieve its purposes. Perhaps it can communicate a sense of product or brand value to consumers without treating them as hostile adversaries—and without engaging in a constant arms race with other marketers to attract, capture, and keep consumers' undivided attention.

Chapter 3

Understanding Attention

A Brain Science Primer for Marketers

"You keep using that word.
I do not think it means what you think it means."
–Inigo Montoya

If there is one principle with which nearly every marketer agrees, it is that marketing must grab a person's attention before it can influence them. In this chapter, we will dig down into the brain science behind attention to learn more about how this seemingly self-evident mental state is actually more elusive than it appears at first glance. We will see that there are several types of attention, that attention can be triggered in several different ways, and that the biggest problem with attention may not be getting it, but keeping it. Then, in the next chapter, we will take a fresh look at marketing's preoccupation with capturing and monopolizing consumer attention, asking whether and how intuitive marketing can operate both in the presence of attention and in its absence.

Aiming the Spotlight of Attention

One common metaphor for human attention is the spotlight. Like a single beam aimed at a performer standing in the center of a dark stage, attention illuminates only a small part of the total scene, leaving everything else in darkness. As the spotlight moves, other areas come into view, but only as regions previously illuminated fall into darkness. The spotlight can only cast light in one place at a time.

This metaphor is appealing to marketers because it's easy to imagine *your* product standing in that spotlight, while your competitors' products get lost in the surrounding darkness. But the spotlight metaphor is flawed. It misses two of the most important aspects of attention—the spotlight is both constantly in motion and fuzzy around the edges.

Despite our best efforts, we cannot fixate our attention on one thing indefinitely. The human brain is too omnivorous and too easily distracted to allocate its attentional focus to one object for any length of time. Even when we are subjectively confident that we are gazing intently at one spot for an extended period, our eyes are in fact imperceptibly jumping all over the visual scene in front of us. It is our brains that stitch all that movement together to create the illusion of a stable image. And this is only what happens during *external attention*. We also devote a significant amount of our attentional resources to monitoring our internal state—engaging in what attention scientists call *introspection*. Whatever is coming in through our senses, our attention is often aimed inward, listening in to our internal monologue and monitoring how we are feeling—whether we are feeling happy or sad, hungry or thirsty, nervous or calm, sleepy or alert. Introspection is a key element of *deliberation*, the conscious cognitive process discussed as part of the cognitive timeline in Chapter 2.

Attention is less like the beam of a spotlight and more like the flicker of a firefly.

It flits from place to place, never stopping in one spot for very long, jumping from external to internal monitoring and back again. Attention is a process and an effort, which is why our brains use it sparingly. It is imperfect. it generally aims where we want it to aim, but it also can't help focusing on some things we would rather ignore and ignoring other things we would rather notice.

Varieties of Attention

One problem with the spotlight metaphor is that it makes attention seem like a single thing. The beacon of attention is either shining on one location or it is shining on another. It is either on or off. But attention is far more complex than that. In fact, it consists of a number of separate functions in the brain that recruit different pathways and regions to accomplish different tasks. If marketers want to understand how attention and marketing really intersect, they need to learn at least a bit about how these different aspects of attention operate in the daily life of the human brain.

What Attention Does: Orienting, Vigilance, and Control

Michael Posner, professor emeritus of psychology and neuroscience at the University of Oregon, has been studying attention in the human brain since the

1970s. Acknowledged as one of the world's leading experts on the topic, Posner first established that human attention was not a single state, but a combination of three basic functions that together give us the capability to control how we observe and interact with the world around us—while simultaneously monitoring and controlling our internal thinking processes. Posner identified three key functions that remain the cornerstones of how scientists study and think about attention today:

- *Orienting.* Our ability to direct our attention to a particular location or object, either automatically or purposefully.
- *Vigilance.* Our ability to maintain our attention on a selected object. Posner calls this function *alerting.*
- *Executive control.* Our capacity to use attention to monitor and control our thoughts, feelings, and behaviors.

Orienting

When marketers talk about attracting attention, "grabbing" attention, or "rising above the clutter," they are usually talking about orienting. This function of attention has to do with selection. Orienting our visual attention to an external object (called *overt attention*) is a highly orchestrated physical process in which the body, the head, the eyes, and the patterns of visual scanning and fixating all collaborate to zero-in on a selected object of attention.

The act of orienting can be triggered automatically by the external stimulus itself (*bottom-up attention*) or it can be voluntarily directed by a goal or purpose (*top-down attention*).

Orienting can also occur without involving any eye or body movement. This is called *covert attention* and is the mechanism by which we become aware of objects outside the center of our visual field. In natural settings, covert attention usually precedes overt attention as a bottom-up signal that directs conscious, overt attention to a new location. The covert sources of the orienting shift may not be consciously experienced. Only the overt target of the shift is noticed as the new focus of attention.

There are two other very important types of visual attention that do not involve moving the eyes. The first is called *feature-based attention* and involves the deployment of covert attention to specific features of a stimulus or scene, such as its color, texture, shape, orientation, movement, etc. The second is called *object-based attention* and involves paying attention to an object as a unified entity, or as a collection of separate objects, rather than as a spatial location or a collection of physical features. Object-based attention becomes relevant for issues like how many objects a person can attend to at the same time, how a set of features or a location in space can become perceived as a single object, or how a foreground object gets differentiated from its background.

All of these aspects of orienting—whether overt or covert, automatic or voluntary, or focused on a location, feature, or unitary object—have important implications for marketing. Although these implications have not, for the most part, been explored by traditional market research models of attention, they have the potential to provide a rich foundation of new insights for intuitive marketing. Findings about feature-based attention, for example, can be used to develop better packages and label designs, given that consumers often spend less than one second scanning crowded store shelves before making a product selection. And findings about object-based attention can be used to help marketers determine how many objects consumers can easily "take in" at one time—a limit that significantly impacts their ability to process and appreciate visually complex stimuli like TV ads and in-store displays.

Vigilance

Vigilance is the process of maintaining attention over time, enabling an object, feature, or scene to remain in attention for longer than a moment. While orienting is the first step in attention, vigilance is the mechanism by which we maintain an alert state of attention toward something for any length of time. Without the ability to maintain vigilance, the act of orienting wouldn't do us much good. Evolutionary biologists believe our ability to maintain a focused state of selective attention is built into our brains today because it provided several evolutionary advantages in the early days of humankind. It allowed us to remain vigilant in a hostile environment, it enabled us to prepare for action, and it gave us time to observe and learn from the world around us.

> **Maintaining attention requires cognitive effort and heavy reliance on *System 2* processing.**

It is much harder than it seems, because the same mechanisms that make it easy to orient attention toward an object also make it easy to orient attention away from that object, toward something else. The ability to maintain attention over time varies from individual to individual, with some of us being much better at it than others. Several cognitive impairments, such as Attention Deficit Hyperactivity Disorder (ADHD), are related to how well the vigilance network functions in the brain. Conversely, an ability to concentrate intensely and maintain selective attention is often associated with productivity and intellectual accomplishment.

Our brains are also very good at tricking us into believing we are maintaining constant attention to a particular object when in fact we are not. As mentioned earlier, eye-tracking studies show that when we believe we are maintaining focus on a single location in our visual field, our gaze is actually roving widely around the scene in front of us. The perception of constant vigilance is an illusion created by our brains, much like a modern video camera can create a *steady-cam* effect that compensates for unintended movement of the camera in the hands of its operator.

Traditional marketers tend to be most concerned with the orienting function of attention and less concerned with its vigilance function.

While they almost universally want their marketing messages to draw people's attention away from competing stimuli and toward their own, they spend much less time thinking about what they want those people to do *after* their attention has been attracted. Do they want the consumer to dwell on the message, engaging in what Robert Heath calls *high attention processing*? Or do they want the consumer simply to take away a rapid, largely emotional, impression from the experience, one from which they can then build positive associations in a more implicit, nonconscious manner? Before brain science revealed the existence these rapid, largely unconscious *System 1* responses, marketers did not realize they had a choice. Today they are starting to understand that they do, and that the choice they make can have both positive and negative repercussions.

Executive control
Executive control is the type of attention we use when we need to resolve a conflict between different possible responses to a situation. Its functions include selecting among competing inputs, resolving conflicts among possible responses, and monitoring and correcting errors. Executive control is the mechanism by which we direct attention inward, paying attention to what we're thinking and feeling, as well as assessing the gap between our current internal state and what we are trying to accomplish at any given moment.

Executive control is very important to people's ability to concentrate, problem-solve, and evaluate alternatives.

The activation of executive control is exclusively a function of *System 2* thinking. Indeed, one of the best ways to define *System 1* thinking is to say it is thinking that occurs in the absence of executive control. As we observed in Chapter 1, *System 1* jumps to conclusions, ignores ambiguity, and suppresses doubt. That's a pretty good definition of thinking without executive control.

Like maintaining a focused state, executive control is cognitively taxing. It requires the expenditure of mental effort and concentration and is therefore something our *cognitive miser* brains would rather avoid if at all possible.

> Many of the *System 1* shortcuts we employ regularly as consumers and shoppers allow us to perform the (usually) useful function of avoiding explicit executive control in marketing, shopping, and consumption experiences.

Traditional marketers appear to have a love-hate relationship with the executive control function of attention. On the one hand, their beliefs about marketing effectiveness tell them they should get people to think consciously about their brand or product if their audience is going to absorb their carefully-crafted marketing messages. But on the other hand, they know that one of the most common results of invoking executive control with regard to marketing is *counter-arguing*, also called *persuasion resistance*. When a person consciously considers a persuasive argument, they may respond by constructing reasons why that argument might not be true, or they may even begin generating alternative arguments that might be more plausible.[1] These responses, of course, are exactly what marketers *do not* want the targets of their messages to do. So marketers are often torn on the topic of executive control.

Bottom-Up and Top-Down Attention

Attention can be triggered in two very different ways, called *bottom-up* and *top-down* attention. Marketers need to understand the differences between these two types of attention, and know whether a given piece of marketing is meant to attract an audience in a bottom-up or top-down manner.

Here is how these two types of attention differ. Imagine you are a guest at a party. You are in a large room with many other people, in which many separate conversations are going on. You are concentrating intently on the conversation in your group when, suddenly, you hear your name spoken across the room. Despite your current object of attention, your unconscious monitoring system hears your name, signals your orienting system, and your attention is automatically and involuntarily diverted toward the source of the sound. This is *bottom-up attention*. It may be covert attention, in that you can orient toward this new sensory experience without moving your eyes, but most likely it will become overt, and you will start scanning the room to find out where the sound is coming from. Bottom-up attention is also called *exogenous attention*, because the source of your attentional shift is located outside your own mind. Bottom-up attention is activated from the outside in.

In contrast, imagine that you are planning to meet a friend at this party. While you are engaged in friendly banter with your fellow party-goers, you are also discreetly scanning the room, trying to spot your friend. You are engaged in *top-down attention*. You are directing your attention voluntarily and effortfully, consciously allocating a certain amount of your attentional resources to a task you have defined for yourself—finding your friend in a crowded room. Top-down attention is also called *endogenous attention*, because it originates inside your mind, as part of a behavioral plan that begins with a goal or intention. Top-down attention is activated from the inside out.

Bottom-up attention

> **Too many marketers believe their goal in life is to attract bottom-up attention at any cost.**

This is why television stations in the US automatically turned up the volume of commercials—until the practice was outlawed in 2012.[2] It is why commercials are filled with extravagant "gimmicks" designed to grab people's attention, such as car crashes, irritating noises, physical pain, disgusting objects, and obnoxious behavior. Such practices *seem* to work. They do grab attention. When measured with traditional *System 2* metrics, such marketing messages are better remembered and often better liked—as little moments of entertainment. But these measures do not take into account the emotional association-building that occurs with every exposure to these messages. As we will see in Chapter 8, repeatedly associating a product or brand with negative stimuli can result in the creation and reinforcement of aversive *somatic markers* that will trigger automatic and unconscious withdrawal reactions to that product or brand when it is encountered in the future—even though there is no logical or causal relationship between the product and the negative attention-grabbing gimmick used in the marketing message.

> **Marketing or advertising that associates a product with an aversive stimulus for the purpose of grabbing bottom-up attention may well prove counter-productive in the long run—with neither marketers nor consumers ever realizing the effect is occurring.**

One of the most interesting brain science findings about bottom-up *visual* attention is the discovery that the visual triggers of bottom-up attention are highly predictable. Neuroscientists have mapped a number of visual elements that reliably attract bottom-up attention when we first encounter a new visual scene. Such elements are said to have *visual saliency*. Some of the most prominent visual saliency elements that automatically draw our gaze include:

- Brightness relative to background
- Certain colors and color combinations
- Distinct borders
- The center of a viewing area
- Tight groupings of visual objects
- Overlapping items
- Movement (especially around the visual periphery)
- Faces and where faces are looking[3]

The effects of visual saliency on eye gaze movements are so predictable that neuroscientists have been able to develop *computational algorithms* that simulate the bottom-up attention patterns of human viewers with up to 90% accuracy, compared to the results of real eye-tracking studies. In other words, software algorithms can scan a visual scene and identify with high accuracy exactly where people will look when they first take in that scene.[4] Such algorithms are now available commercially and can be used to identify the flow of bottom-up attention in response to both static images and dynamic videos.[5]

> **Understanding how automatic bottom-up attention operates can be extremely valuable for marketers, but also for anyone involved in the design of visual interactive displays that need to processed and navigated by humans.**

Top-down attention

Top-down attention usually follows bottom-up attention, often within less than a second. As a part of *impression formation*, bottom-up processing automatically creates a mental *saliency map* of the visual scene, using the elements described above, to predict areas that are more or less likely to yield useful information. This rapid process is inaccessible to conscious awareness. The saliency map is then used to guide a *navigation strategy* that is enacted when top-down attention, driven by the goals and tasks of the viewer, is activated.

Top-down attention can be characterized as the allocation of additional cognitive resources, including conscious *System 2* oversight, to an object flagged for closer scrutiny by bottom-up processes. This interaction of bottom-up and top-down processing highlights an important fact.

> **Attention is not a switch with only "on" or "off" settings, but rather a continuous resource allocation function that can be modulated from "none" to "less" to "more."**

The continuous nature of attention is what makes it possible for researchers like Robert Heath to explore the different ways low and high attention processing can impact responses to stimuli like TV advertising (see Chapter 4).

One of the most important findings from eye-tracking research is that *our goals and expectations determine where we look.* If two people view the same scene with different goals or expectations in mind, their gaze patterns are likely to be completely different. Top-down attention is *endogenous*, it is a function of the purposes of the mind directing it, not the external object or scene toward which it is aimed. This is an important point. When top-down attention is activated, the resulting gaze patterns and behavioral outcomes cannot be explained with reference to the object of attention alone.

> **Scenes or objects do not have a built-in "attention score." The amount and focus of top-down attention allocated to them depends on the goals and expectations of the person viewing them.**

This reality can be very problematic for marketers. Although attention is a conscious *System 2* mechanism—you can't pay attention without knowing you are paying attention—goals and expectations can be activated either consciously or unconsciously. If consumers are unaware of the purposes that are driving their attention, they cannot communicate that information to researchers. This measurement problem goes even deeper. Unconscious goals are often triggered by unconscious emotional reactions or motivational impulses, which in turn may be triggered by unconsciously perceived primes or emotional somatic markers, which can also activate unconscious associations or unconscious approach-withdrawal responses, all of which can directly influence conscious attitudes, preferences, choices, and behaviors.

> **Unconscious goals and expectations that trigger top-down attention are only the top layer of many layers of unconscious processing that remain invisible to traditional self-reporting marketing measurement techniques.**

Sources of Attention

Traditional advertising and marketing are mostly concerned with bottom-up attention. Where does it come from? There are two main sources: *novelty* and *emotion*. In addition, there is one especially important source of both bottom-up and top-down attention: *reward anticipation*. Understanding how these sources of attention work can help marketers adjust the levels of attention they want to attract for different kinds of marketing.

Novelty and Expectancy Violation

Our attention is naturally drawn to novelty. Encountering something "new and different" is one of the most reliable ways to trigger the *orienting* function of bottom-up attention. But how do our brains determine what is novel? The answer has to do with one of the most important brain science findings.

> **The brain is basically a *prediction engine*, that is, an active generator of *expectations* about what will happen next, given what happened before and what is happening now.[6]**

Novelty is what our brains register when a prediction breaks down. When something *unexpected* happens, it creates an *expectancy violation*—a mismatch between what our brains predicted would happen and what actually happened—and that violation typically triggers a conscious emotional feeling every human knows well: *surprise*. It does not take much to create an expectancy violation. Our brains are finely tuned to identify the smallest deviation from normalcy.

Novelty is not an objective property of an object, scene, or situation. It is a subjective property determined by the brain's comparison of *what's expected* with *what's observed*. Because expectations vary from person to person, what might be a novel attention attractor for one person might be perfectly familiar and remain unnoticed for another. Novelty is in the eye of the beholder.

Every marketer is aware that novelty attracts attention. When combined with the assumption that attention is always good for marketing, it is natural to conclude that good marketing should always include a healthy dose of attention-grabbing novelty.

But brain science tells us a more nuanced story. In fact, it tells us two stories that at first glance appear to be completely contradictory. The first, better-known, story says that we are emotionally attracted to novelty. It produces a pleasurable reaction that we seek out and enjoy. But the second story says our natural reaction to novelty is aversion and discomfort, and as a result, we don't like novel things as much as we like familiar things. Taken together, these two stories tell us we're attracted to novelty, but we also distrust it. How can this paradox be resolved?

Let's look at the aversive side of novelty first.

An expectancy violation means that something went wrong.

It signals an error in our predictive model of the world, and that error signifies uncertainty and, potentially, danger. Uncertainty is an aversive state, which people are strongly motivated to diminish and avoid. Taking an evolutionary perspective, we can see why caution in the face of novelty's uncertainty would have survival value for our hunter-gatherer ancestors. As Daniel Kahneman points out in *Thinking, Fast and Slow*:

> To survive in a frequently dangerous world, an organism should react cautiously to a novel stimulus, with withdrawal and fear. Survival prospects are poor for an animal that is not suspicious of novelty. However, it is also adaptive for the initial caution to fade if the stimulus is actually safe.[7]

In the modern world, in which no longer have to worry about man-eating predators behind every bush, the vestiges of these ancient lessons still guide our unconscious and conscious reactions to novelty. Marketers often see the conscious side of this effect when they introduce consumers to new products or packaging designs. More often than not in their focus groups and surveys, they find that the alternative rated most "new and different" is also rated the least liked.

In contrast to this picture of humans as novelty-averse, a second stream of research paints a very different picture, in which humans are seen as enthusiastic novelty-seekers who find in novelty many positive effects, such as pleasure, attraction, curiosity, and learning. At the root of this picture is novelty's association with *dopamine*, a key chemical neurotransmitter that is released in the brain and throughout the body. There are several dopamine systems in the brain. One of the most important, called the *midbrain dopamine* system, has been found to release dopamine in two related circumstances: when we *detect novelty* and when we *anticipate reward*. Since rewards are usually pleasurable to attain, and novel situations often (but not always) end up being rewarding, this system seems to associate novelty with pleasure, a feeling that is incompatible with aversion.[8]

The resolution of this apparent paradox can be found in a deeper understanding of the role of dopamine in novelty detection and reward processing. Russell Poldrack, a neuroscientist from the University of Texas, Austin, has written that it is a mistake to think of dopamine as the "feel good" neurotransmitter, that is, as a direct source of pleasure. Rather, he notes that researchers now see dopamine more as a motivation-driver.

What gets triggered when dopamine is released is not pleasure per se, but an even more important human capability—a motivation to learn and act.[9]

Novelty, because it violates our expectations, attracts attention and creates an opportunity for learning. Paying attention to novelty gives us a way to update our expectations and correct our bad predictions. Dopamine release facilitates this process by motivating us to treat every expectancy violation as a learning opportunity. Whether this leads to pleasure or pain depends on *what* we learn. Only by focusing our attention on novelty, exploring it, and converting it into something familiar can we adjust our expectations appropriately. This is why scientists now believe it is not novelty per se that triggers dopamine release and subjective feeling of pleasure, but the anticipation of a reward that *may* result from the novel situation.

There is a clear implication for marketers. Novelty in marketing needs to be treated with caution. The link between novelty and attention has been known for years. But the link between novelty and aversive emotional reactions, largely occurring outside of conscious awareness, is a more recent discovery. For the most part, this knowledge has not migrated into the "received wisdom" of traditional marketing. We will expand on this topic in Chapter 5, when we look at how the *novelty-familiarity continuum* reveals two "sweet spots" that intuitive marketing can leverage to optimize the mixture of these two important ingredients in marketing messages.

Emotional Display

The second major source of bottom-up attention is emotional display. Just as paying attention to novelty conferred survival advantages to our early ancestors, so did paying attention to the emotional expressions of others. Being able to "read" emotional displays enhances our ability to determine whether others wish us well or ill, or if they are reacting to something in the immediate environment that is also relevant to us. These skills have been passed down to us as attention-grabbing routines which still get triggered automatically in our brains today.

Although it is also true that our own emotional states affect our propensity to pay attention to events and objects around us,[10] what is more relevant to marketing is our ability to detect the emotional "climate" around us, both consciously and unconsciously, and then use that information to guide the allocation of our attention. Our mental machinery for focusing attention on emotions is efficient and deeply ingrained. Researchers have found that both positive and negative emotional pictures can reliably trigger the orienting response of attention after only half a second, and that emotionally-charged pictures displayed for less than a quarter of a second can elicit brainwave activity indicating the onset of attention.[11]

The boundary between conscious and unconscious responses to an emotional display is not a sharp line.

The threshold of conscious awareness emerges gradually out of unconscious processing, passing through an intermediate state that Bernard Baars and colleagues call *fringe consciousness*—a domain of vague feelings of knowledge or familiarity that are consciously experienced but not quite tied to a specific object of thought.[12] Emotional triggering of attention may cross this fringe consciousness threshold, creating moments in which we experience indistinct feelings or intuitions of personal relevance—which could be positive or negative in emotional direction—that motivate us to engage attention and explore a situation more deeply. Researchers have found that such moments may be triggered by exposure to brands or marketing messages,[13] so marketers should want to know whether their efforts to attract attention with emotional displays are creating positive or negative emotional impressions on their audiences.

This question is important because another feature of the relationship between emotional displays and attention is that we pay more attention to negative emotions than positive. This *negativity bias* appears to be a general feature of how humans attend to the world around us. As Roy Baumeister and coauthors observe in an article aptly titled "*Bad is Stronger than Good*":

> *Bad emotions, bad parents, and bad feedback have more impact than good ones, and bad information is processed more thoroughly than good. The self is more motivated to avoid bad self-definitions than to pursue good ones. Bad impressions and bad stereotypes are quicker to form and more resistant to disconfirmation than good ones.*[14]

For allocating attention, bad emotions are stronger than good emotions.

This means that if a marketer or advertiser is trying to maximize the attention-grabbing power of their messaging, they may conclude that negative emotions work better than positive. And if this conclusion is shared by other marketers, it can result in a marketing "commons" filled with an overabundance irritating, annoying, and emotionally grating messages. In this way, the natural negativity bias in our allocation of attention has the potential to turn into a pervasive negativity bias in the marketing we are subjected to everyday.

The risk of excess negativity in marketing is increased by the fact that emotional responses to single exposures of ads or marketing tend to be relatively small. This may motivate marketers to "ratchet up" the negative emotional content to get a bigger immediate response. In addition, when people self-report their responses to stimuli they are exposed to, they often misidentify the emotional arousal generated by negative stimuli as positive emotional valence.[15] All of this combines to improve the attention-grabbing "effectiveness scores" of emotionally negative ads, while hiding the potential longer-term effects on brand and product associations that can develop through repetitive conditioning, priming, and negative association-building.

The use of negative emotional displays to attract attention, like the use of expectancy violations, comes at some risk to the marketer. Many advertising and marketing professionals recognize the short-term weaknesses of these approaches, privately referring to them as "cheap tricks" that contribute little to the brand or product story they want to tell. The brain science research we have reviewed reveals an even more serious problem, going to the heart of how marketing works in the minds of intuitive consumers. The point is worth repeating.

System 1 does not rationally assess or logically scrutinize the associations it observes, it simply records them, strengthens them when they are repeated, and incorporates them into action plans that may or may not ever reach conscious awareness.

By repeatedly associating their products and brands with negative emotions, marketers risk creating invisible but enduring associations in the minds of consumers that can lead to unintended and unrecognized aversive reactions later on in the *consumer cycle*, as marketing audience members interact with products as shoppers and consumers.

Reward Anticipation

Finally, both top-down and bottom-up attention are attracted by potential rewards. Novelty and emotional displays capture attention primarily by activating our *defensive* motivational systems, to increase our alertness and vigilance in the face of uncertainty. Rewards engage attention in a more positive way, by activating our *appetitive* motivational systems, to increase our ability to exploit beneficial opportunities in our environment. Defensive reactions evolved to keep us safe and alive, appetites evolved to keep us active, healthy, and most importantly, procreating.

Rewards come in two broad categories. There are *natural rewards*, also called *intrinsic rewards*, that are hard-wired into our biological nature. These include the rewards we derive from food, sex, and companionship, but also psychological rewards such as autonomy, competence, and a sense of belonging. Then there are *learned rewards*, also called *extrinsic rewards*, that may not be rewarding on their own, but lead to separate outcomes that we learn to be rewarding. Earning money, for example, may not be rewarding in itself, but the money earned gives us access to other rewarding experiences that we desire.[16] These topics are taken up in more detail in Chapter 10.

As we see in the cognitive timeline model, every impression we form through sensory inputs immediately and automatically gets associated with both a *meaning* and a *value*. This value attribute is a mental representation of the *reward value* of that perceived object or situation. The more positive value a stimulus is predicted to have, the more likely it is to attract our attention.[17]

> **Reward anticipation research shows that our brains are constantly updating a "tally sheet" of value that gets adjusted with every object or event we encounter.**

Obviously, how this tally sheet gets updated by marketing and advertising, as well as shopping and consuming experiences, should be of paramount importance to marketers.

What is most interesting about the relationship between reward and attention is that it is not the reward itself that most effectively attracts attention, but the *anticipation* of reward.

> **Novelty and emotion make us aim attention, but reward anticipation makes us sustain attention.**

In other words, novelty and emotion are very good at triggering the *orienting* function of attention, but reward anticipation is much better at maintaining the *vigilance* function of attention. Anticipating a reward is what keeps us focused, even to the point of fixating our attention on addictive stimuli that may overpower the *executive control* function of attention, driving us to engage in habitual behaviors that challenge our capacity for self-control (as many players of *Candy Crush Saga*™ can testify).

The neurotransmitter *dopamine* plays a big role in the relationship between reward anticipation and attention. Release of midbrain dopamine facilitates attention to novelty and emotion because attention to those features facilitates learning. In experiments studying reward anticipation, midbrain dopamine release has been found to increase not only when we pursue rewards, but also when we make accurate predictions about those rewards.[18]

People are especially attentive to emotional rewards that appear irregularly and unpredictably, that is, that provide a *variable reward* pattern.

Our attention is preferentially drawn to activities and situations that produce unpredictable reward streams. Examples include games, puzzles, competitions, and gambling—basically, just about any activity with the potential to produce rewarding outcomes that arrive with uncertainty. We are motivated to maintain attention because we don't know when the next reward will appear. And we continue to maintain attention until we "figure it out," which, for carefully crafted variable reward patterns (such as those generated by slot machines), may be never. We are particularly drawn to variable reward streams for which we believe our own choices and actions can have a causal impact on the production of rewards.

Once a variable reward pattern is "figured out," its ability to attract attention starts to decline, as does midbrain dopamine production when it is later encountered. As it becomes more predictable, and thus more familiar, we do not need to deploy the same level of cognitive effort to extract the reward it yields. With additional repetition over time, extracting the reward may become a *habit*. A habit is the most efficient mechanism our brains have for minimizing the cognitive effort required to perform an action. It is a memorized behavioral sequence that can be triggered by an external or internal *cue* and performed with little or no conscious effort. We may not even be aware of the relationship between the cue and the habit it triggers.[19]

Habits take familiarity and predictability to the next level, replacing a familiar but conscious action with an automatic and unconscious one.

Getting Attention Is Easier than Holding It

Holding attention is hard for two reasons. First, we don't like to pay extended attention to things that we don't care about, or that don't provide potential reward value to us. We may not be able to override our automatic *bottom-up* orienting response to "cheap tricks" that activate a momentary shift of attention, but we can pretty quickly and efficiently use our *top-down* attention to filter out stimuli that are not aligned with our goals and intentions. Second, we are easily distracted. Unless we are deeply concentrating on a particular object of attention—a state of affairs that is relatively rare for a marketing message—our attention can be easily diverted to other objects in our immediate vicinity.

How Distractions Steal Attention

Distraction is a big problem for any marketing effort that depends on holding attention to get its message across. The problem is this: high-attention marketing usually starts out as a distraction that must wrest attention away from wherever that attention was previously focused. Its ability to do this is a function not only of its own bottom-up *attention-grabbing* ability, but also of the *attention-holding* qualities of the previous object of attention.

Brain scientists have been looking at this issue for some time, and a body of research has begun to accumulate around the question of when and under what circumstances we are likely to get distracted when trying to focus our attention on one thing while ignoring everything else around us.

The answer at first seemed relatively simple, but lately it has become more complicated. The simple answer is that we are most immune to distraction when we are concentrating on something—in the language of the scientists, when we are experiencing high *task load*. More recently, some contradictory findings about the effects of task load have prompted scientists to refine the concept.

Today, scientists talk about two distinct aspects of task load: *perceptual load* and *cognitive control load*, each of which appears to have a different impact on distractibility.

This has led to a more nuanced theory of distractions, called the *load theory of selective attention and cognitive control*.[20]

Perceptual load refers to the demand on attention required to visually process the complexity or density of the scene within which attention is being directed. More objects in the scene, more movement, more variety among objects, and more distinct visual features in each object all contribute to increasing perceptual load. In terms of our cognitive timeline model, perceptual load occurs at the initial *form impressions* step in the timeline. Because increased perceptual load consumes greater attentional resources, it has been found to lower the potential for distractors to capture attention away from the current task. Conversely, people who are focusing on a task with low perceptual load are more easily distracted from that task.

Cognitive control load, in contrast, refers to the demand on conscious thinking required to engage in a task. It is a measure of the extent to which a task absorbs the limited capacity of our conscious working memory. It occurs later in the *cognitive timeline*, during the conscious *deliberate and analyze* phase. Higher load on cognitive control often produces subjective feelings of fatigue, mental effort, and frustration.

Cognitive control load has been found to have the opposite effect on distractibility than perceptual load.

> **Greater cognitive control load increases the potential for distractors to divert attention away from the current task, while lower cognitive control load is associated with less distractibility.**

Just about everyone has experienced this effect when struggling to concentrate on a demanding task. Have you ever wondered why checking your Facebook page seems so enticing when you are in the middle of reading a complex report, or just trying to finish your homework? It's because you're experiencing high distractibility due to high cognitive control load.

What do these findings imply for marketing? Assuming marketing starts off as a distractor trying to pull attention away from some other object, this research tells us that effort is most likely to succeed when the competing object requires low perceptual load and/or high cognitive control load. For example, a billboard might be better at grabbing attention when encountered while driving down a lonely, monotonous stretch of desert highway in Nevada than when seen in the middle of Times Square in New York. Conversely, if a marketing message is already holding attention, it is more likely to continue doing so if it has the opposite characteristics: high perceptual load but low cognitive control load. So a visually entertaining but cognitively undemanding TV ad should be better at holding attention during an ad break than an ad with low perceptual load and high cognitive control demands.

What Happens When Distractions Fail to Distract

Most marketers assume that attracting bottom-up attention but then failing to sustain top-down attention is just a missed opportunity that incurs no costs of its own. Recent research on a psychological phenomenon called *distractor devaluation* challenges that comfortable assumption.

> **Virtually all marketing research examines responses to marketing messages *after* attention has been paid to them, but most marketing messages are either intentionally or unintentionally ignored.**

So why isn't more research devoted to understanding this much more common case? What happens when consumers *resist* marketing's attempts to pull their attention away from something else that is currently holding their attention?

Psychologists began looking at the effects of *ignoring distractions* in the early 2000s. As we've seen, paying attention depends on two interacting functions—first, selectively focusing attention on a particular object or feature, and second, simultaneously suppressing attention toward everything else. It has been known since the 1980s that this suppression function works through a mechanism called *inhibition of return*, which makes us less likely to return our attention to objects we have previously identified as distractions unrelated to our current task or goal.[21] Around 2003, researchers began to ask whether there might be other after-effects of suppressing attention that could impact how previously suppressed objects were later evaluated when they were encountered with full attention.

Initial studies looked at responses to simple geometric figures or single letters that were designated as targets or distractors in a search task. Later studies looked at human faces, expressing neutral, negative and positive emotions, and different kinds of tasks. Finally, in 2011, a first study was published looking at online banner ads as distractors. All of these studies produced similar results: Items that had previously been encountered as distractors were later rated more negatively in a conscious evaluation task than either previous targets or similar items that had not been seen previously.[22]

This effect, called *distractor devaluation*, raises an important issue for marketing. When we focus on one thing, we don't devalue *everything* surrounding it, we do so only for a subset of those things. What determines whether something gets included in that subset is whether it produces *goal interference*. People's ability to pay attention to one thing while ignoring other things—that is, their ability to hold *top-down attention* and resist distractions—is an act of deliberate intention. It is a *System 2* function, an exercise of conscious goal pursuit.

> **What gets devalued when pursuing a selective attention goal is anything in the immediate environment that is a perceived as a potential competitor to achieving that goal.**

Everything else just gets ignored or suppressed from conscious awareness, but not devalued. This is not good news for traditional marketers and advertisers, because most advertising is specifically designed to grab bottom-up attention in order to interfere with a person's existing focus of attention. This is exactly what "rising above the clutter" means.

The assumption behind the traditional model has always been that if an interference effort fails, no costs are incurred by the brand or product being advertised. Failed attention capture is seen as free. And maybe better than free. Some researchers have argued, and some evidence has been found to support the argument, that ignored ads may indeed induce a *mere exposure effect*, leading to increased positive feelings even when not consciously noticed.[23] But these studies do not test ads in an explicit goal-interference context, so may miss the most important condition under which distractor devaluation occurs.[24]

Sources of Intuitive Influence: Aligned-Intent Marketing

What can marketers do to sustain attention and avoid the threat of distractor devaluation? Traditional marketing offers no solution because it doesn't recognize the problem. Intuitive marketing offers a more focused solution, one that utilizes the first intuitive mechanism of influence introduced in Chapter 1: *aligned-intent marketing*.

> **If a marketing message is closely aligned with a consumer's goals and intentions, it is more likely to be processed consciously as a contribution to goal pursuit, and less likely to be processed as an interference in need of suppression.**

Attention is paid, but it is *earned attention* because it supports the consumer's currently active task and goals.

Attention is beneficial when marketers want to get consumers to consider something novel—a new product, a "new and improved" familiar product, or a radically new product category (think *iPad* or *Segway*). In such circumstances, existing associations are absent in the minds of consumers and need to be established from scratch. Getting attention and triggering conscious *System 2* thinking about the new item is the best way to lay down those new associations.

Attention is also beneficial when the purpose of marketing is to trigger immediate or short-term action of some sort, such as persuading a person to make a purchase, sign up for an email alert, or make a charitable contribution. In these situations, all three functions of attention—orienting, vigilance, and executive control—are likely to be activated as the consumer considers whether or not to act. These are moments when the consumer becomes a *deliberative decision maker*, that is, when they become motivated to receive and process a persuasive message that aligns with their existing intentions, goals, and expectations and helps them determine whether and how to act. Attracting and maintaining their attention with regard to the proposed action, as well as addressing any doubts or concerns they might generate via *executive control*, are all critical to successfully "closing the deal" and instigating action in such circumstances.

Of the five sources of intuitive marketing influence introduced in Chapter 1, *aligned-intent marketing* directly relates to how marketers can successfully earn and take advantage of top-down attention.

Aligned-intent marketing is intuitive marketing optimized to take advantage of situations in which a consumer's goals or intentions are known, or at least strongly suspected.

In such cases, marketing can be crafted more in terms of the traditional persuasive model, because the purpose of the message is to make it easier or more enticing for the consumer to act on his or her intent. Aligned-intent marketing primarily leverages top-down attention, although bottom-up attention principles can also be used to simplify and facilitate the process of behavior activation.

If we think about the continuum between *long-term brand building* and *short-term behavior activation*, aligned-intent marketing can be employed anywhere along that continuum, but it is more likely to fit with marketing objectives at the short-term activation end of the spectrum.

The closer a consumer gets to an actual purchase or other action desired by the marketer, the more effective aligned-intent marketing will be.

This means marketers are more likely to see opportunities for aligned-intent marketing at the *shopping* and *consuming* stages of the *consumer cycle* than at the *marketing* stage, because it is at moments within these stages that the consumer's intent is most likely to be aligned with the goals of the marketer's message.

In a shopping context, packaging is often the most conspicuous carrier of aligned-intent or earned-attention messaging. On a shelf with dozens or hundreds of products displayed, attracting bottom-up attention with stand-out packaging is often key to becoming a member of a consideration set. But once the consumer has engaged *top-down attention* and is actively pursuing a goal to select and buy one product, the messaging portrayed by the packaging—which may be expressed in design elements, not necessarily words—is processed with earned attention, and its alignment with the consumer's goals and expectations can be a critical element in determining the final choice.[25]

Another context in which aligned-intent marketing can be successfully deployed is online and mobile shopping and information gathering. *Online search ads*—those little textual ads that appear above and to the right of search results in Google and other search engines—are perhaps the best example of marketing messages aligned with consumer intent. Because they are presented based on the search phrase entered by the consumer, search ads tend to be highly relevant to the consumer's interests at that moment, so are more likely to attract top-down attention and be experienced as useful information rather than as annoying distractions.

The value of aligned-intent search advertising on both mobile and online platforms is reflected in how advertisers invest their online spending budgets. Search ads remain the most popular form of online advertising, accounting for 45% of all online ad expenditures in 2018, compared to about 31% for banner ads, 15% for digital video ads, and 9% for other formats.[26] Display formats tend to be much more graphically rich than search ads, but due to the relatively primitive state of targeting algorithms used to select ads to display on web pages and mobile screens, are generally not related to immediate tasks and goals. As mobile advertising continues to exploit what might be called "intuitive search"—inferring consumer intent based on geo-location capabilities or other contextual cues—opportunities for aligned-intent marketing in the digital domain will continue to grow beyond its original beachhead in the domain of online search.

A glimpse into the expanding potential for online and mobile aligned-intent marketing is provided by a 2015 study co-authored by the research firm Forrester and Internet giant Google. In this report, the idea of intent-driven search is extended into a more general model of mobile device-enhanced "micro moments" in which consumers turn to their mobile devices to supplement in-store, real-time buying and information-gathering experiences:

> *Consumers can now interact with brands and products at any moment, from any device. This shift in behavior has fractured the customer journey and path to purchase into a collection of user-initiated, intent-driven actions. … These are instances when we reflectively turn to a device to act on a need we have in that moment, to learn, discover, find, or buy something. They are intent-rich moments where decisions are being made or preferences are being shaped. The proliferation of smartphones fueled this shift, but the concept of "moments" is not isolated to the mobile experience. Customers expect relevant and useful content across devices.*[27]

As marketers continue to develop the infrastructure necessary for "in the moment" goal-aligned and task-aligned marketing, we may be seeing one of the most important ways in which the old world of intrusive, disruptive marketing is going to transition into a new world of earned-attention intuitive marketing.

Chapter 4

Marketing in the Absence of Attention

Bypassing the Noise of Persuasive Marketing

"Shouting 'notice us' just doesn't cut it anymore."
–Bernadette Jiwa[1]

Instead of focusing on short-term transactional wins based on attention-grabbing and overt persuasion, marketers can choose to focus on building longer-term, less volatile, and more sustainable positive mental associations. This approach utilizes the second intuitive marketing influence mechanism introduced in Chapter 1: *low-attention marketing.*

In this chapter, we will discuss three circumstances in which attention may be counterproductive to marketing goals. Contrary to the attention-persuasion model, we will see that these circumstances are in fact quite common. They may even represent the majority of situations in which consumers encounter and process marketing messages.

Pioneers of Intuitive Marketing: Robert Heath

Despite the limitations of the spotlight metaphor, marketers often see their goal as putting their messages at the center of consumers' attentional high beams. They want to "grab" attention, "rise above the clutter" of competing messages, and "stand out" against an undifferentiated background. In other words, they want to elevate their messages from a *distraction* on the periphery of attention to a *target* at its center. But there is an irony in this view.

> **Marketing may work best when it operates around the hazy edges of attention, not at its bright center.**

This opens up the disturbing possibility that much of the time, effort, and money marketers have expended to shout "notice us!" and place their products and brands at the center of consumer's attentional spotlight may have been misspent.

The first person to place this possibility in front of the marketing and advertising industry, in a way that couldn't be ignored or easily dismissed, was Robert Heath.

Origins of the Low Attention Model

In 2001, Robert Heath published an unassuming little monograph called *The Hidden Power of Advertising*. Clad in a modest blue cover, Heath's 100-page report set off something of a firestorm in the world of advertising and marketing. He began by reacquainting his readers with the work of Herbert Krugman who, in the 1960s and 1970s, first proposed the idea that TV advertising was consumed in a passive, low attention state that precluded the possibility of active attention, memorization, and recall that were assumed to be necessary by traditional theories of persuasion. In 1965, in one of the first marketing experiments to employ brain-scanning technology, Krugman used EEG (electroencephalography) to measure a young woman's brainwaves while she watched ads on TV and read ads in a magazine. He found two results that contradicted the then prevailing wisdom about TV advertising. First, the woman seemed to be in a lower attention state when she was watching TV than when she was reading the magazine, which contradicted the current view that TV should attract more attention than reading because it employed two sensory inputs (sight and sound) rather than one. And second, her attention to TV advertising appeared to wane with multiple viewings, which contradicted the widespread belief that TV ads should become more engaging with repetitive viewing, not less.[2]

Krugman's study suffered from a number of methodological limitations which made it relatively easy for critics to dismiss its contrarian findings. As a result, its impact on advertising and marketing practice remained minimal over the next three decades.

Heath's 2001 monograph, along with several follow-up studies he published over the next 12 years, resurrected Krugman's ideas and, leveraging more recent brain science findings and more modern measurement techniques, replicated Krugman's findings. More importantly, Heath began to explore the real paradox at the heart of these findings: how could advertising messages that seemed to attract so little attention have such big effects on memory and behavior, even years later?

Heath's response to this question was to suggest a heretical notion, that attention to advertising might actually be bad, at least in some circumstances (e.g., TV ads) and for some purposes (e.g., brand-building). He developed a position based on

70

four interlocking claims. First, he argued that effective brand-building occurred through emotional connections, not rational persuasion. Second, he claimed that advertising's focus on attention was based on a mistaken belief that advertising needed to persuade, and that a high level of attention was needed to deliver a persuasive message. Third, citing research from neuroscience, he argued that emotional processing was more conducive to long-lasting memory formation than rational processing. And fourth, again citing neuroscience research but also his own studies, Heath provided evidence that emotional TV ads were indeed processed with lower levels of attention than more rational-persuasive ads, at least when the ads were consumed in a natural (passive) TV viewing environment.[3]

Heath concluded from this analysis that brand-building was best achieved through emotional advertising that generated positive feelings and implicit associations with brands through simple repetition, not rational persuasion. High attention to this style of emotional advertising not only failed to increase memory formation, Heath argued, it could actually inhibit it. Heath called his alternative approach to advertising the *Low Involvement Processing Model*, which he later renamed the *Low Attention Processing Model*, or *LAP*.

The Market Research Empire Strikes Back

When Heath's studies first began appearing, the response from the commercial market research community was swift and dismissive. No one had much trouble with Heath's first claim—that emotion played an important role in brand-building. Most ad testing methodologies at the time agreed that emotions were important, although they tended to see emotional displays as just another tool for attracting attention, not as a way to bypass it. Emotions attracted attention, and attention made people more receptive to absorbing the ad's persuasive message.

> What really irritated conventional research providers was Heath's second claim, his critique of the attention-persuasion-recall model of advertising effectiveness, which he called the *information processing model*.

Heath argued that the dominant market research providers of the day had a financial stake in maintaining this model because they had decades of investment in measures and metrics that depended on its assumptions. If an ad is believed to work by attracting conscious attention and exploiting that attention to deliver a persuasive message, then the best measures of ad effectiveness are going to be *reported persuasion* and *conscious ad recall*—that is, measures indicating whether a person's declared likelihood of buying a product changes after seeing an ad, and measures indicating whether a person can spontaneously remember an ad and its message later on, such as a day or three days after seeing it. But Heath argued there was a circularity in this logic that accounted for the continuing dominance of the information processing model, despite its failure to account for the success of many ad campaigns:

> *The assumption that high attention is always beneficial has never been tested, partly because attention is so hard to measure. But then it has never needed to be tested, because of the nature of the metrics used to evaluate the effects of advertising. Historically these have focused on persuasion and recall, and because both have been shown to be facilitated by high levels of attention, it has always been assumed that high attention equates with high recall which equates to high advertising effectiveness.*[4]

Although this quote is from an article published in 2006, the knives came out much sooner, almost immediately after the publication of *The Hidden Power of Advertising*. As early as 2002, representatives of major research organizations began attacking Heath in the advertising trade press. A debate of rather heated tone quickly developed.[5] For the most part, Heath's critics focused on questioning the science behind his *LAP* claims—neuroscience was very unfamiliar to marketers at the time—and defending the logic of their own high attention metrics and models. But there were some unfortunate *ad hominem* elements to the debate as well, which reinforced the impression that Heath had hit a nerve that transcended typical intellectual disagreements.[6]

Vindication and Acceptance

It was around 2006 that measures of unconscious consumer responses to marketing started to become more visible, as neuromarketing vendors began to get significant (although often negative) coverage in the press. Academic studies showing how people could be influenced by unattended or peripherally attended stimuli, including marketing materials, began to be cited and circulated around the market research industry. A pivotal moment inside the industry occurred in 2007, when Les Binet and Peter Field published their first study of the IPA Databank, *Marketing in the Era of Accountability*, in which they found that:

> *The more emotions dominate over rational messaging, the bigger the business effects. The most effective advertisements of all are those with little or no rational content.*[7]

An even bigger pivotal moment occurred in 2011, when Daniel Kahneman published his highly readable bestseller, *Thinking, Fast and Slow*, which summarized his 40 years of research with Amos Tversky and others, culminating in winning the Nobel Memorial Prize in Economic Sciences in 2002. Kahneman's book brought the terms *System 1* and *System 2* into mainstream discourse about thinking processes, and quite suddenly the heretical propositions of Robert Heath in 2001 were looking like the new normal. Product and brand companies began demanding that measures of unconscious processes be included in their research deliverables, and the big research firms—some of whom had forcefully challenged Heath a decade earlier—suddenly began creating "consumer neuroscience" and "neuroscience and emotion" practices to deliver the new metrics. One research company went so far as to re-brand itself "the *System 1* agency."

Heath summarized his research on attention, emotion, and advertising in his 2012 book, *Seducing the Subconscious: The Psychology of Emotional Influence in Advertising*. Although some key issues about attention and marketing remain unresolved—most importantly, the exact nature of the boundary conditions that define when and where attention is and is not effective for advertising success—there is no question that Robert Heath was a trailblazer, seeing what few others could see at the time. As such, he stands out as one of the true pioneers of intuitive marketing.[8]

Sources of Intuitive Influence: Low-Attention Marketing

The traditional view of marketing puts attention at the center of marketing effectiveness. This view is based on three generally unquestioned assumptions.

- Marketing *cannot work* without attention being directed toward it.
- Attention is *always* good for marketing, so attracting attention can never work against the marketer's goals.
- A*ny target consumer* can be made to pay attention to a marketing message, if the right attention-grabbing mechanisms are applied, even if the consumer has no prior interest in or involvement with the product or brand.

Unlike traditional marketing, intuitive marketing does not depend on any of these assumptions. On the contrary, intuitive marketing can be characterized as marketing that works when none of these assumptions are true.

> **When marketing is out of the spotlight—when it is experienced in low or no attention conditions, when attention is more likely to hurt than help it, or when an audience is simply not motivated to pay attention to it—these are the circumstances under which intuitive marketing works best.**

Let's look at each of these circumstances in turn, and see the extent to which marketing can still be effective when attention is either unneeded, unhelpful, or unavailable.

Can Marketing Work Under Low and No Attention Conditions?

Thanks to a large body of research in consumer psychology and neuroscience, we now know that marketing and advertising can influence people when they are paying very little attention to it, or even when they are paying no attention at all to it.

One way marketing messages can be processed by consumers in the absence of direct attention is via *System 1 unconscious monitoring*. As we've seen in our discussion of distractions, concentrating on one thing while ignoring everything else is extremely difficult, if not impossible. This is because concentration is an exercise of *System 2* thinking, driven by the *executive control* function of attention.

> **But no matter how intensely we try to concentrate our conscious mind on one thing, we can never completely disable the *System 1* monitoring function that continuously and unconsciously scans our environment.**

Our unconscious minds never stop looking for things or situations that can potentially harm or benefit us.

Nor can we stop our minds from raising observations to conscious awareness from time to time. Complete distractor suppression is something our brains are simply not designed to do, and it is through this "back door" of *System 1* scanning that distractions can *break through* to produce conscious awareness of marketing and advertising messages, allowing them to grab at least a part of our conscious attention, despite our best intentions to ignore them.

> **It will often to be the case that low attention processing—capturing a thin slice of the consumer's conscious attention—is the best marketers can hope for.**

A second way marketing messages can be processed with little or no attention is via *incidental exposure*. A large number of studies, including those by Stewart Shapiro discussed in Chapter 3, have demonstrated that people can be influenced by advertising and marketing they are not aware of seeing and cannot consciously recall having seen. In another important study published in 2008, for example, Chan Yun Yoo showed that incidental exposure to online ads produced priming effects consistent with encoding in implicit memory, led to improved attitudes toward brands that were only experienced unconsciously, and significantly influenced people's next-day brand choices.[9] Other studies published over several decades have found similar results.[10]

How can marketing succeed under low and no attention conditions? I suggested in Chapter 1 that *low-attention marketing* is an intuitive marketing technique that can be used to influence consumers when they are paying little or no conscious attention to marketing.

Low-attention marketing works largely by creating and reinforcing mental associations with a brand or product through repetitive exposures. The purpose of low-attention marketing is to build long-term associations, not to consciously motivate short-term actions such as product purchases. The mechanisms by which this effect operates are *implicit learning* and *associative activation*—both are key elements in the unconscious process of *determining meaning and value*, which is described in the discussion of the *cognitive timeline* in Chapter 2.

> **Repeated exposure to marketing messages, even when attention is not directly focused on them, unconsciously builds associations in implicit memory, which then can be activated in a shopping context via the processes of** *priming***.**

If the associations built through marketing are appropriately positive and motivationally attractive, this sequence of effects can have a significant impact on consumers' consideration sets, stated preferences, choices, and buying behavior—all with little or no conscious awareness of how those effects were achieved.

Traditional persuasive marketing, in contrast, is designed to be consumed with high attention. It is unlikely to be effective under low or no attention conditions for a very fundamental reason.

> **When marketing designed to consciously motivate short-term action is processed with low attention, the call-to-action part of the message does not register, because it requires conscious** *System 2* **deliberation to do its job.**

In the absence of high attention and *System 2* processing of the marketing message, what remains is uncritical *System 1* association building. And the main associations that get built for such messages are likely to be negative, because the *System 1* takeaway is that this product or brand is associated with intrusiveness, disruption, demand on cognitive resources, and trying to get me to do something I don't want to do—at least at this moment.

Can Attention Actually Hurt Marketing?

One of the most important effects of attention is to activate conscious deliberation, thereby shifting the mind from *System 1* effortless thinking to *System 2* deliberative thinking.

If marketers want consumers to engage in deliberation, grabbing their attention is a good thing to do. If deliberation is not the desired response, grabbing attention is probably a bad idea.

There are also some very good reasons why a marketer might want to *discourage* attention to marketing and conscious deliberation. Here are three.

Persuasion resistance and correction

In 1994, Marion Friestad and Peter Wright published an important paper called *"The Persuasion Knowledge Model: How People Cope with Persuasion Attempts."* Noting that most persuasion studies failed to take into account how people's expectations about persuasion attempts affected their reactions to such efforts, Friestad and Wright posited a more interactive model. Their insight was that, just as people have expectations for products and brands, they also have expectations for acts of persuasion. They called those expectations *persuasion knowledge*. Friestad and Wright were the first to study how people use their knowledge of persuasion motives and tactics to interpret, evaluate, and respond to persuasion attempts by marketers and others.[11]

Key to the persuasion knowledge model is the state of the current *goals and intentions* of the person being targeted for persuasion. As observed by Friestad and Wright and other persuasion knowledge researchers who followed them, when a persuasion attempt is not aligned with the target's current intentions, the most common reaction is resistance.

People do not generally like being a target of persuasion—unless the persuasion attempt aligns with their current goals.

Researchers have identified several coping methods consumers commonly use to resist persuasion, such as discounting the credibility of the persuading agent, objecting to the appropriateness of the persuasion effort, identifying ulterior motives for the persuasion agent, or counter-arguing the content of the persuasion attempt.[12] Before any of these responses can be triggered, however, two important preconditions have to be met: first, consumers' persuasion knowledge needs to be *accessible* to them, and second, consumers need to allocate adequate *cognitive capacity* to make the necessary logical arguments and connections. Both these preconditions require that consumers respond to a persuasion attempt using a deliberative, *System 2* mode of thinking. When researchers have experimentally blocked accessibility and cognitive capacity, thus making deliberation about the persuasion attempt more difficult, conscious persuasion knowledge was less likely to be triggered and resistance declined.[13]

Persuasion resistance cannot be completely suppressed by low-attention marketing.

> **Research on *unconscious persuasion correction* has found that a lifetime of exposure to persuasive messaging seems to arm consumers with unconscious persuasion correction filters.**

These filters discount persuasion attempts even in the absence of conscious deliberation and awareness.

In an intriguing series of studies published by Juliano Laran and colleagues in 2011, consumers were asked to estimate how much they would spend on an upcoming shopping trip. Prior to making their estimates, the consumers were exposed to brand names or brand slogans from two kinds of retailers: "value-oriented" stores (e.g., Walmart, Dollar Store) or "luxury-oriented" stores (e.g., Nordstrom, Tiffany). When people were exposed to luxury store *names*, they anticipated buying more in their upcoming shopping trip. And when they were exposed to value store names, they anticipated buying less. This was the result one would expect from classic priming. But when people were exposed to brand *slogans*, a "reverse priming" effect was observed. People's anticipated shopping spend was lower when exposed to luxury brand slogans, and higher when exposed to value brand slogans. This effect was the same whether the brand names and slogans were perceived consciously or unconsciously.[14] Reverse priming is discussed in more detail in Chapter 14.

These findings show that while attention and deliberation may provide one path to persuasion resistance, automatic processes may be at work as well.

> **Not only is persuasion an uphill battle for marketers, but the more attention demands and persuasion tactics are inflicted on consumers, the more consumers develop persuasion resistance strategies, making the hill marketers must climb even steeper.**

Habit disruption

Habits are the backbone of most shopping and consuming experiences. Researchers estimate that up to 45% of people's day-to-day activities are repeated almost every day, usually at the same time and in the same physical location.[15] Many of these activities involve consumer experiences such as buying and using everyday products and food items. Because habits are basically "thoughtless" activations of rigid behavioral routines that become automatic through repetition, get triggered by environmental or situational cues rather than conscious intention, and involve little or no goal pursuit—either conscious or unconscious—on the part of the consumer, they are hard to change.[16] For brands and products lucky enough to be objects of habitual buying, this confers significant advantages over competitors, providing one of the main reasons why leading brands in any category are so hard to displace.

When consumers pay attention and deliberate, habitual behavior can be disrupted.

An example of inadvertent habit disruption that led to disastrous results is the infamous case of orange juice brand *Tropicana* changing its packaging in 2009. The original carton featured the brand's iconic logo of an orange with a straw stuck in it, topped by the brand name *Tropicana* in a distinctive rounded font. Tropicana brand managers reportedly wanted to give their product a more "premium" image, so they decided to replace the orange-with-a-straw with a rather stylish glass of orange juice—the kind of glass you would encounter in an upscale restaurant or hotel, but probably not on your own breakfast table. The glass was wrapped around the edge of the carton, making it somewhat difficult to recognize as, in fact, a glass of orange juice. The new packaging also got rid of the familiar font, replacing it with a cleaner but more conventional sans serif font, in a new shade of green, and rotated vertically along the edge of the carton.

When the new packaging appeared in grocery store coolers in January 2009, results were immediate and catastrophic. Between January 1 and February 22, sales of Tropicana orange juice fell 19%, generating a loss of $33 million, with competitors picking up almost all of the lost market share. At the end of two months, the new packaging was pulled from shelves and the old package reinstated. Sales almost immediately returned to their prior levels.[17]

What went wrong? Despite a significant marketing effort to "introduce" the new packaging, when shoppers encountered the new design in the grocery store, they didn't recognize it as their old, familiar brand—at least not when they conducted their normal, semi-automatic, habitual search. When the expected situational cue (the old package) failed to appear, they were forced to step out of habitual buying mode and shift to conscious attention mode, perhaps for the first time in months or years. And when that mental shift occurred, when the automaticity of habit was disrupted, their newly activated attention triggered deliberation, and new choices were considered and made. In effect, at least some shoppers said to themselves, "Whoa, it looks like my old standby Tropicana isn't here, guess I'll give this other brand a try."

The lesson speaks for itself. Habit disruption can be very costly for leading brands that rely on habitual buying.

Variety seeking

A habit is relatively thoughtless behavior. Disrupting a habit triggers conscious thinking, that is, deliberation. It does this through the mechanism of attention—specifically, *bottom-up orienting*—which is how we recognize changes or differences in our environment that may have significance, positive or negative, for our well-being or goal attainment. Habitual behavior is, by definition, repetitive and consistent. It happens the same way each time it gets triggered. However, when habits get disrupted, consistency itself may become an object of conscious deliberation. And when consistent, repeated behavior becomes an object of conscious scrutiny, it may itself become construed negatively rather than positively.[18]

In consumer behavior, variety seeking is the opposite of consistency seeking. Quite a bit of research has been devoted to figuring out when, why, and how consumers prefer variety over consistency and vice versa.

> **Interestingly, people are not particularly consistent in their devotion to consistency.**

Researchers have identified a number of drivers of consistency. For example, consistency is often a function of habit, as we have just seen, or it may be a function of conscious brand loyalty. Consistency also reduces *cognitive dissonance*, an unconscious and sometimes conscious unease people feel when their actions are inconsistent with other actions or expressed commitments or beliefs.

Variety seeking can also can serve several purposes. First and foremost, it encourages people to try new things, initiating the process of discovery by which new experiences are converted into familiar ones. Variety seeking also provides an alternative when consistency is construed as a source of boredom or satiation. Studies of motivation associated with variety seeking have found that people believe others see them as more interesting and open-minded when they display a propensity toward variety seeking.[19]

> **When people stop and think about repetitive or habitual behavior, whether that deliberation is triggered by bottom-up or top-down attention, they may very well find themselves questioning that habitual behavior and engaging in variety seeking as a result.[20]**

From a marketer's point of view, encouraging variety-seeking is hardly ever the goal of a marketing message. The purpose of persuasive marketing it to get the consumer to consider buying the marketed brand, not other brands that might meet the same wants or needs. To the extent that habit disruption, attention, and deliberation trigger variety seeking, attention-grabbing may not be the right tactic, especially for an established brand with an established base of habitual buyers, or for a marketing campaign that is focused on *long-term brand building* vs. *immediate activation*.[21]

What If Consumers Just Won't Pay Attention?

We have seen that attention is most likely to work for marketing when it is given, not taken. What are marketers to do if their target audience has little incentive to give them the attention they crave?

Byron Sharp indirectly addresses this question in his excellent book, *How Brands Grow: What Marketers Don't Know*. Sharp's book was a bit of a wakeup call for the marketing industry when it was published in 2010. Based on the pioneering work of Andrew Ehrenberg (see Chapter 12), Sharp presented an impressive compilation of data that contradicted many of the most cherished assumptions and beliefs of traditional marketing. Chief among his findings was an analysis of the frequency of buying among competing brands in a product category. In contrast to the view that brands grow market share by increasing frequency of purchase among their more loyal customers, Sharp's analysis showed that most brands grow by acquiring new buyers who purchase the brand only infrequently. Sharp argued that these "light buyers" are critical to brand growth.[22] He concluded that traditional marketing practices that focus on heavy buyers—such as loyalty programs and targeted marketing—are unlikely to achieve market share growth if they are unaccompanied by mass marketing designed to reach the relatively uninvolved and marginally engaged audience of light buyers.

The findings in *How Brands Grow*, which are generally accepted by marketers in theory if not in practice, raise some serious issues for the traditional *high-attention* model of marketing and advertising. Compared to light buyers, heavy buyers are relatively easy to reach:

These heavy buyers get many more opportunities to see point-of-sale material and packaging changes (and they are presumably very good at learning about regular promotions). These buyers are also far more receptive to the brand's advertising: they notice it more and they find it easier to process and remember.[23]

But light buyers present a much greater marketing challenge. Because they buy so infrequently, they have very little incentive to pay attention to these lightly-bought brands' marketing and advertising. If that advertising is focused on short-term activation, they are unlikely to be influenced by it in the short-term, because they are unlikely to be buying in the short-term. If the message requires attention and *System 2* thinking, they are unlikely to let it past their unconscious *System 1* filters, because light buyers do not automatically associate an infrequently purchased brand with potential reward value. Intuitive marketing provides a solution to this dilemma.

To reach the mass market of potential buyers, including light buyers, marketing must be able to work under low or no attention conditions.

Wishing for greater attention, or pursuing it with increasingly disruptive and intrusive efforts, is not the best recipe for success. Using intuitive marketing, marketers can reach and influence an important part of their market that is unwilling or unable to devote high levels of attention to their product or brand.

Similarly, marketers need to recognize, as every consumer does, that marketing is usually a distraction, not a target. Marketing focused exclusively on attracting attention can—when surrounded by competing marketing messages with similar aims—become its own worst enemy. Not only does it help create conditions that thwart its own objectives, it also trains consumers to become experts at suppressing marketing messages and devaluing the products and brands being offered.

There is a kind of *tragedy of the commons* effect here. By overgrazing the "attentional commons," marketers collectively run the risk of making the marketing environment as a whole inhospitable to the allocation of attention to any of their messages.

As each marketer attempts to wrestle attention away from the rest, treating every other message as "clutter" compared to its own demand for attention, the marketing consumer is surrounded by an environment that is all clutter, all interference, and all noise. Paying sustained attention to anything in such an environment is extremely difficult, especially if consumers are already engaged in some other task that has preferentially attracted their top-down attention.

Intuitive marketing recognizes that attention is sometimes good for marketing, sometimes not. It recognizes that allocating attention takes cognitive effort, and that for most people, in most circumstances, this effort is something they would rather expend elsewhere, not on marketing. Most importantly, intuitive marketing recognizes that whether and how to trigger attention to marketing is a strategic choice, not a universal requirement.

Chapter 5

How We Prefer, What We Prefer

Mechanisms of Consumer Preference

"You can't always get what you want."
–Mick Jagger

What's your favorite brand of soft drink? Of potato chips? Of automobile? To understand at a fundamental level how people answer questions like these, brain scientists have had to ask some far more basic questions. How do human beings develop preferences? How do our brains get from the *idea* of Coca-Cola to a *rating* of Coca-Cola? How do we get from *knowing* a product or brand to *judging* that product or brand? When we say we *prefer* a Ford to a Chevy, what mental processes go into producing that statement? And once we say it, how likely is it to remain the same over time, and how reliable is it as a prediction of future behavior?

For brain scientists, how human beings determine in our conscious *System 2* minds whether we like or don't like something, whether we *prefer* it to something else, is a challenging research question. Where do these *beliefs*, which we as consumers and research participants regularly report to eager market researchers, come from? In order to answer these questions, we need to dig deeper into the relationship between *System 1* and *System 2* processing.

How We Prefer: System 1 Meets System 2

Most discussions of *System 1* and *System 2*, like ours in Chapter 1, emphasize the differences in how the two systems operate, noting how *System 1* is fast, effortless, and largely unconscious, while *System 2* is slow, effortful, and conscious. But emphasizing these differences can lead to an erroneous picture of *System 1* and

System 2 as two separate modes of thinking that function largely in isolation from each other. Nothing could be further from the truth.

> **Because human behavior is born at the intersection of unconscious *System 1* reactions and conscious *System 2* deliberation, it is important to know when and how these two systems interact.**

Overriding Intuition

In fact, humans could not respond to the world around us, make choices, and engage in behavior in the way we do without an ongoing and seamless linkage between these two modes of thought. Instead of the smooth and adaptive way we react and take action within the many environments we encounter every day, human behavior without integration between *System 1* and *System 2* would jerk back and forth between two incompatible modes: at one moment acting automatically and instinctively, using hardwired routines to respond to the world around us, in a manner not much different from a rabbit or a lizard; at the next, engaging in a rich internal monologue, remembering and planning, imagining scenarios of both the past and the future, sitting motionless and vulnerable, essentially impervious to the world around us. Such a creature would have run out its evolutionary clock a long time ago.

System 1 and *System 2* do not operate in such a state of mutual isolation. *System 2* emerged as a function of the *prefrontal cortex*, a much more recent evolutionary addition to our brains that developed not because it replaced the older brain structures that control the automatic reactions of *System 1*, but because it provided an extremely useful additional layer of functionality that interacted with *System 1* to produce some distinctive new human capabilities—planning, analytical thinking, and most important of all, *self-consciousness*. And self-consciousness enables *meta-cognition*, the ability to think about thinking.

Through self-consciousness and meta-cognition, *System 2* provides a layer of flexible control over the output of *System 1*. This is the key to how the two systems interact, continuously and seamlessly.

The older and more automatic *System 1* continues to do its job as environmental observer and sentinel, keeping a constant and largely non-judgmental eye on the world.

> *System 1* **records and remembers. It notes and strengthens associations according to how frequently they occur or how easily they can be processed.**

System 1 prepares for and sometimes, in the case of learned habits, triggers simple actions in response to its observations. It jumps to conclusions, producing a constant stream of approach and withdrawal directives. It is not equipped to assess ambiguity or question what it observes. From time to time, its observations are passed along to System 2, primarily through the mechanism of *bottom-up attention*.

> **Once engaged, *System 2* provides a much deeper, self-conscious assessment of the situation presented by *System 1*.**

System 2 may adjust the simple interpretation provided by *System 1*. It may override an automatic response triggered by *System 1* and replace it with a more considered alternative. It does this by activating *working memory*—that "voice in your head" that signals conscious thinking—and accessing *long-term memory* to identify similar situations, both experienced and learned (see Chapter 12). It assesses similarities and differences. It considers rules and reviews results of actions taken in the past in similar situations. It anticipates outcomes and makes plans. Eventually, it may formulate and direct a different response, a *strategic* response. For example: a fake smile, a carefully modulated display of anger, or a witty riposte.

One incorrect idea, common in popular press characterizations of the unconscious, is the notion that *System 1* is somehow "at odds" with *System 2* and operates against the "better judgment" of *System 2* reasoning. This is not what the science tells us.[1] As Kahneman and others have pointed out, when the conscious mind engages in *System 2* thinking, it often acts as a *controller* of the unconscious processes produced by *System 1*. As such, *System 2* thinking can always override the initial responses of *System 1*. The opposite, however, is not true.

> **Although conscious *System 2* thinking can override unconscious *System 1* responses, *System 1* cannot override *System 2*.**

In other words, the ability to control our thoughts and behavior only works in one direction. Our unconscious minds cannot make us do things our conscious minds do not want to do. This is why alarmist concerns that unconscious suggestions may somehow overrule conscious intentions is misplaced. An advertising campaign cannot "make" a person start smoking if they do not already want to smoke. Flashing subliminal messages on a movie screen to EAT POPCORN cannot make a person buy and consume popcorn if they are not hungry or don't like popcorn.

> **Advertising and marketing cannot turn us into mindless puppets, programmed by evil marketers to act in ways contrary to our conscious desires.**

This is not to say that unconscious processes do not play an important role in how we choose, act, and respond to the world around us. But that role is not one of *controlling* conscious responses. Rather, it is one that comes into play either *before* the activation of conscious thinking, or when the controlling function of *System 2* *fails to get activated*, either because we *choose* not to activate it, or because our capacity for conscious, effortful thinking has been *diminished* by circumstances beyond our control.

Lazy Control

As Kahneman observes in *Thinking, Fast and Slow*, in a chapter appropriately titled "The Lazy Controller," the ability of *System 2* to control *System 1* is limited:

> *For most of us, most of the time, the maintenance of a coherent train of thought and the occasional engagement in effortful thinking ... require self-control. ... Even in the absence of time pressure, maintaining a coherent train of thought requires discipline. An observer of the number of times I look at e-mail or investigate the refrigerator during an hour of writing could reasonably infer an urge to escape and conclude that keeping at it requires more self-control than I can readily muster.*[2]

The issue is not that we don't have the *capability* to override *System 1* "suggestions" with *System 2* thinking, it's that we often fail to make the effort to do so.

In general, this is because our brains are *cognitive misers* that prefer to avoid the expense of cognitive effort whenever possible. In a recent summary of 11 studies published in *Science* by Timothy Wilson and colleagues, the researchers reported that:

> *participants typically did not enjoy spending 6 to 15 minutes in a room by themselves with nothing to do but think, that they enjoyed doing mundane external activities much more, and that many preferred to administer electric shocks to themselves instead of being left alone with their thoughts.*[3]

Our apparent desire to avoid deliberation—even to the point of preferring an electric shock to a few minutes of introspection—is exacerbated by various situational factors, such as when our conscious thought processes get overwhelmed or distracted by time pressures, complexity, or interruptions. In any of these circumstances, we are more likely to let the superficial interpretations and reactions of *System 1* slip through, bypassing the deeper thinking and deliberation that *System 2* would afford. And this is how many of the cognitive biases and misattributions made famous by Kahneman and his behavioral economics colleagues make their way into our default thinking patterns (see Chapter 15 and Chapter 16).

When and how does *System 2* override *System 1*? This is a critical question for both marketers and consumers, because it determines how marketing should be designed to reach consumers in the most effective and least disruptive way.

For the traditional persuasive model of marketing, *System 2* activation is assumed, because it is required for evaluating and memorizing explicit information and arguments about a product or brand. But for intuitive marketing, waking up *System 2* may or may not be the best approach, depending on the purpose and positioning of the message.

Our discussion of attention in Chapter 3 provides a good starting point for understanding how *System 2* thinking is activated by *System 1* processes. Attention is a prerequisite for *System 2* deliberation, so anything that triggers attention—such as expectancy violations, emotional displays, and reward anticipation—may also trigger *System 2*. But this is not quite the whole story.

Attention itself is only a first step in *System 2* thinking.

Once attention is allocated to an object or situation, further *System 2* processing in the form of *analytical thinking* may or may not occur. Whether it does is essentially the difference between *low attention processing* and *high attention processing*, as described by Robert Heath. The term "low attention processing" implies that *some* attention is allocated, but not enough to engage active conscious deliberation and analysis, which may invoke consumer responses unfriendly to marketing goals, like counter-arguing and variety-seeking. But such deliberation is the hallmark of full-blown *System 2* thinking. As summarized in our *cognitive timeline* model, *System 2* control is required for the final three stages of cognition: *conscious goal activation*, *deliberating and analyzing*, and *speaking and acting*.

So what causes *System 2* to fully engage, to overcome our *cognitive miser* tendencies and escalate mental activity *beyond low attention processing* to the more effortful deliberation and analytical thinking required to override *System 1* impulses? There has been a large body of research devoted to this important question over the years, and although the results have not been conclusive, a few findings have appeared consistently. First is the idea that our brains can't shift from effortless to effortful thinking in the absence of either motivation or cognitive capacity. If we are not adequately motivated to engage in deliberation (for example, if we do not feel accountable for an outcome or if a situation is not personally relevant to us), or if our brains are otherwise overloaded with distractions, time constraints, or deliberative thinking with regard to another topic, we tend to stick with *System 1* thinking even when it might steer us wrong. But while motivation and cognitive capacity may be necessary conditions for engaging in *System 2* thinking, they are not sufficient. They do not tell us why or how people come to recognize that *System 1* processes might be producing faulty output that requires a shift to analytical *System 2* output.

Recent research on reasoning and decision making has highlighted the importance of *conflict detection* as a positive source of *System 2* thinking.[4] In a series of studies reported by Gordon Pennycook and colleagues in 2015, they found that a necessary condition for *System 2* override of *System 1* was an awareness of *contradictions* in a situation or information presented or observed. Sometimes these conflicts are noticed only implicitly (that is, observers cannot access why they began thinking more analytically in one situation rather than another) but they result in behaviors, such as slower response times and higher accuracy rates, that indicate greater activation of *System 2* processes. Interestingly, the researchers did not find that greater *System 2* activation always led to greater accuracy. Instead, they found that *System 2* analytical thinking could proceed along either of two paths. Sometimes it led to "cognitive rethinking," in which an original intuitive *System 1* response was replaced by a better, more deeply-reasoned response. But at other times it led to "rationalization," in which analytical thinking was used to further justify or analytically support the original (often incorrect) intuitive response.[5] So these studies provide an important caveat to an assumption people often hold about *System 2*.

> *System 2* thinking is not always *better* thinking. Sometimes more effortful analytical thinking is used to find better answers, but sometimes it is simply used to rationalize intuitive *System 1* responses.

Additional research has highlighted the fact that people have different innate predispositions to engage in analytical thinking, and this impacts their propensity to escalate to *System 2* thinking in different contexts. This "individual differences" perspective is often underappreciated in discussions of the relationship between *System 1* and *System 2*. For example, some people are simply more willing to engage in analytical thinking than others, whatever the context. People who score higher on measures of "open mindedness" also show a greater willingness to think analytically and perhaps question initial *System 1* responses that are based on stereotypes, accessibility heuristics, or other misattributions. These differences represent *top-down* sources of *System 2* activation that are independent of the characteristics of the object of thinking.[6]

> **For marketers who want to better understand the risks and benefits of *System 1* versus *System 2* communication strategies, knowing the cognitive styles that predominate in their targeted consumer base may be crucial to finding the most effective approach.**

One additional finding from research on disfluency and *System 2* activation is worth noting. Several studies have found that the disfluency cues perceived by *System 1* may be *logically or causally unrelated* to whether or not the task at hand requires deliberative thinking. For example, studies have shown that incidental exposure to processing disfluency, such as presenting information in hard-to-read fonts or using hard-to-pronounce words, can trigger *System 2* activation. Even when the disfluency cue has no logical connection to a task at hand, it appears to trigger a conflict detection response, resulting in a more general and diffuse vigilance, which causes the task to be considered more carefully than when the disfluency cue is absent.[7]

For marketers, another way to fully engage *System 2* thinking is with *aligned-intent marketing*. While disfluency can induce conscious deliberative thinking with *unconscious* cues, providing a marketing message at a time and place that aligns with a consumer's goals or intentions can be a more overt way to hold a consumer's attention and trigger conscious deliberation and analytical thinking. But this can be a two-edged sword. *System 2* deliberation that is conducive to a marketer's immediate behavior-activation goals may indeed be reliably invoked by a marketing message that aligns with a consumer's immediate intentions. But equally, unwanted *System 2* byproducts of activation—in the form of persuasion resistance, variety seeking, habit disruption, or distractor devaluation—can also be induced by attention-grabbing marketing that is intrusive, annoying, or otherwise disruptive of immediate goals and intentions.

> **It is always in the best interest of both the marketer and the consumer to know when *System 2* deliberation is a good idea for marketing, and how best to invoke it—through novelty, emotional display, reward expectancy, processing disfluency, or goal alignment.**

The intricate dance between *System 1* and *System 2* processing is perhaps best illustrated by the different ways in which our dual-processing brains respond to novelty and familiarity.

What We Prefer: The Novelty-Familiarity Continuum

The opposing attractions of novelty and familiarity, which seem to tug marketing strategies and practices in two opposite directions, have perplexed marketers since the first marketing messages were crafted.

Do consumers prefer the new and exciting, or are they more comfortable with the trusted and familiar?

When presented as a dichotomy, this question appears to be unanswerable, because good evidence can be cited on both sides of the argument. I believe the way around this dilemma is to view novelty and familiarity not as a dichotomy, but as a continuum. This continuum is the path along which a consumer travels with regard to any product or brand. Novelty necessarily comes first, but over time and through exposure and experience, what's novel becomes familiar.

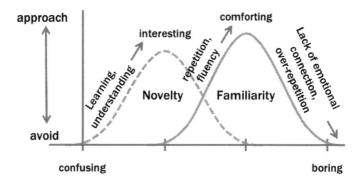

Figure 6. The Novelty-Familiarity Continuum

Figure 6 illustrates one way to visualize novelty and familiarity along this continuum, emphasizing how they contribute to approach and withdrawal motivation. The model can be applied across all three stages of the consumer cycle—from marketing to shopping to product experience.[8] The four steps along this path represent how our responses to objects and situations change as we become more familiar with them, typically passing sequentially through four states: from *confused* to *interested* to *comforted* to *bored*.

Let's take a closer look at the logic of this model, the underlying research on which it is built, and its implications for intuitive marketing and the development of consumer preferences.

Novelty: Getting From Confusing to Interesting

We have already discussed novelty at some length in Chapter 3, characterizing it as a source of attention that, in its pure form, is more associated with negative than positive initial responses. We saw that humans' often-observed positive responses to novelty are not actually a function of novelty per se, but rather a dopamine-triggered attraction to *learning* that can result in a positive response to novelty if and when a novel stimulus is found to be associated with a positive outcome or reward.

Pure novelty both orients attention *and* stimulates vigilance. If not immediately resolved into something familiar, it initially produces a sense of confusion, which triggers an aversive or withdrawal-oriented motivational reaction. Our instinctive response to something completely new and different is to withdraw and observe from a safe distance. This represents the first stop along the novelty-familiarity continuum—*confusing*.

The available research on what causes something initially perceived as *confusing* to become *interesting* is, well, very interesting. Psychologist Paul Silvia was one of the first researchers to begin exploring the relationship between interest and novelty in a 2005 paper titled *"Emotional Responses to Art: From Collation and Arousal to Cognition and Emotion."* In one experiment, Silvia had people read a poem. You can experience the results of this experiment yourself by reading this first stanza from the poem he selected, titled *"The Whitest Parts of the Body"*:

> *Such daring against men*
> *with a throat so big*
> *separated by a hundred years*
> *full of misfortune: the bloody*
> *flux. taken by a fit of madness*
> *prone to eating human flesh*
> *and measured, in due course, by naturalists.* [9]

One group of subjects were told nothing more about the poem and were asked to evaluate it. Not surprisingly, they were not confident they understood it and didn't find it very interesting. A second group of subjects was given one additional piece of information. They were told the poem was about *killer sharks*. When they evaluated the poem in light of this additional information, they felt much more confident they understood it and found it much more interesting than members the other group.[10] You can experience the transition from confusing to interesting yourself by re-reading the stanza right now.

As Silvia remarks in a later study, *interest* is the emotional response that gets us beyond our natural aversion to novelty:

it is because unfamiliar things can be harmful that people need a mechanism that motivates them to try new things. One never knows when some new piece of knowledge, new experience, or new friendship may be helpful. Interest is thus a counterweight to feelings of uncertainty and anxiety .... Interest won't—and shouldn't—always win the tug-of-war between approach and avoidance, but, over the long haul, interest will motivate people to encounter new things.[11]

The mechanism by which we build a bridge between *confusing* and *interesting* is *learning*, and the result of learning is *understanding*.

As we saw in Chapter 3, novelty naturally stimulates curiosity and exploration. If that exploration results in reducing uncertainty regarding the new object or situation, we experience the reduction in confusion as a subjective feeling of *understanding*. And with understanding, something that used to be confusing generally becomes more interesting. If that understanding also supports a prediction that the novel item will not be harmful, or may even be beneficial or rewarding, we also experience a shift from withdrawal to approach motivation with regard to it.

Interesting is an unstable point of appraisal. It has a short shelf-life. If you imagine the novelty curve in Figure 6 as a "hill," a marble placed at the top of that hill would, with the slightest push, roll down one side or the other. If the exploration effort failed to achieve a sense of understanding, the appraisal would roll back to confusing. If the currently interesting item became fully understood and predictable, it would cease to be interesting and the marble would roll forward and bump into the familiarity curve. This tendency for *interesting* to be short-lived means that satisfaction is often a temporary state,[12] but it also works extremely well as an adaptive mechanism. It keeps us exploring and looking forward to the "next big thing," that is, the next opportunity for learning.

As the dopamine model of exploration and learning implies, humans are naturally inclined to try to figure new things out. And we receive a jolt of emotional satisfaction, often below our conscious awareness, when we believe we have reached an understanding of "how it works." Similarly, we are pleased with ourselves when we "get the joke" or "solve the puzzle." But the feeling of accomplishment is temporary— a solved puzzle is no longer an interesting puzzle.

The signature benefit of understanding is that it lowers uncertainty, thereby improving our ability to make more accurate predictions and anticipate what will happen next in the world around us.

As we observe our predictions about a novel object becoming less susceptible to *expectancy violations*, we begin the mental transition toward classifying that object as familiar.

Familiarity: Getting From Novel to Comforting

As novelty transitions into familiarity, our responses and expectations undergo a profound shift. Something that is *interesting* is stimulating: it engages us, it attracts our attention, it often triggers *System 2* deliberation. But this effect, this state of arousal, is effortful and cognitively expensive. As such, it is necessarily temporary. Once the "mystery" of a novel object or situation is revealed, it begins to lose its inherent interest. Once we've "figured it out," the midbrain dopamine drip turns off and we move into the territory of familiarity. "I get it," our brains say in effect, "so what's next?"

Traditional marketers tend to inhabit a world in which novelty and interest are highly valued, constantly pursued, and lucratively rewarded.

The pursuit of novelty by marketers is closely tied to their pursuit of consumer attention, which in turn is seen as a necessary precondition for their traditional specialty—persuasive messaging. Most marketers get into the field because they have a deep affinity for what's new and what's interesting. They enjoy the creative spark that comes from a fresh idea, executed with originality. But with people drawn to novelty overrepresented in the marketing world, there is a potential downside. They may assume that the consumers they serve are just like them, constantly stimulated by a never-ending stream of clever, interesting, and attention-grabbing marketing messages, new products, and innovative brands.

But most people are not like marketers.

Marketing is not the center of most people's lives, as it is for marketers. Consequently, traditional marketers may seriously underestimate the tremendous power and attractiveness of *familiarity* for the average consumer. So let's look more closely at how regular folks respond to familiarity.

People's natural response to familiarity is in almost every way the opposite of their response to novelty. Unlike novelty, which triggers attention, stimulation, conscious deliberation, vigilance, and caution, familiarity can be experienced without much attention, it has a calming rather than stimulating emotional effect, it is processed more automatically than novelty, it triggers less conscious vigilance, and it is associated with approach rather than withdrawal motivation.

Familiarity is based on experience. For an object or situation to be perceived as familiar, it must be connected to accessible *associations* in memory and generate *expectations* that are met regularly and reliably in practice. As illustrated in Figure 6, an optimal level of familiarity might be labeled *comforting.*

Generally speaking, people prefer comforting familiarity to interesting novelty.

This is why the "comforting" peak in Figure 6 is a little bit higher on the approach axis than the "interesting" peak. People's preference for comfort is a major source of familiarity's staying power. While *interest* is a relatively temporary response to something new and different, *comfort* is a more long-lasting response to something familiar. Once an object or situation becomes comforting, it is hard to dislodge as a preference. As we shall see below, comfort is a gateway to trust and habit, two powerful sources of preference that reach well beyond simple familiarity. Comfort means *safety*, and given the choice, people will almost always prefer the safety of familiarity to the riskiness of novelty. Douglas Van Praet captures this dynamic in his book, *Unconscious Branding*:

> *One of the many paradoxes of the human mind is that although we are attracted to the novelty of pattern interrupts, we move toward the complacency of the established and familiar. The number one drive in human behavior and biology is homeostasis, or the seeking of the same stable, balanced, predictable state. Although we are excited by what is new and different, we also seek certainty and stability in our lives, deriving pleasure in the comfort of the known. We learn to love and trust what we are accustomed to, not just in terms of the people and environments we gravitate toward, but in the brands, products, and services we choose to buy.[13]*

Boredom: When and How Familiarity Goes Bad

The risk with familiarity is that it can transform from the approach-oriented peak of *comforting* to the withdrawal-oriented trough of *boring*. Figure 6 highlights two ways to get there. One is through a lack of *emotional connection*. Boredom is an emotion which signals that a familiar object or situation is not engaging a sense of *personal emotional relevance*.

Put simply, if something is well-understood and familiar, but fails to provide—or no longer provides—a sense of emotional reward, our brains classify it as irrelevant to our immediate needs.

The brain's natural inclination for such a stimulus is to ignore it, but if it is brought to our attention by persistent marketers in spite of our desire to filter it out, we will experience it not only as *irritating*, but also as *boring*, and it will become a source of withdrawal motivation. Note that this path does not require over-repetition, but may be helped along by it. It is hard to imagine a familiar object being perceived as *comforting* without an accompanying emotional connection. But if that connection is extinguished by over-repetition, the transition from *comforting* to *boring* can be swift.

The second path from familiar to boring is through *over-repetition*. For marketers, the curse of over-repetition is called *wear-out*. Much has been written about how much repetition consumers can tolerate before they experience over-repetition and boredom. Results are mixed, probably because wear-out is a highly personal effect, depending on the varied interests, intentions, and goals of each individual consumer. Also, wear-out is usually measured via subjective self-reports, while unconscious withdrawal reactions can begin to appear well before a person is consciously aware of them.

Novelty vs. Familiarity: Does It Blend?

Tradeoffs between novelty and familiarity bring to mind a well-known principle of design: *MAYA*, or "Most Advanced, Yet Acceptable." Product and package designers, often struggling with the inherent aversion to novelty and new products discussed earlier, have learned to embrace this principle, first articulated by industrial designer Raymond Loewy:

Provide moderate levels of innovation tied to recognizable elements of familiarity.

Recent studies have provided substantial evidence that the technique works. Examining aesthetic preferences for consumer products in several categories, Dutch researchers led by Paul Hekkert found in 2003 that novelty and category "typicality" (similar to, but not quite the same as familiarity) both contributed to aesthetic preferences, but in opposite and mutually suppressing ways. They found that people preferred novelty only when it complemented rather than contradicted typicality, which is another way of saying that people responded positively when the *MAYA* principle was at work. Similarly, in a 2012 study of aesthetic preferences for chair designs that built on the Hekkert study, Hung and colleagues decomposed novelty into three dimensions—trendiness, complexity, and emotional appeal—and found that preferences were greatest for moderate degrees of novelty along all three dimensions, but declined as designs approached the extremes of either too novel (*confusing*) or too familiar (*boring*).

> **People like their product novelty in small doses, preferably intertwined with the feeling of comfort associated with familiarity and category typicality.[14]**

What do these balancing acts between novelty and familiarity mean for marketers and advertisers? First, they belie any simple answer to the question "which is better for marketing, novelty or familiarity?" As the novelty-familiarity continuum illustrates, neither state is stable, much less permanent. Novelty can slide into familiarity or confusion, familiarity can slip into boredom. Indeed, it may be best to think of any point along this continuum as a momentary balance between two opposing forces—our innate drive to uncover new things in a world that may harm or benefit us, and our equally innate drive to exploit our knowledge and experience to minimize costly expenditures of cognitive effort.[15]

A second implication follows:

> **The relative effectiveness of novelty and familiarity for a given consumer at a given point in time is highly dependent on both the *purpose* and the *placement* of the marketing effort.**

Marketing designed to encourage immediate or short-term behavioral activation will benefit from novelty's proven ability to grab attention, while marketing designed for long-term brand-building will do better when it works quietly in the background, strengthening familiar brand associations without disruption or distraction.

Similarly, the *placement* of a marketing effort must be taken into account. Marketing in traditional passive contexts, like TV viewing, needs to operate effectively under conditions of low attention, in which familiarity is beneficial and disruptive attention-grabbing can produce negative effects. In more active, cognitively-engaging contexts like online goal pursuit or real-world shopping, novelty can be effective in attracting the consumer's already-engaged mind, but will produce positive results only to the extent it aligns with that consumer's intentions in the moment. If novelty-based marketing is not aligned with consumer intent, it is more likely to ignored or devalued because it interferes with the consumer's current intentions and goals.

Chapter 6

Shortcuts to Consumer Preference

Mere Exposure and Processing Fluency

"Preferences need no inferences."
–Robert Zajonc

We tend to think of our preferences as "sticky." We recognize that preferences are subjective, in the sense that the same object may be preferred by me but not preferred by you. But for each of us, the common-sense belief is that we *know* whether we prefer one thing over another. This belief doesn't feel like something we could be mistaken about. But preferences are actually more fluid than that, and in fact they can be influenced by incidental features of *form* or *context* that can act as "shortcuts" to preference formation outside our conscious awareness. In this chapter, we look in detail at two of the most important shortcuts to consumer preference: mere exposure and processing fluency.

The effects of mere exposure and processing fluency on consumer preferences are not the equivalent of Freudian hidden wants and needs. As we saw in Chapter 1, unconscious influences on our beliefs and attitudes can be unrelated to any reasons at all, hidden or otherwise. In terms of our *cognitive timeline* model from Chapter 2, this is because they are products of *impression formation* that directly influence how we unconsciously *determine meaning and value* for what we experience through our senses. In some cases, they trigger *goal activation* and impact *deliberating and analyzing*, but we are generally unaware of how they affect our conscious behavior, that is, our *speaking and acting*.

The story of how conscious preferences can be influenced by unconscious perceptions and implicit associations begins with a breakthrough and highly counterintuitive finding discovered in the 1960s by a young psychology professor at the University of Michigan, Robert Zajonc. With a name impossible to pronounce from its spelling, friends reminded each other, "It rhymes with *giants* and *science*." Zajonc's discovery was easier to pronounce. It was called the *mere exposure effect*. And it changed radically everything we thought we knew about preferences.

Pioneers of Intuitive Marketing: Robert Zajonc

Robert Zajonc led an amazing life. He was born in Lodz, Poland in 1923. In 1939, he and his parents fled to Warsaw ahead of the Nazi invasion. Two weeks after arriving, his parents were killed and he was seriously injured in a German bombing raid. An orphan at 16, he attended an underground University in Warsaw and was later arrested by Nazi soldiers and sent to a forced labor camp in Germany. He escaped, was recaptured, and was sent to a political prison on France. He escaped again, joined the French Resistance, and studied at the University of Paris. In 1944, he made his way to England and worked as a translator for American forces in the European campaign. After the war, he joined the United Nations relief agency in Paris and studied psychology at the University of Tübingen. He emigrated to the United States in 1948, earned a PhD in psychology from the University of Michigan in 1955, and taught and conducted research there until his retirement in 1994. He then moved to Stanford University, where he continued to work until his death in 2008.[1]

Discovering the Mere Exposure Effect

Zajonc first published his discoveries about the mere exposure effect in 1968. In an article titled "*Attitudinal Effects of Mere Exposure*," he described a series of experimental findings that fundamentally challenged the psychological understanding of preferences accepted at the time. According to that understanding, preferences were a result of conscious thinking. Cognitions were believed to come first, in the form of information processing, evaluation, and inferences about a perceived object. Attitudes, in the form of likes, dislikes, and preferences among alternatives, were believed to form only later, based on those prior cognitive processes. In other words, you had to *think about* something before you could form a preference regarding it.

In a series of elegant experiments, Zajonc turned this model on its head. In his most famous experiment, he had volunteers view a long series of simulated Chinese ideograms (mostly nonsense symbols in the style of real Chinese ideograms). Some symbols were shown only once, others up to five times. Participants were then asked to guess whether the symbols represented positive or negative words. Overwhelmingly, the more exposures of a symbol people saw, the more "positive" they rated it. Since the symbols were completely novel and meaningless, there was no way for information processing to precede preference formation. This was the first demonstration of the mere exposure effect.

> **Zajonc showed that people could develop preferences for things based on repetition of exposure alone, without any prior information processing or evaluation; indeed, without even knowing their preferences were being influenced by exposure frequency.**[2]

Later studies by Zajonc and others demonstrated that the mere exposure effect was powerful and ubiquitous, occurring with words, numbers, faces, works of art, music, interpersonal interactions, and many other types of stimuli.[3] It was even found in nonhumans. In one particularly striking experiment, two distinct tones were played to two sets of fertilized chicken eggs. When the hatched chicks were tested for their preferences between the two tones, the chicks in each set consistently preferred the tone they had been repeatedly exposed to before birth.[4]

> **The mere exposure effect has come to be seen as one of the most consistent and persistent psychological phenomena ever discovered.**

Once the mere exposure effect was revealed, Zajonc began probing to discover its boundaries. To settle conclusively the question of whether conscious thoughts might be slipping in as a source of the mere exposure effect, he began to explore whether stimuli experienced below the threshold of conscious awareness—that is, *subliminal stimuli*—could induce liking based on frequency alone. Using new display technologies that started becoming available in the 1970s, Zajonc began testing subjects with stimuli presented for as little as one-thousandth of a second (one millisecond). He found that preferences not only increased for more frequently presented subliminal stimuli, despite the fact that people were unaware of having "seen" them, but even more significantly, he found that the effect was *stronger* for subliminally presented stimuli compared to consciously perceived stimuli. These findings established in very strong terms the validity of Zajonc's original hypothesis: changes in preferences induced by repeated exposures depended not on any prior subjective and conscious evaluations of attributes of the stimulus, but rather resulted from the objective history of exposures alone.[5]

> **When derived from mere exposure, preferences indeed need no inferences.**

Mere Exposure and Classical Conditioning

Since the discovery of the mere exposure effect, much effort has been devoted to pinpointing the mental processes that underlie it. Zajonc made the case that the basic mechanism was *classical conditioning*.

First observed in Pavlov's famous experiments with dogs, food, salivation, and bells, classical conditioning describes a process by which an automatic or *unconditioned response*, which normally follows an *unconditioned stimulus*, can be turned into a *conditioned response*, which now follows a previously neutral *conditioned stimulus*. In Pavlov's case, food was the *unconditioned stimulus*, salivation was the *unconditioned response*, the bell became the *conditioned stimulus*, and after conditioning, salivation became a *conditioned response* to the bell, meaning it could now be triggered even in the absence of food, the original unconditioned stimulus. The mechanism by which this transfer occurs is *repeated co-occurrence in time*—the bell is rung just prior to presenting the food, preferably within half a second. This establishes a *predictive* connection between the bell and the food. When that connection is repeated many times, salivation—a natural unconditioned response to the presentation of food—becomes *conditioned* to the previously unrelated stimulus, hearing the bell. When the bell rings, salivation occurs automatically. Thus are associations built in the mind.

Zajonc suggested the mere exposure effect works through a similar mechanism.[6] In this case, the *conditioned response* is the formation of a positive preference for a repeatedly presented stimulus. What is the *conditioned stimulus*? Zajonc argued it was the *absence* of any negative consequences co-occurring in time with the repeated exposures. As exposures accumulate, the repeated response stimulus becomes *conditioned* by this absence of harm associated with each exposure. Over more exposures, this begins to transform the response stimulus into a *conditioned response*, producing an increase in preference and a greater approach tendency with regard to it. A primitive association is created in memory: "this thing is familiar and safe, I can approach it with confidence."

Zajonc's identification of classical conditioning as the process underlying the mere exposure effect is generally accepted among researchers. Several implications follow. One is that the increased liking effect should not occur if the repeating stimuli *are* accompanied by negativity or harm. As we saw in the discussion of distractor devaluation in Chapter 3, this result does seem to be the case when the potential conditioning stimulus is a distractor that *competes for attention* with a response task. In that situation, liking for the distracting stimulus *declines* rather than increases after the repeated exposures, just as Zajonc's classical conditioning model would predict.

The mere exposure effect is not universal. In fact it may not work in one context that is quite common to marketing and advertising—when an ad or marketing message is competing for attention with an unrelated goal-directed task or intention.

Another implication of the classical conditioning model is that mere exposure can have spillover effects. Because "absence of negative consequences" is such a general and diffuse conditioned stimulus, its conditioning effects might be equally diffuse, extending well beyond increasing the attractiveness of the specific object being presented repeatedly.

Zajonc began exploring this possibility in the late 1990s and found that, indeed, repeated mere exposure could have a wider positive effect—influencing both general moods and attitudes toward other objects completely unrelated to the repeated stimulus. In the first of two experiments published in 2000, Zajonc and colleagues found that when people were exposed *subliminally* to Chinese ideographs at different rates (five exposures each of five ideographs vs. one exposure each of 25 ideographs), those who were shown multiple exposures reported being in better moods than those who were shown only a single exposure.

In a follow-up experiment, after the same subliminal exposure exercise, participants were asked to rate how much they liked images drawn from three groups: one-third from the ideograms presented in the exposure phase (called "old"), one-third from ideograms that were similar, but different from those shown in the exposure phase (called "novel similar"), and one-third from a completely different category (random polygons of different shapes, called "different"). As the mere exposure effect would predict, the "old" ideograms were rated more positively when they had been presented multiple times rather than once. But the "novel similar" ideograms were also rated more positively in the multiple-exposure condition, despite the fact that they were not the ideograms that had been repeatedly viewed. Finally, the completely "different" polygons were also rated more positively after exposure to multiple vs. single ideograms, even though polygons had no direct visual connection to ideograms.[7] The overall conclusion from this classic experiment was clear.

The positive emotions induced by repeated mere exposure are diffuse enough to influence both general moods and the ratings of "things" completely unrelated to the repeated objects producing the effect.

Mere Exposure and Intuitive Marketing

Zajonc's mere exposure effect is an important building block for understanding the science behind intuitive marketing. It demonstrates that positive emotions, such as liking, preferences, and positive moods, do not need "reasons" to come into existence, they can be produced by mental processes that do not involve conscious or inferential thinking at all.

If preferences can be generated by noncognitive sources like repetition, it follows that asking people why they prefer one brand or product over another might be problematic. Zajonc recognized this possibility early on:

We buy the cars we "like," choose the jobs and houses that we find "attractive," and then justify those choices by various reasons that might appear convincing to others who never fail to ask us, "Why this car?" or "Why this house?" We need not convince ourselves. We know what we like.[8]

The fact that people are often unable to articulate, or even recognize, the sources of their preferences has been an entry point for some neuromarketing vendors to claim their measures reveal the "real reasons" underlying consumer preferences, choices, and/or actions. But taking Zajonc seriously means purveyors of these new techniques need to be careful about what they say they are measuring.

Sources of preference that operate directly on *System 1* processes are not deeper "reasons" that lie below traditional articulated "reasons." They are innate or learned unconscious reactions that precede the very act of reasoning.

The precognitive, preconscious nature of the mere exposure effect can make it hard to accept as an explanation for consumer choices and behavior. For many—and probably for most of us when we first encounter mere exposure—it just don't feel like a good answer to the puzzle of where preferences come from.

As reasoning creatures who are fully aware of our own conscious reasoning processes, yet blind to the busy unconscious guidance systems that direct so much of our behavior, bypassing the idea of reasons to explain human behavior feels like a cop-out.

Perhaps this is why some neuromarketers and consultants talk in terms of "hidden reasons" rather than "reasons-free" sources of consumer behavior. But they are not doing marketers any favors by speaking this way. Ultimately, both marketers and consumers need to overcome this natural resistance to understanding how our minds really work. Until they do, marketers will just continue to make the same old mistakes, polluting our "attentional commons" with annoying and intrusive messages designed to provide us with "reasons" for buying one product or another, but in the process assaulting our unconscious guidance systems and offending our sensibilities without telling us anything we really want or need to know.

Feeling the Warm Glow of Processing Fluency

Being familiar is not the only way to create the feeling of familiarity. Another source of perceived familiarity is *processing fluency*.

Processing fluency is the subjective experience of easy mental processing.

Humans tend to assume, in the absence of evidence to the contrary, that easy-to-process things and experiences are familiar things, because in our minds the opposite association is so well-established: things that are familiar are generally much easier to process than things that are novel. This is another example of our unconscious *System 1* monitoring processes making an *implicit associative connection* between two objects or events. A *System 1* associative connection is based on co-occurrence only, not logical reasoning. So when, over a lifetime, *System 1* observes and learns that familiarity and processing fluency tend to co-occur, it does not distinguish between cause and effect. *System 1* is not capable of making the logical inference that A (familiarity) is the cause of B (an experience of processing fluency). Making that inference requires the intervention of *System 2* conscious reasoning, which may or may not occur in any given circumstance. So when *System 1* observes the presence of B (processing fluency), it automatically assumes that A (familiarity) must be present as well. Unless *System 2* is activated to correct this *misattribution*, our unconscious minds will tend to assume that any easily processed item or experience is probably one we are familiar with.

Processing fluency and repetitive mere exposure speak a secret language that can only be heard by *System 1* but significantly and directly influences conscious, self-aware *System 2*.

This is an important connection that is often misunderstood. Processing fluency is not itself an unconscious process. We are *aware* of the subjective feeling of fluency. We know when something feels easy to process. We know when information is easy to extract and use, and when it is not. This is why processing fluency is defined as a *subjective* experience. We recognize it when we are experiencing it, just as we recognize its opposite, processing *disfluency*. What we don't recognize is how it influences what we think and do next. While we are aware of the "warm glow" of processing fluency, we tend to be unaware of two things: what causes that feeling in the first place, and how it regularly and consistently shapes our subsequent thoughts and actions. As we shall see, processing fluency can act as a powerful shortcut to reasoning, judgments, preferences, and choices that feel like products of conscious thought alone, but are in fact heavily influenced by unconscious processes that operate outside our conscious awareness.

> **What is surprising and counterintuitive about processing fluency is how heavily it biases key *System 2* thought processes: reasoning, judgments, and preferences.**

Invoking a feeling of familiarity is only one way in which processing fluency can impact conscious thought processes. When processing fluency causes us to mistake something new for something familiar, we call that a *misattribution*—we have misattributed the fluency effect to (an erroneous) familiarity cause. Processing fluency can also be a source of other misattributions beyond a false feeling of familiarity. In fact, to the extent processing fluency affects *System 2* thinking without conscious awareness of that effect, it can be a prolific source of misattributions across a wide domain of *System 2* thought processes.

> **One of the hallmarks of *System 2* thinking is awareness of the process of thinking itself, which lets us to make inferences about what and how we are thinking. Researchers call this phenomenon *meta-cognition*.**

"Meta" in this context means "self-referencing." so meta-cognition is cognition about cognition, or thinking about thinking. A feeling of easy processing is a meta-cognition. It provides a clue about how thinking is going. Specifically, ease or difficulty of processing provides a clue regarding the amount of effort that is going to be required to complete a cognitive task.

> **Processing fluency impacts conscious thoughts and actions primarily through this mechanism of meta-cognition.**

Fluency researchers describe the process as proceeding through three stages.[9] In Stage 1, various kinds of unconscious *System 1* cognitive processes occur, generating a meta-cognitive feeling of fluency or disfluency. In Stage 2, a conscious *System 2* process occurs in which fluency or disfluency is rapidly assessed using a "naïve theory" to determine (sometimes correctly, sometimes not) the informational value and implications of the experience. Finally, in Stage 3, this interpretation is used to make judgments about the cognitive experience that triggered the fluency or disfluency feeling in the first place. Researchers have found significant impacts of fluency on judgments in several domains that are highly relevant to consumer choice and action.

> **If marketers want to understand how their messages, products, and brand representations trigger fluency and subsequent judgments, it is not enough to know if fluency is occurring or not.**

Marketers need to understand all three stages of the fluency experience: the sources of fluency, the naïve theories people use to interpret the fluency experience, and the judgments that follow from that experience.

Sources of Processing Fluency

A large body of research has been devoted to the question of how and when objects and situations trigger a feeling of processing fluency in the human brain. Several common sources of fluency have been identified, in five general categories: objective attributes of an object, the perceiver's familiarity with the object, the "averageness" of the object within its category (also called *typicality* or *prototypicality*), the degree of consistency or congruency among multiple objects, and the perceiver's expectations for an object.

Objective features. Some objective features that have been found to enhance processing fluency include:

- *Amount of information.* Objects containing less information are more fluent because they are easier to decode.
- *Symmetry.* Symmetrical objects are more fluent, in part because they contain less information due to the redundancy provided by the symmetry. Interestingly, vertical symmetry is easier to process than horizontal symmetry, and both are easier to process than diagonal symmetry.[10]
- *Clarity and contrast.* Higher resolution images and greater contrast between object and background (*figure-ground contrast*) both result in greater fluency, especially when objects are observed only briefly.

All of these objective features enhance *perceptual fluency*, the ease of processing an object itself, as compared to *conceptual fluency*, which refers to the ease of understanding the meaning or significance of the object. Both types of fluency produce similar effects on judgments, choices, and actions.

Familiarity. Familiarity is a function of a person's experience with an object or situation. We have seen how fluency can create a misattribution of familiarity, because *System 1* does not differentiate between co-occurrence and causation. But while fluency can be produced by many sources other than familiarity, it is established beyond a doubt that familiarity itself produces a feeling of fluency, and this feeling is central to the relationships between familiarity, comfort, liking, and preference covered earlier in this chapter. The mechanisms underlying this chain of responses are *repetition* and *implicit learning*. In the realm of consumer behavior, repetition occurs not just across marketing exposures, but across the full *consumer cycle*—from marketing to shopping to consuming and back again, many times over. Implicit learning, in turn, occurs through *conditioning* and *pattern recognition*, the brain's basic unconscious mechanisms for encoding associations between objects or events that co-occur, such as a product and one's experiences with that product across the consumer cycle.

Typicality. Typicality is another important source of processing fluency. Objects that are typical of their category (assuming the category itself is familiar and understood) require less cognitive effort to process, and are thus experienced more fluently. Numerous studies have found that people prefer prototypical and "average" forms over less typical alternatives in a wide variety of contexts, such as color patches, paintings, furniture, music, and human faces.[11]

Marketers will note that this association affords a significant advantage to leading brands in any category, since that top seller often becomes the definition of "typical" for that category. This can result in a virtuous cycle in which the leading brand is preferred because it is the most fluent representative of the category, which is primarily due to the fact that it is the leading brand. Such self-reinforcing cognitive dynamics may help account for the high levels of consistency and stability in brand market shares and repeat purchase rates across categories, as first recognized by Andrew Ehrenberg and codified in his "Double Jeopardy" principle.[12]

Consistency and priming. Another important source of fluency extends beyond the features of an individual object to connections between objects. This is fluency that derives from consistency or congruency between objects or events. A common example is temporal or sequential consistency, in which we repeatedly experience a regular pattern of co-occurrence in time.

If *B* regularly follows *A*, we tend to process *B* more fluently when *A* precedes it.

In addition, repeated co-occurrences of *A* and *B* strengthen the neural connections between the two objects or events in long-term memory, thus facilitating a feeling of fluency for the *pair* as a cognitive unit, even if *A* and *B* on their own are not particularly fluent.

In addition to sequential consistency, fluency can be enhanced by other forms of consistency such as *physical proximity* (things that consistently appear next to each other), *lexical proximity* (words that go together, like doctor-nurse, horse-carriage, cat-dog), or *relationship proximity* (membership in a group or category, like family members, animal pairings, or members of a food group). In each of these types of co-occurrence, consistency is a function of elements being tied together in a relation. Here again we see the basic mechanism of *priming* at work: as one element consistently pre-activates a related element, that consistency breeds neural co-activation, which triggers priming, which creates the subjective feeling of fluency. Consistency is about regularity, and priming is the brain's main mechanism for exploiting regularities.[13]

As we will see in a later section, consistency can be a powerful tool for marketers who want to build on fluency to establish deeper levels of trust, loyalty, and habit in consumers' relationships with their products or brands.

Expectations. Fluency created by these four direct sources—objective attributes, familiarity, typicality, and consistency—can be *moderated* or situationally influenced by a fifth factor, the observer's expectations. Although at first it might seem counterintuitive, researchers have found that processing fluency is more likely to produce conscious feelings (meta-cognitions) of liking or familiarity when it is encountered *unexpectedly*, rather than when it is expected.[14] For example, seeing your family dentist in the dentist's office is a fluent but expected experience that generally does not elicit a strong meta-cognitive sense of familiarity, while seeing your dentist at the airport is unexpected and therefore does.[15] Similarly, finding a product unexpectedly easy to use might generate greater liking for the product than if the product were expected to be easy to use. This interplay of expectations and fluency has potential implications for advertising, marketing promotions, product designs, packaging, and other elements of the marketing mix.

Marketers who understand where fluency is expected and unexpected in their product domains can build *unexpected fluency* into consumer experiences all across their consumer cycle—from messaging to purchasing to delivering to consuming and even to disposing of their products—thereby facilitating positive emotional feelings toward products and brands in new and innovative ways.

Interpreting Processing Fluency

There can be significant variations in how processing fluency impacts judgments, including consumer judgments. These variations are largely a function of the different beliefs or *naïve theories* that consumers might apply to a processing fluency experience in Stage 2 of the processing fluency effect.

When marketers first learn about processing fluency, they often adopt a naïve theory of their own, that increasing processing fluency with regard to a message, product, or brand will always result in more positive feelings toward that object. This is often true, but not always. Processing fluency is a subjective feeling that can be responded to in different ways.

> **How fluency affects judgments and decisions—what marketers really care about—depends on the *naïve theories* that consumers use to evaluate the meaning and interpretation of a fluency experience.**

Consumers' naïve theories about *why* they are experiencing processing fluency in a given instance can have a huge impact on how they interpret that fluency experience. Indeed, researchers have found that naïve theories can reverse the usual effects of fluency: under some interpretations, feelings of fluency can lead to negative judgments and feelings of *disfluency* can lead to positive judgments. For example, in a 2001 study titled *"How pleasant was your childhood?"* social psychologists Piotr Winkielman and Norbert Schwarz divided their subjects into two groups. The first group was asked to recall four childhood events, a relatively easy and therefore fluent task. The second group was asked to recall 12 childhood events, a more difficult and more disfluent task.[16] What the researchers wanted to find out was whether the fluency or disfluency of the recall task would affect a later judgment of how pleasant a person's childhood was, overall. The default expectation would be that the people primed with a fluent recall task would rate their childhoods as more pleasant than the people primed with a disfluent task.

But then the researchers added another element to the experiment. They provided their subjects with different naïve theories to "explain" how their recall experiences might relate to their actual childhood experiences. Some subjects were told that events from *pleasant childhoods* would be difficult to remember later on, while others were told the opposite; that events from *unpleasant childhoods* would be difficult to remember later on. The impact of introducing these different naïve theories was dramatic, to the point of reversing the expected effects of processing fluency on later judgments. Specifically, among subjects who were given the difficult recall task, those who were told that events from pleasant childhoods were harder to remember rated their childhoods as significantly more pleasant than those who were told that events from unpleasant childhoods were harder to remember. A disfluent experience thus led to a positive judgment, the opposite of what one would expect from processing disfluency, simply because a naïve theory was invoked that allowed people to "explain" the disfluency feeling as an indication of a pleasant childhood.[17]

Other instances of this effect have been noted in the consumer behavior literature. For example, one team of researchers found that advertising luxury items in an easy-to-read font caused consumers to rate the products as *less valuable*, because the fluent experience made the items seem more familiar and therefore more common, which contradicted people's default naïve theory that luxury items should be rare and therefore less familiar, not more.[18]

What kinds of naïve theories do people use to interpret subjective feelings of processing fluency or disfluency? In a much-cited paper in the *Journal of Consumer Psychology*, Norbert Schwarz identifies a wide range of meta-cognitive theories people rely on to explain their processing fluency experiences.[19]

- *Theories about "the world out there"* People believe that things that come to mind easily are more common in the world—that is, have a higher frequency or probability—than things that come to mind with difficulty. This is called the *availability heuristic*[20] and explains why people often interpret a fluent experience as something that happens regularly or typically in the world.
- *Theories about "my memory"* People believe the ease or difficulty with which information about a topic can be recalled is an indicator of how much experience they have with that topic. So a person asked to perform a difficult recall task will assume they have less experience with the topic, while a person asked to perform an easy recall task will assume they have more experience the topic.
- *Theories about "how things are presented"* People believe that things experienced with more fluency are experienced for longer durations than things experienced with less fluency. They also believe that visual objects experienced with more fluency have greater clarity than objects experienced with less fluency.
- *Theories about "my knowledge"* People believe they know more about familiar things than unfamiliar things. So when they mistakenly experience something as familiar due to processing fluency, they often mistakenly believe they know more about it than if they experience it disfluently.
- *Theories about "consensus and truth"* People hold the naïve theory that a true statement will be believed by more people than a false statement. They

also assume that a familiar-feeling statement will be believed by more people than an unfamiliar statement. So when the objective truth of a statement is difficult to determine, people tend to judge a fluently presented statement as more likely to be believed by more people, and therefore as more likely to be true, than a disfluently presented statement.

- **Theories about *"what I like"*** Fluency increases positive feelings or "liking" toward objects that are experienced more fluently. People hold the naïve theory that, when choosing between two items, they will probably get more long-term satisfaction from one they like more in the current moment. So when people experience a feeling of liking due to processing fluency, they often mistakenly believe they are experiencing a better choice option, rather than just a positive feeling.

In each of these examples, the naïve theory becomes a lens through which our minds build an interpretive bridge between a *fluency experience* and a *judgment or choice*.

But as noted, each of these naïve theories may *incorrectly* identify the source or sources of fluency and thereby lead to incorrect inferences about the meaning or implications of the fluency experience.

Processing fluency is a function of the *form* or *context* of an object or event—its complexity, symmetry, familiarity, typicality, or consistency—but most commonly-held naïve theories interpret it as a function of the *content* of the object or event. Fluency may have nothing to do with how common or probable an event is, how easily I can remember it, how much knowledge I have about it, how likely it is to be true, or whether I'm likely to prefer it. But the naïve theory I apply to an experience of fluency or disfluency may lead me to draw those conclusions about those judgments, often accurately but sometimes inaccurately.

When marketers consider how processing fluency can affect consumers' reactions to their products and brands across the *consumer cycle*—from marketing message receptivity to product acquisition ease to product consumption satisfaction—they need to be cautious about avoiding too simplistic a perspective. Although fluency can have many positive consequences for brand and product appeal, our takeaway for marketers is that they need to do more than just build in standard indicators of easy processing like easy-to-read fonts, symmetrical designs, and easy-to-understand instructions.

Marketers need to consider, first, what naïve theories their consumers are automatically bringing to these fluency experiences, and second, whether they need to augment their marketing messages with their own interpretive theories in order to influence consumers' inferential processes as they translate their fluency experiences into judgments and buying decisions about a product or product category.

Successfully leveraging processing fluency in marketing requires that marketers understand not only how to make their brands, products, and messages more or less fluent, but also how to make sure their consumers are interpreting those fluency experiences, both consciously and unconsciously, in the manner intended by the marketing team. Only by taking both aspects of fluency into account can marketers accurately calibrate the impact of fluency or disfluency on their consumers' judgments and choices.

Consequences of Processing Fluency

Experiencing processing fluency (Stage 1), combined with interpreting processing fluency via metacognitive *naïve theories* (Stage 2), can have a powerful and direct impact on a wide range of consumer judgments, decisions, and preferences (Stage 3). Here are some of the most important ways a subjective feeling of processing fluency can impact subsequent beliefs, preferences, and judgments.[21]

Truth. When experiencing a fluently presented statement, people tend to apply "consensus and truth" naïve theories to interpret that statement as more truthful than when the same statement is presented disfluently. In making this judgment, people infer that fluency implies frequency, which in turn implies social consensus, which in turn implies truth.

Liking/preference. Using "what I like" naïve theories, people tend to interpret the positive feelings generated by fluency as a valid representation of their more content-based likes and preferences. As first shown by Zajonc, liking can be increased by the mere exposure effect, which also increases a sense of familiarity. In combination, fluency and familiarity reinforce each other and can have a powerful impact on people's subsequent judgments about what they like and what they prefer.

Frequency/probability. In the absence of additional information, people tend to use naïve theories about "the world out there" to judge fluently described events as occurring more frequently or with a higher probability than disfluently described events. This judgment relates once again to the familiarity impression produced by processing fluency. Events perceived as more familiar due to fluency are judged to occur more frequently or to be more probable than events perceived as unfamiliar due to disfluency.

Valuation. People's judgments of value can be affected by processing fluency. For example, studies have shown that recently-offered stocks with easy to process ticker symbols (e.g., KAR) gain more value over their first six months than stocks with hard to process sticker symbols (e.g., RDO),[22] and that people ascribe greater value to currency when it is represented more fluently (e.g., a familiar dollar bill) than when it is represented disfluently (e.g., an unfamiliar dollar coin).[23]

Category typicality. People are more likely to judge a fluently-presented item as typical of its category than a disfluently-presented item. This effect is similar to the familiarity/probability effect of fluency in that a naïve theory about "the world out there" can lead to a judgement that fluency implies familiarity, which in turn can lead to a judgment that a fluently-presented item is more typical of its category than a disfluently-presented item.

Confidence. When information is presented fluently, people tend to be more confident about their evaluation of that information. For example, when instructions are easier to read, people are more confident they have followed the instructions correctly. Similarly, when a task is easier to accomplish, and therefore experienced more fluently, people tend to feel greater confidence in their performance than when the task is harder to accomplish.

Intelligence. People tend to judge the authors of more fluently presented writing as more intelligent than authors of less fluently presented writing.

Risk. Fluency researchers have found a strong relationship between processing fluency and judgments of riskiness. People tend to judge food additives with harder to pronounce names as riskier than additives with easier to pronounce names. They tend to judge amusement park rides as more exciting and scarier (riskier) the harder the ride's name is to pronounce.[24] As with the frequency/probability and category typicality effects, this judgment of increased riskiness is based on naïve theories connecting fluency and familiarity, but in this case, working in the opposite direction. Because disfluency implies unfamiliarity, and unfamiliarity implies novelty and uncertainty, disfluency cues tend to be associated with novelty and therefore heightened riskiness.

Processing Fluency and Intuitive Marketing

Processing fluency can have a wide variety of impacts on consumer judgments and preferences. By digging deeply into the sources, interpretations, and consequences of fluency and disfluency, we have found that the subjective experience of fluency can significantly impact consumer impressions of familiarity, liking, truth, frequency, value, risk, and other attributes of products and brands. However, we have also seen that these fluency-based inferences can be *misattributions*, that is, mistaken beliefs in which the results of fluency are incorrectly attributed to the features of products or brands themselves.

What does this mean for marketers? First, it is a reminder that consumer judgments and assessments are often *not* derived from a conscious assessment of the actual attributes of things and experiences in the world around us. We may *believe* we are making objective inferences about inherent qualities of, say, a brand or product or marketing message, but in fact those inferences may be overwhelmingly influenced by other factors that—if we were consciously aware of them—we would consider to be irrelevant to the judgment task at hand.

> **Often, our judgments are not based on what we think they are based on. We are fooled into mistaking *how* we think for *what* we think.**

Second, the effects of processing fluency remind us that intuitive marketing, unlike traditional marketing, should take into account all three aspects of a marketing message: its *content, form, and context*. A marketer with an understanding of intuitive marketing principles knows that while a consumer may fervently believe they are offering an opinion about the *content* of a marketing message, their opinion may in fact be largely determined by the *form* or *context* of that message. Reaching consumers through *form* and *context* can take much of the burden off of content-centered marketing that mistakenly assumes that consumers only hear and respond to the *content* of marketing messages. Much of the shouting and disruptive noise that characterizes traditional persuasive marketing is directly attributable to this serious mistake.

Given the powerful and sometimes misleading impact of processing fluency on judgments and choices, consumers can also benefit from a better understanding of how and why fluency impacts their marketing, shopping, and consumption experiences. Specifically, heightened awareness of fluency effects can remind consumers to dig below surface-level presentation features when evaluating or comparing products— particularly products that are new and unfamiliar, or when a "best" choice among a set of alternatives cannot easily be discerned. These are the circumstances when consumers are most likely to benefit from deliberative *System 2* assessments of product features or attributes, as opposed to relying on fluency-driven *System 1* thinking.

> **Through experience and education, consumers can learn how to recognize and discount fluency effects, enabling them to direct greater conscious attention and vigilance to a decision task when required.**

Such added effort comes at a cognitive cost, of course. Often—especially when products are familiar or choices are "no brainers"—such added consideration is unnecessary and consumers can safely enjoy the cognitive ease of a quick and effortless fluency-based decision. In such cases, processing fluency is likely to be an accurate cue,[25] not a misleading one, because fluency in consumer decision making often flows from repeated experience, real familiarity, and reliability, not just super-ficial presentation features that may be unrelated to actual product value or quality.

> **In the face of tough marketplace competition, marketers may feel a temptation to use fluency cues to misinform consumers about their products and brands.**

Marketers may see processing fluency as a way to make their products seem more familiar than they really are, or make their advertising claims seem more truthful than they really are, or make their brands seem more unique than they really are.

Marketers may also avoid such temptations and choose to use fluency cues in a more mutually beneficial way—to make consumers' lives easier, less cluttered, and less disrupted—by communicating about their products and brands in ways that can be more quickly and easily processed, thereby fulfilling their own marketing mission while also saving consumers time and precious cognitive effort. Most marketers are well aware that misinforming consumers is never a route to long-term marketing success. Using processing fluency to create false impressions inevitably backfires down the road when marketing expectations meet actual product performance.

> **Consumers who succumb to fluency-based misattributions may later become very unforgiving when those beliefs is contradicted by actual product use or consumption.**

Lasting preferences are developed and reinforced by multiple journeys through the *consumer cycle*, not by one-off, fluently-presented marketing messages. Successful intuitive marketers don't use processing fluency effects to *fake* the product attributes they wish their products and brands had. Rather, they use fluency as a cue to more effectively communicate the benefits and values their products provide through multiple journeys around the *consumer cycle*. In this way, processing fluency can be an effective and powerful tool for influencing consumers without recourse to disruptive persuasion.

Chapter 7

Intuitive Marketing and Lasting Consumer Preferences

Marketing Beyond Mere Exposure and Processing Fluency

"Your preference is a product of your behaviour and not the origin of it."
–Rory Sutherland[1]

People's automatic responses to repetitive exposure and processing fluency may create what appear to marketers to be stable and reliable preferences. But brain science researchers have found that human preferences are often much more temporary and much more easily manipulated than consumers' sincere declarations of brand love might lead marketers to believe.

This is an area where traditional marketing theory has been led astray by the classic economic model of rational choice, which predicts behavior based on assumptions that preferences are stable, consistent, known before choices are made, and known with adequate precision to make the process of choosing among alternatives unambiguous. In contrast to this approach, much of the consumer choice research we have reviewed—and indeed, much of the behavioral economics research tradition (see Chapter 15)—has found those assumptions of economic rational choice to be unrealistic as descriptions of how individuals acquire and use preferences in everyday life. Although it is true the rational choice model often works well in predicting the overall behavior of large aggregates of individuals in economic systems, it can provide a very misleading picture of the role played by preferences in individual consumer choice and behavior.[2] And it is that role that both marketers and consumers care about the most.

The Fragility of Consumer Preferences: Seven Principles

When scientists study how preferences actually get incorporated into consumer decision making (and human decision making in general) they consistently find empirical results that violate the assumptions of economic rational choice. To the extent that marketers fail to recognize these violations, they tend to over-emphasize the importance of managing preferences as a goal of marketing.

> **The path to changing consumer behavior through persuasion seems to pass inevitably through a requirement to change preferences first.**

In the persuasive marketing model, preferences determine product choices, so if you want to change product choices, you must first change preferences. And if you want to change preferences, you must first know what those preferences are, so you have to measure and track them through consumer research. Once you have determined what current preferences are and how you want to change them, your task is to deploy either rational argumentation, demonstration, or emotional appeal to convince people to change their preferences and do what you want them to do. This is the logical foundation on which most of the marketing and advertising we endure today is built.

Brain science has demonstrated that much of this logic is flawed. Preferences play a quite different role in consumer decision making than is assumed by the traditional model. What we know today about the fragility of consumer preferences can be summarized in seven principles.

Preferences are constructed

In 2006, social psychologists Sarah Lichtenstein and Paul Slovic published a book titled *The Construction of Preference*, collecting in one volume over 35 years of research on this topic. Beginning with Lichtenstein and Slovic's examination of the "preference reversal" phenomenon—the finding that people reverse their preferences when they compare alternatives in different ways, such as jointly vs. sequentially[3]—the book documents a wide variety of contexts in which preferences are not independent inputs into choice deliberations, but rather calculated in real time as part of the choice process itself, often in ways that are highly dependent on how, where, and when the choice is encountered.

Since the publication of *The Construction of Preference*, research on this topic has continued to be voluminous and supportive of the basic hypothesis that consumer preferences are indeed more often constructed than not. Recent research has focused on identifying the conditions under which preference construction tends to occur: specifically, how and when preferences are most susceptible to influence by contextual factors, and how and when preferences are most likely to be calculated during choice rather than retrieved from memory prior to choice. These elaborations are important for establishing the boundaries of preference construction. They also provide some significant implications for consumer choice and marketing practices.[4]

> **To the extent that consumers have unstable goals, operate under cognitive constraints, or make choices without prior experience or expert knowledge—three common conditions during the shopping stage of the consumer cycle—their preferences are more likely to be constructed and less likely to be reliable indicators of their future choices, preferences, and behavior.**

To say preferences are *constructed* is not to deny that human beings have *predispositions* that are relatively stable over time. There has been some debate among researchers about the relative strength of these *inherent preferences* versus constructed preferences,[5] but for the most part this debate bypasses the point of primary importance for marketers. The relevance of constructed preferences to consumer choice is not dependent on the existence or nonexistence of inherent preferences, it merely highlights the fact that when consumers cite preferences as causal sources of their decisions, those preferences may actually be constructed as a byproduct of the decision process, even if consumers think otherwise. Expressed preferences may be *misattributed* by both consumers and marketers as more inherent than they really are, which can lead to erroneous conclusions about what consumers really want and need. That is the danger of failing to appreciate the role of constructed preferences in consumer choice.

Some powerful examples of constructed preferences and preference reversal are found in the "choice blindness" studies of Lars Hall and Petter Johansson. In a series of experiments focusing on faces, food items, personality traits, political and moral attitudes, and other stimuli, these researchers asked people to identify their preference between two items represented as pictures, physical items, or survey questions. They then used various tricks to surreptitiously "switch in" the non-preferred item for the just-identified preferred item. Presenting their subjects with the previously non-preferred item, they asked them to explain why they preferred it.

The findings have been consistent across multiple choice categories and presentation methods. In a great majority of cases, people do not even notice the switch and are quite willing to provide extensive rationales for why they preferred the item they in fact didn't prefer.[6] Not only are their preferences constructed in real time, but those "faked" preferences tend to have staying power. When the choice task is repeated without the sleight-of-hand, people are more likely to prefer the item they had falsely been led to believe they preferred in the first task.[7] The act of describing a non-preferred item as preferred actually reversed the original preference order, at least for a short period of time.

Preferences are often consequences of behavior, not sources

The counter-intuitive implication of constructed preferences is that consumers do not access pre-existing preferences from memory to solve choice problems, they actually *discover* what their preferences are by solving choice problems. This process is highly contextual, and those discovered preferences may emerge differently in a later choice situation presented in a different context.

From the perspective of the rational choice model, this depiction of human choice appears quite irrational. But there is a different kind of rationality at work here, originally described by James March in a classic 1978 paper, that might be called *posterior rationality*:

> *Ideas of posterior rationality emphasize the discovery of intentions as an interpretation of action rather than as a prior position …. Actions are seen as being exogenous and as producing experiences that are organized into an evaluation after the fact. The valuation is in terms of preferences generated by the action and its consequences, and choices are justified by virtue of their posterior consistency with goals that have themselves been developed through a critical interpretation of the choice. Posterior rationality models maintain the idea that action should be consistent with preferences, but they conceive action as being antecedent to goals.*[8]

According to posterior rationality, it is rational to *prefer what we do*, rather than to *do what we prefer*, as long as we learn through our choices and improve our ability to pursue our goals over time.

Consumer choice is not normally about applying pre-existing preferences to choice situations, it is more often about literally creating preferences as a consequence of choosing.[9]

Preferences are transient and elastic

Constructed preferences tend to have short half-lives. They change over time as contexts and goals change. In two recent studies by psychologist Dan Simon and colleagues, participants were asked to rate their preferences regarding four features that might be associated with a job offer: office space, salary, vacation package, and commute time. After rating several options for each feature separately, they were shown two hypothetical job offers with different combinations of the four features. After reviewing the job offers, they were again asked to rate the features. In this new context, they "reconstructed" their preferences for the individual features in a manner that supported the job offer they rated as more attractive overall.

The researchers then waited for various periods of time—15 minutes, one week, eight weeks—and asked the participants to rate the four features again. After each interval, their preferences returned to approximately the baseline ratings they had given before considering the two job offers. Their preferences were not only constructed, they were also short-lived and continued to be highly context-dependent. In the second study, Simon found these constructed preferences to be highly *elastic*, changing shape to meet the needs of a particular choice situation, but then "bouncing back" to roughly their original shape when disengaged from that choice context.[10]

Based on these studies and related research, marketers need to think about preferences not only as constructed, but also as both transient and elastic. Simon's work is important because it shows that expressed preferences not only change in response to different choice situations, but also tend to revert to a common baseline in the absence of imposed choice constraints. This reversion to baseline may be a function of inherent preferences hidden beneath preference construction. But as long as those inherent preferences can be so easily overridden in different choice contexts, constructed preferences are more likely to be operative in day-to-day consumer choice and behavior.

Preferences need no inferences

As we saw in our discussion of the *mere exposure effect* in Chapter 6, preferences can be created by repetition alone. Robert Zajonc's great contribution to social psychology was to disprove the seemingly self-evident proposition that our preferences *must* have logic and reasons behind them—we should not be able to have a preference for one thing over another unless we have a *reason* for that preference. But Zajonc's famous dictum that "preferences need no inferences" proclaims just the opposite—that liking and preference can be generated by repetitive mere exposure in the complete absence of reasons or even conscious awareness. If simple repetition can condition our preferences in such a predictable and persistent way, how much should marketers rely on stated preferences as a basis for designing and marketing their products and brands?

Preferences can be primed without conscious awareness

Mere exposure is not the only way preferences can be triggered unconsciously. Preferences are also susceptible to priming via perceived or unperceived environmental cues.

In a fascinating series of experiments and field studies conducted by Jonah Berger and Gráinne Fitzsimons, consumers' product preferences were shown to be subtly influenced by environmental cues of various types.[11] In one study, participants were approached on a college campus and asked to fill out a questionnaire in which they had to choose a preferred item from 20 pictured pairs of common consumer products (e.g., candies, detergents, beverages). Some of these products were associated with the color orange (like the soft drink *Fanta*), others were associated with the color green (like the soft drink *Sprite*), and others were associated with neither color (like the soft drink *Pepsi*). Ostensibly at random, participants were handed either an orange pen or a green pen to complete the questionnaire. Although no explicit mention was made of the color similarities between the pens and some of the products, product preferences were significantly correlated with pen color. Participants who wrote with an orange pen preferred more orange products than participants who wrote with a green pen, and vice versa. As expected, pen color had no effect on the selection of color-neutral products. In this case, incidental exposure to a seemingly irrelevant environmental cue led participants to construct completely different product preferences.

In this study, as in many similar examples,[12] people were completely unaware of the substantial effects seemingly trivial environmental features, observed repeatedly but with low or no attention, could have on their constructed preferences. These are all examples of *System 1* processes bypassing both conscious awareness and in-depth *System 2* deliberation. They illustrate once again a key finding from brain science.

The mental processes human beings use to guide their beliefs and actions do not need to be consistent, sensible, or even consciously accessible to have an impact on their preferences and choices.

Preferences can be implicit

While the mere exposure effect and preference priming remind us that preferences can be *created* without conscious awareness, the resulting preferences are themselves consciously experienced—people are aware of their preference even if they are unaware of the *source* of that preference. Other research has shown that preferences can also be unconsciously experienced, that is, implicit rather than explicit. The existence in consumers' minds of *implicit preferences* that may differ from expressed *explicit preferences* creates another headache for marketers and market researchers. Consumers may be completely honest in reporting their explicit preferences, but those reported preferences may not be good predictors of their subsequent behavior because that behavior may be more influenced by implicit preferences they are not aware they have. Several studies have demonstrated that implicit preferences can and do deviate from explicit preferences, do impact consumer choices independently, and are more likely to do so under time constraints and other forms of cognitive load.[13]

> **Explicit preferences are more predictive of deliberate, controlled choices and actions, while implicit preferences are more predictive of less controlled, more impulsive choices and actions.**

Expressed preferences are unreliable predictors of future behavior

Finally, the elephant in the room for marketers and market researchers is the flip side of implicit preferences: the fact that explicitly stated preferences, extracted from surveys and interviews, the workhorses of self-reporting consumer research, are often *unreliable* predictors of future consumer choice and behavior. The problem is not that stated preferences never predict subsequent behavior, but that they fail to do so dependably, thus making it difficult and risky to allocate product development and marketing resources based on consumer preference data alone.

This lack of reliability in predictions based on consumer preferences is often attributed to variations in how and when preferences are measured. Noting that preferences are most predictive when they are measured just prior to performing a behavior, when they reference a familiar or habitual behavior, and when the behavior is completely under the control of the person expressing the preference,[14] researchers have correctly observed that these conditions are hardly ever fully present in measurements of *consumer* preferences and behavior. Not only are consumers often asked to predict their likely behaviors far in advance, or with regard to products they may be unfamiliar with, but their eventual purchasing decisions are often constrained by many factors outside their immediate control, such as changes in personal finances, changes in situational needs, or event-specific shopping factors such as available time or product shortages.[15]

All of these quite reasonable explanations for the unreliability of behavioral predictions based on preferences still assume, or at least do not question, the belief that consumers have stable and reliable preferences to be measured. They simply acknowledge that many extraneous factors can intervene between the expression of those preferences and a later behavior. But additional research casts doubt on that comforting belief that preferences themselves are not the problem.

For example, researchers have discovered that the very act of asking someone to express a preference can impact their later actions, artificially inflating the apparent association between stated preferences and behavior. This phenomenon is called *self-generated validity* and has been observed in several studies in which the behaviors of surveyed consumers are compared to behaviors of a matching group of nonsurveyed consumers.

In a 2005 study, Pierre Chandon, Vicki Morwitz, and Werner Reinartz examined three large-scale field studies of purchase intent and behavior across three diverse product categories: groceries, automobiles, and personal computers. Using a clever two-stage statistical estimation technique to identify *latent purchase intent* prior to being surveyed, they found that the correlation between latent purchase intent and purchase behavior was 58% greater for consumers who were surveyed than for a matched group of consumers who were not surveyed. After eliminating two alternative explanations—social norms and nonsurvey-related intention modification—they were able to ascribe this difference entirely to self-generated validity.[16] Their conclusion—that simply asking people to express their intention changes their later behavior—has deep implications for traditional market research based on asking questions about consumer preferences.

> *[Survey] studies assume that they can extrapolate the intention–behavior relationship of nonsurveyed consumers on the basis of the relationship that surveyed consumers exhibit. In doing so, the studies ignore the potentially important problem that the measurement of intentions itself might self-generate some of the association between the intentions and the behavior of a particular consumer.*[17]

Why Expressed Preferences Don't Reliably Predict Behavior

The failure of expressed preferences to reliably predict future behavior leads to an even deeper question regarding the nature of opinion surveys as instruments of knowledge acquisition. If we take seriously the idea that human beings are highly intuitive thinkers who operate at both conscious and unconscious levels and respond to the world around them in contextually-sensitive ways that might not be available to their conscious minds, we can begin to make sense of that deeper question:

What are people actually doing when they respond to questions on a survey questionnaire?

The standard answer is that when people say they prefer X over Y on a survey questionnaire, they are simply describing a preexisting state of feeling more favorable toward X than Y. But, as we have seen, that view does not conform with the large body of accumulated evidence that shows expressed preferences to be more often constructed in the moment than accessed from a preexisting memory. So what else might be going on?

One of the first—and still one of the best—answers to this question was put forward in an influential paper written by political scientists John Zaller and Stanley Feldman in 1992 titled "*A simple theory of the survey response: Answering questions versus revealing preferences.*" Zaller and Feldman recognized something that is still missed by many in the survey research field: answering questions on a survey form is a unique cognitive experience that has its own rules, risks, and expectations. Ordinary people do not ordinarily get asked to state preferences, rate products, or predict their future buying behavior using standardized seven-point scales and other measurement devices researchers learn about in graduate school. This leads to a conclusion that is so self-evident it is easy to miss.

> When people respond to questions on a survey, they are not revealing preferences so much as entering into an artificially-imposed social interaction in which they are forced to sample and organize their thoughts and feelings in ways that may be completely foreign to their normal modes of thinking.

So what do ordinary people do when they find themselves in this unique circumstance? Zaller and Feldman's insight is worth quoting at length:

> *Most citizens, we argue, simply do not possess pre-formed attitudes at the level of specificity demanded in surveys. Rather, they carry around in their heads a mix of only partially consistent ideas and considerations. When questioned, they call to mind a sample of these ideas, including an oversample of ideas made salient by the questionnaire and other recent events, and use them to choose among the options offered. But their choices do not, in most cases, reflect anything that can be described as true attitudes; rather, they reflect the thoughts that are most accessible in memory at the moment of response.*[18]

The problem with surveys, according to this perspective, has less to do with *how* they measure and more to do with *what* they measure, or more correctly, what survey researchers *believe* they measure. When preferences are seen as inherently ambivalent and answers to survey questions are seen as results of in-the-moment searches for accessible memory cues, several deficiencies in survey results become understandable. People give inconsistent answers because the attitudes being measured are not pre-formed. People are guessing and reconstructing their preferences every time they are asked, and those processes naturally lead to different answers at different times.

Since the publication of Zaller and Feldman's article in 1992, additional research has revealed that ambivalence is not the only source of variation impacting how individuals express attitudes and preferences. Another potential source of survey answer bias is question *difficulty*. As Daniel Kahneman has observed in numerous articles and presentations, when people are confronted with a question they find difficult to answer, they often replace it mentally with an easier question which they answer instead—usually without being aware of the substitution.[19] This easy-for-hard substitution effect makes survey answers even more suspicious as reliable guides to future behavior. Not only are survey respondents often constructing their answers on the fly, they may also be constructing answers to *different* questions than the ones researchers believe they are asking, and this effect may be occurring outside the awareness of either the researcher or the respondent.

> Expressed preferences are better thought of as stories consumers tell themselves—and market researchers—to make sense of how, what, and why they buy.

Given the fragility and implicit nature of many consumer preferences, marketers are more likely to get generalizable, actionable results by measuring *what consumers do*, not *what they say*, when faced with product or brand choices. Also, marketers need to be aware that consumer behavior can change radically across different contexts and situations. Constructed preferences are deeply influenced by the context within which a choice is made.[20]

Can Intuitive Marketing Build Lasting Preferences?

> Intuitive marketing doesn't focus on changing preferences. It focuses on building associations and expectations.

We need to look at the full *consumer cycle* in order to understand why. *Marketing* alone builds weak and temporary preferences at best. The stated preferences that marketing appears to create in consumers, as measured by self-reports, are fragile and easily changed. To understand how consumers build lasting preferences, marketers must look at the relationships between each of the stages of the consumer cycle: marketing and shopping, shopping and consuming, and consuming and marketing. Strong and stable preferences, expressed behaviorally by loyalty or habit, are mostly a function of product consumption.

> Lasting preferences are never created by marketing alone. They are built up from repeated journeys through the consumer cycle.

Because expressed preferences are largely constructed on the spot, highly susceptible to influence by incidental contextual factors, and quick to change when circumstances change, trying to change consumer behavior by tracking and changing expressed preferences is unlikely to be the most fruitful way to build and sustain lasting consumer relationships.

Intuitive marketing addresses this issue differently. Rather than trying to measure and change expressed preferences one ad or marketing campaign at a time, intuitive marketing aims to influence consumers by building a product or brand's long-term reputation for consistency, reliability, and trust. Consistency sends a strong unconscious signal to consumers that a product or brand is reliable and can be trusted to deliver on its value proposition in the future as well as the present.

> Consistency and reliability are the foundations of trust and trust is the foundation of loyalty and habit in consumer behavior.

Expressed preferences may derive from a trusted relationship or they may be a byproduct of cognitive shortcuts like mere exposure or processing fluency. Cultivating and attempting to change expressed preferences cannot replace developing a deeper understanding of why and when consumers rely on trusted relationships when they seek out, buy, and use "liked" products and brands on an everyday basis.

Sources of Intuitive Influence: Consistency, Reliability, and Trust

In the traditional model of persuasive marketing, the purpose of marketing is assumed to be the achievement of short-term transactional persuasion. In the newer model of intuitive marketing, the purpose of marketing is seen as something very different: the achievement of long-term influence through deep and authentic customer relationships.

> When adopting the intuitive marketing perspective, it would be a mistake for marketers to view shortcuts like mere exposure and processing fluency as final objectives of their marketing efforts.

Because the effects of these processes are relatively easy to measure with modern neuromarketing techniques, neuromarketing research vendors may have an incentive to tell marketers that these effects are all they need to be concerned about in testing their marketing materials. But accepting this advice would be a mistake. Marketers need to recognize that mere exposure and fluency are not ends in themselves, but only intermediate steps along a much longer route to building strong, lasting, and mutually beneficial customer relationships. This is because the kind of liking produced by mere exposure and processing fluency is ephemeral and easily manipulated—it can even turned on and off by leveraging the sources of mere exposure or processing fluency we have reviewed.

> What products and brands need to strive for is not "mere liking" based on shortcuts to immediate preference, but more enduring trust and, through trust, long-term customer loyalty and habit.

What is trust in the context of products and marketing? It is the expectation that a product will perform in the same way and provide the same benefits every time it is used or consumed. In terms of the *consumer cycle*, trust is predominantly a function of *consuming*. It cannot be achieved through *marketing* or *shopping* alone.

> Trust in brands and products is built through a long and often circuitous process. It starts with a surrender of vigilance.

This occurs as a function of experience and learning. As customers engage with a novel product, either directly or through simulated experience via marketing, advertising, or word of mouth, the original vigilance and heightened alertness with which they approach novelty diminishes. Novelty turns into familiarity and vigilance is replaced by a sense of predictability. When familiar experiences are repeated and yield similar results over time, our brains begin to recognize the consistent pattern, which gets encoded into memory as a co-occurrence association—*if A, then B*: "if I use this product, then I get this result." With familiarity comes processing fluency. The disfluency and cognitive effort that accompany learning something new get replaced by the fluency and cognitive ease of a well-practiced, familiar experience. With fluency comes liking, which encourages more repetition, which further enhances fluency. All these steps can occur unconsciously, and the resulting association can be retrieved by *System 1*, spontaneously, automatically, and effortlessly.

The combination of fluency, liking and repetition emerges into conscious awareness as a subjective feeling of positivity—what researchers call the "warm glow" of processing fluency.[21] When we become consciously aware of this feeling with regard to a product or brand, we translate it into a conscious judgment. We think of that product or brand as *reliable*. And reliability makes something worthy of trust—literally *trustworthy*—because reliability implies predictability, safety, consistency, and easy mental processing.

> **Reliability is the foundation on which the mental attribution of trust is built.**

How do consistency, reliability, and trust influence consumers without relying on traditional marketing practices of persuasion? One way to think of this effect is to conceptualize trust as *front-loaded persuasion*. As we saw in Chapter 1, traditional persuasion is the application of intrusive marketing techniques to get consumers to do something the marketer believes they would not otherwise do. The theory behind overt persuasion is that people need to be *convinced*—either through a rational argument or an emotional appeal—to do what you want them to do.

The theory behind trust as a source of intuitive influence is just the opposite.

> **Trust is a mental encapsulation of prior experience that represents not what people need to be convinced to do, but what they *want to do*, combined with how they've already *learned to do it*.**

Familiarity, liking, and fluency, combined with repetition, consistency, and a judgment of reliability lead to a mindset that does not require additional convincing at the moment of choice. In effect, all the persuasion required to move someone toward one choice over another is already *built-in* and condensed into the feeling of trust. Thus, the "choice," when it is made, may not even feel like a choice at all, but more like a simple application of prior learning and experience. This is why trust can be such a powerful source of product and brand influence, much more powerful and much more long-lasting than immediate, transactional persuasion.

> **Trust is an important source of influence not only with regard to products and brands, but also with regard to the organizations that provide products and brands to the marketplace.**

Trust in an organization is represented in the idea of *reputation*. Reputation is an important component of economic transactions that is not well captured by standard economic models of rational decision making. As advertising executive Rory Sutherland has observed, these models, which have informed traditional business and marketing strategies for over 100 years, are "trust-free, psychology-free, context-free, relationship-free and ethics-free."[22]

Unlike rational models, the intuitive consumer model that informs intuitive marketing takes into account all these "nonrational" elements of consumer choice. Companies that invest in developing a *reputation for reliability* are signaling to consumers that they are in business for the long term. They are saying they can be trusted by consumers in *this* transaction because they intend to be around for the *next* transaction, and the transaction after that. The reason companies invest in their reputations is to encourage not just immediate behavior, but future behavior in the form of repeat business.

> **When consumers have a feeling of trust toward a company, they are not only more likely to buy from its current portfolio of products and brands, but also to consider seriously new products or brands it might offer in the future.**

Reputation can act as a buffer against the natural resistance to novelty we discussed earlier in this chapter. Together, trust and reputation contribute to two key sources of sustained repeat business: *loyalty* and *habit*.[23]

Trust is a particularly important commodity when consumers must interact with an anonymous vendor, as they do when they buy online. Online sites have evolved a number of practices to convey trustworthiness, especially to first-time buyers. The most effective of these practices tend to "borrow" reputation from other sources to bolster the trustworthiness of the website. For example, offering reputable payment services like *PayPal, Apple Pay*, or *Google Pay Send*—which in turn borrow their own trustworthiness from the reputations of their parent companies—make sites appear less risky. Similarly, providing genuine reviews of products by real customers gives visitors a *surrogate* for prior experience by letting them see the experiences of other customers. Finally, providing easy-to-find help, including the availability of online chat, lowers risk by allowing customers to get their questions answered in real time. It also conveys an assurance that if customers have a problem with a product or transaction, the site has resources available to help solve it.[24]

From a consumer's perspective, it is "rational" to buy from sellers with good reputations and avoid one-time transactions with less well-known vendors, even if the latter promise lower prices and superior products, especially if there is no potential for repeat business beyond the current transaction. This is because consumers know intuitively that a vendor who never expects to see a buyer again has absolutely no incentive to treat that buyer fairly and offer a product that fulfills the promises of its marketing messages. As Rory Sutherland humorously points out, this is why one should never eat at a restaurant that caters only to tourists. Because none of its customers will ever come back for a second meal, that restaurant suffers no reputational damage if it provides poor service, outrageous prices, and terrible food.[25] Nurturing loyalty and habit makes no economic sense to the owner of a restaurant located right next to a popular tourist attraction.

It is worth mentioning here, in anticipation of an upcoming discussion in Chapter 11, that reliability is only one dimension of reputation that companies may want to emphasize in their product and brand marketing. Brands can also increase their ability to influence consumers nonpersuasively by developing a reputation for supporting the aspirational goals or identity needs of their consumers. Reputation is a powerful cognitive shortcut in the minds of consumers. It is difficult to build, easy to lose, and requires constant attention and care to remain effective and credible over time.

What are the benefits that products and brands derive from trust? In addition to the longer-term benefits of loyalty and habit formation, trust also provides marketers with several immediate transactional benefits.

> **The availability of a trustworthy choice at a point of sale discourages *System 2* deliberation and counter-arguing, decreases uncertainty and risk, inhibits variety seeking and search, increases willingness to try new products presented under a trustworthy brand, and vastly simplifies decision making.**

The intuitive marketing perspective provides clear guidelines for how to build trust in the minds of consumers. Every product and brand must find its own path to trust. But one thing is for sure. Whatever the path, building trust is a long-term project that requires sustained attention to each of the building blocks of reliability and trustworthiness that have been covered in this and previous chapters:

- Make your product experiences fluent and easy to process.
- Use repetition wisely to allow your messaging to build positive associations and connections in the minds of consumers.
- Manage your products along the novelty-familiarity continuum using the *MAYA* ("*Most Advanced, Yet Acceptable*") principle to achieve and maintain

the comfort of familiarity without sacrificing interest or descending into boredom.

- Be consistent in how your marketing presents your products and brands, especially with regard to the key associations you want to build and strengthen in consumers' minds.
- Be consistent in packaging and placement of your products in whatever shopping environments they are offered.
- Most importantly, be consistent in how your products are experienced, each and every time they are used by consumers.
- Close the loop between *product experience* and *marketing messages* by making sure consistency of product experience and reliability of brand performance are regular themes in your marketing.
- Remember that mere exposure, priming, familiarity, and fluency can all activate associations that may predispose a consumer to trust a product, but only repeated, consistent, and satisfying product consumption experiences can seal the deal.

Chapter 8

Emotions in the Marketplace

How Feelings Impact Consumer Behavior

"I've learned that people will forget what you said, people will forget what you did, but people will never forget how you made them feel."
–Maya Angelou

Can we really say that consumers "love" some brands? What drives our likes and dislikes for products and brands, and how do those feelings affect our behavior as consumers?

Traditional marketing seems to have extracted one catch-word from the deluge of brain science information it has absorbed since the emergence of neuromarketing in the last decade. That catch-word is *emotion*. Every nugget of knowledge and insight brain scientists have uncovered about the complexities of forming impressions, determining meaning and value, pursuing unconscious and conscious goals, deliberating and analyzing, and deciding and acting have been distilled down to one simple take-away—*give people more emotion*.

In this chapter, we will see how this simple formulation misses much of the complexity and nuance behind the varied roles emotion plays in consumer behavior, in both conscious and unconscious forms. We will learn that emotional reactions are important sources of consumer behavior in the intuitive marketing model, but they are not direct sources. We will see that unconscious emotions play an important but circumscribed role in triggering consumer choices and actions. We will also see that conscious emotions influence behavior mostly through learning and anticipation, not direct causal effect. And finally, we will see that a new wave of lump-in-the-throat emotional marketing recently flooding Super Bowl and other TV ad breaks is no more likely to create a sure-fire path into the pocketbooks of consumers than is the old model of persuasive marketing aimed at our *System 2* reasoning powers with pitches, demonstrations, and endorsements.

Pioneers of Intuitive Marketing: Antonio Damasio

In 1994, a neuroscientist at the University of Iowa named Antonio Damasio published a book that presented a radical new perspective on the relationship between body and mind. The book was called *Descartes' Error: Emotion, Reason, and the Human Brain.*[1] Its title was a reference to the famous dictum of 17th century French philosopher Rene Descartes: "*I think, therefore I am.*" Reporting on a series of powerful experiments comparing the decision-making capabilities of "controls" (volunteers without brain damage) to patients suffering from *prefrontal cortex (PFC) damage*—that is, damage to the region of the brain where conscious deliberation and analysis takes place—Damasio discovered a surprising fact that contradicted Descartes' belief that human reasoning was separate from and unrelated to the emotional and physical impulses of the body.

What Damasio learned was this: emotions and reasoning are inextricably intertwined in human decision making and, further, when connections between the emotional and rational processing centers in the brain are disrupted by injury or disease, people's ability to reason and decide is severely impaired. In contrast to Descartes' *dualist* view, Damasio found that mind and body could not be separated and that emotion, rather than acting only as a disrupter and inhibitor of reasoning processes, was actually a fundamental facilitator of rational choice. Without access to their emotional reactions and intuitions, Damasio's brain-damaged patients were not just bad decision makers, they were often unable to make decisions at all. Damasio then went further and proposed a mechanism through which emotions had this effect on human choice. He called it the *somatic marker hypothesis.*

Antonio Damasio was born in Portugal and received MD and PhD degrees from the University of Lisbon. He moved to the United States in 1975 to join the Department of Neurology at the University of Iowa, where he and his wife Hannah Damasio, a distinguished neurologist in her own right, began assembling one of the world's largest databases of brain injuries, comprising hundreds of studies of brain lesions and diagnostic images. From these studies, the Damasios began to build a body of evidence identifying the intricate ways emotional control and cognitive reasoning interact in both normal and damaged human brains.

The Iowa Gambling Task

The breakthrough studies that led Damasio to his conclusions in *Descartes' Error* began with a clever experimental procedure developed by Damasio's post-graduate students Antoine Bechara and Steven Anderson. In this task, which later became known as the *Iowa Gambling Task (IGT)*, experimental subjects (called *players*) are presented with four face-down card decks on a table in front of them, labeled A, B, C, and D. They are provided a "loan" of $2,000 (in realistic-looking fake money) to play a gambling game in which their goal is win (or avoid losing) as much money as possible. Each deck contains cards that either add or subtract money from the player's "pot" of winnings (or losses). For example, one card might add $100 to the player's winnings, while another might subtract $1,250. Players do not know how many reward and punishment cards are in each deck, nor what their values are. They also are not told when the game will end. The "gamble" is which deck they choose to select the next card from. As they flip over cards from any of the four decks, they may start to see patterns: some decks appear to provide a better stream of payoffs than others. In fact (but unbeknownst to players), decks C and D are designed to provide smaller rewards but also smaller and less frequent punishments, so are more likely to produce a positive payoff over many plays, while decks A and B have larger rewards, but also larger and more frequent punishments, so are likely to result in a negative payoff over many plays.[2] Players are not told how much they are winning or losing, nor are they allowed to keep written notes of their progress.

As both "controls" and patients with prefrontal brain damage played this game over a period of 100 turns, Damasio noticed some initially similar patterns and then some significant divergences. All players started out by sampling equally from each of the four decks, getting a sense of the payoff potentials of each. After this initial sampling, however, the two groups began to diverge. Controls started making more and more of their choices from decks C and D, recognizing that those decks provided more consistent positive results over time. Patients, in contrast, showed no such recognition, and in fact continued to pick more cards from decks A and B, even when those choices resulted in the loss of their $2,000 bankroll halfway through the game, and required them to get additional "loans" from the experimenters to continue.[3]

To Damasio, it looked like the patients were making choices that had high *immediate* rewards but, in the context of the game, were consistently followed by severe but *delayed* punishments. They were attracted to the immediate gains, but were not affected by the prospect of losing those gains in the more distant future. Damasio knew from prior work with these patients that they shared another symptom that might be relevant to their poor performance in the game: they displayed and often expressed an inability to access normal emotional responses to the world around them.[4] They suffered, in Damasio's words, from "flat emotion and feeling."[5] This led Damasio to hypothesize that their poor performance in the IGT might be a function their inability to access emotions to aid in their decision making, not only in the controlled context of the game, but more generally in the realms of personal, financial, and moral choices in their daily lives.

To test this hypothesis, Damasio and his colleagues took advantage of the fact that emotions originate as physiological changes in the body. We experience emotional states when signals from body state changes are transmitted to the brain. The greater the body state change (for example, changes in heart rate, breathing, body temperature, sweating, etc.), the more intense the emotion. One such change is an increase in the secretion of fluid by the skin's sweat glands. Because human sweat contains salt, and salt conducts an electric current, sensors placed on the skin can trace these increases (even if they are below our ability to see or feel them directly). The measure of electrical flow captured by these sensors is call *skin conductance*. And people's *skin conductance response (SCR)* is a well-known and generally reliable measure of emotional arousal—the higher the skin conductance response, the greater the emotional arousal. Damasio and team decided to measure the SCRs of controls and patients as they played the game in order to see precisely how emotions did or did not enter into their decision-making behavior.

The results confirmed Damasio's hypothesis in two ways. First, as the game proceeded, "controls" began to elicit strong *SCRs* in anticipation of picking cards from the high-punishment decks A and B, but not from the low-punishment decks C and D. Furthermore, *SCRs* showed an *unconscious* anticipatory effect in these subjects.

> **On average, controls started producing skin conductance responses in anticipation of picking from the "bad" decks 30 plays before they *consciously* realized that those decks should be avoided.[6]**

Second, for subjects with PFC damage, *SCRs* were flat throughout the game and unconscious anticipatory recognition of the "bad" decks never occurred. Even when they expressed conscious recognition that decks A and B were "bad," they still chose disproportionately from them. Without access to the emotional warning system tracked by *SCRs*, patients were unable to make "rational" choices to minimize their risk of loss.

This led Damasio to the insight that unconscious emotional assessments were a critical part of rational decision making. Damasio's *PFC*-damaged subjects had lost their brain's connection to emotional "gut feelings." His experiment showed that, rather than being a hindrance to rational choice, emotions were a necessary element. It also showed that this contribution occurred below conscious awareness, prior to the perception of conscious *feelings*.

> **Using Kahneman's *System 1–System 2* language, Damasio's discovery provides a compelling demonstration of what happens when the connection between these two systems of mental processing is severed.**

We saw in Chapter 5 and Chapter 6 that *System 1* and *System 2* are not isolated systems but instead work together to share the load of cognition. What Damasio observed was the profound impact of disrupting the link between *System 1* and *System 2*—producing not a facilitation of rational *System 2* deliberative processing "freed" from *System 1* constraints, but a complete breakdown of people's ability to engage in effective deliberative decision making.

The Somatic Marker Hypothesis

Digging further into the mental machinery by which unconscious and conscious emotions participate in human choice processes, Damasio developed an explanation that has deep implications for the world of marketing: the *somatic marker hypothesis*.

Somatic markers, as defined by Damasio, are *somatic* in the sense that they arise from the body;[7] that is, they are body state changes—sometimes subtle, sometimes not—that signal to the conscious or unconscious mind an *emotional association* with a current choice situation. They are *markers* in that they mark some aspect of the choice situation as either advantageous or disadvantageous, thus biasing the decision-making process toward or away from different options. These emotional markings can be experienced overtly, as "gut feelings" or vague "hunches" that an option is either good or bad, or they can also be experienced covertly, influencing choice and behavior via signal systems operating below conscious awareness. In terms of the *cognitive timeline* model, somatic markers enter into the cognitive flow at either the *determine meaning and value* stage or the *activate goals* stage of cognition. They then influence conscious *deliberation and analysis* that result in choices and subsequent *speaking and acting*.

Some somatic markers are *innate*, activating automatically under certain environmental conditions and operating through evolutionarily-established circuits in the brain. For example, people have an innate fear of sudden loud noises, are naturally repulsed by rotten food, and are predisposed to prefer rounded to pointy-edged objects.[8] These responses are all triggered by somatic markers that come "pre-loaded" in the human brain and run the gamut of emotional arousal from intense to barely perceptible. None of these responses need to be learned through experience. They occur spontaneously and reliably whenever the triggering stimulus is encountered, even when it is encountered for the first time.

Most somatic markers, however, especially those that are relevant to marketing and consumer behavior, are *learned*. They are encoded in human memory during events experienced every day, from birth to death. In effect, when we encounter any person, object, or situation in our daily lives, our brains do a rapid, unconscious recording of our body state (heart rate, respiration rate, perspiration production, etc.). Those recording are encoded in memory as indicators of emotional response—somatic markers—of that experience.

Later, when we have a similar experience, two things happen. First, a somatic marker for that category of experience is retrieved from memory and we experience a similar somatic state (though often less intense than the original), which then becomes an emotional input into any deliberations, choices, or actions that might follow. Functionally, this is a type of *priming*, as we will discuss in depth in Chapter 14. Because the somatic marker triggers an emotional state, priming researchers call this process *affective priming*.[9]

Second, the current encounter produces an update to our somatic marking of that category of experience. Based on current body state signals, our encoded somatic marker for that experience may become more positive or negative. In this way, somatic markers both participate in and are modified by every interaction we have with persons, objects, and events in the world around us.

Based on the somatic marker hypothesis, as well as painstaking testing and rejecting of many alternative hypotheses, Damasio developed a neural model of precisely what was going on in his patients' brains during their poor showing in the *Iowa Gambling Task*. Unlike healthy brains, their damaged brains—which had suffered lesions in a very specific area of the prefrontal cortex—were unable to access the *as-if loop* pathway during choice deliberation. They were able to *imagine* future outcomes in the game (winning or losing). They were even *aware* that decks C and D were more advantageous than A and B. But this knowledge did not change their behavior, they continued to draw disproportionately from the bad decks. Only one element of good decision making was missing.

> **Damasio's patients could not sense the emotional signals—the somatic markers—that connect knowledge to action in normal brains.**

They could anticipate the future quite normally, but those anticipations did not trigger the somatic markers that provided emotional guidance about good and bad choices. This absence of emotional feedback showed up in their failure to generate any skin conductance responses at any point during the task. Unable to read their bodies' responses to poor deck choices, they were unable to modify their actions and strategies even when they knew they were performing poorly.[10]

This was a stunning result. Damasio's discoveries reported in *Descartes' Error* turned brain scientists' understanding of the roles of emotion and reasoning in decision making upside down. In one focused research program, he demolished two longstanding myths about the role of emotions in rational choice, replacing them with a new picture that gave emotion a mandatory role in even the most rigorous, disciplined forms of decision making. He demonstrated that emotion was not just a pesky hindrance to good reasoning (as folk wisdom had warned us for centuries). Nor was it simply a "nice to have" intuitive booster of reasoning, adding nothing essential to what reasoning could achieve on its own.

> **Damasio discovered that reasoning without emotion fails to motivate action because mind and body are inextricably linked in human decision making and behavior.**

The implication for believers in rational-emotional dualism is profound: focusing exclusively on the rational, conscious aspects of choice misses a crucial but previously hidden influence on human behavior—the subtle, often unconsciously transmitted impact of emotional signals in the form of somatic markers.

What Somatic Markers Mean for Marketing

Many marketers and market researchers have taken note of Damasio's pioneering work on emotion and choice. Unfortunately, too many of them have drawn excessively simplistic lessons for marketing, advertising, and sales. Two misconceptions in particular need to be corrected if marketers are to properly understand the implications of somatic markers for their profession.

- Marketers need to avoid confusing somatic markers with conscious feelings of *liking*.
- Marketers need to understand that somatic markers influence consumer choices *indirectly*, not directly.

With regard to the first misconception, Damasio makes clear throughout his writings that there is considerable cognitive distance between activating a somatic marker and experiencing a conscious feeling such as liking. A somatic marker is a re-enacted body state that may not even be experienced consciously. If it is experienced consciously, it needs to be *identified* as one type of feeling or another, and that interpretation, just like any other perception or determination of meaning and value, is always highly context dependent.

> **The same state of emotional arousal can be identified as joy or fear, depending on whether it's being experienced in Disneyland or in a dark alley.**

Somatic markers are not necessarily indicators of conscious liking, or any other discrete emotion for that matter. They are body-state *inputs* into complex behavioral routines, not *outputs*. They may be produced by negative experiences as well as positive ones. Indeed, Damasio and his team have posited that a key evolutionary advantage of somatic markers is their ability to function as *warnings* of potential bad outcomes, just as spiking *SCRs* warned participants in the gambling task that they were selecting from a disadvantageous deck.[11]

> **Marketers naturally want to increase liking for their products and brands, but labeling such feelings as "somatic markers" is an over-simplified and misleading use of the term.**

With regard to the second misconception, somatic markers don't determine choices or make us do things in ways we would not otherwise. They are not "buy buttons" in the brain. They do not "dictate" consumer behavior.[12] Marketers need to understand that somatic markers tend to influence consumer choices in relatively subtle ways that fall far short of forcing consumers to buy one product over another. For example, somatic markers have been found to impact choice and behavior indirectly[13] by:

- Orienting attention
- Priming associations in memory
- Making it easier to hold an idea in working memory
- Influencing the mental ranking of options during deliberation
- Biasing the construction of preferences
- Simplifying the consideration of longer-term consequences
- Triggering motivation and goal pursuit

All of these processes can and should be measured and monitored by marketers who want to understand how consumers respond to their brands and products—and how somatic markers influence those responses. Although somatic markers do not force consumer outcomes in any direct or automatic way, they do influence the mental processes underlying consumer choice and action at several points along the cognitive timeline, both before and after the onset of conscious deliberation.

What marketers need to take away from Damasio's somatic marker hypothesis is this:

> **Consumers are walking emotional thermometers who automatically register the emotional temperature of everything around them.**

They update those readings (a little hotter, a little colder) every time they re-encounter a person, object, or situation they have encountered before.

We do this automatically and usually unconsciously. For marketers, this means it is important to keep tracking the emotional underpinnings of consumer responses to products and brands over time. Damasio's discoveries not only imply that products and brands have an emotional temperature in the minds of every consumer who has ever used them, heard about them, bought them, talked about them, or even thought about them. They also imply that those temperature readings are highly malleable and can change over time with every new encounter between consumer, product, and brand.

Following the publication of *Descartes' Error* and related academic studies, Damasio's interests moved on to encompass other areas where the intersection of emotion and reason play a crucial role, such as addiction, moral decision making, and the neurological foundations of consciousness[14]. We will have an opportunity to return to the topic of addiction in our discussion of *learned needs* in Chapter 10.

Although it was probably never his intention, Damasio's research and insights on the impacts of emotion and somatic markers on decision making have inspired a number of challenges to the traditional model of persuasive marketing over the last two decades, including the work of Robert Heath profiled in Chapter 4. Damasio's investigations into the unconscious emotional drivers that underlie all human choice, including consumer choice, make him one of the earliest and most influential pioneers of intuitive marketing.

How Unconscious Emotions Influence Behavior

Like the role of attention in consumer responses to marketing, the role of emotion in responding to marketing is more complicated than it appears at first glance. Just as most marketers believe—incorrectly, as we saw in Chapter 3 and Chapter 4—that attention is a required pre-condition for marketing effectiveness, so too do they believe that a *positive emotional response* is a required pre-condition for marketing effectiveness. When marketing elicits conscious feelings of *liking*, it is commonly assumed, this directly causes people to engage in the main forms of consumer behavior marketers care about: buying, consuming, advocating, and repeat buying.

> **Attention-in, liking-out: this is the universal equation for successful marketing that most marketers learn in college and their early careers.**

Brain science tells us the road from emotion to consumer behavior is a bit more long and winding. There are two levels of complexity we need to explore. The first is the interplay of unconscious emotions—which brain scientists sometimes call *unconscious affect*—and conscious *feelings*. On top of that, we need to consider how both these types of emotion interact with and influence conscious reasoning, deliberation, analysis, choice, and ultimately, consumer behavior in the marketplace—the conscious stages of the consumer's cognitive timeline.

Are Unconscious Emotions Real?

The first distinction marketers and consumers need to understand is the difference between conscious and unconscious emotion.

Like the idea of awareness without attention, the idea of emotion without awareness is counterintuitive, even a little spooky.

And the further idea that these "unfelt" emotions can have a significant effect on our conscious thinking and actions is even more spooky.

In the late 1990s, the idea of unconscious emotion was still controversial in the academic world. While most psychologists accepted Robert Zajonc's *mere exposure* findings—that emotional states such as *liking* could be induced unconsciously by fluency manipulations as simple as repeated exposure (see Chapter 6)—they still generally believed that the resulting emotion had to be experienced consciously. Brain scientists Piotr Winkielman and Kent Berridge decided to test this assumption, so they went searching for emotions that people didn't know they were having.

Winkielman and Berridge designed a clever experiment to test whether unconscious emotions existed and, if so, how much impact they had on conscious consumer attitudes and behavior.[15] They reasoned that proving the existence of unconscious emotion required two things. First, people had to be unable to report any kind of conscious feeling impacting their behavior. And second, their behavior had to be undeniably the result of an emotional reaction they were not aware they had. So the researchers set up a two-part experiment.

In the first part of the experiment, after participants were asked how thirsty and hungry they were feeling at the moment, they were asked to perform a simple gender identification task. Headshots of individuals were presented on a computer screen and participants had to classify them rapidly as male or female. All the faces had neutral, non-emotional expressions. Easy enough, but what the participants didn't know was that before they saw and classified each face, they were also *subliminally* exposed to another face, flashed up on the screen for only 16 thousandths of a second, so rapidly their conscious minds could not detect it. For some participants, these faces all showed happy expressions; for others, they all showed angry expressions; and for a third group, they all showed neutral expressions. Participants evaluated eight faces in a baseline task (all neutral primes), then evaluated eight more faces in a test task (all negative, neutral, or positive primes).

What Winkielman and Berridge were doing was *subliminally priming* different emotional states in different participants in their experiment. As we saw in Chapter 3 and in our discussion of Robert Zajonc in Chapter 6, subliminal primes are a great tool for experiments, because they allow researchers to induce and study purely unconscious influences on behavior.[16] In this case, participants were being exposed to positive, negative, or neutral emotions outside their awareness. Previous research had confirmed that such exposure induces the primed emotional state in people who see it.[17] So those primed with happy faces were presumably in a more positive emotional state, those primed with angry faces were in a more negative emotional state, and those primed with neutral faces were in an unchanged neutral emotional state. Thus primed, the participants proceeded to the next part of the experiment.

Part 2 consisted of two tasks: a subjective rating of how participants were feeling at the moment (degree of pleasantness, degree of arousal) and a taste test involving a fruit-flavored, sweetened beverage. Half the participants were given the rating task before the taste test and half were given it after.

For the taste test, participants were allowed to pour as much of the beverage as they wanted from an opaque pitcher into a glass and then taste it. They then rated the beverage on several measures: deliciousness, how much they wanted to drink, how well it quenched their thirst, and how much they would pay for a can of this drink. Again unrevealed to participants, the researchers were not really interested in those answers. What they *were* interested in was how much beverage the participants poured into the glass and how much they actually drank. As a final check, participants were given a *prime perceptibility* test to determine if they could consciously recognize any of the subliminal primes they had been exposed to (they could not).

Results provided strong support for the existence and behavioral impact of unconscious emotions. First, participants primed with happy faces poured significantly more beverage into their glass than those primed with neutral or angry faces. But importantly, this effect was significantly large *only* for participants who had described themselves as *thirsty* at the start of the experiment.

Thirsty participants primed with happy faces poured 114% more of the beverage than thirsty participants primed with angry faces.

There was a weak priming effect for those who were moderately thirsty and none for those who were not thirsty. Similarly, thirsty participants drank 280% more of the beverage after being exposed to happy primes vs. angry primes, while people with moderate or low levels of thirst drank approximately the same amount of beverage regardless of which primes they were exposed to. No effects of priming on either drinking or pouring were found for participants who had stated they were feeling *hungry*, but not thirsty, at the start of the experiment.

Finally, the recorded changes in pouring and drinking behavior were *not* accompanied by any changes in conscious feelings. Neither participants' subjective moods nor their felt arousal levels were impacted by the subliminal emotional primes. Whatever emotional effects were influencing their behavior, those effects were not rising to the level of conscious awareness. Participants were completely unaware of the emotional forces that were moving them.

> **Winkielman and Berridge's experiment provided the two proof points they were looking for: participants engaged in behaviors that were undeniably the result of emotions they were not aware of, and they were unable to report any changes in their conscious feeling accompanying those behaviors.**

Unconscious Emotional Priming and Consumer Choice

For marketers, there is a bit of "good news-bad news" here. The good news is that people can indeed be influenced by emotions operating below their conscious awareness and, further, that these emotions can be *induced* by visual stimuli that are not consciously recognized.

The bad news—at least for marketers who see this as a golden ticket into consumers' unconscious minds—is three-fold. First, consumers need, in effect, to be *predisposed to act* in order for unconsciously primed emotions to have an effect on their actions.[18] Only participants who were already thirsty were behaviorally influenced by the subliminally presented emotional faces. Others who were not already predisposed to drink a thirst-quenching beverage were not. This is an important point.

> **Unconscious emotional priming does not cause people to do things they would not otherwise do. It does not change people's minds. Rather, it increases people's motivation to pursue actions they were already inclined to pursue.**

Second, the impact of unconscious emotional primes on conscious consumer attitudes and preferences is short-lived. When the subliminal primes were separated from the expression of subjective ratings in this experiment by only a few seconds, their effect vanished. This is the main reason why, as we saw in Chapter 1, researchers have judged "subliminal persuasion" to be a very ineffective way to advertise or promote products.

Third, this experiment highlights once again that *System 1* effects on conscious behavior do not need to make sense. There is no logical reason why exposure to smiling faces should impact pouring, drinking, or expressing an opinion about a fruit-flavored beverage. Yet sometimes it does. This reminds us of a key finding about the mere exposure effect: Positive emotions induced by repeated mere exposure can influence the ratings of "other things" completely unrelated to the repeated objects producing the effect. *System 1* effects on *System 2* tend to be *diffuse*, not targeted.

In summary, Winkielman and Berridge's findings about unconscious emotions contain nuances that marketers would do well to keep in mind. This does not limit their originality, nor the significant impact they have had on subsequent research about consumer emotions, but it does remind marketers that two caveats are in order:

- This study does *not* show that marketers can effectively influence consumer attitudes and behavior with subliminal primes.
- It does *not* show that consumers can be persuaded to do what they do not want to do by targeting their unconscious *System 1* processes.

If unconscious emotional primes only affect consumer attitudes and behavior when aligned with existing wants and needs, what is their role in understanding and predicting the thoughts and actions of consumers? To answer this question, we must recognize that unconscious emotions cannot be fully understood without taking into account the complementary role of conscious emotions, a topic to which we now turn.

Unconscious Emotions Are for Deciding, Feelings Are for Learning

Antonio Damasio confirmed there is both a *deep divide* and a *solid bridge* between emotion and reasoning in the human brain.

> **Emotion emerges from different locations and activates different processes in the brain than reasoning, yet the two streams of processing intertwine in complex and essential ways.**

When that choreography breaks down, as Damasio discovered, our ability to choose and act effectively in the world is severely constrained.

There is a traditional model of emotion and behavior that says conscious emotion is a direct cause of behavior. This model has dominated thinking about emotion at least since the days of the ancient Greeks. At first glance, it seems to make perfect sense. Don't emotions make us act? If we get angry, we attack our foe. If we experience fear, we freeze or run away. If we feel love, we want to embrace our beloved. But a closer examination reveals flaws in this simple characterization.

Direct emotional causation of behavior certainly makes sense for animals that lack the sophisticated cognitive capabilities of humans. A reptile or lower mammal, for example, might exhibit many built-in reactions to significant events in the course of surviving and/or maintaining well-being that could be interpreted as direct emotional reactions—responses to danger, to the presence of a potential mate, or to the presence of food or drink when hungry or thirsty, for example.[19] Evolutionary biologists speculate that emotions probably evolved originally for the purpose of directly controlling survival-enhancing behaviors.[20] But humans benefit from a more evolved brain that enables us not merely to react to emotions, but to stop, think, and plan what we want to do about them. Because humans have an advanced capacity for self-consciousness and self-regulation, we are not always prisoners of our emotions. We can manage how we respond to them, at least to some extent.

Also, for humans, when we think of examples of conscious emotion causing behavior, we tend to think of negative emotions. This is reflected in how we talk about emotional causation. We say anger *makes* us attack, we say fear *makes* us freeze or flee, but we do not say love *makes* us embrace our beloved. Rather, we say love makes us *want* to embrace our beloved. As any English speaker will confirm, *wanting* to do something is a very different from actually doing it.

Indeed, positive emotions can cause us to *want to do* many things: give a stranger a hug (not recommended), dance in the street, sing in the rain. But that's precisely the problem with the direct causation model. If we can *choose* a response to our felt emotion, then our response is not being automatically triggered by the emotion itself.

Once we acknowledge our uniquely human capacity to decide how to act in response to an emotion, we acknowledge the full array of cognitive machinery that gets activated in between the emotion and the response.

And once we do that, we must leave the "emotion causes behavior" theory behind.

So how do emotion and behavior interact? One approach that has gained support among brain scientists is the *emotion-as-feedback* theory presented by Roy

Baumeister, Kathleen Vohs, and colleagues in their 2008 article, *"How Emotion Shapes Behavior: Feedback, Anticipation, and Reflection, Rather Than Direct Causation."*[21] The essence of their theory is the title of this section:

Unconscious emotions are for deciding, feelings are for learning.

Viewing the emotion-behavior connection as a feedback system rather than a direct causation system not only helps put many empirical results in context, such as Damasio's somatic marker hypothesis and Winkielman and Berridge's unconscious emotion findings, but also provides marketers and consumers with a much more useful and realistic model of how emotions—both conscious and unconscious—can and do influence consumer choices and actions.

Emotion-as-feedback theory draws upon decades of brain science research to answer one key question: *how does emotion help humans survive, adapt, and succeed in the world?* It is built on four basic principles:

- The purpose of conscious emotional *feelings* is not to direct behavior in the moment, but to stimulate thinking, reflection, and learning *after* an outcome or behavior has occurred.
- The purpose of unconscious emotional associations—called *automatic affect* by Baumeister and team—is to facilitate choice and action in the moment without requiring activation of full-fledged conscious feelings *prior to* deciding or acting.
- Unconscious emotional associations are automatically derived from conscious emotional experiences through a process of *associative learning*.
- Over time, what we learn from emotional experiences is to *anticipate* future emotional outcomes and behave so as to pursue the emotions we prefer.

The feedback loop in this theory operates in three steps. First, we *learn* from life experiences which emotions tend to follow from different types of actions and outcomes. Second, over time we *encode* these learned lessons as unconscious emotional associations which bias our subsequent behavior, either without conscious awareness or, at best, with only "quick and simple twinges of liking or disliking."[22] Third, our constantly growing repertoire of conscious emotional learnings and unconscious emotional associations enables us to *anticipate* the likely emotional outcomes of future options, thereby impacting our behavior indirectly by guiding us toward actions that are more likely to achieve the positive emotional states we seek.

Conscious emotion thus influences behavior as a function of learning and anticipation, not direct causation.

What are the implications of this model for marketers and consumers? Does it lead to different lessons and insights for marketing than the "direct causation" model? To answer these questions, we need to look at each of the four principles in turn.

The Purpose of Conscious Emotion

The purpose of conscious emotion is to stimulate thinking and learning after an emotional experience has occurred.

If marketers assume that the purpose of conscious emotion is to stimulate consumer behavior, such as buying or consuming a product or brand, it follows that the most important task for marketers is to understand the consumer's conscious emotion at the moment of interaction with the product or marketing message. From that emotional reference point they hope to infer what the consumer is likely to do as a result. *Emotion-as-feedback* theory says this is not quite right.

> **If marketers want to understand how emotions contribute to consumer behavior, they need to look not just at the conscious—and therefore self-reportable—emotions consumers *say* accompany their exposures to marketing, but also at what consumers *learn* as a consequence of their emotional interactions with products, brands, and marketing communications.**

According to Baumeister and colleagues, conscious feelings are for learning. Empirical research on the activation of conscious emotion provides two insights into why this makes sense: conscious emotions form relatively slowly and they tend to form after, not during, the experiences that trigger them.

First, as we saw in the Damasio and Winkielman experiments, conscious feelings do not unfold fast enough to play a role in many choice and action situations, such as those that trigger 'gut feelings" or subliminally-induced unconscious reactions. Those responses are hard-coded into our *System 1* "jump to conclusions" mental machinery. It takes time to recognize and classify what conscious feelings one might be experiencing in a given situation, which requires overriding our *System 1* impulses and activating our slower, more cognitively-taxing *System 2* deliberative processes. Even diagnosing how we feel, separate from using that knowledge as part of a choice process, takes more time and effort than a rapidly unfolding choice situation may allow, or deserve. This is why evolution has equipped the modern human brain with dedicated "rapid response" circuitry that enables behavior to be activated without required full-blown conscious deliberation and analysis.[23]

Second, most conscious feelings occur *following* an emotion-inducing experience, not during the experience itself. This is true for both negative and positive feelings. Recall situations in which you have felt anger, resentment, or fear. Often, the conscious emotion only occurred after the incident that triggered it—for example, the "slow burn" of anger that follows a perceived insult, or the resentment that festers after being slighted, or the fear that grips you only after you have successfully maneuvered your vehicle to avoid a crash. Positive emotions often become most intense after the fact as well. Even the most unambiguously positive emotions, happiness and joy, tend to follow the events that trigger them. We often need a moment to reflect on whether an incident has fulfilled our hopes and expectations, for example, before we begin to experience the feeling of joy that follows from such a realization.

This view does not deny that conscious feelings sometimes precede and cause behavior directly. But such instances tend to be sporadic and often counterproductive—an insight that is reflected in many folk wisdom adages about *acting without thinking*, such as "look before you leap" and "never reply to an email when you're angry." The point is not that conscious emotion *never* causes behavior, but that "it operates mainly and best by means of its influence on cognitive processes, which in turn are input into decision and behavior regulation processes."[24]

Because consciously felt emotions tend to develop relatively slowly in cognitive time and occur after, rather than during, an emotion-inducing experience, they are particularly well-suited to be sources of learning about what to expect from experiences of various kinds in the future.

Immediate unconscious emotion does not *replace* conscious emotion in explaining and predicting consumer behavior. The two types of emotion are in constant interaction and both contribute to the eventual actions consumers choose to take in the marketplace.[25] Consumers are complicated, emotional effects are complicated, and marketers need to become sophisticated observers of those complications if they want to learn how conscious emotions influence consumer choice and behavior.

The Purpose of Automatic Affect

The purpose of automatic affect is to guide choice and action in the moment.

Unconscious affect, according to the *emotion-as-feedback* theory, is for deciding and acting. This conclusion is derived from a large body of brain research, much of which we have covered, such as Zajonc's studies of the mere exposure effect, the processing fluency literature, Damasio's somatic marker hypothesis, and Winkielman and Berridge's studies of unconscious emotion. In all these examples, we see that automatic affect can subtly guide our choices among competing goals or plans without requiring that we expend costly conscious cognitive effort to do so.

What Baumeister and co-authors are describing here is the *unconscious emotional guidance system*[26] we encountered in Chapter 2. The distinction between *causation* and *guidance* is important because unconscious emotions only influence choice and behavior indirectly. As we saw in Figure 4, unconscious emotional reactions impact behavior by first activating the *motivational guidance system*; specifically, by triggering motivational states of *approach* or *withdrawal*, which may or may not trigger conscious states of *wanting* or *needing*.

> **Even if *liking* is induced and/or experienced unconsciously, as in the mere exposure effect, processing fluency, or subliminal affective priming, it cannot translate into action in the absence of unconscious approach motivation or conscious wanting or needing.**

Recall a key finding in the Winkielman and Berridge experiment: if participants in their study were not thirsty (a conscious feeling of need), they were not influenced by the subliminal happy faces. They did not pour more or drink more of the offered beverage. Only when the induced positive emotion met an existing state of relevant *need* (thirst, which was relevant to drinking, but not hunger, which was not) did the statistically significant effects on behavior occur.

Substantial research has demonstrated that unconscious affect impacts behavior through the activation of approach and withdrawal motivation in the brain.[27] An important aspect of this impact is that it is not very specific. Rather, the dominant element in unconscious affect is its diffuse positive or negative *valence*.

> **Unconscious affect does not contain specific information about how to act, it simply evokes an approach or withdrawal reaction based on positive or negative associations with prior experiences in similar situations.**

The main lesson for marketers is that the influence of unconscious affect on consumer behavior tends to be much more nonspecific and diffuse than marketers might wish it to be. Because unconscious emotional associations contain little specific information, they cannot be precisely targeted. Rather than motivating consumers to seek out a particular product or brand, they are more likely to create a more general motivation to satisfy a more general want or need. Food advertising on TV, for example, is more likely to trigger a broad goal to eat, which can be satisfied in the short term by whatever is in the pantry, rather than a more specific goal to buy the advertised product on the viewer's next grocery-shopping trip.[28]

How We Learn Unconscious Emotional Associations

Unconscious emotional associations are derived from conscious emotional experiences via associative learning.

Implicit learning is the crucial unconscious process by which our brains make connections between all kinds of things and events we experience in our lives, including marketing messages, products, and brands (see Chapter 12). Through *repetition* and *conditioning*, implicit learning enables our *System 1* mental machinery to link together just about any two things that co-occur in time or space. Later, when one element of the association is experienced as a *prime, associative activation* searches memory and brings to mind its counterpart. What Baumeister and colleagues are summarizing in this principle is how this mechanism works specifically with emotion-based learning.

One function our brains perform below conscious awareness is to take lessons we have learned or acquired consciously and *automatize* them—that is, encode them so they can be executed automatically without conscious intervention. This is how humans acquire skills in general.[29] *Emotion-as-feedback* theory suggests a specifically emotional version of this general automatization process:

Conscious emotion leaves an affective residue associated with the memory of the situation and behavior that produced the emotion, and when a similar opportunity arises in the future, the affect can be automatically activated ("lying is bad") so as to guide behavior.[30]

> **What gets automatized through learning is not the full-fledged emotional experience, but the *affective residue* from that experience, which is essentially encoded as simple valence—an answer to the question, "do I want to have that emotion again, right now?"**

This unconscious residue of past emotion then acts as an input into the *unconscious motivational guidance system*, which rapidly and efficiently determines the best course of action—approach or withdrawal—in the current situation. The evoked affective residue does *not* contain specific information about how to act, it merely provides a *summary marker* of whether similar experiences in the past produced positive or negative memories. This is the insight captured by Maya Angelou in her quote at the start of this chapter: long after someone forgets what you said or did, they will still remember how you made them feel.

> **Affective residue outlives factual recollection every time.**

Baumeister and colleagues align their notion of *affective residue* directly with Damasio's concept of *somatic markers*. Both ideas, they note, refer to stored evaluative information derived from past outcomes that can be accessed rapidly and unconsciously to guide both current and future behavior.

For marketers, and in particular for practitioners of intuitive marketing, this depiction of how conscious emotional events get converted into unconscious emotional associations and then, by activating motivational processes and goal pursuit, impact choices and actions, necessitates a radical rethinking of how emotions influence consumer behavior.

> **Rather than focusing on fine-tuning consumers' conscious emotional responses to marketing messages, intuitive marketing focuses on monitoring and understanding the simple *affective residue* produced by every interaction consumers have across every touchpoint with their products and brands.**

It is the conscious emotional *after-effects* of these interactions, not the emotions spontaneously induced by puppy dogs or dancing babies in Super Bowl ads, that matter in building a strong intuitive relationship between a brand and its consumers. Those are the conscious emotions that get translated into automatic emotional associations that create lasting relationships of trust, habit, and loyalty.

Emotional Experiences Influence Behavior through Anticipation

Anticipating emotional outcomes of future actions is the main way emotional learning influences behavior.

The core idea underlying *emotion-as-feedback* theory is that emotions influence behavior not through direct causation, but through anticipation. We have seen how we learn from emotional experiences. What exactly do we learn?

First, we learn that certain emotions follow from the outcomes of certain actions. Emotions provide us with signals as to how we're doing. Feeling a negative emotional outcome (anger, shame, guilt) can stimulate counterfactual thinking (*what-if* speculation) about how we could have gotten better results if we had acted differently. Conversely, feeling a positive emotional outcome (joy, elation, pride) can stimulate strategies and plans to get ourselves into future situations to repeat the behaviors that produced those emotions. In this way, our brains learn to recognize *if-then* rules for relationships in the emotional realm, encoding lessons we can draw upon later, both consciously and unconsciously, to shape our behaviors in favor of pursuing emotionally preferable goals.

Second, we learn that we cannot voluntarily *make ourselves* have an emotion. Emotional feelings are one kind of cognitive event that cannot be turned on or off at will. Emotions can literally overwhelm us, rendering our rational *System 2* processing inoperative, at least temporarily. We can teach ourselves to control our *responses* to emotions, but these efforts at self-regulation are aimed at the after-effects of emotions, not the emotions themselves. This has always been somewhat puzzling to evolutionary biologists and psychologists. Why have humans evolved the ability to self-control our actions and thoughts, but not our emotions?

> **We can choose to walk across the room, or not, and we can choose to redirect our attention and think about something else, but we cannot choose to have, or stop having, an emotion.**

Why should that be? *Emotion-as-feedback* theory proposes an answer: "*you cannot control your emotions because the purpose of emotions is to control you.*"[31] If emotions are a feedback system for facilitating behavioral learning and control, they cannot themselves be self-controllable or they would lose that crucial function. For example, if you could stop feeling guilty simply by act of will, then there would be little need to change your behavior to avoid guilt-producing actions. Guilt would lose its power to steer you to behave in moral or socially desirable ways.

Third, because emotions are beyond our direct control, we learn that they create a kind of predictability. If we repeat an action that triggered a particular emotion in the past, we expect it to trigger that same emotion in the future. In other words, we learn to anticipate the emotional repercussions of our behavior.

Finally, we learn to make better choices. Our ability to anticipate emotional consequences makes us more likely to pursue actions that make us feel good and avoid actions that make us feel bad. In this way, the anticipation of emotion—based on learning across multiple life experiences—becomes more important than the emotion produced by a single experience. Immediate emotional responses provide feedback about actions just performed, but the greater value of this feedback is to help us learn how to act in the future. Anticipating emotional outcomes can help us make better decisions based on deeper experience, increasing our chances of getting better outcomes tomorrow than got yesterday.

Chapter 9

Emotional Displays in Marketing

Intuitive Insights for Traditional Marketers

"What's love got to do, got to do with it?
What's love but a second-hand emotion?"
–Tina Turner

What are the implications of *emotion-as-feedback* theory for marketing? Marketers need to understand not just what emotions consumers are having *while experiencing* marketing messages, but also how those emotional experiences are influencing what they are *learning* about products and brands, and how those emotion-based lessons are impacting what they are *doing* in the marketplace. Once the role of emotion in consumer choice and behavior is properly identified as a feedback system, the emotions consumers feel during marketing exposure become less important than the emotional and motivational outcomes consumers *anticipate* regarding future experiences with the product.

Alert readers will recognize that Baumeister's concept of *anticipation* is quite similar to the concept of *expectations* introduced in Chapter 2. In that discussion, we saw that consumer experiences at each stage of the consumer cycle can subtly and sometimes radically change product or brand associations in consumers' minds, which can then change consumer expectations going into any stage transition—from marketing to shopping, shopping to consuming, or consuming to marketing. Baumeister's concept of emotional anticipation expresses the same basic idea. Anticipation is essentially an expectation applied to a specific upcoming event or circumstance.

A final implication for marketers is that this interplay of anticipation and learning creates a loose, not tight, connection between emotion and consumer action. Unlike the *emotion-in, liking-out* model of traditional marketing, *emotion-as-feedback* asserts a longer-term, more context-sensitive, and dynamic relationship between emotional experience and consumer behavior.

> **A consumer's emotional relationship with a product or brand cannot be inferred from a single, one-time emotional response to an advertisement or other marketing message.**

Rather, it is a function of a complex interaction, over time, between what each consumer experiences, what they learn, what they anticipate, and—as we will see in this chapter—what they remember.

Liking: The Most Overrated Emotion

In 1991, the Advertising Research Foundation, an industry-funded think tank and trade organization, published the results of a large study called the *Copy Research Validity Project (CRVP)*,[1] which found that the single best predictor of an ad campaign's success—measured as sales in the markets where the ad was run—was how much respondents *liked the ad*. Based on this result, *ad likability* quickly became the most popular measure for pre-testing advertising adopted by both advertisers and ad agencies.[2] From this beginning, the legend of *liking* as the key emotional basis for advertising and marketing effectiveness was born.

Years later, the *CRVP* results were revealed to suffer from a statistical defect called the "ecological fallacy." This is a flaw in statistical reasoning in which a correlation between two groups' average scores is assumed to imply a correlation at the level of individuals within a single group. In the *CRVP* study, ad liking was measured in one group, market performance in another. There was a strong correlation between the two averages over a number of ads and markets. However, when researchers later conducted a study of this correlation at the individual level, they found that an *individual's* liking of an ad was unrelated to *individual* purchasing behavior.[3] This is not an uncommon result in social science research.[4] It means that liking an ad about a product does not *cause* someone to buy that product, as might mistakenly be inferred from the original study. Rather, it usually means that one or more intervening variables are influencing both ad likeability and product sales, causing them to covary in relative unison at the aggregate level.

In contrast to the situation in 1991, today brain science provides us with a number of candidate processes—perceptual, emotional, motivational, and evaluative—that can impact both aggregate levels of likeability and aggregate levels of sales, without necessarily strongly correlating at the individual level.

As we have seen, liking can be induced in many ways that are independent of any properties of the "liked" object itself.

- Along the *novelty-familiarity continuum*, the comfort and sense of safety produced by familiarity can be interpreted as liking.
- According to the *mere exposure effect*, liking can be induced by repetition alone.
- According to *processing fluency*, liking can be induced by ease of mental processing.
- According to the *somatic marker hypothesis*, unconscious or barely conscious positive affect can be interpreted as liking in a choice or decision-making task.

Each of these processes can induce a feeling of liking, aimed at a particular object, even if the object itself is not "really" the source of that impression or evaluation. Meanwhile, our always-on *System 1* is monitoring and indiscriminately recording all such co-occurrences of objects and emotional reactions, whether the emotion is "real" or induced by *form* or *context*. When a consumer conditioned with such learned associations goes shopping, those associations may become activated by cues in the shopping environment, thereby unconsciously biasing their decision-making and purchasing behavior. Similarly, the same automatic activations might influence a different consumer's behavior in a different context, such as answering "likeability" questions on a survey form or in an interview.

> **If people only bought what they liked, they would never buy anything new.**

But people do overcome their natural aversion to novelty and try new things. We learn what we like by observing the outcomes of our actions. We learn to "like" things that make us feel good, and "dislike" things that make us feel bad. These evaluations are always *post-experience* and subject to adjustment as we learn more and gain more experience. Brain science tells us that the traditional marketing view of liking as a source of consumer action has, for the most part, gotten the causal arrow backwards: rather than buy what we like, we tend to like what we buy.

From an intuitive marketing perspective, liking is overrated. For intuitive marketers, the purpose of emotional display in advertising and marketing is not to trigger immediate good feelings of liking that attract attention and increase persuasion, but to build and reinforce automatic emotional and motivational associations for the long-term that can be reliably activated at points of sale and points of consumption. Traditional marketers are correct in their belief that emotional display in marketing can trigger targeted emotions such as liking, but the impact of those emotions on intuitive consumers is complicated. Simply injecting more and more emotion into ads and other marketing materials does not provide a direct path to consumers' hearts or, more importantly, their pocketbooks.

How Consumers Remember Emotion in Marketing

In order to serve as anticipatory guides for evaluating future behavioral outcomes, emotional experiences must first be recorded in memory. It turns out the processes by which emotional events get encoded, consolidated, and retrieved in the human brain have some interesting properties of their own that add to the challenges marketers face when they try to understand and leverage consumer emotions in marketing. We will discuss the brain science behind memory in greater detail in Chapter 12 and Chapter 13, but for now we need to note a few important findings that relate specifically to emotional memories.

Memory operates via three deeply interrelated processes in the human brain:

- *Encoding* is the input process of memory. It is how we process sensory impressions at the moment of perception and attention.
- *Consolidation* is the storage process of memory. It is how we stabilize and strengthen encoded impressions in long-term memory.
- *Retrieval* is the output process of memory. It is how we gain access to encoded and consolidated memories, either by unconscious activation or by conscious acts of recollection.

Emotion, or more correctly, the emotional impact of an experience, has been found to influence all three of these stages of memory processing. And at each stage, the emotional content of an experience can alter the course of memory processing, resulting in memories that differ in significant and predictable ways from memories with little or no emotional content.

> To understand how we learn from emotional experiences, we must also understand how the process of learning itself is affected by the emotions that trigger it.

Encoding Emotional Memories

Emotional memories are special. They have a persistence and vividness that other memories lack. Because of this persistence and vividness, we tend to have greater confidence in the accuracy of emotional memories. But while brain science confirms that human beings do remember emotional experiences more readily than non-emotional experiences, it also tells us our confidence in the accuracy of those memories is often misplaced.

We saw in Chapter 3 that *emotional display* captures attention. The way in which we experience emotion when we encounter emotional display is by reenacting in our own minds the emotions we observe, thus experiencing the displayed emotion, or some slightly less intense version of it, in our own bodies and minds. We *feel* the emotion because we feel its physiological effects—the lump in the throat, the sweaty palms, the goose bumps, etc. We also automatically *evaluate* the emotion. We unconsciously assess its relevance to our immediate situation, its motivational implications (approach or withdrawal), its alignment with our current or future goals, and the degree to which it might require immediate physical action in response. All of these responses happen in the first few milliseconds of exposure to the emotional display. And all of this mental and physiological activity directly impacts what we encode in memory about the emotional event we are experiencing in the moment.[5]

> **Memory researchers have found that when we encounter emotionally-charged experiences, we tend to focus more on the central features of the emotional event or object and less on the peripheral details.**

Memory encoding reflects this biasing of emotional perception, with the result that our superior memory for emotional events is skewed. We are more likely to remember how we felt, and perhaps the immediate source of that feeling, but our ability to recall the details of the surrounding context is actually diminished when compared to neutral memories.

Elizabeth Kensinger, a psychologist and neuroscientist at Boston College, has documented this *tradeoff effect* of emotional memory. Her research confirms that emotional arousal enhances memory encoding of an event, but does so only for some aspects of the event, not all. Details of the event that do not directly relate to the emotion itself tend to be more inaccurately remembered, or forgotten altogether. What is particularly interesting is *which* aspects of the event are more likely to be remembered. Details that relate to the spatial location of an emotionally-salient object, or details that would help identify a similar object in the future, tend to be remembered. But the order of events in time, contextual details, or any decisions made about the emotional object, tend to be forgotten or remembered incorrectly.[6]

> **When people experience and internalize an emotional display, they do so at a cost. They tend to strongly and vividly encode *what* triggered their emotion, but not *when* or *why*, or in *what context*, or with *what consequences*.**

Kensinger's tradeoff effect occurs when encoding both positive and negative emotional experiences, but somewhat differently in each case. Across a number of studies, Kensinger and colleagues have found that memory for negative visual images often includes more item-specific visual details than memory for positive images. People are less successful at encoding which *specific* balloon or butterfly they have seen, for example, but they find it relatively easy to encode which snake, or gun, or dirty toilet they have seen.[7] This is another example of a brain science principle we first encountered in Chapter 3, the *negativity bias*: humans expend greater cognitive effort keeping track of negative things that may hurt us than positive things that may benefit us. Whether we're allocating attention or stimulating memory, bad emotions get priority processing over good emotions.

The discovery that emotion-related experiences "narrow" memory encoding implies some dangers for marketers who want to wrap their products and brands in emotionally-saturated narratives. When emotional content is deployed in advertising or marketing to capture an audience's attention and direct that attention to a traditional informational-persuasive message, findings such as Kensinger's suggest that while the emotional event may be successfully transcribed into memory, the associated message may not.

If the product or brand is not deeply embedded in the emotional moment, it is likely to be evaluated as peripheral to the central emotion, and therefore unlikely to survive the transition from sensory impression to lasting memory.

Strong emotional display may make it more difficult to remember accompanying marketing messages like product benefit statements, feature demonstrations, competitive comparisons, or celebrity endorsements. It may simply overwhelm them.

Consolidating Emotional Memories

The storage of information in memory is not completed immediately after encoding. It takes some time—measured in hours, not seconds—for memory traces to stabilize in a consolidation process that is largely dependent on a region deep in the brain called the *hippocampus*. During this consolidation phase, memories are fragile and susceptible to disruption. Some memories may be strengthened by consolidation, and thus become easier to remember later, others may be weakened and become harder to remember.[8]

Brain scientists have learned that when an impression activates an emotional response, the resulting physiological arousal triggers another brain region, the *amygdala,* which plays a central role in emotional reaction and processing. Amygdala activation signals to the hippocampus that the memory trace has emotional relevance, which then triggers a more intense consolidation process. Researchers have found that this interaction accounts for the greater memorability of emotional events vs. non-emotional events in later memory retrieval.[9]

This consolidation period is critical not only for the likelihood that an experience will be remembered, but also for what elements of the experience will be remembered. Additional studies by Kensinger and colleagues have found that the memory tradeoff for emotional experiences tends to increase over time, especially if the time delay includes a period of sleep. Even a single night's sleep can be sufficient to alter and strengthen the connections between amygdala and hippocampus that impact later memory retrieval, resulting in enhanced retrieval of negative vs. neutral information after a period of sleep compared to no sleep.[10]

> **Over time, and especially following a period of sleep, the tradeoff effect of emotional experiences increases, causing emotional memories to get stronger and surrounding memories of context and background details to get weaker.**

For marketers, these findings represent another challenge for using emotion in marketing. Market researchers tend to ask consumers about their emotional reactions to marketing materials immediately following exposure to those materials. This immediate reaction may be quite different from what consumers later consolidate in memory and learn from that exposure, as the *emotion-as-feedback* theory suggests. When emotional memory biases are added into the equation, the value of immediate emotional reactions becomes even more problematic, as different periods of memory consolidation may produce quite different memories of the marketer's message, and therefore quite different lessons to be activated when the consumer next engages in shopping or buying.

> **Timing matters. Marketers need to think about how best to use emotional display when the purpose of marketing is short-term behavior activation vs. long-term brand building.**

And there is another kind of tradeoff here. When marketers want to encourage short-term behavior activation, traditional persuasive messages highlighting information that aligns with consumer intent may be most effective. Immediate emotional reactions may interact with this short-term goal, but they are also less likely to contribute to persuasion, as strong emotions detract from the kind of cognitive

159

deliberation short-term persuasion requires. When marketers want to encourage long-term brand building, emotional display can be much more relevant, but it is the longer-term learning, consolidation, and retrieval of emotional memories that is most likely to play a role, not the immediate emotional reaction.

> **For both short-term activation and long-term brand building, immediate emotional reactions to intense emotional displays are unlikely to provide a sure path to potential marketing effectiveness.**

Retrieving Emotional Memories

Learning from emotional experiences depends on what we remember about those experiences. Three brain science findings are relevant to understanding how and why emotion affects memory retrieval:

- Biases in encoding and consolidation produce predictable memory errors during retrieval of emotional events.
- We tend to be more confident about the accuracy of our emotional memories than we should be.
- What we remember depends on whether the discrete emotions we experienced (happiness, anger, sadness, etc.) occurred as a part of *goal pursuit* or as a result of *goal attainment*.

Biases in memory retrieval of emotional events

The first finding is a confirmation that biased encoding produces biased retrieval. Because the central features of emotional events are preferentially encoded and consolidated in memory, they are also preferentially recalled. Numerous studies have confirmed that people are better at remembering emotionally-arousing experiences than neutral ones, both in real-world situations where emotional intensity is high and in laboratory settings where induced emotional intensity is relatively low.[11]

But these studies also confirm that not all aspects of emotional experiences are equally retrievable, nor are they equally likely to be retrieved accurately. Specifically, in both real-world and lab settings, although recalled emotional memories tend to be more vivid than non-emotional memories, they are also more distorted in ways consistent with biases introduced during encoding—people easily recall the emotion itself and its proximate cause, but have difficulty recalling peripheral elements that surround the emotional event, such as its timing, context, or consequences. Elizabeth Kensinger's *tradeoff effect* thus occurs at both encoding and retrieval time for emotional memories. It does not occur for retrieval of non-emotional memories, in which central and peripheral details tend to be remembered with equal frequency and accuracy, although with significantly less vividness and more forgetfulness.

The problem this creates for human memory is a higher risk of misremembering the details connected to emotional vs. non-emotional events.[12] Emotional memories contain holes and gaps. As we've seen at several points throughout this book, when such gaps exist in our mental representations of the world, our unconscious minds often *construct* perceptions and beliefs to fill them. We construct perceptions of the external world during *impression formation* (Chapter 2), we construct feelings of familiarity and comfort when exposed to processing fluency (Chapter 6), we construct preferences and attitudes (Chapter 7), we construct evaluations of liking and disliking (this chapter).

> **It should come as no surprise to learn that we construct large parts of our memories as well, especially our emotional memories.**

The problem of false memories has been particularly well-documented in the legal realm, where mistaken eyewitness testimony has been recognized as a leading cause of wrongful convictions, as later determined by DNA-based reversals. Research on "eyewitness misidentification" has been consistent in its findings that eyewitnesses are in fact quite poor at identifying perpetrators and details of crimes, and such testimony should be treated with great caution and skepticism in criminal trials.[13]

Although involving less extreme emotions and profoundly less serious consequences, emotion-induced false memories create problems for marketing as well. One of the most common is the problem of *brand misidentification*. When the emotion in an advertisement is memorable, but the product or brand featured in the ad is peripheral to the emotion displayed, the brand may either be poorly remembered or, worse yet, incorrectly remembered as a competing brand. The problem involves a specific aspect of memory, called *memory binding*, which represents the mind's ability to conjoin various features of an object, person, or event into a coherent whole. Memory binding is particularly susceptible to the selective memory biases produced by emotional memory encoding and retrieval.[14]

Unwarranted confidence in emotional memories

Unwarranted self-confidence in the correctness of our memories is the second feature of emotional memory retrieval that has great relevance to marketers. When combined with people's tendency to misremember details surrounding emotional events, it creates serious difficulties for interpreting the accuracy of consumer self-reports in traditional market research. Why are we so confident in our emotional memories when so much evidence tells us those memories are in fact less reliable than we imagine them to be?

Memory researchers believe our subjective confidence in the accuracy of our own emotional memories derives from the vividness with which these memories can be retrieved and "replayed" from long-term memory. We take this vividness as an indicator that the memory must be accurate as well. Since we usually have no independent record against which to compare our vivid memories, the process tends to be self-confirming. And since such memories tend to come to mind more often than less emotional memories, this sense of confidence in their accuracy gets reinforced every time we mentally reenact them. Details that were initially missed or ignored get *reconstructed* with each recollection. Over time, we convince ourselves of the accuracy of many peripheral details that we have, in actuality, constructed out of thin air. As a result, even as we recount the most arousing emotional experiences of our lives, the accuracy of our memories deteriorates over time as our confidence in those memories increases.[15]

At first glance, this over-confidence in our emotional memories may appear to be a bug, not a feature, of the human brain. However, the adaptive advantages of our unwarranted confidence become clearer when viewed in an evolutionary context.

The human brain evolved not to be a perfect recorder of all experienced events, but to keep us safe and alive.

Our ongoing confidence in our emotional memories—for which we are indeed very good at capturing the "gist" of the experience, if not all its peripheral details—makes it easier for us to react quickly and efficiently in a subsequent time-critical situation. As Swiss psychologist Tobias Brosch and colleagues observe in 2013 review of research on emotion, perception, attention, memory, and decision-making:

> *In new or uncertain situations, we use memory information about similar previous situations to guide our thoughts and actions. In situations that require a rapid response, for example when confronted with an immediate threat, a hesitation to use a memory we are unsure about may be very costly. Enhanced confidence in memories from emotionally charged situations may lead to faster action in critical situations, even if the details of the memory are not absolutely accurate.[16]*

This disconnect between actual emotional memory and subjective confidence may have helped our ancestors stay safe and secure out on the savannah, but it creates difficulties for marketers and market researchers today. Just as lawyers and judges must be cautious about eyewitness testimony in criminal trials, so marketers and market researchers must be cautious about eyewitness reports of emotions relating to brands and products in consumer surveys and interviews.

People do not always know what they know. Even their most confident responses to research queries may, despite their best intentions, steer marketers in wrong directions.

Pregoal and postgoal emotions affect memory differently

The third feature of emotional memory retrieval that is relevant to marketing is a more recent discovery. Earlier studies of emotional memory focused on *arousal* as the key attribute of emotion that caused the differences in memory performance observed by Kensinger and others. The more arousing an emotional event, the more it seemed to produce a *tradeoff effect* or *memory narrowing* in later memory retrieval. But when researchers began to look more closely at the role of *valence*, they found that positive and negative emotions often produced different results. However, even those results were not consistent. Some positive emotions seemed to produce more *memory broadening* than narrowing, and some negative emotions seemed to produce memory broadening as well. Something was missing in the equation.

Since around 2009, memory researchers have started zeroing in on the missing element. It is *goals*; specifically, how the emotion induced by the experience or emotional display relates to a person's currently active goals, intentions, and purposes.

What researchers found when they began exploring the effects of different *discrete* emotions on memory, rather than general levels of arousal or valence, was that an emotion's relationship to an individual's goals made a big difference in how and to what extent that emotion impacted memory.

Specifically, emotions triggered prior to goal attainment (*pregoal emotions*) tend to produce memory narrowing and poor recall of peripheral details, while emotions triggered after goal attainment (*postgoal emotions*) tend to produce memory broadening and better recall of peripheral details.[17]

Taking into account these new findings about how emotions relate to goals, researchers have reconciled many of the inconsistencies in the earlier literature. Both positive and negative emotions that precede goal attainment—such as *hope*, *fear*, or *desire*—narrow the scope of people's attention to information that is central to their goals. This narrowed focus impairs memory for peripheral details, leaving people vulnerable to poor recall, misattribution, and false memories concerning those details. In contrast, both positive and negative emotions that follow goal attainment or failure—such as *happiness, sadness,* or *pride*—broaden the scope of people's attention, producing better recall of peripheral details and greater resistance to misattribution, misinformation, and false memories.[18]

> **According to this *motivational perspective* on emotion and memory, the goals or motivations associated with an emotional experience determine the breadth of memory encoding that accompanies it.**

Pregoal emotions (also called *goal-activating emotions*) like *hope* and *fear* are triggered when the attainment or failure of a goal is *anticipated* but has not yet occurred. These discrete emotions are associated with a motivation to approach or avoid the object of emotion and, as such, are high in *motivational intensity*.[19] When people are experiencing high motivational intensity, they are more inclined to pay attention to and encode to memory *only* those aspects of the experience that are most relevant to their active goal pursuit, while paying less attention and devoting less memory to other aspects of the experience. The result is the *tradeoff effect* or *memory narrowing* found by Kensinger and others.

The opposite effect occurs for *postgoal emotions*—such as *happiness* and *sadness*—which are triggered when goal accomplishment or failure has already occurred. In such circumstances, people pay attention to and remember a broader range of aspects of the situation. Researchers speculate this happens because doing so facilitates deliberation and learning that can be applied to future experiences in which the same or similar goals are being pursued. Motivational intensity is low, so focus is less concentrated and more elements of the situation are considered. The result is the broadening of attention and memory observed by researchers during goal-attainment emotion activation.[20]

> **The lessons we learn from emotional experiences may be quite different when the emotions occur during goal pursuit than when they occur after goal attainment or failure.**

Pregoal emotions are likely to produce very detailed and narrow memories that can facilitate lessons focusing on *how* to pursue similar goals in the future, but not much beyond that. Postgoal emotions are likely to produce less detailed and more expansive memories, taking in more of the context and background of the emotional experience. This provides an opportunity for broader lessons to be learned; for example, not just lessons about *how* to pursue a goal, but perhaps lessons about *whether* a goal should have been pursued in the first place.

Three Ways to Influence Consumers Using Emotional Displays

Looking at emotional memory as a function of motivational intensity aligns well with Baumeister's *emotion-as-feedback* theory. Central to that theory is the idea that we can make our lives better by learning to anticipate future emotional outcomes that we want to achieve or avoid. Emotional memory research adds to this theory by reminding us that our capacity to learn from emotional experiences is influenced by a wide range of factors over which we have little control, including the arousal and valence of our emotions, their pregoal or postgoal timing, and their motivational intensity. All of these factors affect both the accuracy of our memories and the confidence with which we recall them.

> **Emotion is not the panacea for marketing success. Just as attention has limits as a gateway to marketing effectiveness, so too does emotion.**

When advertising or marketing messages are accompanied by highly emotional displays, the emotions triggered by those displays may cause important facts and associations about a product or brand to be missed, ignored, misattributed, or forgotten. Consciously experienced emotion can easily overwhelm our receptivity to non-emotional information and block our ability to encode, consolidate, and retrieve such messages.

Any individual piece of marketing or advertising tells a story. That story gets internalized by those who see it and hear it. They understand it and *feel* its emotional impact by mentally simulating and reenacting its key elements in their own minds. They learn from it by witnessing what kinds of outcomes it produces. Even when those outcomes are an obvious fiction created by marketing storytellers, their unconscious *System 1* processing takes note. It records the emotional lesson just as automatically and faithfully as it does when the event occurs in real life. And it does so with all the same biases, gaps, and later reconstructions.

Emotional displays in marketing are not a *consistent* source of marketing success because emotion is a complex instrument. When it is used by marketers without awareness of its many subtleties, it can produce quite unexpected results. When it is used knowledgeably, it can be tuned to achieve a wide variety of marketing ends. *Emotion-as-feedback* theory and emotional memory research tell us marketers can use emotion in marketing and advertising in three very different ways.

Leveraging pregoal emotions in marketing

The first way marketers can use emotional displays in marketing and advertising is to tell stories that emphasize *pregoal emotions* in the hopes of triggering motivational states that will cause consumers to activate and pursue goals resulting in consumer action—a purchase, a shopping trip, a consumption experience, or some other action along the path to those outcomes. If emotion can trigger a goal, it can trigger action toward achieving that goal.

This is the most common way emotion is used in traditional persuasive marketing and advertising. Often this usage is covert rather than overt because it involves the communication of negative rather than positive emotions. Persuading consumers to want or need something in their lives, perhaps something they didn't know they wanted or needed beforehand, often involves reminding them of what they're missing, and why they should *feel bad* about it.

Following this logic, much of traditional advertising focuses on increasing motivational intensity by using an emotional display to suggest that some aspect of our current state should induce in us a negative emotion such as *fear, shame, disgust,* or *guilt.* Perhaps the problem is with the clothes we wear, the car we drive, the whiteness of our laundry, or the color of our hair. After this emotional activation, the informational part of the message is designed to come to our rescue and provide the solution: a product or brand that will fill the void, give us what we are missing, and allow us to overcome the negative feelings the ad so cleverly helped us feel in the first place. This is not a formula for using emotion to improve people's lives or anticipate better emotional outcomes in the future. At best, negative pregoal emotions are deployed by marketers to make us feel worse so we will seek their recommended solution to bring us back to equilibrium.

Negative pregoal emotions may motivate us to avoid losses or repair damages, but they do little to motivate us to make gains or improve our overall well-being.

Leveraging postgoal emotions in marketing

The second way marketers can use emotional displays in marketing and advertising is to tell stories that emphasize *postgoal emotions* like *happiness* or *sadness.* The purpose of these stories is not to motivate immediate goal pursuit, but to stimulate longer-term learning to help achieve better emotional outcomes in the future.

Postgoal emotions featured in marketing and advertising stories are usually positive. They demonstrate the good feelings we associate with goal accomplishment—*happiness, pride, satisfaction, comfort.* In these stories, goal pursuit is presented as something that happened in the past. Goals have already been reached, and motivational intensity is low. Emotional displays featuring postgoal emotions, when internalized, enable broader memory encoding and access to a wider range of details and consequences. More nuanced and contextualized lessons can be communicated, encoded, consolidated, and later retrieved.

> **Marketing that uses positive postgoal emotional displays is more aligned with the principles of intuitive marketing because it enacts feelings that accompany aspirational success and identity-affirmation, rather than feelings that accompany perceived inadequacy and self-doubt.**

Displays of postgoal emotions in marketing stories can also be negative but, unlike pregoal negative emotional displays, they do not focus on immediate wants or needs to stimulate motivational intensity. Rather, they represent the emotional costs of prior goals being unattained or aspirations being unfulfilled. They get stored in memory as reminders to act differently in the future in order to achieve better results and avoid unwanted emotional outcomes. Advertisements or marketing messages that use postgoal negative emotions are relatively rare. When they do appear, they often depict emotional displays of *sadness* or *regret* regarding the misfortunes of others in order to encourage greater empathy or altruism in the future.

Leveraging small emotional rewards
The third way marketers can use emotional displays in marketing and advertising is to provide simple, even nonsensical entertainments that provide *small emotional rewards* as a standalone experience. When repeated in a non-disruptive and cognitively fluent way, such pleasant experiences can build unconscious positive associations with a product or brand through the process *emotion-as-feedback* theory calls *automatic affect* formation, which in turn can produce what Baumeister and colleagues call *affective residue* and Damasio calls *somatic markers*. These unconsciously learned associations can then be activated later, via *priming* and *associative activation*, at a point of sale.

Providing *small emotional rewards* is the fourth mechanism of intuitive marketing influence introduced in Chapter 1.

Sources of Intuitive Influence: Small Emotional Rewards
You see an ad for *Doritos*™ that contains a funny joke. Unlike most TV advertising, which you are sure you ignore, it makes you laugh out loud. You see it again and pay a little more attention this time because you remember you enjoyed it. After seeing it a few more times, it starts to become familiar, and finally, a little boring. But before you can become consciously irritated by it, it is taken off the air and replaced

by another, similar ad with a slightly different joke, which also makes you laugh. And that is followed by yet another. This ad campaign goes on for months, or even years. You come to expect the next edition of the now familiar setup. The ads are a source of entertainment in their own right. And what about the actual product depicted in the ads? The jokes all tend to involve "wanting" the great taste of *Doritos*, but other than that the product has little to do with the humor in the ad. Even so, it is always there, every time, bringing you that *small emotional reward* you have come to expect. Later, standing in the "salty snacks" aisle at your local supermarket, about 50 choices are arrayed in front of you. Without much thought, you grab a bag of *Doritos*. What just happened?

In an era of "big emotion" in advertising, when marketers want to present their products and brands alongside a giant tug on our emotional heartstrings, the idea of *small emotional rewards* may seem a little underwhelming. But we have seen that marketers' hopes for big emotional displays can be thwarted by the vagaries of human attention and memory. "Big emotion" can make informational details fuzzy and memory fickle. So the expected emotional transfer between "loving that cute puppy in the ad" and "loving our brand of beer" may just not be there.

Marketers' hopes for emotion in marketing might benefit from being a little less ambitious and a little more persistent.

Small emotional rewards operate through both conscious and unconscious brain processes. On the one hand, they are consciously perceived. But the way in which they impact later consumer behavior is generally not accessible to conscious awareness. We recognize an emotional reward when we experience it, but we do not have conscious access to how it translates into an unconscious affective marker capable of shaping our choices and behavior toward its associated product or brand at a later point in time. That process happens behind the scenes, so to speak, where it leverages the process of *classical conditioning*, which we first encountered in our discussion of Robert Zajonc's *mere exposure effect* in Chapter 6. Zajonc hypothesized that repeated exposure increases liking because repetition creates a feeling of positive affect, which then gets transferred, through classical conditioning, to the object or event being repeated. More recently, researchers have begun using the term *evaluative conditioning* to describe this "liking" variant of classical conditioning, because its effect is to change our *evaluation* of the associated object, the product or brand.[21] We will discuss the complexities of evaluative conditioning in Chapter 13.

Conditioning in general is the process by which two ideas get associated in memory so that when we think of one, we can more readily think of the other. The chief mechanisms behind classical conditioning are *repeated co-occurrence* and *pattern recognition*. Our brains recognize a pattern of B occurring along with A and, over time, we create an *associative connection* between the two events. We may be consciously aware of this connection or not. Research on evaluative conditioning has found that conscious awareness of the connection between A and B—called *contingency awareness* in the academic literature—tends to produce stronger conditioning effects, but there is also substantial evidence that conditioning without awareness can occur as well, especially when there is a potential for *source confusability* between B and A; that is, when the experienced feeling of positivity generated by B can be mistakenly attributed to A because A and B are presented simultaneously.[22]

In a typical 30-second TV ad, when one of the events is an emotionally rewarding display and the other is the presentation of a product or brand, our brains use our emotional response to the display to update a *somatic marker* for the product or brand. That update does not record into memory the full-fledged emotional experience depicted in the ad, but rather updates a simple indicator of the *affective residue* or emotional valence produced by the experience. Since we're assuming the experience successfully generates a small emotional reward, we can also assume this update consists of a small *positive* bump in the *automatic affect* associated with that product or brand.

Even if the emotional reward is never depicted as being *caused* by the product or brand, our brains experience the co-occurrence and give the product or brand "credit" for the emotional reward.

Unlike consciously accessible lessons forged through *System 2* deliberation and analysis, small emotional rewards are *felt* consciously, but transfer positive feelings to a product or brand through unconscious emotional associations and markers that are automatically captured in long-term memory through *associative learning*, a process described as part of *emotion-as-feedback* theory in Chapter 8 and discussed in more detail in Chapter 12 and Chapter 13. Small emotional rewards are thus a non-persuasive means for establishing robust automatic associations with positive valence in the minds of consumers. They operate through a kind of reciprocity. Brands reward consumers with a moment of pleasure, consumers reward brands with an emotional edge at a point of sale.

Providing *small emotional rewards* is a "win-win" for consumers and marketers. Consumers get a moment of pleasure free from disruptive persuasive tactics, marketers get a free uptick in *automatic affect* associated with their product or brand.

Enjoying a joke is not the only type of "free" emotional reward that can be provided by advertising and marketing, although it is one of the most effective. Basically any type of *surprise* or *expectancy violation* can attract attention and interest, as we saw in Chapter 3. Visual or verbal puzzles are a good source of emotional rewards, provided the puzzle can be solved. An example is the long-running *Absolut Vodka* print ad campaign, in which the iconic shape of the *Absolut* bottle is "hidden" in different graphic and artistic images that can be decoded by reading the short text at the bottom of the page. In one popular example, the bottle shape is formed by a configuration of yellow taxis stuck in a big-city traffic jam above the phrase *ABSOLUT NEW YORK*.[23] Other types of puzzles and surprises that tend to provide small emotional rewards are depictions of impossible or imaginary events or places, such as the surreal action sequences in the *Old Spice* "Smell Like a Man" ad campaign discussed in Chapter 3.

Finally, two of the most often used sources of small emotional rewards in ads and marketing are pets and babies in recurring roles and situations. An iconic example from British advertising is the *Andrex* puppy. *Andrex*® is a toilet paper brand that for over 40 years has featured a cute Labrador puppy who can't seem to avoid getting tangled up in mounds of toilet paper, which he manages to do in different ways in ad after ad, year after year. In one of the longest-running campaigns in advertising history, the puppy has helped *Andrex* maintain market dominance for decades, achieving an unassailable position as Britain's number one non-food brand, its sixth largest grocery brand, and the market leader in its category in every one of those 40 years since its introduction.[24]

The key element in effective small emotional reward marketing that marketers need to keep in mind is *repetition*. In each of the successful ad campaigns just cited, a common feature is persistence, often extending over a period of years, even decades. Conditioning does not work without repetition.

One-off Super Bowl ads are unlikely to strengthen emotional ties to products or brands if such feelings did not already exist in consumers' minds.

The challenge in long-term marketing campaigns based on small emotional rewards is to avoid boredom. The best long-running campaigns address the risk of boredom by using the techniques described in Chapter 5 to blend the novelty of a fresh emotional reward with the familiarity of an easily recognized setup or context.

The often-missed lesson for marketers is that it is not the immediate conscious feeling—the emotional *tingle* that comes over us when we experience an ad or marketing message—that has the greatest impact on our subsequent behavior as consumers.

> **It is the unconscious accumulation of small emotional rewards, perhaps only loosely connected to the product or brand, that we collect over months and years, that leaves the memory traces that influence us most powerfully as consumers.**

Diffuse and seemingly inconsequential pleasantries can play an outsized and underappreciated role in consumer behavior, unconsciously guiding our choices and actions in the marketplace, unencumbered by any conscious feelings of persuasive pressure.

Chapter 10

Wants, Needs, and Goals

The Foundations of Consumer Motivation and Action

*"Thoughts are to the Desires as Scouts and Spies, to range abroad,
and find the way to the things desired."*
–*Thomas Hobbes, Leviathan, 1651*

Evoking emotion is not the key to triggering consumer behavior—evoking motivation is.

In this and the next chapter, we explore how marketing can more effectively address the wants and needs of consumers. First, we see how *wants* and *needs* are different kinds of motivators that drive consumers to action in different ways. Then we examine how wants and needs get translated into goals, and how marketers' understanding of goal activation and pursuit—in both their conscious and unconscious forms—is the key to long-lasting product and brand success in the modern marketplace. We conclude this chapter with a look at *basic psychological needs* and *intrinsic goals*—universal motivators of human action that most marketers have yet to incorporate fully into their understanding of consumer behavior. In Chapter 11, we will describe some of the key behavioral signatures of both conscious and unconscious goal pursuit—how goals get activated, what goal pursuit looks like, and what happens when goal pursuit ends. We then discuss the last of our five sources of intuitive influence without persuasion: connecting to consumers' aspirations and identity goals. We close Chapter 11 with an addendum on the *replication crisis* in psychology and science more generally, highlighting its implications for the study of goal and behavior priming.

Wanting and Needing:
How Desire and Compulsion Move Us

In contrast to both liking and preferring, wanting and needing are motivational drivers, direct calls to action, and powerful triggers to begin acting in pursuit of a goal—to satisfy the want or need. They can be automatically or consciously activated. They are both longer-lived and harder to change than likes or preferences.

Wants Are Different Than Needs

In everyday speech, we tend to use the phrase "wants and needs" without differentiating between the two terms, but in fact "wants" and "needs" represent very different objects of motivation. Consider these two statements:

- I *want* a new car.
- I *need* a new car.

What images and connections come to mind when reading these two statements? Wanting has a voluntary feel to it. If I *want* a new car, that probably means it's a discretionary decision, something I could choose *not* to do if necessary. But if I *need* a new car, that feels more mandatory, there is an implication that something bad could happen if I did not get one. Not getting what you *want* may be frustrating, but not getting what you *need* is more serious. Why? Because needs don't just go away if they are not satisfied. Failure to satisfy a want usually means only that some positive outcome may not be attained. But failure to satisfy a need means that some negative outcome is likely to occur. Thwarted wants don't do damage, but thwarted needs do.

Wants are based on *desires*. Desires are things we would like to have, but may not be able to acquire at the present time. Inherent in the notion of a desire is the idea that it may not be met. We use terms like *wish* or *longing* to describe a desire that is difficult or impossible to attain. Needs are different, they are based on *compulsions*. We seek to fulfill needs because we must. Unlike wants, needs cannot be put off forever. They must be met in relatively short timeframes or something bad will happen.

Human needs can be classified into three main categories: *physiological, psychological*, and *learned*.

- *Physiological needs* arise because the body must regulate and maintain itself to remain healthy—we need food, water, warmth, etc. We are naturally compelled to satisfy those needs.
- *Psychological needs*—also called *identity needs*—arise from cognitive and emotional motivations shared by all humans. These include what most

psychologists consider natural and universal human needs for belonging, self-esteem, and accomplishment.

- *Learned needs* are derived from recurring and habit-forming episodes of reward-seeking. They are not "natural" in the same sense as physiological or psychological needs.

Physiological needs derive from the body's requirement to maintain *homeostasis*, a balance between internal bodily processes and the external environment. Our bodies warn us if we get too hungry, or too thirsty, or too hot or cold, because such states threaten our ability to maintain a functioning homeostasis. Worst case, if we fail to maintain homeostasis, we die. So our human brains—like the brains of all living creatures—have evolved to monitor all these states closely. And our bodies come equipped with numerous alarm systems to tell us when we are exceeding optimal parameters: we begin seeking food or water, we begin sweating or shivering, and so on.

These signals often appear in the form of *cravings* or *urges* to change our physiological state. We feel a *compulsion* to seek action to regain homeostasis. The motivation to act drives us forward. Satisfying these cravings or urges creates a powerful sense of reward, which then contributes to *conditioning*, which in turn strengthens our motivation to take similar actions the next time similar cravings or urges appear. And they do appear, because physiological compulsions are never permanently satisfied. As the body burns energy and enters different environments in its daily pursuits, the cycle repeats—imbalance, craving, reward, imbalance, craving, reward. Such is the human condition.

Psychological needs share many of the features of physiological needs. They get activated by imbalances between current and optimal states. They create compulsions to change state. But for psychological needs, the state that needs to be changed is mental rather that physical. Research shows that all humans constantly monitor their feelings of self-worth and accomplishment, as well as their sense of belonging in their social community. When threats to these psychological needs are perceived, either consciously or unconsciously, behaviors are triggered to bolster self-image—to bolster *identity*. Sometimes these behaviors are accompanied by conscious intention, sometimes not. These drives can be as powerful as the compulsions regulating physiological health. They also are never permanently satisfied.

Learned needs are "artificial" in the sense that we create them ourselves as we discover rewarding outcomes from recurring behavior. They can vary widely from person to person, because they arise from life experiences. Unchecked, learned needs can become *addictions*, harmful sources of behavior such as obsessive-compulsive disorders, compulsive shopping, overeating, or drug addiction.

Learned needs feel very much like natural needs when we are experiencing them. Learned needs may start out as relatively innocent wants or desires. Satisfying the need may produce both pleasure ("liking" the experience) and a sense of reward. As with natural needs, satisfying learned needs is only temporary. The need will reappear, perhaps even stronger than before, triggering another round of craving and temporary satiation.

Over time, learned needs can become more insistent. A relatively benign form of this insistence is *distraction*—we find ourselves focusing on the need and its temporary satisfaction more than we would like. A more harmful form of insistence is *dependence*—our compulsion to satisfy the need becomes so strong we are unable to control it. Dependence on satisfying a learned need can take over a person's life, causing deep and sometime irreparable damage that the victim feels powerless to repair. At that point, the behavior has become an *addiction*.

The process by which learned needs become addictive behaviors is one that brain scientists have been studying for decades. It involves a disassociation in the brain between the original *liking* and *reward* that accompanied satisfaction of the learned need and the motivational *wanting* that drove it.[1] Over time, wanting continues and even increases in intensity, but liking decreases and eventually disappears altogether. This is the paradox of addictive behavior. The learned compulsion remains and demands satisfaction, often at the expense of other wants and needs, while the original feelings of pleasure and reward are extinguished. The result is a repeating pattern of compulsive behavior that is difficult to control or moderate. Whether it is a relatively harmless distraction like checking one's social media status every five minutes, or a debilitating and life-threatening dependency like a gambling or drug addiction, the compulsion takes on a motivational life of its own, becoming what brain scientists call an *irrational want*—a learned need that produces behavioral cravings unaccompanied by any trace of immediate or expected liking.[2]

Wants, Needs, and Marketing Messages

How are these distinctions relevant to marketing? Marketers are in the business of connecting their products and brands to consumer wants, physiological needs, psychological needs, and learned needs. Marketers have traditionally addressed these different motivators in different ways, but with a common purpose—to persuade unmotivated consumers to become motivated to buy a particular product or brand. Intuitive marketing offers a different approach, focusing on aligning products and brands with *existing* psychological needs of consumers, rather than trying to motivate consumer action directly. Finally, marketing to learned needs presents novel ethical challenges that marketers have only recently begun to consider.

Traditional marketers prefer to speak in the language of wants, not needs. As we saw in Chapter 9, most marketing uses emotional stories to highlight deficiencies that consumers should want to fix, thus triggering a desire to solve the newly-recognized problem using the marketer's recommended product or brand. Wants are easier targets for marketing than needs because they can be tailored to be satisfied specifically by the product being marketed.

> **Wants in traditional marketing messages are *manufactured* to be met by the unique features and capabilities of a given product or brand.[3]**

Physiological needs are a more challenging marketing target than wants because they are less easily tailored to the benefits of a specific product or brand. All humans need water, for example, but why should we want to buy *Evian* vs. *Dasani* vs. *Perrier*? Perhaps more fundamentally, why should we want to buy bottled water at all, when we can fill our glass for free from the kitchen faucet? When we observe how bottled water is marketed, we see the answer. Marketers don't sell bottled water as a way to satisfy the physiological need to quench thirst, they sell it as a way to satisfy various discretionary wants: to display status, to indicate sophisticated taste, or to signal available disposable income.[4]

Psychological needs are also commonly translated into wants in persuasive marketing by presenting narratives in which social status or self-esteem are threatened, often covertly, only to be "made right" by the advertised product or brand. When traditional marketers craft an ad that shows a person feeling shame or guilt for failing to buy the right air freshener, for example, they expect viewers to internalize the emotion and trigger a want to correct the psychological imbalance induced by the ad by purchasing the recommended product. Overtly, consumers are being asked to buy the product because they should "want" to make their homes smell fresher. Covertly, they are being offered the product as a way to rehabilitate their self-image after embracing the embarrassment of allowing their homes to smell bad.

Intuitive marketing also invokes psychological needs, but in a more overt and positive way than is typically found in traditional persuasive marketing.

> **Rather than emphasizing *threats* to consumer status or self-image, intuitive marketing emphasizes *opportunities* for people to achieve aspirational and self-affirmation goals by positioning products and brands as partners in those motivational pursuits.**

References to psychological needs are thus more direct and transparent. Intuitive marketing assumes people are more attracted to products that align with their aspirations and identities than to products that provide nagging reminders of their personal failings or inadequacies.

Marketing to Learned Needs

Marketing to activate learned needs raises ethical questions for marketers. What obligations do marketers have with regard to products and brands that create, promote, and benefit from learned needs that motivate compulsive, possibly addictive behavior? It is true that such products essentially sell themselves. No marketing campaign can match the motivational momentum produced by a product that triggers craving just by coming to mind. Only recently have marketers begun to grapple with the ethics of promoting products that can exacerbate compulsive and addictive behaviors in consumers.

In 2012, Nir Eyal self-published a short book titled *Hooked: How to Build Habit-Forming Products*.[5] It immediately drew a large readership and was republished by Penguin in 2014, at which point it became an international bestseller. In *Hooked*, Eyal lays out a highly accessible and easily understandable model for creating and shaping learned needs in online and mobile applications and platforms. The "hook" model involves four steps:

- Create a *trigger* that draws people's attention to the app.
- Guide people to perform a simple *action* in response to the trigger.
- Provide *variable rewards* from performing the action.
- Ask people to make a small *investment*, such as spending time, providing information, or buying something.

Each cycle through the process increases the desire to revisit the app one more time, building up a learned need that at best becomes a healthy habit, but may also become a distraction from other pursuits or, at worst, a dependency. The key element in this model is Step 3: providing *variable rewards*. As Eyal observes:

> *Variable rewards are one of the most powerful tools companies implement to hook users .... Research shows that levels of the neurotransmitter dopamine surge when the brain is expecting a reward. Introducing variability multiplies the effect, creating a focused state, which suppresses the areas of the brain associated with judgment and reason while activating the parts associated with wanting and desire. Although classic examples include slot machines and lotteries, variable rewards are prevalent in many other habit-forming products.*[6]

We encountered *variable rewards* back in Chapter 3 when we looked at the process of "holding" attention. We see here that this form of reward is particularly effective for creating habitual reward-seeking that can, in some cases, lead to compulsive or addictive behavior. The learning mechanism involved is another form of conditioning called *operant conditioning*. In operant conditioning, as opposed to classical (or evaluative) conditioning, a behavior is reinforced and learning is achieved by repeatedly following the behavior with an immediate reward. Simply put, behavior that is rewarded increases in frequency and behavior that is punished decreases. Rewards that are *variable* in their pattern of delivery (technically referred to as *variable ratio rewards*) amplify the learning and habit-forming effect of operant conditioning.[7] A *learned need* is created and then strengthened by every repetition of the behavior. Over time, the anticipation of gaining the reward *this time*, rather than the reward itself, becomes the primary driver of the behavior. As Eyal notes, this is how slot machines and lotteries work. It is how any "user" of a variably-rewarding product can become "hooked."

Although there have always been products capable of producing compulsive behavior through ingestion of substances—cigarettes, alcohol, and habit-forming drugs come to mind—the modern online technology industry is the first to have compulsive *behavior*, rather than compulsive substance abuse, built directly and positively into its business model. Most commercial Internet-based applications and platforms are funded by advertising in the app or on the platform. Profits are dependent on finding new ways to put more "eyeballs" in front of those ads. The more hours consumers spend inside the app or platform, the more profitable the business becomes. This dynamic has created an industry in which a direct business benefit accrues from maximizing the amount of time people spend using an app or staying on a platform.

This was the business context into which Nir Eyal dropped *Hooked* in 2012. Given what the mammoth tech industry was trying to do, it's easy to see why the book immediately became a huge success. Although Eyal explicitly warned against the dangers of using the *Hooked* model for unethical manipulation, not all readers seemed to notice that part of the message. Almost overnight, "hooking" people into "habit-forming" and "addictive" technologies became the common language of Silicon Valley, venture capitalists, and tech centers around the world. Despite Eyal's focus on habit formation as a way to improve people's lives and well-being, too many of his readers found instead a recipe for winning in the marketplace by relying exclusively on a company's ability to cultivate compulsive and addictive behaviors in its consumers.[8]

By 2017 nearly three billion people worked, played, and socialized on Internet platforms like *Google*, *Facebook*, *Instagram*, and *Twitter*, and over four billion people owned smartphones.[9] It is encouraging that at least some technology giants began

179

to look more closely at the potential downsides of all this "hooking" and "addicting" of people's time and attention on their platforms. Google, for example, created a position called *Design Ethicist* in 2013. Its first (and only?) incumbent, Tristan Harris, described his job as studying "how the design, affordances and choice architectures on digital screens affect users' behavior, thought patterns, relationships and general well-being."[10] Harris left Google in 2016 and founded an organization called *Time Well Spent* to develop and promote guidelines for designing "technology that cares about helping us spend our time, and our lives, well—not seducing us into the most screen time, always-on interruptions or distractions."[11]

What responsibilities do marketers have when their job is to encourage usage of a product designed to produce learned needs and habit-forming behavior? Eyal wrote several posts in his *Nir & Far* blog addressing this question.[12] Arguing that any engaging activity is bound to produce its share of compulsive and even clinically addictive over-users, he admonished tech companies to recognize their ethical obligation to identify and help users who might develop addictive responses to their products.[13] This is reflected in a 2017 article titled *"Tech companies, if you create addicts, you need to help them."*[14]

For marketers at companies selling variable-rewarding products, taking on this additional obligation means continuing to promote the app or platform through traditional marketing channels while also crafting programs around indicators, messaging, and interventions to assist those who might fall prey to compulsive or addictive responses. But that is just a first step. For both Eyal and Harris, as well as others who have written about the problems of technology distraction and dependence,[15] product companies need to go beyond simply providing recovery and withdrawal assistance for those who might become addicted to their apps or platforms.

> **Companies have an obligation not just to help addicts, but also to help people avoid becoming addicts.**

Given that the purpose of habit-forming platforms and applications is to maximize users' time on the site or in the app, embracing this ethical position may seem at odds with the overall business model driving the product. This can create a real challenge for marketers who, in effect, are being asked to help the company sink the hook, but not too deep.

If marketers want to make these products less susceptible to abuse by distraction or dependence, they need to become advocates for consumers' self-interests and well-being. As Eyal makes clear in *Hooked*:

The Hook Model is fundamentally about changing people's behaviors; but the power to build persuasive products should be used with caution. Creating habits can be a force for good, but it can also be used for nefarious purposes.[16]

While it is perfectly appropriate—and profitable—to provide the most engaging and immersive experiences possible, it is also important to give consumers affordances and tools of self-control that enable them to moderate the more habit-forming and disruptive aspects of the app or platform. Harris provides a useful list of guidelines:[17]

- Make it easy for people to stop using an app or unsubscribe from a service if they choose to do so.
- Respect people's attention. Help them attend to one thing at a time, minimize task-switching, interruptions, and other unnecessary choices.
- Measure success by net positive contributions to people's lives, not by number of transactions, swipes, clicks, etc.
- Be realistic and transparent about the full range of impacts of your product, both positive and negative.
- Treat your users as people whose time, attention, relationships, and lives matter, not as puppets whose purpose is to do things you want them to do.
- Accept that app and platform design decisions deeply influence and constrain people's freedom of choice. Don't pretend people only do what they want to do and freely choose their behavior.
- Recognize that the way you frame and organize choices deeply influences what people choose. Frame choices in ways that enable people to make the best decisions for them, not just the most profitable decisions for you.
- Accept that it is your responsibility to minimize psychological costs (compulsions, guilt, stress, anxiety) that arise from using your product.[18]

> **These guidelines for designing apps and platforms bear a strong resemblance to the principles and mechanisms of intuitive marketing.**

If online and mobile products that promote and exploit artificial learned needs are essentially self-marketing machines, they can be approached by marketers in one of two ways: either as vehicles for traditional persuasive marketing or as opportunities for intuitive marketing.

Habit-forming apps and platforms that ignore the legitimate needs and interests of their users are misusing the "hook" formula to produce a covert and coercive kind of persuasion. They create and exploit learned needs that benefit the platform, without much consideration for any conflicting needs or wants of the user. Like persuasive marketing, they focus on immediate transactional compliance rather than longer-term relationship development. When they do achieve long-term relationships, they do so by creating compulsions, not by supporting aspirations, self-affirmation, or the well-being of the consumer.

> **People who are distracted or become dependent on habit-forming, variable-rewarding apps or platforms do not feel in control of their time, attention, or lives.**

They find themselves doing things they don't really want to do—whether it's constantly checking their email, monitoring their likes on *Twitter*, or being lured into another session of *Candy Crush*. All the mechanisms of persuasion resistance discussed in Chapter 4, both conscious and unconscious, are likely to be triggered. Intuitively, people feel worse off than they did before, but they may not know why, and they may not know how to feel better. Along with the learned need, they develop a kind of learned helplessness.

Alternatively, deeply engaging apps and platforms can be designed as agents of influence, not persuasion. Starting from a deeper understanding of the existing and ongoing wants and needs of their audiences, they can become enablers of people's natural *psychological needs*—needs for autonomy, competence, and belonging. Online and mobile apps and platforms can build strong positive relationships by employing the tools of intuitive marketing: aligning with personal intent, lessening demands on attention, building trust through consistency and reliability, providing small emotional rewards, and connecting to people's aspirations and identities.

Such an approach to app or platform self-marketing may appear to sacrifice revenue in the short-term, but the brain science of goals and motivation tells a different story for the long-term.

An audience of consumers driven by learned needs and compulsions is likely to be more volatile and resentful, and ultimately less profitable, than an audience of satisfied, trusting, and supportive consumers who feel a close, two-way emotional bond with an app or platform that helps them feel like they are being the best versions of themselves.

The Centrality of Goals in Consumer Behavior

Wants, physiological needs, psychological needs, and learned needs all motivate action. They *move us* to do something. How do they do this? Wants and needs produce a *tension* in our lives that we feel *compelled* to relieve. This tension creates a perceived or unperceived gap between our *current physical or psychological state* and our *desired or needed state*. To relieve this tension, we mentally construct *goals* which we then begin pursuing to satisfy the want or meet the need.

A *goal* is a mental representation of an envisioned *end-state*. *Goal pursuit* is a behavior aimed at achieving a goal by following a *plan* or *strategy*. A goal has a purpose: to satisfy a want or need. A goal has an outcome: it is either achieved or not achieved. The *want or need* is the motivator, the *goal* is the objective, the *plan* is how to get there, *goal pursuit* is the behavior we engage in while the plan is being executed, and the *outcome* is either success or failure in achieving the goal.

In the *cognitive timeline*, goal activation plays a central role and occurs at the boundary of unconscious and conscious processing. It is placed at that point (see Figure 2) because goals can be activated and pursued either consciously or unconsciously. Brain scientists speculate that unconscious goal pursuit is possible because the brain structures that enable conscious awareness of goal pursuit operate independently from the structures responsible for "running" a goal pursuit process.[19] As a result, goals can become active and guide behavior independently of conscious intention and awareness.

> **Individuals may or may not be aware that they have a goal, that they have a plan, that they are pursuing a goal, or that they have achieved a goal.**

Goals are central to all human behavior, including consumer behavior, because they are the most flexible and adaptive way we have to direct our actions in the external world to help us successfully satisfy our internal wants and needs.[20] Goals are the mental mechanisms by which we direct our efforts to relieve the persistent tensions created by the ongoing motivators that operate in our lives: our desired wants and our more demanding physical, psychological, and learned needs. Conscious awareness can enter into goal activation and pursuit in four ways:

- Goals can be *consciously* activated and *consciously* pursued.
- Goals can be *unconsciously* activated but *consciously* pursued.
- Goals can be *consciously* activated but *unconsciously* pursued.
- Goals can be both *unconsciously* activated and *unconsciously* pursued.

In the first case, goal pursuit is entirely conscious. We consciously set a goal, we consciously pursue it, and we are consciously aware of the result. In the second case, we know we are pursuing a goal, but we don't know how or why the goal was activated in our minds. This is what happens when a goal is *primed* unconsciously but pursued consciously. In the third case, the opposite effect occurs: we are aware of consciously setting a goal, but unaware of at least some aspects of goal pursuit that are occurring unconsciously as a result of goal setting. Finally, in the last case, both the goal and its pursuit are invisible to us. We don't know we are pursuing a goal and we don't know why. Brain scientists generally use the term *unconscious goal pursuit* to describe the third and fourth cases only, but sometimes the term is used more loosely to include the second case as well. A more accurate term for the second case, to avoid confusion, is *unconscious goal activation*.[21]

Conscious goals and conscious goal pursuit are what we usually think of when we think of goals.

All humans consciously strive to achieve conscious goals. As consumers, our conscious goals tend to focus more on satisfying constructed wants than meeting underlying natural or learned needs. This is in part because the ubiquitous marketing world that surrounds us encourages us to convert our harder-to-satisfy needs into easier-to-satisfy wants that can be met, at least temporarily, by acquiring and consuming a marketer's products or brands. It is also because our *cognitive miser* brains always prefer less effort to more.

Conscious Goal Pursuit

Conscious goal pursuit is characterized by two phases: *goal setting* and *goal striving*.[22] Because wants are discretionary, we have to make a conscious decision to act on them. We need to have an *intention* to get the process going. The first step in activating an intention—one that can motivate us to act—is *goal setting*. Once we have set a goal in our minds, we can consciously carry it through to completion. That is *goal striving*. Unlike unconscious goal pursuit, goal striving requires ongoing attention and vigilance to shepherd the goal to completion. Research on conscious goal pursuit has focused on two questions: What makes people decide to set a goal? And what makes goal striving more or less likely to succeed? Answers to both questions have important implications for understanding how people respond to marketing messages.

Goal setting often occurs in response to the demands or requests of others, such as teachers, employers, or parents. Marketing messages are also a kind of external demand or request to engage in goal setting. A persuasion-oriented ad, for example, is essentially an "ask" that a consumer set a goal—a goal to buy or consume the advertised product, usually at some unspecified date and time in the future. Extensive research on how *assigned goals* get converted into *personal goals* raises some serious questions about whether goals can be assigned effectively in this way, especially if the marketing message is presented in the typical manner of a 30 second ad or a rapidly-scanned marketing display or print ad. Researchers have found that assigned goals are most likely to be adopted as personal goals when they are:

- challenging rather than easy
- specific rather than vague
- aligned with existing goals rather than standing alone
- assigned by a source viewed as authoritative, legitimate, and trustworthy[23]

None of these criteria are likely to be met by the kind of conscious goal assignment communicated in a traditional persuasive marketing message. The goal an ad wants us to adopt is generally quite simple ("buy our stuff"); when and how to accomplish the goal is usually not specified ("next time you can"); the goal is likely to be at odds with existing goals (especially if the purpose of the ad is to change behavior); and the brand sponsoring the ad is unlikely to be seen as particularly authoritative or trustworthy (unless the viewer is already familiar and comfortable with the brand).

> **Given these features of traditional persuasive advertising, marketing messages may not be the best way to get consumers to set personal goals to buy or consume a given product.**

Not all conscious goal-setting is assigned. People can and do set goals for themselves. According to motivation researchers, self-assigned goals are more likely to result in goal striving and successful outcomes when they are based on intrinsic *psychological needs* such as autonomy, competence, and belonging. But setting goals based on intrinsic needs is not enough to ensure success. In addition, goal striving must be accompanied by both a sense of *efficacy* and a sense of *agency*. In other words, goals based on authentic psychological needs (not ephemeral wants) are most likely to be achieved, but only when people are also confident they know how to achieve their goals (*efficacy*) and believe their efforts are self-determined, freely taken, and not imposed by others (*agency*).[24]

> **Marketers should know what conscious personal goals are important to the people who buy their brands and consume their products.**

Rather than trying to replace or interrupt those goals with more immediate goals to buy or consume, they should consider asking how their products and brands can become more intertwined with their consumers' self-generated goals and aspirations.

Unconscious Goal Pursuit

In unconscious goal pursuit, goals are not consciously set. They are activated by objects or events in the environment around us. Nor are they consciously pursued. They produce actions which we may not be aware we are performing or which we misattribute to other causes or reasons. These counterintuitive features of unconscious goal pursuit have made it an intriguing and sometimes controversial subject for social psychology and neuroscience research since it was first experimentally observed[25] in the early 1990s. Thousands of studies have been reported in the academic literature.

> Unconscious goal pursuit implies, correctly, that much of the mental processing that underlies our efforts to satisfy our wants and needs is hidden—both from ourselves and from those whose job it is to understand our motivations and help us achieve our goals.

To date, the implications of unconscious goal pursuit for understanding and predicting consumer behavior have not been fully appreciated or addressed by marketers and market researchers.

The discovery of unconscious goals and their role in human behavior was an outgrowth of three well-established research findings in brain science. The first was the overwhelming evidence that *situational factors* could have a powerful impact on behavior, often overriding the effects of more obvious internal sources such as attitudes, personality, or values. The second was the general acceptance of *dual process* models of the mind—originally introduced by cognitive psychologists in the 1970s and popularized by Daniel Kahneman in his *System 1-System 2* model— which distinguish between conscious mental processes and automatic, implicit, or unconscious ones. And the third was the recognition that situational factors could impact behavior by *priming* all kinds of *mental representations*, such as stereotypes or attitudes, which could then influence a person's judgments and behavior without conscious awareness.[26]

For early researchers of unconscious goal pursuit, these three findings provided a foundation upon which a theory of unconscious motivation could be built. Like stereotypes and attitudes, goals are mental representations that should also be susceptible to activation through *priming* via situational cues. Given the *dual-processing* capabilities of the human mind, this activation could in principle occur through either the conscious or unconscious processing systems. And if unconscious activation and pursuit of goals could be established experimentally, this would provide a causal path for explaining how *situational factors* could influence human behavior, even in the absence of conscious awareness.

Since the 1990s, brain science research on unconscious goal activation and pursuit has been extensive. Overwhelmingly, the research has supported the theoretical results initially hypothesized. The biggest challenges have emerged from attempts to replicate the priming mechanisms used to trigger unconscious goals in experimental settings, a topic we will take up in the *Addendum* to Chapter 11. More fundamentally, almost three decades of research has confirmed that goals can be unconsciously primed; they can be pursued without conscious awareness; and they can provide an efficient mechanism for satisfying basic wants and needs while our conscious minds focus on other endeavors, such as planning future actions, learning from past actions, and evaluating alternative scenarios for action.

> **Perhaps the most important implication of unconscious goal research is that it firmly establishes the precedence of the unconscious over the conscious as a source of human thought and behavior.**

Just as scientific evidence eventually compelled us to abandon the "obvious" notion that the sun rotates around the earth, so the discovery of unconscious goal pursuit forces us to reject the "obvious" notion that we only direct our behavior through conscious thoughts and plans. As summarized in the brief discussion of *unconscious behavioral guidance systems* in Chapter 2, that common-sense notion has been displaced today by a new understanding, one in which unconscious processes influence every conscious mental function we deploy to direct our choices and actions: not just motives and goals, but also perceptions, emotions, and evaluations. The ease with which unconscious goal pursuit fits seamlessly into this larger framework of unconscious behavioral guidance is one of the main reasons it has gained broad acceptance in social psychology and neuroscience.[27]

Unconscious goal pursuit also appears to be a mental mechanism with significant evolutionary advantages. Specifically, it allows us to be highly responsive to features in our local, immediate environment that might benefit or harm us, even while our conscious minds are preoccupied with other tasks and goals. All our automatic, unconscious capabilities—to detect novelty and familiarity, to sense internal need states, to automatically assign emotional valence of objects and situations, to infer emotional states of others, to trigger approach or withdrawal reactions, etc.—would have no effect on our pursuit of wants and needs if we were not subsequently motivated *to act* in response to those signals. And the mechanism brain science has identified as the source of that *motivation to act*, operating below our conscious awareness, is unconscious goal activation and pursuit.

Evolutionarily, the primacy of the unconscious makes sense because every successful living creature must have a capacity for automatic goal activation and pursuit in order to ensure its survival and propagation. For evolutionary biologists, unconscious goal-directed behavior is a given, since no equivalent to human consciousness exists at lower levels in the animal kingdom.[28] Our human brains are products of a long history of evolutionary development.

> **Human consciousness has evolved *on top of* pre-existing unconscious behavioral guidance systems, but does not replace or eliminate those systems.**

Rather, conscious and unconscious processes operate together in the human mind, providing us with an ability to comprehend and control the world around us with unprecedented power. Whether this ability will prove to be good or bad for humans and our planet in the long run remains to be seen.[29]

For marketers, it is relevant that unconscious goal pursuit can be more closely associated with deeper physical, psychological, and learned needs than conscious goal pursuit. The latter—at least in the marketing realm if not in other aspects of daily life—tends to be aimed at more superficial wants. While wants can be relatively easy to trigger and activate with marketing messages, this effort, as we have seen, can lead to unintended as well as intended consequences. If marketers want to become partners and enablers of their consumers' intrinsic goals, as the intuitive marketing perspective suggests, then they need to learn how to align with the deeper *identity needs* of their consumers—needs consumers are pursuing every day, both consciously and unconsciously, well outside the bounds of temporary consumption goals that marketers typically try to impose on them.

How Goals Get Activated

> **Conscious goals get activated by *intentions*. Unconscious goals get activated by *primes*.**

But ultimately, conscious goals get activated only after certain unconscious processes have happened first.

Conscious Goal Activation

As described earlier, conscious goals get activated by an *intention*. While the unconscious sources of that intention and the associative activations that bring it to mind may not be accessible to conscious awareness, the intention itself is. The process involves a strong element of *System 2* processing. For example, a look in the mirror might trigger an intention to go on a diet. Adopting an intention involves a conscious *if-then* analysis: *if* I lose weight, *then* I will feel better about wearing a swim suit on the beach this summer. Or the same intention might be adopted for a different reason; for example, because my doctor has warned me that my current weight is unhealthy. That triggers a different kind of calculation and a different set of stakes for goal setting, goal striving, and the likelihood I will accomplish my goal. Events and occasions can also be a source of goal activation. The start of a new year, for example, is often the trigger to adopt new goals in the form of New Year's Resolutions, usually without much success after a few weeks.[30]

Conscious goal activation is the first step in *goal setting*, which can be influenced by a wide variety of factors, some recognized consciously and some not. Among the most important influences on goal setting are efforts to satisfy basic needs of autonomy, competence, or belonging. We often are drawn to goals that increase our ability to act independently, improve our ability to perform a task, or allow us to become more integrated into a desired social group.[31] Such goals are more likely to be successfully attained when they are accompanied by feelings of self-confidence (*efficacy*) and self-determination (*agency*).

We also tend to set conscious goals based on a vision of our *possible selves*. As defined by psychologists Hazel Markus and Paula Nurius in an influential paper in 1986:

> *Possible selves are the cognitive components of hopes, fears, goals, and threats, and they give the specific self-relevant form, meaning, organization, and direction to these dynamics. Possible selves are important, first, because they function as incentives for future behavior (i.e., they are selves to be approached or avoided) and second, because they provide an evaluative and interpretive context for the current view of self.*[32]

A *possible self* is not quite a prediction; it is more an aspiration. It is obviously self-relevant because it maps our hopes, fears, and goals into a mental image of a future self—one we aspire to become or hope to avoid becoming. It can be a powerful source of conscious motivation in two ways. First, it provides a mental "yardstick" in the form of a personal future against which any encountered decision point, opportunity, or threat can be evaluated. Second, it facilitates the construction of a hierarchy and sequence of aspirational goals that can define a path toward the achievement of the envisioned possible self. Researchers have found that our ability to overcome obstacles in conscious goal pursuit is significantly strengthened when a goal is seen as instrumental to achieving a higher-order *possible-self* goal to which we are strongly committed.[33]

Unconscious Goal Activation

Ultimately, every conscious intention emerges out of prior unconscious processing. Working backwards through the *cognitive timeline*, intentions arise as part of *activating goals*, but are shaped by prior unconscious processes operating as part of *forming impressions* and *determining meaning and value*. Once a conscious goal comes to mind, its motivational intensity may be strengthened or weakened by additional conscious *deliberation and analysis*, as when a person's commitment to a lower-order goal gets increased by its connection to a higher-order goal.

> **But every goal has its origin in unconscious processing, whether it leads to a conscious intention or not.**

The underlying mechanism that triggers both conscious and unconscious goal activation is *motivational priming* (also called *goal priming*, *behavior priming*, and sometimes *social priming*).[34] In its most general sense, *priming* is the mechanism by which activation of one thought or concept increases accessibility to other thoughts or concepts that are connected in memory. Through the process of *associative activation*, one thought leads to another.

Brain scientists differentiate between multiple types of priming (see Chapter 14). One type—variously called *associative priming*, *semantic priming*, *trait priming*, or *perceptual priming*—is the unconscious process by which one thought triggers another. Associative priming activates related ideas or *semantic constructs* in memory. The more strongly past experience connects two thoughts in memory, the more likely exposure to representations of one will *facilitate* thinking of the other, at least for a relatively short period of time. If I'm exposed to the idea of a *taxi* in a story or picture, for example, I'm more likely to answer *fare* instead of *fair* in a spelling test (even though *fair* is the much more common spelling).

A second type of priming, *motivational priming* or *goal priming*, operates more broadly, in that it not only triggers thoughts in the form of representations of desired end-states (goals), it also elicits plans, actions and behaviors consistent with pursuit of those end-states. In other words, what gets primed is not just a related idea, but a want or need that can be satisfied by observable behavior.

The idea that goals can be activated and pursued outside of conscious awareness builds upon a large body of research in the 1970s and 1980s that showed how other mental representations, such as *trait concepts* (honesty, aggressiveness), *attitudes*, and *group stereotypes*, could be activated automatically by the presence of primes or cues in a person's environment. For example, a series of influential studies by social psychologist Russell Fazio and colleagues found that people can have attitudes they are unaware they have, which in turn can be activated by environmental cues and subsequently guide behavior, all without conscious awareness. Simply being exposed to an *attitude object*—say, a photo of a loved one or, more relevant to marketing, an image of a product or brand—can automatically elicit learned attitudes toward that object, which can then influence subsequent conscious thoughts and/or behaviors.[35] Similarly, extensive research on racial, demographic, and social-group stereotyping has found that learned stereotype associations can be automatically triggered by direct or indirect exposure to group members, even among individuals who firmly believe they do not consciously hold the associated beliefs and biases.[36]

These findings of mental representations being automatically activated by exposure to environmental cues and primes were further corroborated by Antonio Damasio's discovery in the 1990s of *somatic markers*. As described in Chapter 8, Damasio saw somatic markers as learned emotional associations, based on past experiences, that could be triggered automatically and guide subsequent behavior whenever similar experiences were encountered later on.

Given these consistent findings that automatic behavior could be activated by priming different types of mental constructs—trait concepts, attitudes, stereotypes, somatic markers—researchers began to ask whether *goals*, another type of mental construct, could also be primed by environmental cues and produce unintended behavioral effects. The principle underlying such as effect would be the same—an automatic association in memory between mental representations of *environmental features* (people, places, things) and mental representations of *meanings and values* (attitudes, preferences, expectations). Both representations would need to be *repeatedly* paired in memory to form the automatic association between the two. If goals are also mental representations, it follows that they should be amenable to automatic activation by the same principle.

> **If a goal has been pursued *often and consistently* in a given context in the past, then encountering that context in the present can automatically activate that goal.**

If I habitually competed with my brother when we were growing up, then simply having him enter the room, or perhaps even glancing at a photo of him, might automatically activate the goal of competition in the present.[37] And this effect could occur even if I had no *intention* to compete with anyone at the present time or in the present circumstances. That's the theory behind unconscious goal activation.

Can Products and Brands Activate Goals?

Of particular interest to marketers is whether unconscious goals can be activated by representations of products and brands, such as packages, logos, and slogans. These effects have in fact been studied extensively, and the results indicate that exposure to products, brands, and marks can indeed activate unconscious goals—but often in ways marketers might not expect.

As with priming in general, motivational priming of unconscious goals using products, brands or marks as primes is possible, but can produce broad, imprecise, and even illogical results.

A good example of these diverse results can be found in an influential study of TV food advertising and children's eating behavior, published in 2009. Researchers Jennifer Harris, John Bargh, and Kelly Brownell wanted to see if watching TV ads for high-sugar, low-nutrition foods—similar to those typically shown during children's viewing hours—impacted the eating behavior of children. They divided 118 children into two groups who watched a cartoon show with two embedded ad breaks; one group saw sugary-cereal and salty snack ads; the other group saw ads about games and entertainment products. The children were also given a bowl of *Goldfish* crackers and were told they could have a snack while watching. The dependent variable in the experiment was the volume of crackers the children ate while watching the TV show. As predicted, those exposed to food ads ate 45% more crackers than those exposed to non-food ads. The researchers concluded that "the effect of food advertising was consistent with an automatic link between perception and behavior and in line with most other recent demonstrations of behavioral priming effects."[38]

In a follow-up experiment, Harris and colleagues looked at the effects of food advertising on adult eating behavior. In this study, 98 college students watched a TV comedy with two ad breaks. One groups saw a mixture of non-food ads and four ads for low-nutrition snacks emphasizing fun and excitement; a second group saw the same non-food ads plus four ads for nutrition-oriented snacks emphasizing good health and high nutritional value; and a third group saw only non-food ads. Participants were not offered a snack during the TV viewing, but were offered a range of snacks of varying nutritional value (from carrots to trail mix to chocolate chip cookies) while engaging in a later interview session. Results again showed a strong priming effect. Participants who saw snack ads ate more than those who saw non-food ads, who in turn ate more than those who saw nutrition-oriented ads. However, the most interesting finding—from a marketer's point of view—was the observation that priming effects were *diffuse*. Rather than priming consumption only of the advertised foods, the ads primed consumption of foods in *all* the offered categories. Low-nutrition snack ads increased consumption of both unhealthy and healthy snack options, including vegetables.[39]

> **TV ads for food products in both experiments did not necessarily activate more eating of the advertised product, they just activated more eating.**

These results contradicted food industry claims at the time that advertising only affected brand preferences, not overall nutrition.[40] They also showed that food advertising triggers a *flexible* eating goal, one that can be satisfied in many ways, rather than a product-specific consumption or purchasing goal. Finally, the priming effects observed by the researchers occurred regardless of participants' state of hunger—in the adult study, the amount of food consumed after viewing snack advertising was completely unrelated to participants' reported hunger. The effect was *automatic*, it occurred even in the absence of a conscious want or need to consume food.

Harris's experiments have important implications for marketers. Goal priming produced by advertising is real and potentially powerful, but it is also imprecise and often illogical, even counter-intuitive, with regard to the behaviors it triggers. Once again, we see that goal priming is not a simple or predictable tool for marketers to use in their efforts to influence consumers.

Key to the food-ad priming studies is the fact that food has one very strong and biologically hard-wired association that is almost too obvious to mention—food is associated with eating. Thus, activating the idea of food, through a TV ad for a tasty food product or some other priming mechanism, is very likely to trigger an eating goal. Studies have shown that other brands and their marks (logos, slogans) can also activate goals consumers associate with them, provided the brand has built a strong learned connection with a goal, and that the goal is attractive or desirable to the consumer.

Evidence for this effect has been observed for several popular brands, but not for just any well-known brand. Rather, it has been found for brands that are well-known and also known to *stand for something*—that is, brands that represent a value or aspiration that consumers want to adopt as their own, either tactically in a given situation, or more broadly as a life goal.

Before it became a technology behemoth dominating multiple categories with products like the *iPod, iPad,* and *iPhone,* Apple was a niche player in the personal computer business that tried to differentiate itself as the computer brand for a specialized niche: creative, innovative, and visionary people who "think different." From the moment it introduced its Macintosh computer in 1984, Apple marketed its connection with *creativity* aggressively and consistently. Its "think different" ad campaign launched in 1997 associated the brand with acknowledged creative geniuses like Picasso, Hitchcock, Edison, and Jimi Hendrix. When it rolled out its *iPod* music player in 2001, its unique white earphone cables signaled that its users were innovators who adopted a new and creative way to buy and enjoy music.

In a study published in 2008, Tanya Chartrand and fellow Duke University researchers Gráinne and Gavin Fitzsimons decided to test whether Apple's association with creativity could produce unconscious goal activation. Specifically, they asked if priming with the Apple logo could trigger an unconscious goal to be more creative, without any conscious awareness that such an effect was taking place. To answer this question, they devised an experiment in which 341 students engaged in a distraction task while they were *subliminally exposed* to either the Apple logo or the IBM logo. The logos were displayed on a computer screen for only 13 milliseconds—too fast for conscious awareness—and were masked by small random-colored boxes whose location participants had to track on the screen. Then, either before or after a filler task, participants were asked to complete an "unusual uses" task, in which they had to generate as many unusual uses as possible for a brick. Nowhere in this task was any brand or the concept of creativity mentioned.

Results revealed substantial evidence for unconscious goal activation. On two measures of creativity devised by the researchers, participants primed with the Apple logo performed significantly more creatively. First, they generated significantly more unusual uses for a brick: an average of 7.68 uses vs. 6.10 uses for IBM-primed participants. Second, their first three uses were rated as significantly more creative, based on independent ratings by two judges, averaging 8.44 on the judges' scale vs. 7.98 for IBM-primed participants.[41]

The researchers also conducted two follow-up studies. Experiment 2 was a conceptual replication that found a similar unconscious goal activation effect for the Disney brand and the goal of *honesty*. Pre-testing showed that Disney was a brand associated by the target population of college students with the concepts of *honesty* and *sincerity*. An equally popular entertainment brand, the *E! Network*, was not associated with either of these concepts. In this experiment, participants were primed *supraliminally*; that is, they were primed with logos they were aware they were seeing, they just didn't know why. Primes were presented as part of a "typographical ratings" task, in which participants were asked to rate five versions of either Disney or E! logos, along with several other brand logos. Following an intervening task, they were presented with a series of questions in which they had to choose between socially-desirable but dishonest actions they might have taken in the past vs. more honest but less socially-desirable actions they might have taken.

The researchers' measure of *honesty* was the extent to which participants admitted to the less socially-desirable actions in answering these forced-choice questions. As in the first experiment, the researchers found significant evidence of unconscious goal activation. Participants in the Disney-primed condition answered significantly more honestly than participants in the E! Network-primed condition.[42]

The second follow-up study, Experiment 3, added an important caveat to the earlier findings about unconscious goal priming. In this experiment, the Apple vs. IBM brands were primed in a different way (showing images of various products, including desktop computers displaying Apple or IBM logos) and the "unusual uses" task was then repeated as in the first experiment. But one more step was added: participants were asked to rate themselves on a scale of *creativity motivation*—that is, how motivated they were to be and to appear to be a creative person. While the overall effect of Apple vs. IBM priming on creativity was replicated for both measures of creativity, the researchers also found that creativity motivation moderated this effect in a significant way. The Apple prime had a significant effect on the performance of creativity-motivated participants, but it had no significant effect on the performance of participants who rated themselves low on creativity motivation.

The researchers' conclusion from this third experiment is important for understanding the limits of goal-priming using brands. Brand exposure activates goal-directed behavior only when the brand has an established connection with the goal in question and the individual exposed to the brand has a pre-existing personal or situational motivation to pursue the goal in the current circumstances. In this case, only participants who possessed a *personal goal* to be creative were unconsciously influenced by the Apple brand and its implicit association with creativity. For participants who did not feel a strong need to be creative, priming Apple brand had no effect on their creativity performance.[43]

Brand priming has also been found to activate more immediate and situational goals, in addition to the broader "life goals" examined in the Apple and Disney studies. In another series of studies published in 2008, Chartrand and colleagues found that unconsciously priming consumers with retail store brand names strongly associated with "prestige" or "thrift" could trigger quite different goal pursuit paths when consumers were presented with luxury and low-cost alternatives in a subsequent choice task. Across a wide range of products—sports socks, apartments, and sound systems—participants primed with "prestige" store brand names (*Tiffany, Neiman Marcus, Nordstrom*) were more likely to select high-end, expensive choices, while participants primed with "thrift" store brand names (*Walmart, Kmart, Dollar Store*) were more likely to select lower-end, inexpensive choices.[44]

How did the mechanism of unconscious goal activation work in this instance? In these experiments, the goal was to make a choice between alternatives that clearly highlighted prestige vs. thriftiness as choice criteria. Although the brand primes were not *directly relevant* to this task (no stores were mentioned in describing the products), their well-established associations with prestige or thrift were *goal-relevant* to the task at hand. In the immediate context of making these binary choices, the brand primes activated an unconscious goal to prioritize prestige or thrift. That goal, in turn, helped resolve the choice in a quick and efficient manner, successfully pushing participants—unconsciously—in the primed direction. As with the Apple and Disney examples, it was the fact that these retail brands *unambiguously stood for something*—in this case, prestige or thrifty shopping—that made them work as primes for activating unconscious goals in the specific task situation.

As Chartrand and colleagues summarized their results:

These studies enable us to make the following claims: First, activating consumer choice goals in a purportedly unrelated priming task alters subsequent choices. Second, the observed effects are in line with the theory of nonconscious goal pursuit. ... Finally, ... subliminal exposure to environmental features such as brand names can serve as the primes that activate the goals.[45]

Chapter 11

Consumer Goals in Action

The Dynamics of Consumer Motivation and Action

"Thinking is for doing that accomplishes goals."
–Cesario, Plaks, and Higgins[1]

In the marketing world, goals connect consumers' impressions, emotions, memories, wants, and needs to product and brand preferences, choices, and actions. In the *consumer cycle*, exposure to *marketing* is largely a passive, mental experience, but both *shopping* and *consuming* involve motivated actions driven by conscious and unconscious goals at many levels. For marketers, understanding how and when consumers acquire, pursue, and accomplish (or fail to accomplish) goals relating to product acquisition and consumption is *the* central task of their jobs, because goal activation and goal pursuit are the primary drivers underlying all forms of consumer behavior.

Marketers can choose to look at this central task in either of two ways.

They can view their job as the *creation* of consumer goals; that is, as the imposition of new acquisition and consumption goals meant to interrupt and supersede prior goals the consumer might be pursuing. This is the approach of traditional persuasive marketing. Grab the consumer's attention, use persuasive arguments to distract them from their current goals, then redirect them to adopt a new goal, one that directly favors the marketer's product or brand.

Alternatively, they can view their job as helping consumers achieve their *already-existing* goals. They can position their products and brands as *enablers* of consumers' ongoing goal pursuit efforts, whether short-term and instrumental or long-term and aspirational. This is the approach of intuitive marketing. Like traditional marketing, intuitive marketing seeks to influence consumers. But it does so by aligning with consumers' existing motivations and goals, primarily in the service of positive psychological needs, rather than by attempting to impose new, short-term, transactional goals on consumers using disruption, distraction, and persuasion.

> **Intuitive marketing does not shape people's goals, it is shaped by people's goals.**

The Means and Ends of Goal Pursuit

Whichever approach marketers decide to pursue—imposing their own purchase and consumption goals on consumers or positioning their products and brands as enablers of consumers' deeper aspirations and self-affirmation goals—they need to understand how goals operate as a mechanism for translating consumer wants and needs into expectations, choices, actions, and habits. In the previous chapter, we examined how conscious and unconscious goals get activated based on very different processes. In this chapter, we complete our discussion of goals and motivation by focusing on two additional questions:

- What does goal pursuit look like?
- What happens after goals are achieved or not achieved?

Both these questions are important to understanding how goals impact consumer choice and behavior.

> **Perhaps the most interesting finding in this line of research is the discovery that conscious and unconscious goals get pursued quite similarly despite the fact that they originate quite differently in the human mind.**

What Goal Pursuit Looks Like

Although the processes underlying conscious and unconscious *goal activation* are quite different, the processes underlying conscious and unconscious *goal pursuit* are surprisingly similar.[2] In fact, it is the similar "signatures" of conscious and unconscious goal pursuit that allow brain scientists to observe and measure goal pursuit actions when actors themselves are unaware they are pursuing a goal. What is similar is the presence of *motivational properties* that accompany both conscious and unconscious motivated behavior. These properties are present only when behavior is goal-directed. They are not present when other types of priming occur, such as semantic or stereotype priming. They also differentiate goal pursuit from other mental processes such as liking, evaluating, or choosing.[3]

Goals operate over extended periods of time

For both consciously and unconsciously activated goals, one important indication that motivated goal pursuit is occurring is the presence of behavior persistence over time. Unlike unmotivated priming effects, which dissipate rapidly, motivational priming activates goals that continue to influence behavior until the goals are either achieved or abandoned.

As discussed in Chapter 10, motivational states persist over time because they create a *tension* that produces a *drive* to close a *gap* between an existing condition and an end-state condition represented by the goal. This gap may be voluntarily defined (a "want") or it may be a function of an internally-generated compulsion, either physiological, psychological, or learned (a "need"). Whatever the source of the motivation, we continue to be *moved* to close the gap until some sort of positive or negative resolution is achieved.

Goal pursuit persists in the face of obstacles

A related feature of goal pursuit is persistence in the face of obstacles. An obstacle may be physical or social; for example, handling unpleasant materials or interacting with a disliked individual. Researchers have found that when people are primed for goal pursuit, they are more able to overcome such obstacles than when they are not.[4] This, again, has been found to be the case for both conscious and unconscious goal pursuit.

As a feature of unconscious goal pursuit, persistence in the face of obstacles is one way in which motivation can lead to open-ended and adaptive behavior, even in the absence of conscious executive control. An active unconscious goal can operate on whatever goal-relevant elements happen to occur in the local environment, including obstacles.[5] This flexibility,[6] combined with the persistence of goal pursuit over time, increases the likelihood that an envisioned goal will be achieved, even in the absence of conscious monitoring and control.

If interrupted, goal pursuit is resumed at the first opportunity, even if more attractive alternative activities are available

Another way in which persistence of goal pursuit is maintained over time is through resistance to interruptions. In an often-cited example of this effect, participants in a goal priming experiment were interrupted during a task in which some of them had been unconsciously primed to pursue an achievement goal. Shortly after starting the task, an interruption was staged that lasted about five minutes. Following the interruption, participants were told they could either return to the original task or start another task that was significantly more "fun" than the one just interrupted (based on pre-testing). Despite the opportunity to abandon the first task for the more attractive alternative, achievement-primed participants were more likely to return to the first task than were participants who had not been primed with an achievement goal. This result replicated similar results for conscious goal pursuit, in which readiness to resume an interrupted activity has been found to be a strong indicator of high goal commitment.[7]

The intensity of goal motivation increases over time until fulfilled

Finally, not only does goal pursuit persist over time, overcome obstacles, and resume following interruptions, it also appears to increase in intensity the longer an active goal remains unfulfilled. Again, this is a classic feature of conscious goal pursuit, most prominently displayed when goals are associated with physiological or psychological needs like quenching thirst or countering an ego threat.

An example of increasing goal motivation intensity is found in the study of "thrift" and "prestige" goal priming described in Chapter 10. In that series of experiments, participants were first unconsciously primed to activate mental representations of thriftiness or prestige/luxury prior to making some consumer choices. In one experiment, the choice tasks were delayed by either 3 or 8 minutes with an unrelated filler task. Consistently across three types of products (crew socks, apartments, and sound systems) the percentage of participants choosing the primed option (either thrifty or prestige) was significantly higher after the 8 minute delay than after the 3 minute delay, suggesting that a longer delay between priming and goal achievement increased the impact of the primed goal on consumer choice.[8]

All of these features of conscious and unconscious goal pursuit increase our chances of satisfying our goals in the face of delays, obstacles, or interruptions. They make us more adaptive and more strategic as we strive to fulfill our wants and needs in a complex world in which the path from *A* to *B* is hardly ever a straight line. In the world of consumer behavior, they leave a trail of evidence that allows marketers and market researchers to determine if and when consumers are actively pursuing goals, and what goals they are pursuing, when they engage with products, brands, and marketing messages.

When Goal Pursuit Ends

Goal pursuit leaves distinctive behavioral "signatures" while it is in process. It also produces distinctive and observable effects when it ends, successfully or unsuccessfully. What happens when goal pursuit ends? Success or failure in achieving goals pursued either consciously or unconsciously can affect people in several ways.

Once fulfilled, goal motivation dissipates rapidly

A goal is fulfilled when the gap between the current state and the end-state defined by the goal is closed. At that point, people must be able to disengage from the goal pursuit process, as it is no longer adaptive to continue pursuing a goal that has already been met. This is especially important when a goal is a subgoal or sequential goal that must be fulfilled before another goal can be pursued. The motivating drive behind the first goal must be released in order to activate the motivation required to pursue the second goal.

An interesting byproduct of this tendency for motivation to disappear quickly after goal accomplishment is the situation that arises when a goal is met prematurely along the way to an otherwise planned outcome. For example, in another variation of the thrift/prestige priming study, the researchers gave primed participants two choice tasks in sequence. In the first task, participants could satisfy the "thrift" or "prestige" goal with either a hypothetical choice or a real choice. In the hypothetical-choice condition, they were asked to "pretend to choose" between thrifty and prestige brands of crew socks. In the real-choice condition, they were told they could keep the socks they selected. Later, after a five minute filler task, participants were taken to another room and given a second opportunity to fulfill their primed thrift or prestige goal. In this task, they were asked which of two drawings they would like to enter as a prize for participating in the study. One drawing had a "thrifty" prize (a generic $25 watch and $75 in cash) and the other had a "prestige" prize (a name-brand $75 watch and $25 in cash).

This is where the results get interesting. In the first choice task, priming affected people's selections in both the hypothetical and real choices. Participants primed with "prestige" were three times more likely to select the prestige choice than the thrifty choice, whether the choice was presented as hypothetical or real. According to the principle of rapid goal dissipation, that choice should have extinguished the primed motivation, so the second choice should *not* have been affected by the prime. This is what happened, but only when the first choice was real. When the first choice was hypothetical, the goal was not extinguished and priming significantly impacted the second choice as well.[9]

Some important implications for marketers and market researchers follow from this example.

First, especially when it comes to unconscious goals that cannot be consciously monitored, goal satisfaction can be achieved in flexible and unanticipated ways. If a marketer is priming "prestige" at the entrance of a store, for example, in order to increase sales of a prestige product located at the back of the store, they need to be sure that some other "prestige" experience—perhaps involving a completely different category of product—doesn't extinguish their goal-priming effect before their product is even reached. This once again speaks to the complexity of predicting priming effects in a shopping context in which consumers are assaulted by many potential primes at once, all competing to influence consumer behavior.

Second, goal motivation is not likely to be satisfied by "thinking about" goal achievement; it is only satisfied by "real" goal achievement. While real choices can satiate unconsciously held goals, hypothetical choices may not.

> **If researchers want to study goal activation and pursuit in shopping contexts, they need to be cautious about using hypothetical choices, such as purchase-intent questions, as measures of the actual motivational impact of products, brands, or messages.**

Researchers need to keep in mind that goal satiation effects may produce disparities in choice responses between otherwise identical real and hypothetical choices.[10]

The outcome of goal pursuit, whether the goal is achieved or not, can have a significant impact on subsequent mood and behavior

Several effects have been documented as consequences of successful or unsuccessful goal pursuit. Studies have found that even when goal pursuit occurs outside of conscious awareness, goal completion or goal failure can affect our mood, our performance, our self-esteem, and our behavior toward others. Among these effects are two with large implications for marketing: effects on *mood* and effects on *self-esteem*.

Goals and mood. Brain scientists distinguish between moods and other conscious emotional states by noting that most emotions tend to be reactions to things or events in our environment. Conscious emotions or *feelings* tend to be about something, relatively short-lived in duration, relatively intense, and in most cases, we can identify what they are about. Moods are different in that they are less intense, longer-lasting, and most importantly, without a clear target or object. Feelings also tend to be reflected in facial expressions, while moods often are not. Moods are sometimes described as a diffuse mix, or rolling average, of emotional feelings over time.[11]

Have you ever been in a bad mood but couldn't figure out why? Such states have been called *mystery moods* by researchers. In an ongoing research program led by Tanya Chartrand at Duke University, mystery moods have been found to emerge from three common origins: success or failure in unconscious goal pursuit, automatic evaluations of one's environment, and social interactions. With regard to goal pursuit, Chartrand has reported that mystery moods can be induced in lab experiments by priming unconscious goal pursuit and then facilitating or thwarting goal achievement. After priming the concept of *achievement*, for example, she gave participants an anagram completion task which was easy to complete for some participants, but impossible for others. As expected, successful goal pursuit led to more positive moods and unsuccessful goal pursuit led to more negative moods. Significantly, because goals were induced unconsciously, participants were unaware that they were pursuing an achievement goal and were unable to attribute their mood to their success or failure in that task.[12]

The relationship between unconscious goals and mystery moods has also been found to be two-way.

> **Not only do the results of goal pursuit affect our moods, but our moods affect what goals we choose to pursue and how we choose to pursue them.**

Studies have found that mystery moods influence where we focus our attention and how we process information. We tend to pay more attention to aspects of our environment that reinforce or provide plausible explanations for our mystery moods. This can easily lead to misattributions of the sources of our moods, because the true sources are hidden from our conscious awareness.

With regard to information processing, researchers have found that we often treat moods, including mystery moods, as sources of information.[13] We make inferences about what kind of situation we are in by reflecting on our moods. When we are in a positive mood, we tend to utilize broad, superficial, and heuristic forms of information processing, because we perceive our environment to be safe and supportive. When we are in a negative mood, in contrast, we feel more uncertain about our surroundings, and therefore tend to employ more systematic, vigilant, detail-oriented, and analytical information processing.

> **Positive moods encourage ongoing *System 1* processing, while negative moods trigger more deliberative and analytical *System 2* thinking.**

This relationship between unconscious goals and mystery moods has many significant implications for marketers, market researchers, and consumers. Retailers, for example, want their shopping environments to elicit and support positive moods in their customers, even if those customer enter the store in a negative mood. But retailers are often unaware of the myriad of possible elements in a store environment that can trigger negative mystery moods, which consumers may then mistakenly attribute to the retailer as a brand or even to the specific product they are seeking. Factors such as unhelpful store personnel (who may be either too attentive or not attentive enough), out of stock products, narrow aisles, lack of cleanliness, or long lines at checkout can all contribute to the formation of negative mystery moods that may impact not only the current shopping trip, but also associations and expectations that may over time subtly shift implicit brand evaluations and the likelihood of future visits—all without any conscious awareness on the part of the consumer.

Consumers can also benefit from a greater understanding of the effects of mystery moods, both positive and negative, on their shopping and product consumption decisions and experiences. Researchers have found, for example, that people in sad moods, when asked to participate in a staged taste test, tend to eat more. But they have also found that this effect goes away when people are informed that eating will not improve their mood or emotional state. Similarly, several forms of impulsive or compulsive consumer behavior have been traced to efforts by consumer to alter or respond to negative mystery moods. Researchers see such cases as goal prioritization dilemmas: an immediate goal to feel better assumes precedence over other, longer-term, more strategic goals (such as saving money or engaging in behavior that will produce more long-term benefits).[14]

Goals and self-esteem. A second important consequence of success or failure in unconscious goal pursuit is its effect on self-esteem. Maintaining self-esteem is one of the most universal of human psychological needs. High self-esteem results from satisfying basic *identity needs* which, when met, contribute to feelings of self-worth, intrinsic value, and well-being.[15] When not met, those same identity needs motivate us to engage in compensatory thoughts and actions that enable us to reaffirm and replenish our damaged sense of self-worth. Researchers have found that feelings of self-esteem can be highly variable, even over the course of a single day, and that changes over time in how we feel about ourselves can be connected to goal pursuit outcomes.

Every human being knows the feelings of pride and satisfaction that can accompany the achievement of a consciously-pursued goal. We also know the feelings of frustration and self-doubt that can accompany a failed goal. What brain scientists have found in laboratory experiments is that these effects can be replicated when goals are activated and pursued unconsciously.

In one series of experiments, participants were primed with an achievement goal, using both subliminal and indirect exposure to achievement-related words to induce an unconscious goal priming effect. They were then asked to complete a modified intelligence test—half were given an easy version of the test and half were given a very difficult version. Following that task, both mood and self-esteem were measured using standard psychological questionnaires. Results confirmed that participants who were primed with an unconscious achievement goal reported higher self-esteem after completing the easy task than after completing the difficult task, whereas no such difference was found for participants who were not primed for achievement. These results were replicated in a second experiment using a different priming technique and a different easy/difficult achievement test. In summary, self-esteem was consistently found to be lower after unconscious goal pursuit failed and higher after unconscious goal pursuit succeeded.[16]

> **Of particular relevance to marketers and consumers is what happens after people experience self-esteem damage following goal pursuit failure.**

Because maintaining a positive self-image is a powerful and innate human need, threats to self-esteem tend to be met by a range of protective or restorative measures, any of which might produce behaviors that are otherwise hard to explain, even for the person experiencing them. Strategies to bolster self-esteem in the face of goal pursuit failure include:

- *Self-serving attributions.* After failure, people tend to attribute failure more to external causes than to their own behaviors or capacities.
- *Self-affirmation.* After failure, people tend to reevaluate or reinterpret experiences and events in ways that reaffirm their personal integrity and value.
- *Social comparison.* After failure, people tend to compare themselves to others who are "worse off" relative to themselves.

All of these mechanisms have been observed in responses to both conscious and unconscious goal pursuit failure.[17] What are the implications for marketing?

As we saw in Chapter 10, marketing messages are often efforts to persuade consumers to adopt goals to correct personal failings or inadequacies by purchasing or consuming particular products or brands. Such efforts, since they involve pointing out deficiencies that consumers may believe they share, can indeed activate goals to buy. But purchasing a product may not lead to the larger benefits promised by the marketing message. A "super whitening" toothpaste, for example, may in fact whiten teeth, but it is unlikely to improve one's social life or attractiveness, as promised by the suddenly-attractive model flashing twinkling teeth in a TV ad.

Persuading a consumer to adopt a purchasing goal may meet a marketer's immediate, transactional need to sell product, but it does not necessarily meet the longer-term, more aspirational needs of the consumer. Traditional marketing messages, to the extent they highlight personal flaws and then promise (or hint at) unrealistic benefits, can set up an unconscious goal pursuit process that is bound to end in failure. That, in turn, can produce a threat to self-esteem that the consumer may try to relieve—also unconsciously—with protective or restorative behaviors that have nothing to do with the message or product that triggered the goal in the first place.

> **In the worst-case scenario for the marketer, the consumer may use self-serving attributions or self-affirmation to bolster self-esteem by blaming the product or brand for the goal pursuit failure.**

People respond differently to goal pursuit success or failure when the goal is aspirational and indeterminate vs. immediate and finite

One of the ways in which goal pursuit operates is by increasing the *mental accessibility* and *implicit positive value* of stimuli that are relevant to achieving a currently active goal. This makes such stimuli stand out both perceptually and emotionally. They become more likely to "come to mind" and, because of their increased positive evaluation, more motivationally attractive (i.e., approachable). For example, studies have shown that when an *achievement* goal is activated, people notice and exhibit significantly more implicit positivity toward words like *books*, *classes*, and *library* than they do when an achievement goal has not been activated. Such fast and spontaneous increases in accessibility and implicit positivity are believed to facilitate approach motivation toward objects that may help in meeting an active goal.[18]

What happens to these positive evaluations once a goal is either achieved or abandoned is more complicated. When a goal is achieved, accessibility and implicit positivity toward goal-relevant stimuli usually diminish rapidly, along with motivation. This is believed to happen because those stimuli are no longer relevant to our current, post-goal state. "Disengaging" accessibility and implicit positivity for such stimuli makes it easier to shift our focus to the next active goal we seek to pursue.[19]

Complications arise when we begin to consider the question of what constitutes *completion* of a goal pursuit task. Some goals, especially goals to satisfy physiological needs like hunger or thirst, can be easily and unambiguously met. We know we are no longer hungry or thirsty when our bodies tell us that need has been satisfied. But what about goals that are more difficult to interpret as finished or complete? For example, we have discussed a number of experiments in which an achievement goal is unconsciously activated, followed by a task that people can strive to complete, or not. People primed for achievement tend to perform better on such tasks. But does that mean they have completely satisfied their goal? A goal to achieve can underlie persistence in academic or professional performance over a lifetime. Is it ever *satisfied*? Similarly, is a goal to bolster one's self-esteem ever completely satisfied?

When researchers led by Sarah Moore at the University of Alberta examined goal completion effects following activation of long-term, aspirational goals, as opposed to more immediate and easily evaluated goals, they found different results. After priming participants for achievement, Moore and colleagues found that implicit positivity for achievement-related words *increased* rather than decreased after successful completion of an achievement-relevant task. They attributed this difference to the nature of the goals activated in their study vs. earlier work:

> When a goal is finite and easy to evaluate as being finished or not, success may lead to decreased implicit positivity, which would essentially reflect disengagement from the goal. … In contrast, for goals that are ongoing or indeterminate, success may signal that the person should continue with the goal pursuit while failure may suggest that the person should wait for a better opportunity.[20]

This conclusion leaves us with two quite different possibilities when goal pursuit ends. On the one hand, goal-pursuit motivation usually decreases rapidly after successful goal completion, and this is often accompanied by decreased implicit positivity toward goal-relevant stimuli.[21] On the other hand, implicit positivity for goal-relevant stimuli can also increase after successful task completion, but only if the goal in question is long-term and indeterminate, not immediate and finite.

If achieving a goal is experienced as part of a broader and more enduring goal pursuit, it may remain active after the current goal has been achieved, or even after the goal has been thwarted, as long as it continues to be an active motivational objective for the person pursuing it.

For marketers, these differences in how people react to goal achievement or failure after satisfying immediate vs. ongoing goals presents both challenges and opportunities. The challenge is that triggering a short-term purchase or consumption goal may not be as long-lasting, nor as positive for the product or brand, as a marketer would like it to be. According to the research on goal pursuit and completion we have reviewed, immediate transactional goal achievement may actually contribute to a decline in positivity toward the product or brand in question. This raises concerns for the traditional persuasive model of marketing, which is based on the idea that ads and marketing messages exist to persuade consumers to engage in one-time, transactional acts of buying or consuming; acts which (the model assumes) the consumer would not be motivated to engage in without the persuasive *push* of the marketing message.

The opportunity, in contrast, is that marketers may be able to establish longer-term, more robust positivity toward their products and brands, as well as more sustainable bonds with their consumers, by aligning their offerings with consumers' more enduring goals and needs. This leads us to the fifth and potentially most powerful source of influence utilized by intuitive marketing: connecting to people's aspirations and identity.

Sources of Intuitive Influence: Aspirations and Identity

Human beings are *strivers*. We are always pursuing one goal or another.

Often marketing tries to use this striving against us. It uses emotions to remind us that we are failing, that we are falling short of achieving our goals. Marketers tell us we are not handsome enough, tall enough, blonde enough, rich enough, or popular enough. Also, persuasive marketing tries to get us to replace our goals with the marketer's goals.

> **Marketers have a choice: they can work *with* human goals and aspirations, or they can work *against* them.**

Intuitive marketing takes the first route. Persuasive marketing too often takes the second route.

Connecting with aspirations and identity can be thought of as a special case of aligned-intent marketing. In this case, the intent is to engage in activities and pursue goals that contribute to the attainment of personal aspirations and self-esteem enhancement.

Innate Human Needs and the Goals That Satisfy Them

Do humans have *innate needs* that we all try to satisfy, regardless of age, gender, race, ethnicity, or nationality? The surprising answer that emerges from decades of research led by University of Rochester psychologists Edward Deci and Richard Ryan is *yes*. According to Deci and Ryan's *Self-Determination Theory (SDT)*, all humans are motivated by three *basic psychological needs* which "when satisfied yield enhanced self-motivation and mental health and when thwarted lead to diminished motivation and well-being."[22]

Edward Deci originally formulated his *basic needs* hypothesis in the 1970s, based on a series of studies he conducted on what he called *intrinsic motivation*. At a time when most psychologists believed that human motivation could only be activated externally—by rewards, threats, or punishments—Deci observed that human beings often seemed to be motivated to do things just because they were interesting and enjoyable—a type of motivation he called *intrinsic*, as opposed to outside-in motivation, which he called *extrinsic*. Attempting to understand this behavior more deeply, Deci began searching for the underlying needs that intrinsically motivated behavior seemed to fulfill. He and Ryan initially discovered two candidates[23]—a need for *self-determination* and a need for *competence*. They later added a third, a need for *relatedness* or *belonging*.[24] They called these three motivators *basic* or *innate psychological needs*:

- *Autonomy* is the need to feel self-directed and in control of one's actions. People are more motivated to pursue activities they voluntarily and freely choose for themselves, as compared to activities they feel are imposed on them by other people or external circumstances.
- *Competence* is the need to feel accomplished and capable. People are more motivated to pursue activities they feel competent to accomplish. They are also motivated to pursue activities that allow them to increase their competence through practice and repetition.
- *Belonging* is the need to feel connected to others. People are more motivated to pursue activities that make them feel closer to others and that can be pursued in a supportive social context. This need is called *relatedness* by Deci and Ryan.

As developed in the 1990s and 2000s, *Self-Determination Theory* took the concept of basic needs much further, arguing that these three needs were not just "nice to have" but were innate, essential, and universal. A person's ability to fulfill them, the evidence seemed to say, was a fundamental source of psychological well-being.

Deci and Ryan called the three basic needs *nutriments*: "In SDT, needs specify *innate psychological nutriments that are essential for ongoing psychological growth, integrity, and well-being.*"[25]

Fulfilling these basic psychological needs, Deci and Ryan argued, was a *necessary condition* for the development of a well-integrated, meaningful, and satisfying *sense of self*. Accordingly, basic needs might also be called *identity needs* because, when met, they sustain a positive *personal identity* based on feelings of self-worth, intrinsic value, and well-being.[26]

Throughout their research, Deci and Ryan have studied how the goals people pursue on a daily basis and throughout their lives relate to fulfilling basic identity needs and contributing (or not contributing) to personal well-being. Their findings indicate that the pursuit and attainment of some life goals provide relatively direct satisfaction of basic needs, thus enhancing well-being, while the pursuit and attainment of other goals does not contribute to, and may even detract from, basic need satisfaction. Specifically, they studied differences in the importance people place on *intrinsic aspirations* (goals such as affiliation, personal growth, and community that directly satisfy basic needs) and *extrinsic aspirations* (goals such as wealth, fame, and image that at best only indirectly satisfy basic needs). In these studies, they found compelling evidence that:

> *… placing strong relative importance on intrinsic aspirations was positively associated with well-being indicators such as self-esteem, self-actualization, and the inverse of depression and anxiety, whereas placing strong relative importance on extrinsic aspirations was negatively related to these well-being indicators.*[27]

If some goals do not fulfill basic needs and fail to lead to well-being, then why do people pursue them?

Returning to the idea that basic needs are *nutriments*, SDT posits that if people are subjected to social contexts in which basic needs are not met, or inadequately met, a deficit in need fulfillment is created that can motivate them to pursue *extrinsic goals* as a substitute or compensatory mechanism. Such contexts could be a childhood home, a school, a workplace, or a community that harbors direct obstacles to basic need fulfillment: excessive control that obstructs autonomy, inadequate or overwhelming challenges that obstruct competence, or a lack of social connections that obstruct belonging. Failure to nurture any or all of the basic needs, SDT researchers have found, not only decreases initiative, responsibility, and well-being, but also increases stress, anxiety, and psychopathology.[28]

The key insight of SDT is that goals pursued to meet the basic identity needs of autonomy, competence, and belonging will, if successfully achieved, contribute to lives that are more meaningful, fulfilling, and satisfying.

Conversely, if ways to fulfill basic needs are not available, people will pursue substitute or compensatory goals that ultimately do not contribute to psychological growth, integrity, or well-being. Deci, Ryan, and colleagues have identified and studied several such *extrinsic aspirations* or compensatory goals, including financial success (wealth), social recognition (fame), and appearance (image). What is distinctive about these extrinsic goals is that they are not need-satisfying in themselves, but are aimed at more distant outcomes that presumably heighten one's status in the eyes of others. In other words, they are aimed at satisfying future wants, not current needs. Investing in extrinsic goals like wealth, fame, and image, even when successfully achieved, may not contribute to health or well-being. Not only do such goals fail to satisfy the three basic needs directly, they also distract from investing time and effort on more intrinsically-focused goals. In addition, extrinsic goal pursuit tends to occur in more controlled, pressured, and competitive environments, which are often rather stressful and unpleasant. Such environments may themselves be antithetical to the satisfaction of basic needs and may create obstacles to well-being as a result.[29]

Aspirations, Identity, and Intuitive Marketing

What does the existence of innate human needs and goals mean for marketing and marketers?

First and foremost, it means that a basic assumption underlying the traditional persuasive model of marketing—*that consumers are unmotivated until motivated by marketing messages*—is out of touch with modern social psychology and neuroscience. Consumers are *not* inherently unmotivated actors who can only be moved this way or that by external carrots and sticks.

When we act as consumers, we are not passive vessels waiting to be filled up by marketing messages aimed at imposing marketers' preferred shopping and consumption goals on us.

Instead, we are naturally motivated actors who are constantly pursuing our own ongoing *intrinsic goals*, driven by innate psychological needs for autonomy, competence, and belonging. Pursuing and achieving these intrinsic goals is far more central to our *identities* and *aspirations* than internalizing the *extrinsic goals* imposed by traditional marketing.

Second, the existence of innate identity needs and intrinsic goal pursuit means that consumers do not need to be *persuaded* to act—as long as their actions are aligned with basic need satisfaction and intrinsic goal pursuit. We saw in Chapter 4 that traditional persuasion techniques require disrupting and diverting consumers' attention.

We see here that traditional persuasion also requires disrupting and diverting consumers' internally-driven motivations and intrinsic goal pursuits.

211

Traditional marketing asks people to stop pursuing their intrinsic goals in order to start pursuing extrinsic goals that usually involve activating negative emotions and self-images. Such diversionary efforts may succeed in motivating action in the short-term, but they require constant pressure to do so. That pressure, in turn, can contribute to diminished well-being while at the same time increasing the clutter and noise of overlapping marketing messages which, when encountered as a whole, produce the distracting and intrusive cacophony that many consumers find overwhelming and exhausting.

Third, aligning with innate identity needs and intrinsic goal pursuit allows products and brands to speak to consumers not as *disrupters* of basic needs and aspirational goals, but as *facilitators* of those needs and goals, which consumers are already pursuing as they strive to lead better, more enriching lives. Products and brands that are able to take on such roles are powered by marketers who have a deep understanding of how their consumers perceive and pursue aspirations and basic identity needs in the context of acquiring and consuming their products.

Intuitive marketing offers marketers a new way to support and align with consumers' aspirations and identity goals, one that minimizes the disruption of traditional marketing and provides a path toward longer-lasting influence, without applying the heavy hand of persuasion. The basic idea is simple.

The goals that move people are seldom the goals that marketers would like to impose on them.

Every human being has their own aspirational goals that motivate them to satisfy intrinsic aspirational and identity needs of autonomy, competence, and belonging. Marketers can use intuitive marketing to align their products and brands with these powerful aspirations and intrinsic needs in people's lives.

Addendum: Replication Failures and Behavior Priming

Despite extensive evidence for priming in general and behavior priming in particular, there has emerged in recent years a backlash against this research, based largely on the publication of a number of *replication failures* of highly-cited priming studies.[30] Some observers have suggested these results are symptomatic of a deeper *replication crisis* (sometimes called a *reproducibility crisis*) that is variously described as implicating behavior priming research in particular, priming research in general, social psychology and psychology in general, all the social sciences, or indeed, the entire enterprise of science.[31] Certainly the breadth and depth of this debate is beyond the scope of this book's discussion of brain science and marketing, but it does require addressing one key issue of relevance to both marketers and consumers.

> **Do these replication failures change our understanding of priming as a source of consumer choice and behavior? And, if so, how?**

Replication is one of the most important tools of scientific inquiry. After an experiment or study is completed, the original authors or other researchers often try to repeat it to see if they get the same results. The more times the same results are achieved, that stronger and more reliable the conclusions are taken to be. Conversely, if the study fails to replicate, this can be a valuable result as well. It means researchers have more to learn about the original study; either about the causes or mechanisms that produced its results, or about some hidden aspect of the original procedure that inadvertently impacted the outcome. There are two basic kinds of replications. A *direct replication* attempts to repeat a study exactly, to see if the same result occurs. A *conceptual replication* attempts to generalize a study to see if its findings are applicable to a wider domain; for example, to a wider population of people, a different time and place, or a different experimental procedure.

Failed replications have indeed become a significant issue in psychology. In a massive, multi-lab replication effort launched in 2012 and completed in 2015, researchers attempted to replicate 100 studies—many of which focused on priming—from three psychology journals. They found that while 97% of the original studies reported statistically significant results, only 36% of the replications did. Overall, the *effect sizes*[32] found in the replications were only about half as large as in the original studies, implying that the original studies may have seriously overestimated the magnitudes of the effects they were measuring.[33]

> **What these results highlight, first and foremost, is that there does appear to be an overabundance of positive and perhaps exaggerated results in the published psychology literature.**

It should be noted that excessive positivity in published research is not a problem confined to psychology, or to priming studies. In clinical medicine—generally considered a more "scientific" field—an analysis of 49 studies with over 1,000 citations each found that out of 46 reporting positive treatment findings, 16% were later contradicted and 16% were later shown to have been overestimated. Only 44% were successfully replicated, while 24% were never subjected to replication. So even in this more rigorous field, at least 32% of highly-cited results failed to replicate (and possibly more, because a quarter of the studies were never challenged against later replications).[34]

Naturally, practitioners and commentators want to know why replication failures seem to occur with such frequency, and what this means for the scientific status of the underlying mechanisms and processes being studied.

One source of the problem is prevalent throughout academic science: the norms and practices of scientific publishing. Scientific journals have a natural bias to publish positive results. Positive results are more interesting, more newsworthy, and presumably more prestigious to publish in your journal than negative findings. So academic journals in all fields tend to select the most positive studies, with the largest effect sizes, for publication. That bias, in turn, affects the submission strategies of researchers, all of whom have strong career incentives to get published. Researchers therefore tend to submit their positive findings to journals and put their negative findings aside. This leads to what is called the *file drawer problem* in which negative results do not get reported, resulting in a skewing of published findings in an artificially positive direction.[35] That some of these positive findings should fail to replicate, given they come from a positively-biased sample of all research conducted, should not be completely unexpected.

This publication-driven pressure to find and report positive results—usually measured by finding statistically significant results at the *p=.05* level[36]—can also have a biasing effect on how scientists conduct their research. A problem called *p-hacking* occurs when data is collected and analyzed in multiple ways that artificially increase the likelihood that a significant result will be found.[37] A similar bias can be achieved by continuing to collect and analyze data until a significant result appears, and then stopping. These practices exist alongside other questionable research practices— such as p-value rounding, strategic inclusion or exclusion of outliers, exclusion of nonsignificant results, and post-hoc story-telling—that exploit inherent flexibilities in data collection, analysis, and reporting to increase the odds of obtaining a positive result.[38] Again, these practices can infect any scientific discipline; they are not unique to psychology as a field or priming as an area of study. Statisticians have shown how easy it is for questionable research practices to generate false-positive results "significant at p=.05" even for datasets that that contain completely random and unrelated numbers.[39]

Replication Failures and Behavior Priming: Five Lessons

Although factors such as publication bias and questionable research practices have conspired to make replication failures more common throughout science than many nonscientists would expect, replication failures in goal priming research have raised deeper questions and criticisms, leading some observers to question whether *behavior priming* itself—the proposed mechanism underlying unconscious goal activation—exists at all.[40] Without going too deeply into the details of this wide-ranging and at times highly acrimonious debate, five conclusions seem to have emerged as generally (if not universally) accepted.

Behavior priming is real

The basic idea behind priming—that exposure to an incidental stimulus can unconsciously influence a person's subsequent memory, judgment, and choices—has been observed, replicated, and accepted as a basic building block of human cognition at least since the early 1950s.[41] The question is whether behavior—actual physical actions—can be added to this list of *things priming can influence.*

A large-scale meta-analysis of behavior priming research published in 2016 provided a positive answer. Led by University of Pennsylvania psychologist Evan Weingarten, the analysis examined the results of over 350 tests from 133 studies in which incidentally-presented words were used to prime actions of various kinds. Effect sizes were calculated for behavior differences between primed and non-primed (control group) participants across all 350 tests. Statistical tests revealed a significant overall positive effect of priming on behavior, but of a relatively small size. The researchers concluded that behavior priming was indeed real, but smaller in its average impact than had been reported in some highly-cited early studies. An additional test for *publication bias* found some impact of publication vs. non-publication on effect sizes, but not enough to invalidate the overall findings.[42]

Another important study also published in 2016 by Keith Payne and associates provided further evidence for the replicability and reliability of behavior priming effects. In a series of six experiments, nearly 1,000 participants engaged in a gambling game in which they made betting decisions under conditions of relative certainty or uncertainty. While deciding whether to bet or pass, participants were primed in various ways with both hidden (*subliminal*) and observable (*supraliminal*) primes. The researchers found that when the outcome of the bet was uncertain, all these forms of priming significantly influenced bet or pass behavior in all six experiments.[43]

A distinctive methodological feature of the Payne experiments was the use of a *within-subjects* design, rather than a *between-subjects* design, which is much more common in published behavior priming studies. In a within-subjects design, each individual is exposed to both primed and unprimed treatments, the effects of which are then compared *for each subject.* In a between-subjects design, individuals are randomly assigned to two groups, either primed or unprimed, so the comparisons are made *between groups*, not "within" individuals. Within-subject designs are generally preferred to between-subject designs because they have greater *statistical power*; that is, they are less likely to miss an effect or difference that actually exists. This is because they eliminate errors caused by differences between individuals, which are only partially controlled by randomization in a between-subjects design. Given the strong evidence for behavior priming found in their within-subjects study, Payne and his co-authors suggest that high-powered methodologies may be required both to confirm the reality of behavior priming effects and to replicate results in a consistent way:

> *Here we provided evidence that primes can produce replicable effects on human behavior. Our procedure captured the defining elements of previous priming studies, in that ostensibly irrelevant primes influenced behavioral responses, and appeared to do so unintentionally. These studies used a within-subjects experimental design with high statistical power, which was created based on a priori theoretical predictions. We believe that these results provide important evidence for debates about the reality and replicability of priming phenomena. Whatever the reasons for particular replication failures, we find evidence that primes can reliably affect behavior when high powered methods are used.*[44]

Behavior priming is highly contextual

Much of the early behavior and goal priming research was predicated on a belief that priming effects should be consistent and universal across people and situations. More recently, critics of priming have implicitly adopted this belief when they argue that replication failures must be due to a flaw in the underlying priming mechanism, because priming effects should be reproducible by any researcher, anywhere in the world, with any population of individuals, at any time (even years after the original study)—as long as the experimental procedures and stimuli are identical.

When examined directly, this assumption of universality has been found to be mistaken. Instead, a large body of research now reveals that behavior priming is highly contextual. It varies in predictable ways based on a wide range of individual differences and experimental contexts. For example, in the Weingarten meta-analysis, the priming effect was found to be twice as strong when the primed behavior was known to be *personally valued* by participants.[45]

> Some people were more motivated to engage in the primed behavior because they valued that behavior as relevant to achieving a personal goal, while others were less motivated because the primed behavior had less relevance to them.

This was an individual difference effect.

This finding parallels the results from the Apple-creativity study discussed earlier. In that case, researchers found that people who scored high on "creativity motivation" were the ones who experienced a priming effect when exposed to the Apple logo. Weingarten's meta-analysis shows that this effect is not limited to *creativity* as a motivating value, but occurs across multiple studies in which motivation can vary in the participant sample, such as when priming involves behaviors associated with achievement, altruism, group affiliation, or other values that may (or may not) align with personal goals and aspirations.

Variations in experimental contexts can also produce divergent results that may be incorrectly interpreted as priming failures. For example, studies have found that exposing participants to primes in a group setting vs. a private setting results in different behavior effects for the same primes. Similarly, priming effects have been found to differ based on a person's physical surroundings. In a study of stereotype activation and "fight or flight" threat response, Joseph Cesario and colleagues found that different physical surroundings influenced white people's reactions to priming with images of black male faces. For participants who implicitly associated black male faces with danger, priming with black faces in a confined space made "fight" related words more accessible in a sequential priming task, while the same priming in an open outdoor area made "flight" related words more accessible.[46] In a field study of the effects of physical context on voting behavior, Jonah Berger and colleagues found that people were more likely to vote in favor of a school funding initiative when their polling place happened to be a school.[47]

In each of these examples, the effect of priming on behavior is not universal and direct, but dependent on other factors that appear contextually, either in the minds of participants or in the physical or procedural features of the situation. Researchers call these factors *moderators*. Moderators are elements in an experiment that can literally make an effect appear or not, based on their presence or absence. "Creativity motivation," for example, is a moderator in the Apple-creativity experiment. "Personal value" is a moderator across multiple studies in the Weingarten meta-analysis. "black-danger association" and "confined space vs. open space" are moderators in Cesario's stereotype priming experiments. "Polling place" is a moderator in Berger's voting study.

Looked at from an evolutionary perspective, it makes sense that behavior priming *should* be highly contextual rather than universal. As Joseph Cesario notes in an article aptly titled *"Priming, replication, and the hardest science,"* the human brain has not evolved to be an invariant stimulus-response engine. Its survival value is a function of its ability to find adaptive responses across different circumstances and in the face of different wants and needs. As stated in the opening quote for this chapter, thinking is not *just* for doing, it is for doing that *accomplishes goals*. The conceptual mistake early priming studies made was to assume that every human brain would respond the same way to the same primes. Instead:

> *With the exception of purely reflexive behaviors, it is difficult to find many examples in which behavior is executed inflexibly in response to a stimulus without regard to other information in the surrounding environment.*[48]

It should not be surprising that priming operates differently on different individuals who have different experiences, different mental connections, and different purposes. This of course makes the challenge of replication even harder, especially if the moderators affecting the outcomes are unknown to the researchers conducting the experiment.

What might appear to be a failure of priming may instead be a failure to identify and control the moderators that are differentially impacting participants in an original study vs. a replication attempt.

Behavior priming depends on motivational relevance

What gives moderators the power to moderate behavior priming outcomes? Generalizing from a wide range of studies, psychologists Baruch Eitam and Tory Higgins have focused on the *motivational relevance* of a mental representation activated by a prime as the key moderating element.

According to Eitam and Higgins, a prime makes a mental representation accessible as a potential trigger of behavior only if that representation contains information that is relevant to the pursuit of an outcome a person is *already* motivated to achieve.

Citing several studies in which the effects of priming are found to depend on the motivational value of the primed concepts, Eitam and Higgins make a case for the importance of pre-existing goals as moderators of outcomes in priming studies. For example, studies have demonstrated that people's goal-directed behavior toward being thin or egalitarian is moderated by the value of those concepts in their minds—primes successfully activated goal-related concepts, but only if the goal itself was already important to the individual. Similarly, researchers have found that priming words related to 'socializing' can influence people's social behavior, but only for individuals who view socializing as a personally relevant value. And several other studies have found priming success or failure to be a function of the motivational relevance or irrelevance of the primes introduced in the study.[49]

Eitam and Higgins further argue that there are three basic kinds of motivational relevance that can cause a primed mental representation to become cognitively accessible and available for behavior priming:[50]

- *Value relevance* occurs when a representation activated by a prime is relevant to an existing want or need.
- *Truth relevance* occurs when a representation is believed to be factually correct or morally right.
- *Control relevance* occurs when a representation contributes to determining how much control one has, or can potentially have, in a given situational context.

As priming researchers have developed a greater appreciation of the moderators that can influence behavior priming outcomes, diagnosing replication failures has become more difficult. Simple answers, like dismissing priming as a "fake" phenomenon, have for the most part been replaced by more nuanced examinations of the many moderators that can make priming effects appear or disappear in different contexts, at different times, and for people who hold different motivational interests or aspirations.

This is not to say that every failure to replicate a highly-cited behavior priming study can be explained away in terms of missing moderators or other conceptual causes. Looking back, many early priming studies did indeed suffer from methodological weaknesses that made them highly susceptible to *false positive* results.

Many early behavior priming studies were methodologically flawed

Faced with numerous replication failures, priming researchers now acknowledge that many studies conducted in the 1990s and 2000s were methodologically flawed in various ways. Even defenders of priming as a general psychological phenomenon admit to a "near certainty" that more than a few priming results have been published using methodologies, designs, and statistical tests that are now recognized as "suboptimal" and likely to contribute to false positive results.[51]

A clear-eyed assessment of the priming literature prior to the emergence of the *replication crisis* around 2011 cannot help but conclude that many factors conspired to push the field toward a reckoning. Priming research became a victim of its own novelty. Prestigious journals rewarded articles that emphasized simple, eye-catching, and counterintuitive results. Negative or null findings were unable to find a publishing outlet and ended up in the file drawer. Positive findings began to draw popular press attention, researchers began publishing best-selling popular accounts of their priming work, and science popularizers like Malcolm Gladwell spread the word about the powers of unconscious priming to wider and wider audiences.[52]

In response to this burgeoning demand, young researchers in search of tenure and senior researchers in search of funding focused more and more attention on discovering and documenting the most subtle and unexpected examples of priming effects: sitting in a professor's chair improves performance on an intelligence test; viewing pictures of attractive women makes men more willing to purchase expensive items and engage in risky behavior; hand-washing after viewing a disgusting video decreases the severity of moral judgments; being exposed to faint images of $100 bills increases endorsement of social inequality. Many of these studies proved in retrospect to be extremely difficult to replicate.[53]

Although excluded or uncontrolled moderator variables are often cited by original authors as reasons for priming replication failures, most cases cannot be attributed to missing moderators alone.

> Too often, priming studies have relied on small-sample, low-powered experimental designs that, ironically, make it easier to find significant positive results but harder to have confidence in the replicability of those results.

This problem is exacerbated when prestigious journals are biased toward publishing only the most subtle and unexpected positive effects. Such effects, by their very nature, have a low prior probability of being true. Indeed, the more "surprising" a result turns out to be, the more statistical power is required to identify it reliably. As one assessment of low-powered priming studies has noted, "When designing studies that examine an a priori unlikely hypothesis, power is even more important: Studies need large sample sizes, and significant findings should be followed by close replications."[54] Constrained by tight funding and pressures to maximize publication output, authors of many of the most highly publicized and counterintuitive priming findings were unable to meet either of these key criteria in their original research.

Recent examinations of statistical significance levels in published priming studies have also revealed evidence of publication bias and p-value hacking when looking at the distribution of reported significance levels across a large number of studies. One analysis of 3,500 statistical tests found a suspiciously high number of reported p-values right below the criterion level of $p=.05$, the traditional cutoff point used by journals to indicate a valid positive result. Such a finding cannot be explained by chance. It must come from various manipulations—deliberate or unintentional—by which researchers adjust the "stopping point" of their data collection as soon as they can generate a p-value below .05.[55] A survey of over 2,000 psychology researchers conducted in 2012 revealed that this and other questionable research practices were much more prevalent in the field than had earlier been suspected and appeared to constitute "prevailing research norms" rather than rare research lapses.[56]

Psychology is responding positively to the replication crisis

To its credit, once the field of psychology began to recognize these methodological flaws and questionable research practices in the wake of the replication crisis, it moved quickly to make significant changes.

In 2011, a highly-influential article titled "*False-positive psychology: Undisclosed flexibility in data collection and analysis allows presenting anything as significant*" revealed just how damaging to scientific credibility questionable research practices could be. It showed, among other things, that a combination of various research practices commonly employed at the time could increase the likelihood of a false positive result at the $p=.05$ level to as high as 60%. In 2017, the authors were asked to provide a retrospective: how had the field changed in the intervening five years? Their response was encouraging:

> *Our field has changed a lot since then. Most notably, there is now a dramatically increased focus on replicability and transparency. In 2010, approximately 0% of researchers were disclosing all of their methodological details, posting their data and materials, and pre-registering their studies. Today disclosure, data posting, and pre-registration are slowly becoming the norm, particularly among the younger generation of researchers.*[57]

Other changes are equally promising. Journals are changing their policies to publish more negative findings and replications.[58] Funding agencies have started paying for replication research.[59] New initiatives like the *Berkeley Initiative for Transparency in the Social Sciences* are providing institutional support for open research practices that increase replicability and transparency of research across the social sciences.[60] And statisticians are introducing new statistical practices and measures that go beyond the severe flaws of null hypothesis significance testing to emphasize effect sizes, confidence intervals, and meta-analytic techniques.[61]

Perhaps most importantly for the future of the field, graduate students and researchers are now getting better statistical and experimental design training. Questionable research practices are much better understood and strategies for avoiding them are now being taught in graduate programs around the world.

Implications for Marketers and Consumers

Nonscientists often make the mistake of believing that an individual "finding" in a single academic paper is the fundamental unit of scientific discovery. That is, they read a paper (or read *about* a paper), they see what it claims to show, they see it is reported to have a 19-in-20 chance of being true ($p=.05$), so they assume it must be both true and generalizable. This misconception is reinforced by popular science news and articles, in which a new finding—especially one that is surprising or counterintuitive—is described as a "new truth" that can be directly applied to real-world situations, often situations involving marketing or consumer persuasion.

As the replication crisis shows, there are many biases in the scientific enterprise. There are also many reasons why a single finding might not replicate.

The power of science emerges not from any single study, but from the slow cumulation and convergence of many findings, often over hundreds of studies and decades of research.

The real fundamental unit of discovery in science is the *evolving body of knowledge* produced by a *research community* of scholars and practitioners who focus their work and careers on understanding a slice of reality or human behavior.[62]

Marketers and consumers need to look at the body of knowledge around priming as a whole, whether labeled *social priming, motivational priming, goal priming*, or *behavior priming*. What they should take away from this body of knowledge, especially following the intensive scrutiny it received as a part of the replication crisis, can be summarized in a few bullet points:

- Priming is a real phenomenon. Failure to replicate individual studies can be traced to many causes, none of which nullify the reality of the underlying psychological mechanism.
- Human thoughts and behavior are influenced by peripheral cues in our environments and mental representations in our minds, both consciously and unconsciously.
- Effect sizes of behavior priming are not as large as many early studies reported. Priming regularly produces predictable results in highly controlled laboratory environments, but its effects in the real world, where people are exposed to large numbers of competing primes at every moment, are much less certain and predictable.
- The problem of competing primes is likely to be even more troublesome in shopping contexts and cluttered advertising environments, where multiple marketing messages and cues are competing against each other to influence consumers, both consciously and unconsciously.
- The priming effects of marketing on consumer behavior are unlikely to be universal and reliably predictable, because they can be moderated by different contextual features as well as different beliefs, goals, and attitudes in the minds of consumers.

- *Motivational relevance* is a key predictor of priming effectiveness. If consumers are not already motivated to pursue a particular goal or outcome, priming is unlikely to have much of an effect on their subsequent thoughts and behavior.
- This means that priming is unlikely to be effective as a persuasion technique in marketing—assuming the marketer's purpose is to instill a *new goal* to consider, purchase, or consume a product or service. Priming is more likely to be effective when it acts as a trigger associating a product or service with an *existing goal or aspiration*, one that is already active in the mind of a consumer.

The replication crisis in behavior priming research is an example of science working as it is supposed to work, with a body of knowledge self-correcting both its findings and its methods in light of new information emerging over time. The message to marketers and consumers is fourfold:

- Draw lessons not from single studies and single results, but from cumulation and convergence across a body of studies.
- Remember that scientific results are always tentative, never certain.
- Keep in mind that what looks too good to be true probably is.
- Don't throw out the baby with the bath water.

Chapter 12

How Consumers Learn Without Trying

Implicit Learning, Memory, and Marketing

"Advertising seldom seems to persuade."
– Andrew Ehrenberg[1]

How do consumers learn? Why do they store some experiences in memory but not others? If it's not persuasion that sparks learning, what exactly is it?

This chapter and the next describe the mechanisms and the conditions under which human memory translates consumer reactions to marketing into learning, knowledge retrieval, and subsequent behavior. It's a story of choices and actions that do not need to rely on attention, persuasion, or logical thinking. It starts with a simple but profound question: How do we get from a thought to an action?

The short answer—as we saw in Chapter 10—is that human behavior comes from goals that get activated, either consciously or unconsciously. Activation is the process by which thoughts turn into goals to perform actions. As Joseph Cesario and colleagues observe in the quote at the top of Chapter 11, "Thinking is for doing that accomplishes goals."

A goal *motivates* a body at rest to become a body in *motion*. A goal is a thought. It comes from one of two sources: a sensory input received directly by our peripheral nervous system (which may come from outside or within the body) or another thought retrieved from memory.

So where does consumer behavior come from? It comes from goals that get activated by thoughts that themselves get activated either by sensory experiences or retrieved memories. Goals, in turn, facilitate action by making some ideas stored in memory more *accessible* than others, either consciously, through *ease of recall*, or unconsciously, through *priming*. And the strength of that *accessibility* is a function of the two types of *learning without trying* we will examine in this and the next chapter: *implicit learning* and *conditioning*.

225

Pioneers of Intuitive Marketing: Andrew Ehrenberg

Andrew Ehrenberg is probably the least well-known pioneer of intuitive marketing, once you get outside the relatively small and specialized segment of the advertising research world within which he is a legend. That segment focuses on the study of law-like consumer behavior in *populations* of consumers—not the much more varied (and much less law-like) patterns of choice and action made by individual consumers.

Like Robert Zajonc, Andrew S.C. Ehrenberg's early life was shaped by the rise of Nazism and the approach of World War II. Born into a prominent academic family in Germany in 1926, he and his parents fled to London in 1939, following escalating Nazi persecution of his father, an outspoken Christian theologian. He attended public school in England and pursued a doctorate in mathematical statistics at Cambridge University. Remarkably, in light of his later contributions to the field, he failed to receive the degree because his dissertation on the unscientific aspects of statistics was rejected by the University.[2]

Ehrenberg's early choice of a controversial dissertation topic foreshadowed his career-long interest in questioning "received wisdom" in statistics and, later, marketing. Although mild-mannered and gentlemanly in person, Ehrenberg was an iconoclast at heart and was not afraid to challenge the most sacrosanct beliefs of the marketing profession, including perhaps the most sacrosanct belief of all: that the purpose of advertising is to persuade. His case against that concept, first proposed in 1974, was still causing ripples a quarter century later. As one academic observer wrote in 2000:

> "The assumption that advertising equals persuasion is so ingrained in the USA that a challenge elicits much the same reaction as questioning your partners parentage."[3]

Ehrenberg began teaching as a Lecturer in psychological statistics at the Institute of Psychiatry in London in 1951. Four years later he moved into commercial marketing research and consulting, joining a firm that pioneered the use large-scale consumer panels to collect detailed data on household purchases over time. From close statistical examination of those large datasets, long before computers made such tasks quick and easy, he began to observe the law-like patterns underlying consumer behavior that would remain the center of his work for the rest of his career.

After founding his own research company in 1963, Ehrenberg began publishing the first of over 300 articles and five books in marketing science. He returned to academia in 1970, joining the faculty of the London Business School. In 1992, he became Professor of Marketing at London Southbank University, where he founded the industry-supported *Research Development Initiative* that would later expand to become the *Ehrenberg-Bass Institute for Marketing Science* at the University of South Australia.

Ehrenberg achieved the rare honor of being awarded the Gold Medal of the British Market Research Society twice, in 1969 and 1996. He also received an Honorary Fellowship of the Royal Statistical Society in 2003 and an Honorary Doctorate (finally) from the University of South Australia in 2005. In 2010, he received a Lifetime Achievement Award of the Advertising Research Foundation. He died in London at the age of 80 in August 2010.

Repetitive Advertising and the Consumer

Andrew Ehrenberg initially raised the case against persuasion as the purpose of advertising in his 1974 paper, *"Repetitive Advertising and the Consumer."* The basic problem with persuasion, he argued, was that consumers seldom changed their attitudes toward brands. Since the goal of persuasion is to change attitudes, this looked to Ehrenberg like a serious problem for the persuasion model. Based on studies of dozens of brands, representing both fast-moving consumer goods and less-often purchased durable goods, he found that consumers perceived very little differentiation between brands in any given category, and purchased in predictable ways, not by shifting their attitudes toward one preferred brand, but by consistently selecting among a subset of brands viewed as "good enough" to meet their purposes. Ehrenberg based this conclusion on a number of empirical facts that marketers still find hard to accept after more than forty years of validation, such as:

- Most products, especially in fast-moving consumer-goods categories, are functionally indistinguishable from each other. There are seldom plausible grounds for persuading consumers to switch from one brand to another.
- In many categories where advertising spend is heaviest, such as carbonated beverages, overall demand is flat or declining, not growing. So advertising is not creating new demand even in categories where it is most heavily concentrated.
- Small and medium brands survive year-in and year-out, even though their consumers are exposed to vast amounts of advertising from leading brands in their category.
- Four out of five new products fail. Yet there is no evidence that highly advertised new products have a higher success rate than less advertised new products.

If advertising doesn't persuade people to change their attitudes and behavior, then what does it do? According to Ehrenberg, advertising's primary effect is to reinforce *memory* for brands, so that advertised brands are more likely to be remembered when a consumer is considering a purchase. But ads don't have this effect on their own. In contrast to the persistently popular *AIDA* model of advertising effectiveness—in which ads are presumed to persuade consumers to buy a brand by first attracting *Attention*, then engaging *Interest*, then triggering *Desire*, and finally providing a path to *Action*—Ehrenberg proposed that brand choice behavior proceeds along a different path, which he called the *ATR* model—consumers first gain *Awareness* of a brand, then make a first or *Trial* purchase, then are *Reinforced* to develop a repeat buying habit for the brand.[4]

In Ehrenberg's view, advertising can play a role at all three stages along this path, but not by itself and usually not through persuasion.

- Advertising may "create, reawaken, or strengthen" brand and product *awareness*, but in this role it competes with many other sources of awareness, such as word-of-mouth, observed consumption by others, and accidental encounters with new brands. Awareness may lead to additional information search for a newly discovered brand or product, but at this point in the process the consumer is merely acquiring new information, not changing attitudes or habits.

- Advertising is "one of the factors which can facilitate" a *trial purchase*, but this does not require a prior belief that the brand is special or superior compared to other brands in the category. Indeed, one of Ehrenberg's most robust findings is that consumers tend to have very similar attitudes toward all brands in a category,[5] so there is very little basis for creating a persuasive argument that knowledgeable consumers will find credible.

- Advertising, finally, may *reinforce* repeat buying of a known brand. For Ehrenberg, this function—keeping a brand *salient* and readily accessible in a consumer's memory—is the key to what advertising does:

The role of repetitive advertising of well-established brands is … predominantly defensive—to reinforce already developed repeat buying habits. The consumer tends to perceive advertising for the brands he is already buying, and repetitive advertising enables the habit to continue to operate in the face of competition. The consumer does not have to be persuaded to think of his habitual brands as better than the others, but has to be reinforced in thinking of them as at least no worse.[6]

Advertising: Strongly Persuasive or Nudging?

In a 1997 article co-authored with Neil Barnard, "*Advertising: strongly persuasive or nudging?*," Ehrenberg described the law-like patterns of buying behavior that informed his views of advertising and persuasion. The key question he needed to answer was whether and how consumer markets were segmented.

> **Do consumers fall into distinct segments of *loyals* and *switchers*, as most marketers believe, or are they essentially segments-of-one with *split-loyalties* across several brands, from which they choose on any given shopping trip based on exigencies of the moment?**

The answer is important because it determines how advertising ought to work. If the market consists of *loyals* and *switchers*, then advertising should be strongly persuasive with the purpose of increasing a brand's number of *exclusive loyalists*, either by recruiting from the population of switchers or by converting consumers loyal to competing brands. But if the market consists predominantly of consumers with *split-loyalties*, each with his or her own unique repertoire of habitually-bought brands, then marketers should see very little switching of exclusive loyalty from one brand to another. Instead, they should see a steady pattern of *split-loyal buying* within each consumer's repertoire. In that case, the best strategy for brand advertising would be to focus on reinforcing the brand's presence in consumers' consideration sets by *reminding* or *nudging* them to keep the brand fresh in mind. Brand memory reinforcement, not loyalty recruiting, would be the main purpose of advertising.

To answer this question of whether consumers tend to be exclusive loyalists or split loyalists, Barnard and Ehrenberg used a model of consumer buying behavior called *the Dirichlet*. Named after a 19th-century German mathematician, the Dirichlet is a probability distribution that, among many other uses, generates a remarkably accurate model of consumer buying behavior in multi-brand, non-segmented markets. Ehrenberg began working with the Dirichlet in the early 1970s.[7] Numerous studies have since validated its predictions across hundreds of product categories, countries, and time periods, and it is today used to benchmark brand performance at many of the largest and most sophisticated consumer product companies in the world.[8]

What Ehrenberg and Barnard reported in their 1997 paper was overwhelming evidence in favor of the *unsegmented split-loyal* view of buying compared to the *segmented loyalist-switcher* view.

Matching the predictions of the Dirichlet model, consumers tended to buy multiple brands in a given category at predictable frequencies determined largely by each brands' overall market share and a few simple assumptions about how consumers choose within a category.

Rather than switching loyalty exclusively or even semi-exclusively from one brand to another, consumers were quite willing to sample among multiple brands. Even the heaviest purchasers of a leading brand, for example, were found on average to make about 50% of their purchases from other brands in the category (across a wide variety of categories).[9]

Given the accuracy of the Dirichlet predictions about consumer buying, Ehrenberg and Barnard argued that its assumptions need to be taken seriously as descriptions of actual consumer buying. Summarizing their findings on segmentation, loyalty, and brand buying, they observed:

> *All in all, there is no systematic evidence in the literature that rather homogeneous, distinct, and substantial segments of 'loyals' or various 'switchers' can clearly be identified. Instead it seems that consumers mostly follow a great variety of split-loyalty patterns. This leads … to closely predictable numbers of just how many behave in the various different ways.[10]*

The strong evidence in favor of split-loyal buying reported by Ehrenberg and Barnard provides both empirical and theoretical support for Ehrenberg's *reinforcing-and-nudging* view of advertising:

> *There would therefore be little point in devoting advertising or other resources to try to persuade these elusive switcher segments to drop their other brands or, more generally, to make your brand's franchise abnormal, compared with all other brands.[11]*

Ehrenberg's findings on split-loyal buying imply significant challenges not only for the role of persuasion in advertising, but also for the role of attention in advertising. Brand growth must be driven primarily by acquiring new customers, not by increasing the loyalty or purchasing frequency of currently "heavy-user" customers. This creates a big problem for traditional marketing. As we saw in Chapter 4, if half your customers are very low frequency buyers for whom your brand is functionally indistinguishable from its competitors, no marketing innovation is likely to both grab their attention and persuade them to change their buying habits. But this does not stop marketers from trying, which unfortunately has led to much of the clutter and escalating efforts to "rise above the clutter" we see and hear in so much marketing and advertising today.

Brand Advertising as Creative Publicity

Ehrenberg made his "closing argument" on advertising and persuasion in "*Brand advertising as creative publicity*," published in the *Journal of Advertising Research* in 2002.[12] In this article, he summarized his views on advertising, persuasion, loyalty, and consumer behavior by focusing on three key distinctions: how publicity differs from persuasion, how salience differs from loyalty, and how distinctiveness differs from differentiation.

Publicity vs. persuasion

Ehrenberg settled on the term *creative publicity* to describe the function he felt advertising performed best. Publicity, he argued, may convey new information, but for the most part it is about reminding already-knowledgeable people that a particular brand is (still) available in a category. Much of what marketers think of as persuasive advertising is actually more about publicity than persuasion. Ehrenberg identified seven tactics commonly used by advertising, noting how each is more likely to reinforce memory than change attitudes.[13]

- *Proclaiming the brand.* As in the *Coca-Cola* tagline "Coke is it" this mode of advertising is a simple reminder meant to reinforce memory connections to the brand. It "lets consumers attach or re-attach … prior associations of their own to the brand, once the advertisement has reminded them of Coca-Cola again."
- *Linking the brand to the product.* This is advertising that says, in effect, "Brand X is a kind of product." For example, "X gets clothes clean" is essentially saying that X is a laundry detergent. "Experienced consumers (i.e., most) would know that X is much like other laundry detergents. But the advertising reminds them of X: so when they need more detergent, they can just think X."
- *Providing information.* Information may appear in the guise of a *reason to buy* but, as Ehrenberg notes, "Information can only be new at most once. It soon becomes a mere reminder."
- *Establishing distinctiveness.* This is advertising that emphasizes some creatively memorable, but functionally meaningless feature of a product; for example, "*Life Savers*, the candy with a hole in the middle." Such a connection can make a product more memorable without attempting to change attitudes toward the brand.

231

- **Appealing to emotions.** Here Ehrenberg dips into research by Zajonc, Damasio, and Heath (without going into details regarding the mental mechanisms involved) to note that emotional association-building and a potential for priming occur when a brand is repeatedly paired with a positive emotional display. As we saw in our discussion of *small emotional rewards* in Chapter 9, Ehrenberg concludes that "Feeling good about the product and/or liking the advertising … is seldom strongly persuasive but perhaps memorable."
- **Proffering a reason.** Some advertising does present a reason for buying a brand. Experienced consumers, however, usually find such appeals unpersuasive, knowing that any reason offered to buy one brand in a category is likely to be equally valid for other brands as well. "Nonetheless, saying 'Better' or 'Best' keeps the brand in front of the public and provides some reassurance" that it is worthy of a place in the consumer's consideration set.
- **Making a hard sell.** Finally, some ads do try to convince people to buy something here and now. While a hard-sell, like a promotional discount, may have a short-term impact on sales, the effect dissipates rapidly. "But it can act as a reminder—a rather intrusive way of drawing renewed attention to the brand." Ehrenberg also notes, as we saw in Chapter 4, that hard-selling is most likely to work when the consumer is in a state of *aligned intent.* "Hard sell in advertising might help the already persuaded to 'close the sale' themselves."

After working through each of these traditional advertising tactics, Ehrenberg summarized his conclusions about advertising and persuasion:

> *Basically our view is that advertisements can be effective [or "act"] simply through publicizing the brand memorably, without having to "persuade" consumers that the brand is better than they thought before. Such publicizing works through the brand's "Salience."*[14]

Salience vs. loyalty

Salience is the term Ehrenberg adopted to describe how easily a brand comes to mind in personally relevant choice situations. Salience consists of "awareness and memory traces, *plus* familiarity, *plus* assurance." In a world of split-loyal consumers, salience is not exclusive—it does not require identifying and then marketing to a single, definable segment of loyalists. Rather, it is a property that, for any given consumer, can be shared by multiple brands within a category. Which brand gets selected in a given buying situation is be a function of many factors that, over time, may seem to be semi-random:

An individual usually has a consideration set of several competitive brands that he or she may choose to buy over a series of purchases (and others not). Opting for one or another salient substitute on any specific purchase occasion need then be for no special reason. But the choice can also vary with the context—availability, a desire for variety, a mood, an advertising or retail display, an offer, or a whim of the moment.[15]

For salience to influence consumers in the marketplace, neither loyalty nor persuasion is required.

Salience "is not an attitudinal concept."[16] Brands become more salient to individual consumers through ongoing usage and repeat buying. Such repeated exposures can "breed subsequent liking through various processes," such as the *mere exposure effect* or *posterior rationality* ("I use it, therefore I must like it"). For Ehrenberg, salience goes beyond traditional awareness to include familiarity and some degree of assurance that the brand will continue to do what it has acceptably done in the past. This sounds quite similar to one of our *five sources of intuitive influence* introduced in Chapter 1: attracting customers through *consistency, reliability, and trust.* As we saw in Chapter 6 and Chapter 7, shortcuts to consumer preference produce short-lived and relatively weak effects, so consumers who experience a brand via multiple journeys through the full *consumer cycle* of marketing, buying, and consuming are more likely to view it with the "broad salience" required "to become and remain in one's 'consideration set' as a brand that one might or does buy."[17]

Distinctiveness vs. differentiation
Perhaps Ehrenberg's most controversial finding is that advertising works not by persuading consumers to prefer the unique features and benefits of one brand over its competitors, but instead by making one brand more mentally accessible than its competitors—that is, not to make it more *preferable*, but to make it more *memorable*.

Instead of trying to persuade experienced consumers that every advertised brand is better or best, we should accept that advertising mostly needs to refresh, and may occasionally enhance, acceptance of the brand as one to buy and/or to consider.[18]

The problem for marketers is that true differentiation is very hard to come by in most product categories. Products that do the same thing tend to do it in pretty much the same way. And this is reflected in the beliefs of brand users, most of whom tend to see all brands in a category as similar. This does not mean that they buy all brands with the same frequency. As predicted by the Dirichlet model, frequency of purchase within a category is highly correlated with market share. So it is not so much the performance or "unique selling proposition" of a product that determines its sales levels, but more its combination of mental and physical availability.

Distinctiveness, unlike differentiation, refers to any aspect of a brand that helps it stand out in its competitive landscape.

> **Distinctiveness does not imply *better*, only *different*—different in a way that is memorable, like the hole in a *Life Savers* candy or the foil wrap and distinctive shape of a *Hershey's Kiss*.**

Many seemingly incidental aspects of a brand can increase distinctiveness, such as colors, packaging shapes and designs, fonts, taglines, symbols, spokespersons, etc.[19]

Creating and publicizing distinctiveness associated with a brand is, in Ehrenberg's view, one of the most important ways advertising can increase a brand's salience in consumers' minds. But nothing is certain:

> *In principle, to decide, people could simply toss a mental penny ("Oh I don't know—I think I'll have that one"). In practice, however, consumers mostly seem to find choosing a familiar and even habitual brand convenient and reassuring.*[20]

Ehrenberg's Legacy: A Kinder, Gentler View of Marketing?

Andrew Ehrenberg believed his *ads-as-creative-publicity* model was a largely accurate description of how most advertising actually worked. Decades of empirical research supported this view, while the same research disconfirmed many of the assumptions and beliefs underlying the alternative but widely-accepted *ads-as-persuasion* model. Accordingly, he didn't believe advertising would change much in practice if more marketers were to embrace his perspective. What needed to change, in his view, was not advertising practice, but rather "the way advertising is generally thought of, talked about, and evaluated." That, he concluded, "would be theory coming into line with practice."[21]

Ehrenberg both anticipated and provided much of the empirical groundwork for intuitive marketing:

- He identified the importance of repetition in advertising.
- He used deep empirical analysis and modeling to debunk the widely-held view that advertising was all about persuasion.

- He showed that brands could grow more by attracting new low-frequency buyers than by increasing buying among current high-frequency buyers.
- He proved that the idea of exclusive loyalty—of powerful brand "lovemarks" that represented "loyalty beyond reason"[22]—was largely a myth.
- He identified *salience*, not *persuasion*, as the more appropriate goal for advertising.
- He identified *memories*, not immediate *feelings*, as the real means by which marketing and advertising could most effectively influence consumer choice and behavior.

In all these efforts, Ehrenberg challenged the assumed causal connections between *advertising* and *attitude change*—assumptions that still drive most thinking about marketing effectiveness and evaluation today. In so doing, he articulated a more realistic, less intrusive, and less disruptive path to consumer influence, one which directly anticipated at least three of our five intuitive marketing paths to influence: *small emotional rewards*, *aligned-intent marketing*, and enhancing *trust* (assurance) through *consistency* and *reliability*.

Perhaps most significantly, Ehrenberg pioneered the idea that advertising and marketing are about building *networks of connections in long-term memory* that can be evoked at later points in time to facilitate consumer choice and action. His work leads to a counterintuitive conclusion that is still not fully appreciated by marketers and market researchers:

> It is not our *immediate* emotional or logical reaction to a single ad or marketing message that matters most, it is what we *learn* and *remember* from repeated exposures to ads and marketing that has the greatest impact on our choices and actions as consumers.

In order to leverage Ehrenberg's ideas today, marketers need to brush up on what brain science has to say about the complex mechanisms, both unconscious and conscious, by which memories are formed, consolidated, activated, and retrieved.

A User's Guide to Human Memory Systems

Human memory is complex. Brain science has found that our brains provide us with several distinct but interconnected memory systems that work in different ways and in different timeframes to give us an overall coherent picture of ourselves and our world, as well as a capacity to think about the past, present, and future. As we saw in Chapter 9, human memory is both fallible and largely constructed. Brain scientists believe our memory systems evolved this way not to provide us with an accurate recording and retrieval of everything we experience in our lives, but to help us pursue and achieve our wants, needs and goals, from the most instantaneous actions to pursuits that last a lifetime.

Multiple Interacting Systems of Human Memory

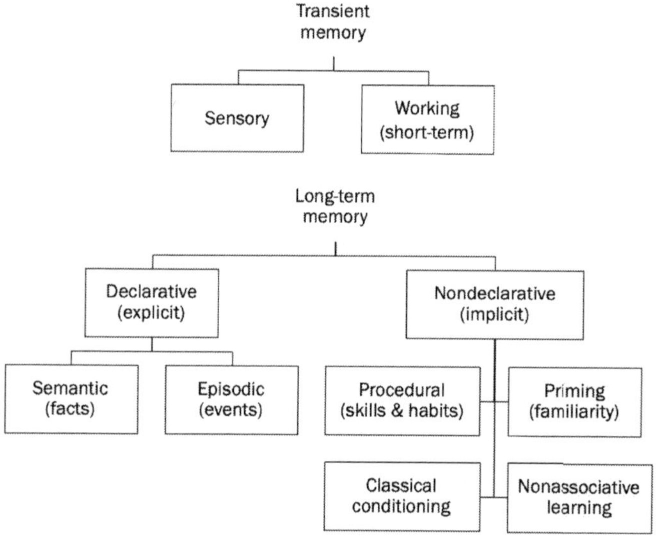

Figure 7. Organization of Human Memory Systems[23]

Figure 7 illustrates the taxonomy brain scientists use today to classify the major systems that make up human memory. At the top level of organization, two very different types of memory operate. *Transient memory* refers to temporary storage and information processing systems that hold information for only short periods of time. The two major branches of transient memory are ***sensory memory*** and ***working memory***. Accompanying these active input-output systems are a number of specialized systems which store memories more or less permanently. These are collectively called ***long-term memory***. Both transient and long-term memory systems have important implications for understanding how marketing strategies—both persuasive and intuitive—can succeed or fail as sources of consumer influence.

Sensory memory

Sensory memory is a holding area for sensory information that is kept for a few seconds or less. Because information flows into our brains through multiple sensory paths, we have multiple sensory memory systems. **Iconic memory** is a fast-decaying store of visual perceptions, **echoic memory** is where we temporarily store auditory inputs, and **haptic memory** is a storage area for touch stimuli. Brain scientists believe we have separate sensory memory systems for each of our five senses. All of these memory systems provide only very short-lived storage. Iconic memories, for example, tend to fade in less than a second. Echoic memories last a little longer, but usually decay in five seconds or less. The purpose of sensory memory is to retain impressions of sensory inputs for a short period of time after the input is no longer present. Thus, sensory memory is part of *impression formation* in our *cognitive timeline* model (see Chapter 2).

Sensory memory systems operate as *System 1* processes, completely automatic and outside conscious control. They allow us to create impressions of smooth continuity in the world we perceive. Iconic memories, for example, last from 0.2 to 0.4 seconds, just the right amount of time to make sequential visual inputs blend together into a continuous flow. Similarly, echoic memory lasts from 2 to 4 seconds, just the right amount to time to allow us to follow spoken language and connect individual word sounds into meaningful sentences.

Experiments has shown that sensory memory systems are vast, essentially limitless in their capacity, but also superficial. Visually, for example, we capture only high-level perceptual features such as color, size, and shape, but not deeper conceptual features such as meaning or function. As we saw in Chapter 2, our brains process *every* signal our senses receive in this way, all unconsciously. Most of these signals rapidly "fade away" through the processes of automatic sensory memory decay, but some trigger *bottom-up attention* or are perceived as relevant to an active goal (and are therefore activated by *top-down attention*) and thereby move into our second memory system, short-term memory.

> **Marketers should be familiar with the natural decay rates built into sensory memory systems.**

While sensory memory evolved to create a smooth impression of continuity in the natural world, marketers mostly communicate to consumers via artificial media such as video and audio. If marketers present media stimuli at a faster pace than our sensory memory is designed to handle, they risk producing results that literally cannot be perceived. In the visual realm, this has been documented in a phenomenon called the *attentional blink*.[24] When two visual stimuli are presented in sequence, with only 0.3 to 0.5 seconds between them, the second stimulus usually cannot be detected. If an important marketing element like a logo or product image is conveyed within that attentional blink time window, as might occur in a particularly fast-paced video ad, it may never be perceived or consciously processed at all.

Working memory

Also called *short-term memory*, working memory consists of things we are aware we are currently thinking about. This includes sensory inputs that have been selected for attention, plus other thoughts that have been retrieved from long-term memory and brought to consciousness for consideration and evaluation. Working memory is thus a part of *System 2* processing and gets activated during the conscious *deliberate and analyze* stage of the *cognitive timeline*. Unlike sensory memory, working memory has a very limited capacity (roughly between 4 and 9 "chunks" of information at a time) and a longer, but still relatively short duration of about 20 seconds before memories start to decay. The term *short-term memory* emphasizes the durational limits of this memory system, while the term *working memory* refers to our ability to actively maintain and manipulate information in short-term storage. Unlike sensory memories, information in working memory can be maintained for longer periods of time through *rehearsal*; that is, by repeating the information over and over, either mentally or aloud, until it is no longer needed. Otherwise, information in working memory tends to turnover quickly, as new objects of attention or deliberation "come to mind" via sensory inputs, long-term memory retrieval, or a combination of the two.

> **When marketers or market researchers ask consumers questions—on surveys or in interviews or focus groups—they are relying on consumers' short-term working memory system.**

The outputs of working memory, as we have seen in our discussions of fluency (Chapter 6), preference construction (Chapter 7), emotional memories (Chapter 9), and goal-states (Chapter 11), are highly dependent on a number of factors, including current context, immediate goals, and the relative strength of associative networks in long-term memory. Working memory is not just *biased* by what easily comes to mind in a given situation, it *is* what easily comes to mind. And this can be a major source of discrepancies between what consumers *say* and what they *do*. In order to get a fuller picture of the sources and consequences of consumer behavior—not just consumer opinions—marketers and market researchers must develop a deeper understanding of the complexities of memory, in particular, the operations and functionality of human long-term memory.

Long-term memory

Long-term memory is where all knowledge, including all brand and product knowledge, resides in the human brain. How knowledge gets into long-term memory, how it gets retained and consolidated, and how it gets retrieved, are all extremely active areas of research in the brain sciences. Long-term memory is composed of several memory subsystems that provide different capabilities to support different memory functions.

In contrast to sensory memory and working memory, long-term memory has no known capacity or duration limits. No one, to scientists' knowledge, has ever "run out" of long-term memory capacity. Similarly, information stored in long-term memory is surprisingly resistant to decay. One study, for example, found that even 50 years after graduation, people can remember the names of around 90% of their high school classmates from yearbook photos.[25] Although we do tend to forget long-term memories that no longer have personal importance or get "overlaid" by more recent memories, personally relevant memories can easily last a lifetime, even if not accessed over periods of years or decades.

At the highest level, long-term memory can be divided into *declarative* and *nondeclarative* forms of memory.

Declarative memory is "the kind of memory we have in mind when we use the term memory in everyday language."[26] We experience declarative memory as a conscious thought or mental representation of information in working memory.

> As the term implies, declarative memory is experienced as a *recollection*; we can "declare" or describe such memories.

Because information retrieved from declarative memory is consciously available, this system is also called **explicit memory**. There are two main types of declarative or explicit memory.

- **Semantic memory** is memory of facts or beliefs about the world. Knowing that *Tide* is a brand of laundry detergent that usually comes in a bright orange container is a semantic memory. We experience semantic memories as facts or beliefs that we can retrieve on demand, even if we do not have any associated recollection of how or when we learned them.
- **Episodic memory** is a specific recollection of a personal experience. It refers to our ability to re-imagine an event or episode in its original time, place, and context. Episodic memory is *cinematic*; it is consciously available as a kind of "time travel," a mental replay of something we experienced in the past. Remembering the first time you tried to use a clothes washer, put in too

239

much detergent, and flooded the laundry room in your college dorm—that's an episodic memory.

How these two forms of declarative memory interact is a subject of some debate. Brain scientists are still unsure how semantic memories become decontextualized from their episodic origins,[27] but generally agree that *consciousness* and *intention* are defining features of both. Whether retrieving *facts* or *events*, we do so by making a conscious effort to "call up" the memory and transfer it into short-term working memory for further consideration or deliberation. Declarative memory thus operates as part of *System 2* processing in the human brain.

Nondeclarative Memory: Where Experience Goes to Hide

Nondeclarative memory is so named because it is not consciously available and therefore cannot be "declared" or described by the person experiencing it.

> Importantly, nondeclarative memory retrieval is not experienced as conscious recollection. Rather, it may be experienced as a disposition, a part of personality, a preference, or an attitude about the world.

The effects of nondeclarative memory are observable only indirectly, as changes in behavior or performance. Unlike declarative memory, nondeclarative memory is acquired unintentionally and effortlessly. When it influences behavior, it does so without conscious awareness of its existence or its impact. Nondeclarative memory is thus a central mechanism of *System 1* processing. Because it cannot be observed directly, its impact on human behavior can be easily underestimated. As Larry Squire—a leading memory researcher and author of the framework shown in Figure 7—has noted, that would be a mistake:

> *The unconscious status of nondeclarative memory creates some of the mystery of human experience. Here arise the habits and preferences that are inaccessible to conscious recollection, but they nevertheless are shaped by past events, they influence our current behavior and mental life, and they are a fundamental part of who we are.*[28]

Nondeclarative memory is also called ***implicit memory***, because it operates implicitly and undetected. There are four main types of nondeclarative or implicit memory.

- ***Procedural memory*** is "how to" memory expressed in skills and habits. The classic example is memory of how to ride a bicycle. Once the skill is learned, it becomes automatic and can be translated into action with little or no conscious thought. Some procedural memories can be described verbally (how to form a G-chord on a guitar) while others cannot (how to juggle). Although *motor skills* are most often cited as examples of procedural memory, the same mechanisms underlie the formation of *habits* like brushing your teeth before bed, buying popcorn at a movie, or picking out your usual brand of orange juice at the grocery store.

- *Priming* is a form of implicit memory that makes one thought or action more likely to occur if it is preceded or accompanied by another, cognitively connected, thought or action. As we have seen in numerous examples, priming comes in many forms. Depending on the type of priming and the situational context, it can be either a powerful or weak influence on human behavior. Functionally, priming is a distinct memory system that leverages *familiarity* to optimize our ability to "detect, produce, or classify an item based on a recent encounter with the same or related item."[29]

Often misunderstood as a source of persuasion by marketers and market researchers, priming facilitates speed and efficiency of mental processing, but does not change attitudes.

- *Classical conditioning* is an implicit memory system that encodes memories based on repeated co-occurrences of events in the world. Unlike priming, classical conditioning *can* change attitudes. *Evaluative conditioning* (introduced in Chapter 6 and Chapter 9 and discussed in detail in Chapter 13) is a form of classical conditioning that occurs when an initially neutral object, such as a product or brand, is repeatedly paired with a positively-valued object, such as a well-liked person, place, or experience. The effect of the conditioning is to increase *liking* for the initially neutral object, essentially transferring positive valence from the first object to the second, through repeated pairing. As with other forms of nondeclarative memory, classical conditioning can create learning without effort or conscious awareness of the underlying processes.
- *Nonassociative learning* is an implicit memory system that enables learning from repeated or prolonged exposures to a single stimulus. While both priming and conditioning depend on *associative learning*, in that they make or activate connections in memory based on associations between one thing and another, *nonassociative learning* occurs in response to repeated exposure to one thing only. The two main forms of nonassociative learning are *habituation* and *sensitization*. Habituation occurs when the strength or

probability of a response to a stimulus diminishes as the stimulus is repeated or prolonged. An example is habituation to noxious odors, which tend to be acutely sensed when first experienced, but then seem to become less intense over time. Sensitization is the opposite effect; the strength or probability of a response to a stimulus is *amplified* by repeated exposures. Sensitization often involves amplifying responses to other stimuli in addition to the one being repeated. Repetition of a painful stimulus, for example, may intensify one's startle response to an unexpected loud noise.

In addition to operating differently with regard to conscious awareness and intention, declarative and nondeclarative memory systems also produce different kinds of learning. Declarative forms of long-term memory are well suited for rapid learning from specific events (sometimes called *single trial* learning), whereas nondeclarative memory enables slower learning over time and repetition of events.

Interacting together, the three major systems of memory—*sensory, working*, and *long-term*—provide a range of capacities and functions that enable us to remember and learn from the past, apply that knowledge to the present, and anticipate the consequences of our actions in the future. They allow us to perceive the world as a coherent whole, as a reality that has continuity over time. Figure 8 summarizes how brain scientists view the interactions among these three memory systems today, including how we remember and forget information at each stage of the memory process.

Information Flow In and Out of Human Memory

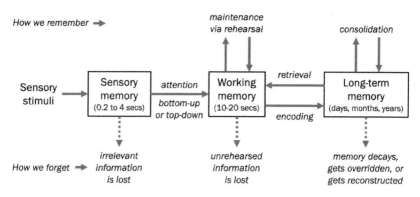

Figure 8. Information Flow through Human Memory Systems

With this basic understanding of human memory systems now encoded into our declarative memory systems, we can turn to the key question of this chapter: How do consumers learn about products and brands, often unconsciously and without effort, and what are the implications of these learning processes for marketing and marketers?

How Implicit Learning Puts Thoughts in Our Heads

Implicit learning is not the same as implicit (nondeclarative) memory. Implicit learning is a form of *memory encoding* that is not consciously experienced. Implicit memory is a *stored result* of either implicit or explicit learning that is not accessible to conscious retrieval.

Implicit learning can occur within implicit memory systems, but it can also occur as a byproduct of explicit knowledge acquisition. For example, within implicit memory systems:

- *Classical conditioning* and *nonassociative learning* are both systems that enable implicit learning.
- *Priming* is not itself a type of learning, but depends on prior learning. It can only operate if either explicit or implicit learning has already taken place to establish a cognitive connection between two concepts or ideas.
- *Procedural memories* are usually learned as a consequence of explicit practice or rehearsal, but once a skill has been mastered, it can be executed with minimal explicit memory involvement.
- *Habits* are usually both acquired and carried out less consciously and explicitly than learned skills, although they can be learned through explicit practice and repetition as well. "Bad habits" also tend to require dedicated conscious effort to break.[30]

Implicit learning can occur as a byproduct of explicit learning because the two main branches of long-term memory enable our brains to record different aspects of the reality we are experiencing. This is a subtle point that marketers often miss.

While explicit learning helps us encode semantic and episodic information about a single object or event (*object recognition*), implicit learning helps us place that object or event in a broader context (*pattern recognition*).

Implicit learning helps us *classify* an object or event, determine its *probability or frequency* of occurrence, establish its *emotional valence*, estimate its *motivational relevance*, and calculate its potential *reward value* (given our immediate and long-term goals and purposes). All these learnings develop unconsciously and incrementally over repeated—not single—exposures. They update the *associations* we attach to an object or event, and they alter the *expectations* we bring to bear the next time we encounter a similar object or event.

When we view marketing in the context of the full *consumer cycle*, we see why incremental, implicit learning of associations and expectations is so important to understanding consumers' deeper relationships with products and brands. As people make multiple journeys through the full cycle of marketing, shopping, and consuming, their learned associations and expectations evolve, often slowly but always cumulatively. This evolution of implicit learning over time is not normally addressed by traditional marketing, which tends to focus on promoting explicit learning from a single marketing message. Intuitive marketing, in contrast, focuses on the depth and direction of implicit learning over cumulative exposures to marketing, shopping, and consuming experiences. Where traditional marketers ask "will *this* ad increase sales?" proponents of intuitive marketing are more likely to ask "how will this ad change or reinforce the associations and expectations consumers bring to their next experience with our product or brand?" For intuitive marketers, it is positive learned associations, not persuasive pitches, that lead to increased sales in the long-run.

Implicit learning was originally discovered by researchers studying language acquisition and recognition. The term *implicit learning* was first coined by psychologist A.S. Reber in 1967, in an article devoted to exploring the question of how humans come to recognize the rules of a language when they cannot explicitly articulate those rules. For example, how do we know that "conler" could be a word in English, but "xzylk" could not? To test whether people were learning language rules implicitly, Reber showed participants a series of "words" between 5 and 8 letters long that consisted of a set of five letters—say M, V, R, X, and T—presented in different orders and combinations. For some participants, these "words" were generated by a hidden logic such as 'words must begin with an M or V' and 'every R must be followed by an X'. For other participants, the words were randomly generated from the five letters with no underlying logic. Following each displayed sequence of letters, participants were asked to guess whether it was a "correct" word or not. What Reber found was that the more words people saw, the better they got at recognizing the grammatically correct ones, whereas their guessing rates did not improve for the random words. When asked to articulate how they knew some words were correct, most people could not do so. They *recognized the pattern*, but they could not consciously *describe the rules* that generated it.[31]

Reber's experiments with artificial grammars showed that human brains can learn not only from single events, but also from patterns and rules hidden in recurring events.

And this learning occurs without any conscious awareness, intention, or effort. Literally, it is learning without trying.

Neuroimaging research has confirmed that explicit and implicit learning depend on different structures and circuits in the brain. Explicit learning—that is, the formation and retention of declarative memories—requires activation of the *hippocampus* and surrounding cortical structures in an area deep in the brain called the *medial temporal lobe* (MTL). This is known because patients with damage to these structures display an inability to form and retain new memories of facts (semantic memory) or events (episodic memory). However, implicit learning of nondeclarative memories by such individuals appears to remain intact. They can learn new habits and procedures, they can be primed, and they can be influenced by classical conditioning.[32]

For many years, implicit learning was defined only negatively. It was learning that did *not* activate the brain structures implicated in explicit learning and was *not* accompanied by conscious awareness of the learning process. But recently a positive definition has emerged. The key element in this definition is *neuroplasticity*, the brain's ability to "rewire" its neural connections adaptively and unconsciously in response to patterns and regularities in experiences over time.

Implicit learning is not a separate learning system located in a specific region of the brain, it is an emergent property of general neuroplasticity.

It's how the brain responds to experience, whether or not explicit learning is occurring as well. As psychologist and leading learning researcher Paul Reber has put it:

> the capacity for changes in functioning reflecting memory are embedded in every circuit and connection in the brain; that is, every neural connection (synapse) has the potential to be adjusted to reflect experience. ... [W]e should expect to find implicit learning and memory phenomena whenever perception and/or actions are repeated so that processing comes to reflect the statistical structure of experience.[33]

This emerging view of implicit learning has several important implications:

- It is a very primitive capability, one we share with all other sentient species.
- It has survived because it is a highly adaptive mechanism that increases our ability to respond successfully to the world around us, even those parts of that world we're not paying conscious attention to.
- It explains how many of the mental mechanisms we have discussed—such as *System 1* thinking, priming, processing fluency, and somatic markers—actually operate in our brains.
- It establishes a neurological foundation for how intuitive marketing works.

We unconsciously treat the influx of marketing messages that bombard us daily as a statistical flow. We do not absorb most ads and marketing messages directly (the exception is when we are in a state of *aligned intent*).

Our capacity for implicit learning records the flow of messages around us, which we automatically and effortlessly classify by type, frequency, positive or negative valence, reward value, and other *natural assessments*, all without conscious awareness.

This is how almost all marketing gets encoded and stored in our long-term memory systems.

Chapter 13

Can Consumers Be Conditioned?

Evaluative Conditioning in the Lab and the Marketplace

"It is beyond dispute that pairing stimuli can result in changes in the liking of those stimuli."
–Jan De Houwer[1]

Implicit learning is an unconscious memory process human beings use to acquire knowledge when they are not explicitly trying to acquire knowledge. When we are not paying attention—when we are distracted, daydreaming, or simply unmotivated to put effort into learning something *explicitly*—our implicit learning processes are still hard at work, observing, recording, classifying, and connecting every sensory experience our conscious mind is deciding to ignore. Much of this input is immediately discarded (see Figure 8 in Chapter 12), but much of it ends up represented in nondeclarative long-term memory, ready to be "brought to mind" when prompted by repetition, a similar circumstance, or an environmental cue.

In this chapter, we consider one of the most important ways consumers learn implicitly and effortlessly: the nondeclarative memory process called *evaluative conditioning*. Operating both above or below our threshold of conscious awareness, evaluative conditioning can contribute in important ways to producing the thoughts and feelings that consumers access when they confront—either reflectively or reflexively—a choice or action in the marketplace.

Evaluative Conditioning: Not So Simple After All

We saw in Chapter 6 that *classical conditioning* was the mechanism Robert Zajonc identified as the basis for his *mere exposure effect*, the nearly universal increase in conscious feelings of liking that results from repetition alone. Scientists use the term *evaluative conditioning (EC)* to describe this particular type of classical conditioning because it involves changing evaluations or attitudes toward things we experience, based on repeated pairing of those things with other things that are already evaluated positively. For Zajonc, repetition alone, *as long as it occurs without any co-occurring negative or aversive consequences*, can produce this EC effect.[2]

Marketers have taken a special interest in evaluative conditioning because it appears to be a simple and painless way to increase liking for products and brands. Although repetition is built into almost every traditional marketing campaign, most marketers do not rely on repetition by itself to build positive feelings toward their offerings. In addition, they are likely to adopt a more direct conditioning approach by repeatedly pairing their product or brand with a second stimulus—perhaps a celebrity, a cute animal, or a happy setting—that is already known to be positively evaluated. In the language of classical conditioning, the product or brand is called the *conditioned stimulus (CS)* and the already-liked object or setting it is paired with is called the *unconditioned stimulus (US)*.

The basic idea is to get some of the positive feelings for the second stimulus (called the *unconditioned response* or *UR*) to "rub off" on the product or brand, producing a *conditioned response (CR)* in which the product or brand becomes more positively evaluated in consumers' minds due to its proximity to the already-liked stimulus. And the mechanism by which this transference of positive feelings occurs is called evaluative conditioning.

Unfortunately, this is about as far as most marketers go in their understanding of how conditioning operates. When we look at the work of brain scientists who have studied evaluative conditioning in depth, we find a much more complex picture of when, where, and how this seemingly simple process of "rubbing off" occurs—and often doesn't. For marketers who want to understand the pros and cons of evaluative conditioning as a source of consumer learning and attitude change, brain scientists have discovered some important complications and limitations that need to be considered.

We have already seen in Chapter 9 that *liking*, at least in the marketing world of products and brands, is predominantly ephemeral, constructed in the moment, sensitive to form and context as well as content, and easily misattributed. Throughout previous chapters, we have seen how liking can be artificially inflated by familiarity, repeated mere exposure, or processing fluency. We have also seen in Chapter 10 and Chapter 11 that lasting positive feelings for products or brands—that is, liking that persists beyond immediate circumstances and marketing "tricks"—is derived and reinforced by *motivational intensity*, which is itself driven by wants and needs of various kinds, the activation of goals to meet those wants and needs, and the successful achievement of those goals. How does evaluative conditioning fit into this mix?

Jan De Houwer is a Belgian psychologist who has devoted over two decades to studying the intricacies and underlying dynamics of implicit learning, conditioning in general, and evaluative conditioning in particular. He has also written extensively about the implications of these processes for marketing and consumer behavior, most directly in a 2007 book chapter titled "*Conditioning as a source of liking: there is nothing simple about it.*"[3] De Houwer begins his overview by emphasizing that evaluative conditioning undeniably exists.

But while its existence may be beyond dispute, there are still many unresolved issues among brain scientists about the processes that produce evaluative conditioning (or fail to produce it), the nature of the evaluative transfer it enables, the permanence or longevity of this effect, and the circumstances under which evaluative conditioning can be undone. All these debates have implications for how and when *EC* can be successfully deployed by marketers to increase liking for their products and brands. As highlighted by De Houwer and others, three types of factors appear to be critical to determining evaluative conditioning success in marketing and consumer contexts:

- How the *CS* and *US* are paired
- Awareness of the *CS-US* pairing
- Prior familiarity with the stimuli being paired

Conditioning Depends on How the CS and US Are Paired

Evaluative conditioning is not a "sure thing." Its success, strength, and longevity can be influenced by a number of *moderators*. As we saw in our review of *behavior priming* in the previous chapter, moderators are variables that can affect the strength of a relationship between a *cause* (in this case, an *EC* procedure in which a CS and US are repeatedly paired in some way) and an *effect* (an increase in liking for the CS based on prior liking of the US). Moderators can determine when an effect will occur and how strong it will be. Order and number of *US-CS* pairings are both known moderators of evaluative conditioning.

Order of CS-US pairing

Several early *EC* studies found conditioned changes in the liking of the CS to be larger when the *CS* consistently preceded the *US* (*forward conditioning*) than when it followed the *US* (*backward conditioning*)[4] A recent meta-analysis of 214 *EC* effects under a wide variety of conditions found similar average effect sizes for forward and backward conditioning, but far fewer studies and a wider range of reported effects for backward conditioning.[5] At a minimum, these results show forward conditioning to be a more reliable *EC* procedure, while not denying that backward conditioning may produce positive results as well, although with less certainty.

Simultaneous presentation of *CS* and *US*—such as superimposing an image of the *US* on a positively-valenced *CS* background image—was also found in the meta-analysis to produce positive average conditioning effects. This result fore-shadows more recent studies that provide intriguing evidence that simultaneous *CS-US* presentation may be necessary for evaluative conditioning to occur outside of conscious awareness.

Number of CS-US pairings

A second potentially important moderator variable is the number of times *CS* and *US* stimuli are paired. Overall, studies have found that evaluative conditioning becomes stronger as the number of *CS-US* pairings increases, but also exhibits a threshold effect: after a certain number of pairings, additional pairings no longer lead to a strengthening of the effect or might even produce a weakening of the effect.[6]

Conditioning Depends on Awareness of CS-US Pairings

A *mediator* is a variable that accounts for (or explains) the relationship between two variables that co-occur, such as *CS-US* conditioning (a presumed cause) and increased liking of the *CS* (an observed effect). A mediator is thus a *necessary condition* for the observed relationship to occur. When the causal impact of a mediator is fully accounted for, the connection between the presumed cause and the observed effect may go away—statisticians say it has been "explained." In contrast, if the effect is still observable when the mediating variable is not present, then that variable is not strictly speaking a mediator; it is rather a *facilitator* that enables and perhaps even enhances the observed effect, but does not constitute a necessary condition for the effect to occur.

By far the most disputed question in EC research is whether a person's conscious awareness of the *CS-US* connection, called *contingency awareness*, is a mediator without which the *EC* effect could not occur. This question has theoretical and practical significance for marketers, because a *yes* answer implies that evaluative conditioning cannot operate through unconscious, automatic, and effortless *System 1* processing; it must be the result of conscious, deliberative, and effortful *System 2* processing.

What is contingency awareness? In a controlled laboratory experiment, contingency awareness exists when participants consciously recognize the *CS-US* pairing pattern being used in the conditioning procedure. This recognition can be confirmed either directly, by asking participants open-ended questions about the relationships they observed, or indirectly, by asking participants to match *CS*s with candidate *US*s that might or might not have been paired with them during the procedure. Whichever method is used, it needs to confirm *which* aspects of the *CS-US* relationship participants are aware of. There are three possibilities:

- They might guess and be aware of the *hypothesis* being tested.
- They might be aware of the *identity* of the paired *US*(s).
- They might be aware of the *valence* of the paired *US*(s).

Awareness of the hypothesis underlying an EC experiment is a danger to experimental validity. If participants are aware of the experiment's purpose, they may conform their answers to what they believe the experimenter wants to hear. This is also called *demand awareness* and is usually grounds for dropping a participant's data from study results.

The other two contingencies participants might be aware of—*US identity* and *US valence*—can influence attitudes toward the *CS* to the extent that participants can make a logical connection between the *CS* and *US*(s). For example, a brand of bottled water might be repeatedly paired with an idyllic image of a pristine mountain stream. If I'm aware of that pairing, I might infer (correctly or not) that the bottled water comes from that pure mountain stream, or is otherwise as pure as I imagine mountain stream water to be. As a result of this reasoning, I might make a *conscious decision* to increase my liking for the brand of bottled water. The key assumption is that I must form a *conscious proposition* about the *CS-US* relationship before that relationship can influence my liking of the *CS*.[7]

There is no question that evaluative conditioning in the presence of contingency awareness can produce real and strong conditioning effects.

Study after study has confirmed that *EC* effects are both larger and more robust when people are contingency-aware than when they are not. In the previously cited meta-analysis, the average *EC* effect was found to be almost three times as large for participants classified as contingency-aware than for contingency-unaware participants.[8]

Despite the fact that evaluative conditioning appears to work best in the presence of contingency awareness, a large number of studies have found that it also works when people are *not* aware of *CS-US* contingencies. Although these effects tend to be smaller than contingency-aware effects, a meta-analysis of 48 samples of contingency-unaware participants found average effect sizes that were significantly greater than zero.[9] These results have two important implications: first, contingency awareness is more likely to be a *facilitator* of evaluative conditioning than a *mediator*; and second, automatic processes do have a role to play in conditioning, making adoption of the *propositional account* of *EC* premature at best.

Recent methodological innovations have given evaluative conditioning researchers new tools for measuring contingency awareness and, more importantly, separating the effects of awareness-based explicit learning from the effects of implicit attitude learning. In a series of studies led by Mandy Hütter and Steven Sweldens, researchers have demonstrated that previous measures of contingency awareness were strongly biased in favor of classifying *EC* effects as contingency-aware, mainly because they failed reliably to separate conscious contingency memory from unconscious conditioned attitudes. Using a new *process dissociation procedure* to separate memory and attitude components of EC effects, Hütter, Sweldens, and colleagues found not only that contingency *unawareness* was much more common in *EC* experiments than previously estimated, but also that *EC* could indeed occur in the absence of contingency awareness.[10]

In a follow-on study,[11] Hütter and Sweldens speculated about the mechanisms and boundary conditions for contingency-unaware *EC*. Using their new method for dissociating effects of memory for the *CS-US* pairings from effects of attitudes conditioned without memory for the pairings, they found evidence for contingency-unaware conditioning when the *CS* and *US* appeared *simultaneously*, but not when they appeared *sequentially*, even when the *CS* preceded the *US* by only half a second. They concluded from this finding that the likely mechanism underlying automatic attitude transfer in evaluative conditioning was *implicit misattribution of evaluative responses*.

Misattribution is a cognitive process we first encountered in Chapter 6 in our review of *processing fluency* and *familiarity*. We also encountered it as central to Robert Zajonc's explanation for the *mere exposure effect*, in which people can mistakenly attribute liking to an object based on repeated exposure alone.

> **Just as people regularly misattribute *familiarity* to something that is processed fluently, or *liking* to something that is experienced repeatedly, it appears they can also misattribute liking for a *CS* that is repeatedly paired with an already-liked *US*, but only if the two are perceived *simultaneously*, not one after the other.**

In presenting these findings, Hütter and Sweldens provided new evidence in support of the *implicit misattribution model*, a theory of evaluative conditioning introduced in 2001 by Michael Olson and Russell Fazio.[12] As noted by Jones, Olson, and Fazio in 2009, the key condition underlying implicit misattribution is *source confusability*—the extent to which liking for the CS might be mistakenly attributed to the US. Source confusability can be varied experimentally to reveal boundary conditions for implicit evaluative conditioning:

> *Broadly, source confusability is high when the CS and US are compatible in the sense that evaluation evoked by the US could plausibly have been evoked by the CS, when the source of the experienced evaluation is ambiguous, and when the CS and US are processed in close temporal continuity. Some minimal level of source confusability is necessary for EC to plausibly occur through implicit misattribution.[13]*

Although the debate over propositional-learning vs. associative-learning accounts of evaluative conditioning continues unabated,[14] this latest round of findings about simultaneous vs. sequential *CS-US* pairing should be of practical interest to marketers. In the absence of attention and contingency awareness, which are often missing when people encounter advertising and marketing messages, marketers can still boost liking for their offerings through evaluative conditioning. To do so, these findings from Hütter and Sweldens suggest the first thing they need to do is present their products or brands simultaneously with the already-liked person, object, or setting, not before or after.

> **In evaluative conditioning without contingency awareness, what leads to source confusability is not *constructing a logical proposition* that one *should* like the CS because one already likes the US. Rather, it is *failing to pay enough attention* to the conditioning procedure to properly differentiate the CS and US as separate stimuli, each with separate emotional associations.**

What gets "confused" is not the logical relationship between the CS and US, but the source of the subjective feeling of liking that is in fact triggered by the US alone, even though the CS is *simultaneously* present.

This explanation has some resonance with Robert Zajonc's finding, discussed in Chapter 6, that the positive feelings produced by the *mere exposure effect* tend to be *diffuse* in that they can influence both general moods and the ratings of other objects in the immediate environment, even when those objects are completely unrelated to the repeated objects *actually* producing the effect.[15] It is possible that what appears to be successful evaluative conditioning in the absence of contingency awareness may in fact be a byproduct of repetitive mere exposure, thus bypassing the awareness requirements that significantly enhance the strength of *EC* effects in most laboratory experiments.[16]

Conditioning Is Inhibited by Prior Familiarity with the *CS*

A final obstacle marketers must face when considering evaluative conditioning as a way to increase liking for their products and brands is substantial evidence that conditioning works best when the *CS* is novel or neutral in valence prior to pairing with the *US*.

Several studies have found that evaluative conditioning does not overcome prior preferences. It is easier to create a new attitude using *EC* than change an existing one.

Significantly, this finding has been reproduced in studies looking directly at evaluative conditioning of attitudes toward brands. In an early but influential study published in 1991, Terence Shimp and colleagues examined *EC* effects for three categories of cola brands: unknown (small regional brands unfamiliar to participants), moderately-known (*RC Cola* and *Shasta Cola*), and well-known (*Coke* and *Pepsi*). Their findings confirmed that *EC* effects were strongest for the unknown and moderately-known brands and weakest for the well-known brands. They ascribed this result for well-known brands to two factors:

First, in line with conditioning-theory predictions, highly familiar brands, such as Coke and Pepsi in the present experiments, are so well-known that little opportunity remains for additional learning and attitude enhancement. Second, the operation of ceiling effects made it unlikely that the conditioning groups' attitudes could be enhanced enough by the CS-US pairings to become significantly more favorable than the control group's already-favorable attitudes. [17]

Neither of these factors would appear to be limited to the soft drink category or to the consumer context of the early 1990s. Indeed, a conceptual replication of this study published in 2008 by Bryan Gibson, again using *Coke* and *Pepsi* as brand stimuli to be conditioned, found similar results. After a pretest that classified participants into three groups—*Coke*-lovers, *Pepsi*-lovers, and *Coke-Pepsi* neutrals—a *simultaneous-presentation-multiple-US* conditioning procedure was carried out. Gibson then looked for changes in both explicit and implicit attitudes, using survey questions to measure the former and an *Implicit Association Test* to measure the latter.

The results both confirmed and extended the 1991 findings. For explicit attitudes, none of the groups showed any effects of conditioning on attitudes. For implicit attitudes, a conditioning effect was observed, but only for participants who were initially neutral with respect to the two cola brands; participants who had prior strong attitudes for one brand vs. the other once again proved impervious to conditioning.[18]

Gibson also looked at whether and under what circumstances conditioning of *implicit attitudes* toward mature brands might have an impact on product selection. In a second experiment, both main findings from the first experiment were replicated: the EC procedure did not change explicit attitudes toward the *Coke* and *Pepsi* brands and only participants who were initially neutral toward the two brands showed any evidence of implicit attitude change. Participants were then given a chance to select a "prize" for their participation—either a can of *Coke* or a can of *Pepsi*. The choice was offered in two ways. Half the participants were simply asked to choose which prize they would prefer. The other half were first asked to memorize an eight-digit number, then make their selection, then repeat the number back to the experimenter. The purpose of the memorization task was to create *cognitive load* to limit the amount of cognitive resources participants could allocate to the choice task.

The results were intriguing. Among participants who displayed implicit attitude change after the conditioning procedure, the distractor task made a difference. For participants who chose under cognitive load, conditioned implicit attitudes successfully predicted their product choices. But for participants who chose without distraction, conditioned implicit attitudes had no effect on their product choices. This finding represents a small ray of hope for evaluative conditioning of attitudes toward well-known brands.

> Although established *explicit* attitudes appear to be impervious to change via conditioning, *implicit* attitudes may be responsive to *EC* procedures and may subsequently influence product purchase decisions, but only when consumers are otherwise distracted or selecting products impulsively rather than deliberatively.[19]

Overall, the prospects for using evaluative conditioning to improve attitudes toward mature brands remains dim. This is largely because mature brands are already deeply embedded in long-term memory and connected to complex webs of associations, beliefs, and feelings that have been built up over years or even a lifetime of journeys through the *consumer cycle*. While *forming* positive attitudes toward a young and unfamiliar product or brand may be quite amenable to evaluative conditioning, *changing* established attitudes toward well-known brands appears to be much harder.

Evaluative Conditioning In the Real World

On the one hand, this review of evaluative conditioning suggests some positive news for marketers: there is solid evidence that liking for brands and products can be facilitated and improved by pairing them with other positive stimuli. This effect appears to be achievable both with and without awareness. On the other hand, evaluative conditioning does not always work, because the process appears to be sensitive to any number of disrupting influences: some situational, some procedural, and some motivational.

Researchers have used cleverly-designed and carefully-controlled laboratory experiments to explore how these influences can interfere with conditioning efforts. But in the real world of marketing practice, where external distractions and internal motivations both remain outside marketers' control, there is more likely to be disruption than facilitation.

> Like other shortcuts to consumer preference and liking we have examined, evaluative conditioning is not a silver bullet for marketers.

Many of the complexities revealed in laboratory studies of *EC* have obvious implications for using *EC* in advertising and marketing. Conditioning consumers in the marketplace is possible, but hardly simple, and is subject to several caveats and limitations that revolve around a wide variety of confounding factors, including order and frequency of presentation, motivational readiness, contingency awareness, and prior familiarity with products or brands being conditioned.

For marketers, these lab results don't easily translate into actionable guidelines for marketing practice. Lab studies are designed to achieve generalizability and reproducibility by carefully controlling or manipulating a multitude of potential external and confounding factors in each experiment. But in the real world of marketing, that control is replaced by countless competing attractions and distractions of the shopping experience. Nothing is controlled, everything is subject to change, and the result is that conditioning effects become must harder to achieve.

> Only a few studies have looked at how conditioning effects might be weakened or extinguished by marketplace *disrupters* following a conditioning procedure.

In one notable example, Steven Sweldens, Stijn Van Osselaer, and Chris Janiszewski published a series of experiments in 2010 that examine three potential disrupters consumers might plausibly encounter in a dynamic marketplace after being conditioned by an advertising or marketing campaign:

- *US reevaluation*: what happens when a US used to condition a product or brand changes its emotional valence from liked to disliked.
- *Retroactive interference*: what happens when encoding new information causes a previously learned association to become less accessible.
- *Persuasion correction*: what happens when a previously learned association is revised or rejected because it is seen as an unsolicited persuasion attempt.

Sweldens and colleagues tested how these disrupters would impact brand evaluations conditioned in different ways. Their baseline experiment involved conditioning an unknown brand of Belgian beer by pairing images of the beer (the CS) with emotionally positive images of people engaged in fun activities (the USs).[20] For one group of participants, the CS and US were presented *sequentially* (first CS, then US), with a half-second delay between them. For others, they were presented *simultaneously*, with the CS image superimposed on the US image. In addition, half the participants saw the CS paired with a *single* US image; the other half saw the CS paired with a rotating series of *different* (but all emotionally positive) US images. To test the effects of these different conditioning procedures, changes in liking for the target Belgian beer were compared to changes in liking for other unknown Belgian beers which were paired with emotionally neutral images. Thus, conditioning was varied across two dimensions: sequential vs. simultaneous CS-US presentation and CS pairing with single vs. multiple USs.

The researchers hypothesized that these different conditioning procedures would all produce positive conditioning, but would do so by engaging *different learning processes*, which in turn would have different implications for post-conditioning effects like US reevaluation, retroactive interference, and persuasion correction. Specifically, they argued that pairing a CS repeatedly with a *single* already-liked US—either sequentially or simultaneously—would produce an *indirect affective response* to the brand in which later exposure to the brand would activate thoughts of the already-liked US, allowing the brand to benefit *indirectly* from the good feelings associated with the US. They further speculated that this type of learning would require *contingency awareness* to operate successfully, because participants could only retrieve a positive response to the brand if they consciously recalled its prior connection with the US.

In contrast to this learning process, Sweldens and colleagues suggested that repeated *simultaneous* pairings of the CS with *multiple* already-liked USs would produce a *direct affective response* to the brand in which the positivity associated with the USs would be transferred *directly* to the brand through the process of misattribution discussed above. Later exposure to the brand would trigger positive feelings without any need to activate thoughts of the *US*s at the same time. Crucially, this type of learning would *not* require contingency awareness to operate successfully, because participants would (mistakenly) attribute their affective response to the brand, without needing to bring the *US* to mind at all. To test these hypotheses, the researchers added each of the three post-conditioning disrupters to their baseline experimental design.

US reevaluation

In Experiment 1, participants completed the baseline conditioning task as described above. To simulate a *US* reevaluation, a second task was added, beginning with a warning that "inconspicuous-looking people can commit serious crimes." After this warning, each *US* image was shown three more times. For some of the pictures—the *to-be-reevaluated US*s—felonies (e.g., murderer, rapist, arsonist) were consistently displayed at the bottom of each image. Other neutral and positive *US*s were also shown three more times, but without an accompanying felony label. The conditioned beer brands were not included in any of these images. Participants were then asked to rate their attitudes toward each of the brands.

For brands paired with *US*s *not* subjected to reevaluation, all four conditioning procedures produced significant conditioning effects. Ratings for brands paired with positive images were higher than ratings for brands paired with neutral images, whether *CS-US* pairings were *sequential* or *simultaneous* and whether brands were paired with *single* or *multiple* positive images.

For brands paired with *US*s that *were* subjected to reevaluation, results differed for different conditioning procedures exactly as predicted by the researchers. When the target brand was paired repeatedly with a *single* positive *US*, the conditioning effect was erased by post-conditioning reevaluation. Brands paired with devalued positive stimuli were found to be less liked than brands paired with non-devalued positive stimuli, and no better liked than control brands paired with neutral *US*s. In contrast, when the target brand was paired *simultaneously* with *multiple* positive *US*s, the original conditioning was not diminished by post-conditioning reevaluation. Brands paired with devalued positive stimuli were liked just as much as brands paired with non-devalued positive stimuli, and remained more liked than control brands paired with neutral *US*s. All these results were consistent with the authors' dual learning process model.

Additional evidence supporting the dual learning process model was obtained from an analysis of *contingency awareness* under the different conditioning procedures. As predicted, contingency awareness was high when the target brand was repeatedly paired with a *single US* scene. The size of the measured *EC* effect was also significantly greater for contingency-aware participants vs. unaware participants. But this often-observed relation between contingency awareness and evaluative conditioning disappeared for participants exposed to the *simultaneous-multiple-US* conditioning procedure. For them, awareness of *CS-US* pairings was not above chance level and had no impact on their brand evaluations. All these results were consistent with the idea that *indirect affective responses* are dependent on contingency awareness but *direct affective responses* are not.

Retrospective interference

In Experiment 2, a different learning task was added after initial conditioning. Participants were asked to learn the names of the brewers of eight new Belgian beers not included among the original conditioning stimuli. This task simulated the kind of retroactive interference people might experience in a real-world encounter with advertising. The results revealed that memory interference disrupted the conditioning effect for participants who were exposed to the *sequential-single-US* conditioning procedure, but failed to do so for those who were exposed to the *simultaneous-multiple-US* procedure.

The authors interpreted this result as more evidence in favor of their dual-learning-processes model. An *indirect affective response* to a brand, they argued, could be disrupted by retroactive interference because it required invoking memories of the liked *US* before the emotional response to the *CS* could be accessed. *That* memory task was disrupted by the second memory task, producing extinction of the *EC* effect. In contrast, *direct affective responses* to the brand did not require accessing memories of the US, so were unaffected by the retroactive interference task.

Persuasion correction

In Experiment 3, a persuasion correction warning was added to the conditioning task. After initial conditioning, participants read a warning reminding them that the positive images they just viewed "contain no valuable information about the taste or quality of the beer." The warning went on to advise participants "not to rely on the pictures the beers were shown with when you determine your attitudes toward the beers."[21]

Some participants were thus explicitly warned to be aware of, and to correct for, any *EC* effect on their brand attitudes. Once again, results varied by conditioning procedure. For participants subjected to *sequential-single-US* conditioning, the persuasion warning lowered the *EC* effect, but did not eliminate it, confirming that *indirect affective responses* to a brand could be mitigated by not extinguished

259

by persuasion resistance. For participants subjected to *simultaneous-multiple-US* conditioning, however, activating persuasion knowledge did not significantly reduce the EC effect. *Direct affective responses* to the brand remained resistant to later persuasion correction.

All of these potential disrupters of evaluative conditioning—US reevaluation, retroactive interference, and persuasion correction—are likely to be found in the real-world marketplace.

Learning, Evaluative Conditioning, and Intuitive Marketing

Several lessons for marketers follow from this extended journey through the annals of evaluative conditioning research. We can summarize them in a series of bullet points:

- *Contingency awareness* is a key variable in creating *EC* effects.
- Conditioning-with-awareness is more likely to succeed when the product or brand appears *before* the already-liked person, place, or thing, rather than after.
- Conditioning-with-awareness is more likely to succeed when a logical proposition can be formed that connects the product or brand to the already-liked stimulus—that is, when the relationship between *CS* and *US* "makes sense." It is less likely to succeed if there is no plausible proposition connecting the *CS* and *US*.
- Conditioning-with-awareness produces stronger EC effects than conditioning-without-awareness. However, it is more susceptible to later *extinction* by post-conditioning disrupters like *US* reevaluation, retrospective interference, or persuasion resistance—all of which can commonly occur in the real-world marketplace.
- Marketers need to recognize that their advertising and marketing efforts will most likely be experienced *without the attention* and *goal-relevance* required to produce contingency-aware conditioning.
- Conditioning-without-awareness is more likely to succeed when the product or brand is presented *simultaneously* with the already-liked stimulus, because simultaneous presentation enhances the possibility of inducing *source confusability* and *misattribution* in the minds of consumers.
- Conditioning-without-awareness does not require the relationship between *CS* and *US* to "make sense" because it does not require forming a conscious proposition that logically and plausibly connects the two stimuli.

- Conditioning-without-awareness produces weaker EC effects and also requires more repetitions to be successful. However, it is less intrusive and less likely to be weakened by post-conditioning disrupters like *US* reevaluation, retrospective interference, or persuasion resistance.
- *Conditioning in general* is less likely to work with mature or well-known products and brands, because it is easier to condition a new attitude than to change an existing attitude.
- Despite strong evidence that conditioning of consumer attitudes can *increase liking* (or disliking) for previously neutral stimuli, there is much less evidence that conditioning can predictably *change behavior* in the marketplace.

Conditioning research provides an important window into the minds of consumers who respond to advertising and marketing in both conscious and unconscious ways. Evaluative conditioning in particular is not a simple process by which positive feelings for people, events, or places can be easily "rubbed off" onto accompanying products or brands. Decades of brain science research have revealed a much more complex story.

Conditioning itself is highly conditional: it occurs or fails to occur under a wide variety circumstances that include the context of the conditioning effort, the conditioning procedure itself, and degree to which the target of conditioning—the consumer—is alert, cognitively engaged, and motivated to embrace the conditioning effect.

Conditioning researchers have established that *EC* can operate through both conscious and unconscious learning processes. Implementing conscious (or contingency-aware) evaluative conditioning shares many underlying principles with the traditional model of persuasive marketing. Attention and propositional reasoning are assumed to be necessary for conditioning to be noticed, absorbed, and later remembered at a point of sale. We have seen that this type of *EC* effect can be achieved regularly and consistently in carefully controlled laboratory experiments, producing what Sweldens and colleagues call an *indirect affective response* to the conditioned stimulus. Outside the lab, however, conscious evaluative conditioning—like persuasive marketing more generally—has also been found to be vulnerable to reversal or extinction due to several circumstances over which marketers have little or no control. The conditions it requires and the mental processing it demands are not always available when advertising and marketing are encountered in the marketplace.

Implementing unconscious (or contingency-unaware) evaluative conditioning shares many underlying principles with the intuitive marketing perspective.

In contrast to contingency-aware evaluative conditioning, contingency-unaware *EC* requires neither attention nor goal-activation to achieve a conditioning effect for a product or brand. It operates more slowly and produces weaker effects than contingency-aware conditioning, but compensates for those limitations by enabling an implicit learning process that is more resistant to extinction and subsequent reevaluation. It produces a *direct affective response* to the conditioned stimulus that does not depend on creating and maintaining a consciously-accessible, ongoing association in declarative memory between the conditioned product or brand and the already-liked *US* with which it is paired in advertising or marketing. We have reviewed several factors that facilitate successful achievement of this type of evaluative conditioning: simultaneous rather than sequential presentation of *CS* and *US*; pairing the *CS* with multiple positive *US*s rather than one; and repeated but nonintrusive pairing of *CS* and *US* over an extended period of time.

Chapter 14

Priming and Knowledge Accessibility

How Priming Brings Knowledge to Mind

"People don't have to think of a brand as being different to come to buy it.
They just have to think of it at all."
–Martin Weigel[1]

In our discussions of the *cognitive timeline*, we picked a convenient starting point—forming an impression—in a sequence of steps that actually represents a continuous loop of mental and physical activity. We entered the timeline by asking what happens when we encounter some stimulus in our environment. But starting at that point runs the risk of making our brains seem more passive and reactive than they really are. Why does *that* impression enter our cognitive timeline? Why not some other aspect of the rich and complex sensory environment we experience at every moment? The answer relies on the fact that our brains are not passive observers, but rather *active predictors* (Chapter 3). We don't just see what happens to be "out there" at a given moment. Thanks to our *unconscious behavioral guidance systems* (Chapter 3 again), we are always anticipating. We see what we want to see and what we need to see. Our attention, whether triggered top-down or bottom-up, is directed at specific features of our environment that past experience tells us can be either beneficial or dangerous to our well-being and continued survival. This is where priming enters the scene.

Priming Brings Learned Associations to Mind

Priming helps us bring to mind—sometimes via *System 1*, sometimes via *System 2*—*stored knowledge* that may help us successfully navigate any situation we find ourselves in.

Learning adds information to our memory systems and connects new information to "old" information already encoded. This occurs through both explicit and implicit modes of learning. Priming is the automatic way we gain access to that information based on our needs and goals at any moment. Learning encodes aspects of new experiences and connects them to prior experiences. Priming facilitates the process of *retrieving* those memories. This is how priming brings learned associations to mind.

> **Priming *biases* one of our most basic cognitive functions: *knowledge accessibility*.**

Here the term *bias* is used statistically, not pejoratively. It simply means that priming is a nondeclarative (implicit) memory function that makes some knowledge stored in our memory systems *more likely to be accessed* at a given point in time than other knowledge, and this happens as a consequence of our rapid and unconscious interpretation of our immediate circumstances (through both *impression formation* and *determining meaning and value*). Biased knowledge accessibility is critically important, because it fundamentally affects how we *use knowledge*—to judge, decide, and act.

Priming as a General Mechanism of Memory Retrieval

When Endel Tulving and Daniel Schacter first introduced the idea of priming as a separate and distinct memory system in 1990, they noted that priming bore similarities to other memory systems already identified, but operated in a unique way to provide a unique function that could not be subsumed under other systems. At that time, three memory systems outlined in Chapter 12 had been identified by memory researchers: the explicit *semantic* and *episodic* memory systems and the implicit *procedural* memory system. Priming shared some features with both procedural and semantic memory:

> *Priming resembles procedural memory in that it enhances perceptual skills. It also resembles semantic memory in that it involves cognitive representations of the world and expresses itself in cognition rather than behavior.*[2]

But priming also appeared to be distinct in several ways. Semantic and episodic memory systems enable constructing and consciously accessing *cognitive representations* of things (semantic) and events (episodic). Priming also operates on cognitive representations, but does so without invoking explicit or conscious recollections of prior knowledge or experiences. Procedural memory resembles priming in that it is also an unconscious memory process, but it lacks the capacity to access cognitive representations of the external world, a key feature of priming.[3]

The purpose and function of the priming memory system identified by Tulving and Schacter remains the centerpiece of our understanding of priming today. As they put it, the function of priming is "to improve identification of perceptual objects."[4] Marketers should take note.

> **Brain scientists believe the purpose of priming as a mechanism of memory retrieval is to improve identification and classification of perceived objects, *not* to increase persuasion.**

In a classic demonstration of priming, if a person is asked to complete a partial word like G R __ __ __ , they are much more likely produce one response if the question is preceded by a list of fruits (apple, pear, banana) and a different response if it is preceded a list of colors (red, blue, yellow). Those prior lists act as primes; they trigger access to cognitive representations associated with each category in semantic memory, producing a bias toward GRAPE in the first instance, and GREEN in the second. In neither case is there any expectation that the priming exercise will produce an increased positive attitude toward either grapes or the color green.

Ever since Tulving and Schacter's initial identification of priming as a separate memory system, memory researchers have expended considerable effort trying to determine the underlying brain processes through which priming operates. The dominant model, which we first encountered in Chapter 2, emphasizes the mechanism of *associative activation*, also called *facilitation* or *spreading activation*. The basic idea is that encoded learnings are stored in long-term memory as nodes in associative networks that connect strongly or weakly to other nodes in constantly growing and highly dynamic configurations. These networks are massive and over-lapping and are built up over a lifetime of learning. When one node is activated by a prime, other nodes connected to it are also activated—at varying levels depending on their *strength of association* with the prime node within the memory network. Originally applied to the processing of semantic knowledge only,[5] the model has since been applied to a much wider range of cognitive representations.[6]

Although more than one version of the associative activation model has been developed, all variants share two common assumptions:

First, priming exerts an influence on judgments and behavior by increasing the accessibility of previously formed concepts and knowledge in memory and, therefore, the likelihood that they will come to mind at the time a target response is generated. Second, primed content is more likely to influence a response when the primed content is relevant to the response (i.e., the primed content is diagnostic).[7]

Central to these models is the principle that the "influence" of a prime on a subsequent response—that is, the likelihood that the primed content will be activated either consciously or unconsciously—is a function of the *strength of association* between that content and the prime preceding it. Strength of association, in turn, can vary from moment to moment depending on a wide variety of both rapidly and slowing changing factors, such as priming frequency, priming recency, the expected usefulness of associated concepts in the current situation, and the immediate and long-term wants, needs, and goals of the person experiencing the prime.[8] Associative activation has also been shown to be sensitive to cognitive load and mental state: individuals are more likely to activate closely associated ideas when they are under time or task pressure, but are more able to access broader and weaker associations when they are in a more relaxed or exploratory state of mind.[9]

Scientists believe priming has evolved as a distinct capability in the human brain because it helps us recognize things that may be beneficial or harmful to us. Priming leverages what we have learned in the past to make some thoughts and actions more accessible in the present.

Importantly, priming does not create preferences, but rather brings *previously learned preferences* to conscious awareness.

When a child hears the sing-song melody of an ice cream truck coming down the street, that sound activates a network of learned associations connected to it. In turn, it makes more accessible in the child's mind a wide variety of knowledge and thoughts about ice cream in general and the approaching ice cream truck in particular. As any parent can attest, the ice-cream-truck melody is very likely to *prime* and make more accessible to the child a *goal construct*—to acquire and consume ice cream—and a supporting *plan of action*—to relentlessly badger Mommy and Daddy until that goal is achieved.

Like conditioning, priming is a much more complex mental phenomenon than it appears to be at first glance, or as it is commonly described in introductory marketing texts. We have encountered several varieties of priming throughout this book. In Chapter 8, we observed *affective priming*, a type of priming in which emotional states are activated by environmental features and past experiences. In Chapter 10, we identified two general classes of priming: *associative* and *motivational*, the former priming *perceptions* or *concepts*, the later priming *goals*. In Chapter 11, we discussed at length how priming can trigger behavior directly via *behavior priming*.

The ubiquity of priming as a feature of so many mental processes—all of which contribute directly or indirectly to consumer choice and behavior—requires us to take another look at all these forms of priming in light of three key questions:

- How are these forms of priming *similar*, in that they are all functions of a single memory system, the nondeclarative system called "priming" by memory researchers?
- How are these forms of priming *different* in terms of how they impact human choice and behavior?
- What are the implications of these different forms of priming for both traditional persuasive marketing and intuitive marketing?

What Priming Primes: Knowledge Content and Cognitive Processes

In a recent comprehensive review of priming as it relates to consumer psychology, Chris Janiszewski and Robert Wyer provide a useful taxonomy of types of priming. They begin by specifying two general categories of priming: *content priming* and *cognitive process priming*. They observe that "Priming occurs because the processing of the prime stimulus makes *content*, and the *cognitive processes* used to comprehend and manipulate this content, more accessible."[10]

Content priming

Content priming is the priming of knowledge or information. Janiszewski and Wyer identify four general types of knowledge that can be stored as nodes in associative networks and primed: *semantic, affective, goal* (motivational), and *behavior* (motor actions). In addition, each of these type of knowledge can be primed either *directly* or *indirectly*. *Direct priming* occurs when a prime increases accessibility to content as a direct consequence of experiencing the prime (*A* primes content *B*, which influences response *C*). *Indirect priming* occurs when a prime increases accessibility to content *associated with* the directly primed content, but it is this associated content, not the directly primed content, that influences a subsequent perception judgment, or overt behavior (*A* primes content *B*, which primes content *C*, which influences response *D*).

Further complicating this picture, content priming can produce effects that are either consistent with the meaning of the prime (called *assimilative* effects) or inconsistent with the meaning of the prime (called *contrast* or *reverse* or *negative priming* effects). For example, in our discussion of *persuasion resistance* in Chapter 4, we reviewed a study by Laran and colleagues in which luxury brand *logos* presented as primes produced *more* expected purchasing in an imagined shopping trip (consistent with the meaning of the primes), but luxury brand *slogans* produced *less* expected purchasing, a reverse priming effect in the second instance and an assimilative priming effect in the first.[11] Anticipating assimilative or reverse content priming effects is one of the thorniest problems facing marketers who want to incorporate priming into their marketing strategies. We take up this problem in a later section of the chapter.

Semantic priming is the priming of non-episodic knowledge and beliefs. Semantic content includes knowledge about persons, events, objects, attributes, and the relations between them. It also includes beliefs about oneself and the world in general, including lessons derived from personal experiences, "naïve theories" of cause and effect (see Chapter 6), beliefs about other people's predispositions and traits, and learned steps required to attain a goal. Semantic priming includes at least three subtypes we have discussed before: *perceptual priming, conceptual priming,* and *trait priming.*

- **Perceptual priming** is a *direct* semantic priming effect that facilitates the identification of repeated or familiar stimuli. Importantly, perceptual priming does not necessarily lead to a subsequent evaluative or behavioral response.
- **Conceptual priming** is an *indirect* semantic priming effect that produces increased accessibility to concepts with associated meanings, like *doctor-nurse, horse-buggy,* or *dog-cat.* The effect is indirect because additional category knowledge must be retrieved before the connection can be activated. Like perceptual priming, conceptual priming does not necessarily lead to a subsequent evaluative or behavioral response.
- **Trait priming** (also called *stereotype activation*) is semantic priming that makes personality or attitude traits of oneself or others more accessible. It can have either direct effects or indirect effects. As an indirect effect, trait priming is more likely than other types of semantic priming to facilitate downstream effects beyond associated meanings, such as subsequent judgments and behaviors.

Our example above ("apple primes grape," "yellow primes green") is an instance of *indirect conceptual prim*ing. Activating the concept "apple" makes the fruit category concept more accessible, thus making "grape" more accessible and more likely to come to mind as a solution to the word completion task G R __ __ __ . If we had preceded our word completion task not with various fruits, but with the word GRAPE repeated many times and the word GREEN repeated fewer times, then completing the task with the word GRAPE would have been an example of *direct perceptual priming;* no intermediate category knowledge retrieval would be required to prime the solution.

Semantic content priming – bringing a unit of knowledge to mind based on exposure to another unit of knowledge – has been found to be a relatively weak and short-lived form of priming. Unlike primed goals, which tend to persist over time, overcome obstacles, and increase in intensity until the goal is achieved, primed semantic representations tend to decay rapidly in memory, are easily overridden or disrupted by subsequent sensory inputs, and appear capable of impacting subsequent judgments or behavior only immediately after priming, if at all.[12] This is why the supposed scourge of innocent consumers – subliminal persuasion – has been found to be surprisingly ineffective when tested in controlled laboratory conditions.[13]

Affective priming is the priming of emotional states. It works based on two assumptions. First, emotions can be represented as semantic concepts in memory networks.[14] And second, thoughts, beliefs, goals, and behaviors that have been experienced alongside emotional states can, through learning, become associated in memory with those emotional states and later act as primes to make those states more accessible.

Direct affective priming occurs when an affective prime makes an affective state, such as a mood or conscious feeling, more accessible. The primed affective state, in turn, can have downstream influence on subsequent judgments and actions. *Indirect affective priming* occurs when an affective state is primed by non-affective knowledge content, such as a thought, goal, or action. Here again, the primed affective state can influence downstream judgments and actions.

An important feature of affective priming is that it does not lead to behavior directly. As we saw in Chapter 8, neither conscious emotion nor unconscious affect are direct causes of behavior. Conscious emotion is best viewed as a source of learning and a guidepost for planning and anticipation. When it does evoke behavior directly, such as when anger leads to a physical attack, the results are usually regrettable. Unconscious affect can only trigger behavior indirectly, by activating a motivational state of wanting or needing. As we saw in Chapter 10, it is motivation, not emotion, that drives behavior, either consciously (through intention) or unconsciously (through activation of the unconscious motivational guidance system).

Goal priming is the priming of goals or motivations to act. Unlike other semantic concepts, goals have a unique property: they can both activate and be activated by motivational states.

Direct goal priming occurs when a goal consciously or unconsciously activates other knowledge concepts related to its attainment, which in turn may stimulate behavior directed toward that end. For example, we saw in Chapter 10 that priming the concept of "prestige" could make a goal to acquire expensive product options more accessible, resulting in a bias toward selecting higher-priced options in a later comparative shopping task.[15] *Indirect goal priming* occurs when nongoal knowledge (semantic, affective, or behavioral) is primed and then spreads to an associated goal through the process of associative activation.

Interestingly, many of the priming studies that have failed replication attempts in recent years (see the *Addendum* to Chapter 11) have been indirect goal priming studies. Prominent among these have been efforts to prime goals with *semantic content*, such as priming a "high performance" goal by exposing people to words associated with "achievement," or priming a goal to perform well on a general knowledge test by priming people to think about the qualities of a generic "professor."[16] Similar failures to replicate have been reported with efforts to prime goals with *behavioral content*, such priming a goal to be physically clean after reading a description of unethical behavior.[17] In contrast, efforts to prime goals with *affective content* have been more robust; for example, numerous studies have replicated the priming effects of positive and negative emotional content on mood-maintenance and mood-repair goals, respectively.[18]

Behavior priming is priming that makes a behavior or physical action more accessible following exposure to an associated prime. Behavior priming is possible because representations of physical behaviors can be encoded as nodes in semantic memory networks. As a consequence, those behavioral representations can be activated by associated cognitive content, including associated semantic, affective, goal, or behavioral knowledge.

Direct behavior priming occurs when observation of a behavior increases accessibility of cognitive representations of that behavior, producing a greater likelihood that recently observed behavior will be replicated in subsequent behavior. Perhaps the best example of direct behavior priming is *mimicry* – the tendency of people to adopt the behaviors, postures, and mannerisms of others with whom they are interacting. Mimicry usually occurs without conscious awareness and has come to be seen as an evolutionary adaptation that facilitates trust, cooperation, and coordination within human groups. Researchers have found that mimicry increases rapport and liking among individuals, but only if the mimicry is not consciously identified as a manipulation tactic. Direct behavior priming via mimicry is one of the most robust and replicated findings in social psychology research.[19]

Indirect behavior priming occurs when the activation of a semantic, affective, or goal prime makes behaviors associated with that prime more accessible and therefore more likely to be performed following exposure to the priming content. Because much of human behavior is goal-directed, indirect behavior priming is often a consequence of indirect goal priming. Goals, in turn, can be primed by any combination of semantic, affective, goal, or behavior priming. This means there may be many intermediate cognitive steps between experiencing a content prime and engaging in a primed behavior.

An inability to reproduce those long strings of contingent steps may help explain the poor replication record of some early indirect behavior priming studies. As Janiszewski and Wyer's model suggests, indirect priming is requires multiple cognitive steps.

> **Humans do not jump from a semantic category like "the elderly" to a behavior like "walking slowly" in a single leap; they must activate a whole sequence of intervening cognitive steps – including, possibly, multiple cascades of semantic, affective, and goal priming – in order to complete the connection.**

Given that any one of those steps could be disrupted by the kinds of moderators and mediators we reviewed in Chapter 11, it should not be too surprising that replicating indirect behavior priming effects is much harder than initially believed.

Cognitive process priming

In addition to making *knowledge content* more accessible, priming can also make *cognitive processes* that *act on knowledge content* more accessible. Cognitive processes in this context are mental operations used to manipulate, transform, or reorganize knowledge or information. For example, we might process new information in a more holistic or piecemeal manner; we might engage in deep vs. superficial information search; we might focus attention on differences vs. similarities in a comparison task; or we might choose to perform a behavior quickly vs. slowly. Any of these cognitive processes can be primed, thereby increasing the likelihood the same process will be used in subsequent content-processing tasks.

Direct process priming occurs when activating a particular cognitive process makes that process more accessible and therefore more likely to be activated in a subsequent task. It is the process itself, not the content it acts on, that functions as the prime. *Indirect process priming* occurs when the prime is not a cognitive process, but the target is. In this case, the prime could be a semantic concept, an affective state, a goal, or a physical action. Any content prime can make a cognitive process more accessible if that process is associated in memory with the content that primes it.

Janiszewski and Wyer's taxonomy of priming variants may be exhausting to wade through, but it provides a useful lesson for marketers and market researchers:

> **Priming is complicated. It is *not* a simple mechanism that can be easily implemented in real-world marketing.**

Some forms of priming are stronger and more robust than others. Some produce longer-lasting effects than others. A single prime can make many different kinds of knowledge content accessible – from semantic concepts to emotional states to motivational goals to plans and actions. Through indirect priming, different types of primes can prime each other, and even do so in a cascade of priming effects, each triggering the next like a row of tumbling dominoes.

Perhaps most significantly, while brain scientists and market researchers may be able to isolate one type of prime and measure its impact on one type of target in a laboratory experiment, marketers must make decisions and implement strategies in a complex, uncontrolled world in which consumers are surrounded by a cacophony of competing marketing messages and potential primes, sponsored by thousands of competing products and brands, all clamoring for attention and consideration across many channels and touchpoints. In such a context, priming is not a simple tool marketers can implement in predictable ways to shape and control consumers' responses to products and brands. Rather, it is an important memory retrieval system that helps determine what knowledge comes to mind, in what contexts, and with what downstream effects on thoughts and actions, as consumers navigate the complex world of products and brands marketers have created for them.

Ultimately, it is *what* knowledge becomes accessible to consumers, not *how* it becomes accessible, that should be the top concern of marketers.

Understanding and Avoiding Reverse Priming

One of the most perplexing features of priming is the fact that similar-appearing primes, of even the same prime, can have opposite or reverse priming effects in different circumstances. Several possible explanations for reverse priming effects have been suggested by priming researchers.

In the Laran priming study discussed in Chapter 4, the authors emphasized the roles of both conscious and unconscious *persuasion resistance* as a source of reverse priming. They demonstrated that people perceived slogans, but not brand names, as having *persuasion intent*, which triggered resistance. When participants were given reasons to think of slogans as creativity efforts, rather than persuasion efforts, the reverse priming effect disappeared. They also found evidence that reverse priming was associated with unconscious goal activation. Testing the hypothesis that slogans triggered an unconscious *bias correction* goal, they found that when participants were provided with an alternative means of satisfying such a goal, the reverse priming effect again disappeared. Finally, they demonstrated that persuasion resistance could be activated without conscious awareness. In a final experiment, they were able to induce reverse priming simply by repeatedly presenting the word "slogan" *subliminally* in the corner of the computer screen while participants read sentences about saving or spending money at the center of the screen. The result was reverse priming when "slogan" was presented and positive priming when a neutral word was presented.[20]

For traditional marketers who view persuasion as the ultimate goal of marketing, these findings raise some red flags. As Laran and co-authors observe when considering the broader implications of their study:

> *It is quite likely that the triggers and consequences of automatic correction are much broader than the current research suggests. For instance, it is plausible that the reverse priming effect documented here is just one of many consequences that would result from correction. Negative evaluations of the marketing tactics involved, or of persuasion tactics in general, are other potential candidates. It is also plausible that slogans are just one of many persuasion tactics that could activate automatic correction. ... This view would predict that persuasion tactics activate a nonconscious goal to correct for bias that not only leads to a reverse priming effect on behavior but also underlies automatic negative effects on attitudes.[21]*

Another factor regularly identified as a source of reverse priming is *awareness of the prime*. For example, in several early studies of priming and evaluative judgment, researchers found a positive (or *assimilative*) priming effect when the prime was not remembered at the time of evaluation, but a reverse priming (or *contrast*) effect when the prime was remembered. Recalling the prime, in turn, was more likely if the priming effort was "blatant"—that is, obvious and easily recognizable as an effort to influence the later judgment task.[22]

This effect has also been found to be influenced by *motivation* and *capacity*. If a person is aware of a priming effort and knows or suspects its purpose is to bias their judgment, there is a higher likelihood they will consciously search for an alternative basis for judgment, resulting in a contrast or reverse effect for the presented prime. This effect, however, is only likely to occur if the primed individuals are both *motivated* and *able* to engage in the required awareness and correction effort. If they are unmotivated or unable to identify an alternative basis for judgment, the prime is more likely to have its expected assimilative effect.[23]

Reverse priming resulting from awareness of the prime depends on the prime being recognized consciously and subjected to a conscious *System 2* deliberative process. It follows that any situational factor that stimulates *System 2* thinking is also more likely to produce contrast vs. assimilative priming effects. One such factor is time. The longer a prime is presented, the greater the likelihood it will attract attention and trigger deeper and more complex processing.

> **Exposing consumers to primes for longer periods of time may increase the risk of reverse priming, an effect that might seem paradoxical to a traditional marketer for whom more exposure is always seen as preferable to less.**

In looking for a more general cause of reverse priming, some researchers have identified the *applicability* or *extremity* of the prime as a critical factor. In one often-cited study by psychologist Paul Herr, participants were primed with either moderately hostile or extremely hostile historical figures and then asked to judge the likely hostility of an ambiguously-described individual. Priming with moderately hostile figures produced the expected positive priming effect, but priming with extremely hostile figures, such as Charles Manson or Adolf Hitler, produced a reverse priming effect, leading Herr to conclude that reverse priming was more likely when the prime represented an exemplar that was outside the range of applicability for the subsequent judgment task.[24]

This effect has also been observed with *extremely positive* primes. In a study led by Michaela Wänke, priming the name of a "star" German politician was found to have a reverse priming effect on ratings of colleague politicians of lesser stature. Interestingly, this reverse priming effect was itself reversed when the shared political party affiliation of the "star" and his colleagues was also made accessible, implying that the inapplicability of an extreme prime can be moderated by directing explicit attention to a category membership shared by the extreme prime and a less-extreme target.[25] This finding highlights the role of *applicability* (or *diagnostic relevance*) in positive priming, as well as its absence in reverse priming. If a shared feature is activated that provides a *rationale* for associating an otherwise inapplicable prime to a target, that inapplicability can be "corrected" as part of the priming process, making the prime less likely to trigger a reverse priming effect on the target perception or behavior.

> **Although *awareness of the prime* requires conscious processing of the prime/target relationship to produce a reverse priming effect, both *bias correction* and *applicability/extremity* as sources of reverse priming have also been found to occur in the absence of conscious intervention.**

Unconscious reverse priming was first observed by psychologists Jack Glaser and Mahzarin Banaji in 1999.[26] Using an implicit affective priming design, Glaser and Banaji exposed participants to two types of *subliminal primes*: relatively neutral words about food (e.g., turnips, pancakes) and words with more extreme positive or negative emotional associations (e.g., heaven, toothache). Following subliminal presentation of these primes, participants were asked to speak aloud a series of positive or negative words that had racial-stereotype connotations (e.g., jazz, slum, hockey, skinhead). This "speak aloud" technique was used to ensure that no conscious evaluative goals were activated by the target task. The dependent measure was the response time required for participants to speak the target word after it appeared on a computer screen. The expected result was for faster response times when prime and target words were emotionally congruent (positive-positive or negative-negative) and slower response times when the prime and target were emotionally incongruent.

While the expected result occurred for most prime-target combinations, a few exceptions stood out. Most prominently, when the target words were race-related, a reverse priming effect was observed for the more emotionally extreme generic word primes, but an assimilative effect was observed for the more neutral food word primes. For example, participants should have responded faster when negative racially-associated target words were preceded by negative prime words (such as toothache-slum or toothache-skinhead), but they did not. Instead, they responded faster for positive-negative and negative-positive combinations than for either of these negative-negative combinations.

After conducting several follow-up experiments to explore these results in more depth, Glaser and Banaji concluded that unconscious reverse priming in their experiments resulted from an *implicit bias correction* process that was triggered by the emotional extremity of the generic word primes, both positive and negative, especially when those words were associated with a positive or negative race-related target word. This correction process appeared to produce an *overcompensation effect* on participants: extreme negative primes ended up acting like positive primes and extreme positive primes ended up acting like negative primes. Thus, both *extreme primes* and *bias correction* were found to operate as unconscious as well as conscious sources of reverse priming.

> Glaser and Banaji showed that reverse priming can be induced by an implicit bias correction process that automatically counters precisely the kinds of persuasion efforts regularly seen in traditional marketing efforts.

This short excursion into the world of reverse priming highlights a significant challenge for practitioners of persuasive marketing—the existence of both conscious and automatic *persuasion resistance* and *bias correction* in consumers' responses to marketing and advertising messages. Like evaluative conditioning, priming is not a simple and foolproof technique for bending the thoughts and actions of consumers to the purposes of marketers. Consumers are not passive observers ready to be triggered and guided by the manipulations of marketing and advertising campaigns; they are active participants who *form impressions, determine meaning and value*, and *unconsciously activate goals* based on every sensory input they experience, including persuasive marketing messages. These unconscious mental processes, in turn, are not conjured up in the moment, they are dependent on learning and memory. Ironically (for marketers), one of the lessons people learn from a lifetime of exposure to marketing and advertising is that persuasive messages often need to be resisted because they are biased to serve the purposes of the messenger, not the recipient.

Priming, Salience, and Knowledge Accessibility

Priming is important to marketers because it influences knowledge accessibility. Every prime consumers are exposed to has a downstream effect on their subsequent thoughts, choices, and actions in ways marketers would like to understand and, if possible, influence. But because any single prime in the real world does not operate in isolation, every priming effort mounted by marketers must contend with other primes also present in the consumer's immediate environment. And those primes are working independently to make more accessible different or even opposing thoughts in the consumer's mind. It is the *cumulative effect* of all these primes, not the isolated impact of any one of them, that influences how consumers respond—and that is true whether the consumer is passively viewing a marketing message, shopping in a stimulus-rich retail environment, or actively using or consuming a product.

Priming in a Noisy World

Real-world priming can be thought of as a competitive battle among many combatants, each trying to influence consumers in a different way. Because associations between nodes of memory cannot be observed directly, researchers typically measure strength of association by observing knowledge accessibility results of various kinds.

The "winner" in a competitive priming contest is usually assumed to be the prime that most closely aligns with the observed response. In contrast to a lab experiment, where it's possible to isolate the effects of a single prime—say, a can of *Pepsi*—the situation when a consumer is standing in front of a grocery store cooler is quite different. In that context, the can of *Pepsi* does not stand alone. It must compete as a prime with the can of *Coke* sitting right next to it, as well as the other 96 varieties of soda displayed in the cooler.

What knowledge comes to mind in such a situation? That's the more general question of *knowledge accessibility* that brain scientists have been contemplating for many decades.

> **Just as evaluative conditioning can be one source of priming, priming can be one source of knowledge accessibility. But it is not the only source.**

To understand how and why knowledge accessibility impacts the many ways consumers interact with marketing, products, and brands, we must return to the concept of *bias*. As partially self-aware human beings, we tend to hold the naïve belief that when we confront a situation requiring a judgment, choice, or action, we bring to mind *all relevant knowledge* applicable to that situation; that is, we access all the knowledge we have at our disposal to understand, diagnose, and select the best path of action in the circumstances we face. But that belief—like many beliefs we hold about how our minds work—is incorrect. The reality confirmed by a substantial body of brain science research is quite different.

> **Our judgments and decisions are typically based on only a small subset of the knowledge we could potentially apply.**[27]

The knowledge that comes to mind when we face a judgment or choice task is the knowledge that *most easily* comes to mind. And what most easily comes to mind is not necessarily the best or most relevant knowledge that *should* come to mind. Rather, it is *biased* by all sorts of factors that a "rational" decision maker would classify as irrelevant or even damaging to a rational choice, such as familiarity, mere exposure, fluency, somatic markers, conditioning, priming, and mood, to name a few. Yet all these factors—and many others—do influence knowledge accessibility in consumer contexts.

> **If marketers want to understand why consumers do what they do and buy what they buy, they must understand how and why *biased knowledge accessibility* enters into consumer judgments, choices, and actions.**

How does knowledge accessibility operate in a context of competing stimuli (and competing primes) like the beverage shopping situation just described? Several discrete steps involving both unconscious and conscious processing are required to fill in the picture.[28] First, knowledge cannot be accessible if it is not available. *Availability* simply means that knowledge must be acquired and stored in memory before it can become accessible. It must have been learned in some way—either explicitly or implicitly. Second, knowledge accessibility needs to be distinguished from *knowledge activation*. To be accessible is to have a *potential for activation* in a given circumstance. To be activated is to literally "come to mind" as an object of conscious *System 2* attention. All available knowledge has more or less potential for activation, which will vary under different conditions and over time. Third, knowledge activation needs to be distinguished from *knowledge use*. The same knowledge that comes to mind as a result of activation may be used differently in different circumstances. Reverse vs. positive priming provides a good example. A prime may make a particular unit of knowledge more accessible, that knowledge may become activated in a given situation, but once activated, the same knowledge may be used in different ways; for example, to facilitate a particular judgement or choice (positive priming), or to resist that judgment or choice (reverse priming).

Salience and Knowledge Activation

Why does one unit of knowledge "win out" over all the other possible candidates to become activated in the presence of a target stimulus or situation? Accessibility is a necessary condition for activation, but it is not sufficient.

> **Researchers view knowledge activation as a function of accessibility plus two additional features: *applicability* and *salience*.**

Knowledge applicability refers to the relation between the features of a stored unit of knowledge and the attended features of a stimulus or situation:

> *The greater is the overlap between the features of some stored knowledge and the attended features of a stimulus, the greater is the applicability of the knowledge to the stimulus and the greater is the likelihood that the knowledge will be activated in the presence of the stimulus.*[29]

Salience refers to those properties of a target stimulus or situation that draw conscious attention. An accessible unit of knowledge becomes more applicable in a given situation, and therefore more likely to be activated, the more it relates to the *salient features* of the target stimulus. Salience in this formulation refers to properties of the target that make it more likely to be noticed and therefore more likely to be brought into conscious awareness. Salience can be broad or narrow, encompassing properties of the target situation as a whole, particular features of the target stimulus, the context within which the target stimulus appears, or relationships among any of these properties.

This definition is similar to the concept of *brand salience* introduced by Andrew Ehrenberg when he observed that increasing salience in the minds of consumers is the most useful function advertising can perform (see Chapter 12). Both definitions regard salience as something that attracts attention, not something that produces liking or preference. Ehrenberg's concept is somewhat broader in that it goes beyond attention to highlight how salience can be enhanced by additional features of a brand, such as its familiarity or trustworthiness.

> For both Ehrenberg and knowledge accessibility researchers, salience is a key variable for understanding the path from knowledge availability to accessibility, applicability, activation, and eventual use as part of a judgment, choice or action.

Contextual Sources of Knowledge Accessibility

It is not possible to cover the full range of factors that can influence knowledge accessibility in consumer contexts, but psychologist Robert Wyer has provided some useful guidelines in a 2008 review of research on this topic, titled *"The Role of Knowledge Accessibility in Cognition and Behavior: Implications for Consumer Information Processing."*[30] Wyer argues that knowledge accessibility and its associated biases can have a significant impact at all stages of consumer judgment and choice; from what aspects of a situation get noticed, to how meaning and value get assigned, to what gets learned and represented in memory, to how inferences and judgments get made, and finally, to what choices get made:

> *Processing at each of these stages typically requires the activation and use of previously acquired concepts and knowledge. Therefore, it may depend in part on which of several potentially relevant subsets of this knowledge happens to be most accessible.*[31]

Wyer organizes his review of knowledge accessibility around four general principles that together provide a useful framework for understanding how and why one knowledge unit gets accessed in a given consumer situation, while others do not. Wyer's principles look beyond *strength of association* as the predominant source of knowledge accessibility to address a key issue:

> What happens when a stimulus is equally associated with more than one concept or unit of knowledge?

Which knowledge "wins out" and comes to mind in such a case? These principles can be thought of as describing the "tie breakers" for knowledge activation when strength of association does not yield a single solution. Each has important implications for marketers and market researchers.

> ***Principle 1.*** *People rarely retrieve and use more knowledge than is necessary to attain the objective they are pursuing. When each of several knowledge representations is sufficient to attain this objective, the first representation that comes to mind is most likely to be applied.*[32]

This principle is a reminder that all human brains are cognitive misers. We prefer to expend no more mental energy on any task than we absolutely have to. When we need to assess our situation or make a decision, we do not conscientiously comb our memories like a detective searching a crime scene, we usually only pick up the first piece of evidence that seems sufficient for the purpose at hand and base our response on that.

For marketers, this principle has two important implications. First, it is crucially important to understand *which* associations immediately come to mind when consumers think about or encounter your product or brand. Often, unless consumers are motivated to engage in more cognitively-taxing *System 2* deliberation and analysis, those initial thoughts will be the ones marketers need to focus on, reinforce in their messaging and, if necessary, replace with more congenial associations. Second, it follows that searching for deeper or more obscure associations with a product or brand, in the hopes of unearthing some connection previously missed, is probably a fool's errand. Rather than going deeper, marketers need to go wider.

In addition to knowing what immediately comes to mind when consumers think about their own brands, marketers should know what comes to mind when consumers think about their competitors' brands, as well as their category as a whole.

If a brand does not have *salient* features that are *distinctive* in its category, no amount of advertising or marketing is going to make it more accessible in consumers' minds than any other brand that provides equivalent features and functionality.

> ***Principle 2.*** *The accessibility of a unit of knowledge in memory is an increasing function of both the recency with which it has been activated in the past and the frequency with which it has been activated. The effect of recency decreases over time, whereas the effect of frequency persists.*[33]

This principle addresses the overriding importance of timing and repetition as sources of knowledge accessibility. When two concepts or units of knowledge are equally applicable in a choice or judgment situation, the one that was most recently activated—even if in a completely unrelated circumstance—is more likely to be activated again. That's the *recency effect*. In the absence of a recency "winner," the concept or knowledge unit that has been most frequently activated in the more distant past is the one most likely to be activated again. That's the *frequency effect*. Frequency and recency both reinforce salience, keeping a brand or product fresh in consumers' minds. Neither needs to invoke persuasion or content differentiation.

> **The lesson is that advertising and marketing budgets may be better spent repeating the message "we're here" than declaring the message "we're different."**

Principle 3. If people have interpreted information on the basis of recently activated concepts and knowledge, the effects of this interpretation on later judgments and decisions about its referent will persist over time.[34]

This principle highlights how learning contributes to the persistence of knowledge accessibility biases. Once a judgment has been made, a representation of that judgment may be stored in memory without an explicit connection to the activated knowledge that contributed to its formulation. Later, that judgment may be retrieved and used as a basis for other judgments and decisions. As a result, any knowledge accessibility bias embedded in the initial judgment may be carried over into subsequent judgments, allowing the initial bias not only to persist, but to do so without conscious awareness. The more times this occurs, the stronger the association becomes, as Wyer's *Principle 2* states.

For marketers, this principle implies a *primacy effect* that can have a significant impact on consumers' evaluations of products and brands over time. It also helps explain why it is so difficult to overthrow a leading brand in an established category. Leading brands usually achieve that status because they have managed to create positive associations with their category before other brands appear on the scene to challenge them. Once such positive associations are established in consumers' minds, leading brands benefit from familiarity and fluency effects and are extremely difficult to displace. Thanks to this primacy effect, learned associations can continue to bias knowledge accessibility in a self-reinforcing way for years or even decades.

Traditional persuasive marketing has no solution to this dilemma for non-leading brands, other than to recommend new and louder ways to persuade consumers to change their minds. As we have seen, this is often self-defeating because consumers are naturally inclined to resist blatant persuasion attempts and discount biased information that conflicts with their currently-active goals and motivations.

Intuitive marketing offers a different approach. Rather than trying to convince consumers to transfer existing associations from a leading brand to a challenger brand, an intuitive marketing strategy would search for new associations not yet "owned" by the leading brand—preferably associations that would align with consumers' natural higher-level goals around aspirations and personal identity (see Chapter 11)—and leverage those associations to establish *new primacy effects* that would benefit knowledge accessibility for the challenger brand at the expense of its competitors.

> **Principle 4.** *Knowledge that becomes accessible in memory for reasons that are unrelated to a judgment or decision will influence this judgment or decision if participants either are unaware of the conditions that activated the knowledge or, alternatively, are unaware of the relation between these conditions and the judgment or decision to be made.*[35]

This principle summarizes the role of *awareness* in determining whether inappropriate knowledge activated at a moment of judgment or choice gets corrected. *Principles 1-3* highlight how easily biased knowledge can be brought to mind when people are faced with an judgment or choice. Under what conditions is such biased knowledge likely to be recognized and corrected? As we saw with evaluative conditioning and priming, awareness of the conditions impacting a memory encoding or retrieval process—in this case knowledge activation—can play a significant role in determining what outcomes that process produces. If people are unaware of why they activated a unit of knowledge as part of a judgment or choice task, they are unlikely to question it, or correct it if necessary. This, in turn, can lead to erroneous judgments or suboptimal choices. We have seen only one exception to this principle: the special case of *unconscious persuasion resistance*, which seems to be an implicitly learned and relatively automatic response to a lifetime of exposure to unwanted persuasion attempts.

Wyer adds a second part to *Principle 4* that is worth considering separately:

> *Even if people are aware of the biasing influence of judgment-irrelevant knowledge, they may not be motivated or able to correct for its influence or, alternatively, may not know how much they should adjust their response to compensate for its effect.*[36]

This statement emphasizes that awareness alone does not guarantee a correction effort even when the knowledge that gets activated is known to be biased. Conscious correction is likely to occur only if an individual is both *motivated* and *able* to apply the cognitive resources required to override or adjust questionable activated knowledge. This means that under conditions that hinder motivation or capability, such time constraints, distractions, or other forms of cognitive load, people will typically fail to correct knowledge that comes to mind, even if they know it is not really relevant or appropriate to the task at hand.

For marketers, understanding how knowledge accessibility impacts consumer evaluations and choices is crucial to understanding how consumers make decisions in the marketplace. Here are some key points marketers need to keep in mind when considering how consumers access knowledge about their products, brands, and marketing messages.

- When making a judgment or choice, consumers generally access only a small portion of the knowledge available to them.
- The knowledge that comes to mind most easily is what gets activated.
- Two factors make knowledge come to mind more easily: the *recency* and *frequency* of prior activations of that knowledge.
- Interpretations based on recently accessed knowledge tend to persist.
- *Primacy* in establishing strong associations with a product or brand can provide a significant marketing advantage.
- Consumers generally *do not recognize* when they apply inappropriate or irrelevant knowledge to a judgment or choice situation.
- Consumers generally *do not correct* the knowledge biases that impact their marketplace judgments or choices.
- When consumers do correct knowledge biases, they usually must be both *motivated* and *able* to do so.

> **Taken together, conditioning, priming, and knowledge accessibility determine what "comes to mind" when consumer choice takes place.**

Conditioning is the cognitive process through which implicit learning can establish and reinforce associations between brands, products, and marketing messages. Priming is the ubiquitous unconscious memory retrieval mechanism through which stored associations can become more accessible and influence downstream consumer responses in both intuitive and counterintuitive ways. Knowledge accessibility can be triggered by priming to make some thoughts more accessible than others. The knowledge that gets activated as a result of conditioning and priming is necessarily partial and may be significantly biased by all the encoding and retrieval processes that precede it.

Chapter 15

The Challenge of Behavioral Economics

Rethinking Rationality in Consumer Behavior

"As we have seen again and again, an important choice is controlled
by an utterly inconsequential feature of the situation"
–Daniel Kahneman[1]

Are consumers rational? For many years, marketers followed the lead of economists and assumed they were. Beginning in the 1950s, a few iconoclastic social scientists began examining whether the behavioral assumptions underlying neoclassical rational choice theories matched how real people thought and acted in real economic situations. Their findings came as something of a shock: people did not act *at all* like rational actors when they made choices. These findings were at first greeted with skepticism, if not downright derision, by classically trained economists. But eventually, they spawned a robust and influential subdiscipline that came to be call *behavioral economics*. In this chapter, we cover the origins and findings of behavioral economics and considers their implications for both traditional and intuitive marketing.

Although behavioral economics reveals unequivocally that people are not consistently *rational* in the pursuit of their interests, this does not mean they are *irrational*, as that term is typically understood. People do, in fact, consistently and methodically pursue their interests, and those interests tend to be overwhelmingly beneficial to them. Even when the *logic* they use in pursuing their desired ends fails to meet the strict criteria of rationality as defined by rational choice theory, the ends they pursue—that is, their goals and objectives—are far from irrational, random, or chaotic. Behavioral economics has taught us that people use *heuristics* rather than strict logic to make most everyday decisions. Heuristics offer a kind of *shortcut logic* that violates the rules of rational choice, but, by and large, makes people predictable and helps them survive and prosper in a complex and demanding world.

Rebels at the Gate: Herbert Simon and James March

The seeds of what later became known as behavioral economics were planted in the late 1950s when social scientists like Herbert Simon and James March began to explore whether the theoretical assumptions of neoclassical economics—assumptions about how people thought and behaved as economic actors—were accurate descriptions of how people actually thought and behaved when they made decisions in the real world. The question these researchers asked was whether economic actors were *rational* in the ways described in economic theory. That definition of rationality was based on a few key assumptions, such as:

- Rational actors have *complete information* about any choice they make, including knowledge of all alternative choices, probabilities of all possible outcomes, and costs and benefits of each alternative.
- Their *preferences are stable* across alternatives, do not change over time, and are *revealed* by the choices they make.
- Their preferences are *consistent across alternatives*: if they prefer *A* to *B* and *B* to *C*, they also prefer *A* to *C*.
- Given complete information, complete alternatives, and stable preferences, rational actors are able to accurately *calculate* or *compute* the relative value or *expected utility* of each alternative available to them.
- Rational actors *always choose and act* in a manner that is consistent with maximizing their expected utility.

Most economists who ascribed to this *expected utility* or *rational choice model* of economic behavior did not claim the model was an accurate depiction of how actual human beings made real-world decisions. They considered the assumptions to be valid and useful because they enabled the construction of hypotheses that (most of the time) yielded accurate predictions about individual-level and market-level behavior. They argued that these predictions were successful because individuals acted *as if* they were behaving in accordance with the assumptions of the model. From their perspective, the rational choice model was never meant to be a realistic depiction of the underlying psychological mechanisms of human behavior; its assumptions were always seen as rationalizations of rational actions, not explanations.[2]

Despite these efforts by rational-choice economists to isolate economics from the messy world of psychology and observable human behavior, some social scientists decided to take a peek anyway. Because these scientists were interested in *describing* economic behavior, rather than *rationalizing* it in terms of a set of abstract assumptions, they came to be known as *behavioral economists*.

The initial shot across the bow of rational choice was fired by economist-political scientist-cognitive psychologist Herbert Simon in his 1955 article, "*A Behavioral Model of Rational Choice*." As the title implied, Simon positioned his critique as a revision within the traditional rational choice model, not as a repudiation:

> *Broadly stated, the task is to replace the global rationality of economic man with a kind of rational behavior that is compatible with the access to information and the computational capacities that are actually possessed by organisms, including man, in the kinds of environments in which such organisms exist.[3]*

Noting that "One is tempted to turn to the literature of psychology for the answer," Simon rejected that idea because he felt psychology did not yet possess the knowledge or theories required to fully explain the mental processes underlying human choice. Instead, he proposed setting down a "marking stone" metaphorically halfway between economics and psychology as a more reasonable goal. His "marking stone" emphasized three major deviations from the rational choice model.

- First, all relevant information is never "known" prior to making a choice. Instead, decision makers gather information in a series of steps that are constrained by time, effort, and cognitive capacity.
- Second, all alternative choices are never "known," nor can they be completely evaluated before a choice is made. Instead, a limited number of alternatives are selected and examined *sequentially* and *incompletely* as part of the choice process.
- Third, decision makers do not have the capacity, knowledge, or skills to perform the complex calculations required to determine the relative value of alternatives available to them. Instead, they use computational *shortcuts* to make a best guess as to which alternative should be selected.

Simon's conception of constrained rational choice was further developed in a book he co-authored with James March in 1958, titled *Organizations*.[4] One of the most influential social science texts of the 20th century, *Organizations* codified Simon's model of rational choice in terms of three ideas: *bounded rationality*, *incomplete information*, and *satisficing*. These concepts would become the foundations upon which modern behavioral economics would be built.

For March and Simon, the "boundedness" of rationality was situational. Complete rationality was inhibited by three factors: the vastness of information and multiplicity of alternatives potentially relevant to any nontrivial choice situation; the limited computational capacity of the human brain to combine, parse, and evaluate all that information; and the inherent limitations of time available to make the decision. Given these constraints, human decision makers had to make choices based on knowledge that was not only partial, but also incomplete in the sense of being ambiguous and uncertain. Simon coined the term *"satisficing"*—a clever mashup of "satisfy" and "suffice"—to describe how decision makers coped in practice with these constraints. Rather than searching for and computing the optimal choice in a given situation, humans typically *satisficed* by searching for alternatives only up to the point at which a sufficient solution, based on the limited information available, was found.

> **Bounded rationality is a theoretically messy but behaviorally realistic model of choice under conditions of incomplete information and limited computational capacity.**

Under these conditions, decision makers tend to make choices by satisficing rather than optimizing. They cope with the complexity and uncertainty of choice by selecting the first alternative that appears to be "good enough" to meet the requirements of the situation.

After writing *Organizations*, Simon's interest in organizational behavior waned as he focused more on cognitive psychology and computer science, where he made major contributions to the fields of artificial intelligence and expert systems. March continued to develop his ideas about bounded rationality and decision making, producing another classic work with Richard Cyert in 1963, *A Behavioral Theory of the Firm*, and several other important contributions to theories of bounded rationality, organizational learning, and human choice throughout the following decades.[5] In a major acknowledgement of the growing importance of behavioral approaches of economic decision-making, Simon was awarded the Nobel Memorial Prize in Economic Science in 1978, the first non-economist to be so honored.

Underlying Simon's formulation of bounded rationality was a belief that humans could and would be more rational if circumstances allowed. Simon held the *normative* view that some type of rationality, however limited by situational complexity, was always to be preferred. This belief was not shared quite so dogmatically by March, who observed that human choice sometimes needed to spring from nonrational sources:

Individuals and organizations need ways of doing things for which they have no good reason. Not always. Not usually. But sometimes. They need to act before they think.[6]

288

As it turned out, March's intuition about the inherent rationality of human choice proved to be more prescient than Simon's.

Pioneers of Intuitive Marketing: Daniel Kahneman and Amos Tversky

Generally considered the fathers of behavioral economics, Daniel Kahneman and Amos Tversky first crossed paths at the Hebrew University of Jerusalem in 1969, when Kahneman invited Tversky to speak to his graduate seminar on *Applications of Psychology*. Tversky at the time held a view of human rationality similar to Simon's: he believed people were basically rational in how they approached choices—at the very least, their naïve reasoning processes were roughly in line with "rational" statistical thinking. In his talk to Kahneman's students, he recounted a series of recent studies at the University of Michigan which seemed to uphold that view.

Kahneman found Tversky's characterization of human decision making shockingly out of touch with his own experience and research results. In Kahneman's view, the subjects described by Tversky were not acting like naïve but essentially rational statisticians at all. Rather, they were *irrationally* jumping to conclusions based on inadequate evidence. And this was the same sin, Kahneman speculated, that the Michigan researchers were committing; they too were jumping to conclusions that fit their "naïve statistician" theory, ignoring what to Kahneman were much bigger and much more consequential implications of their work.[7]

Kahneman and Tversky's first study together was designed to test the Michigan hypothesis that people used a naïve but essentially rational form of statistical reasoning when they made judgments about probabilities and likelihoods. They created a questionnaire in which people had to answer questions that could only be answered correctly with sound statistical reasoning. For example:

The mean IQ of the population of eighth graders in a city is known to be 100. You have selected a random sample of 50 children for a study of educational achievements. The first child tested has an IQ of 150. What do you expect the mean IQ to be for the whole sample?

This question essentially asked people how they would update their estimate of a sample mean based on new information; in this case, one actual data point from the sample. A trained statistician could calculate the correct answer precisely using a formula called *Bayes Theorem*.[8] A non-statistician, reasoning on the basis of an intuitive grasp of probabilities, might not be able to calculate the exact adjustment needed, but they should be able to intuit that this new information demanded an upward adjustment, at least a bit. The correct answer is 101—if one child has an IQ of 150, the sample of 50 is likely to have a slightly higher average IQ than the population as a whole. Only one *wrong answer* was of interest to Kahneman and Tversky. That was 100, the answer that failed to adjust at all for the new information. That answer would represent a non-statistical, non-rational mode of thinking.

Kahneman and Tversky decided to do something subversive. Rather than test their questionnaire on college students, as was the usual procedure for psychology experiments, Tversky gave the questionnaire to *professional statisticians*, first at the 1969 meeting of the American Psychological Association and later at a conference of mathematical psychologists (the most "scientifically sophisticated" psychologists, as they liked to think of themselves). The results were nothing short of jaw-dropping: overwhelmingly, the professionals violated their own expertise; a majority estimated that the sample mean should still be 100.

They presented their results in a 1971 paper titled *"Belief in the Law of Small Numbers,"* a tongue-in-cheek reference to the most well-known principle of modern statistics—the Law of Large Numbers—which states that small samples are less likely to represent true population values than large samples or multiple samples drawn from the same population. They argued that their respondents were ignoring the inherent variability of small samples, assuming that the average for the 50-child sample in the IQ question, for example, would be *representative* of the average for the total population. Even after the one extreme outlier was revealed, they answered the question as if they expected the values to "cancel each other out" as more data was examined. More low values would compensate for the initially observed single high value and the average would settle back to 100.

Judgment Heuristics

The mode of thinking Kahneman and Tversky discovered with their questionnaire needed a name. They called it the *representation hypothesis*. Later, they would call it the *representativeness heuristic*. The name highlighted what seemed to be going on.

> **People, even professional statisticians, were acting as if they thought a sample drawn randomly from a population should *represent*, or *look like*, the population as a whole.**

But that's not how random sampling works. Small samples display random variations compared to a population. Those variations only disappear as the sample size becomes closer and closer to the population size. Even an "intuitive" statistician should have realized that.

With their *"Law of Small Numbers"* paper, the two psychologists presented a new idea that would eventually shake economic thinking to its core. This idea was that errors in thinking like the representative heuristic were not inconsequential momentary mistakes, nor were they mere naïve misunderstandings of randomness; they were fundamental cognitive *biases* to which even highly-trained scientists were susceptible:

> *The true believer in the law of small numbers commits his multitude of sins against the logic of statistical inference in good faith. The representation hypothesis describes a cognitive or perceptual bias, which operates regardless of motivational factors. … His intuitive expectations are governed by a consistent misperception of the world rather than by opportunistic wishful thinking.*

In rapid succession, Kahneman and Tversky produced a series of papers over the next few years that both deepened and expanded their concept of judgment heuristics. In 1972, they published more findings on the representativeness heuristic in a paper titled, *"Subjective Probability: A Judgment of Representativeness."* For example, they reported asking Israeli high school students the following question:

> *All families of six children in a city were surveyed. In 72 families the exact order of births of boys and girls was G B G B B G.*
>
> *What is your estimate of the number of families surveyed in which the exact order of births was B G B B B B?* [9]

When the students answered this question, 80% decided the second sequence was less likely than the first. Why? Because it looked less like a random sequence *should* look. It did not *represent* the image of randomness they had in their heads as well as the first sequence. But in fact, both sequences were equally likely.

Although Kahneman and Tversky discovered representativeness in judgments about random sequences, they quickly determined that the impact of this heuristic on human judgement went far beyond incorrectly understanding randomness.

In *"On the Psychology of Prediction,"* published in 1973, they explored the ways in which the representativeness heuristic influenced how people made predictions in everyday life. A prediction, they wrote, was basically a judgment projected into an uncertain future. When making predictions, people—both naïve and sophisticated in terms of their understanding of statistics—seemed to make the same mistakes they made when judging results of random processes:

In making predictions and judgments under uncertainty, people do not appear to follow the calculus of chance or the statistical theory of prediction. Instead, they rely on a limited number of heuristics which sometimes yield reasonable judgments and sometimes lead to severe and systematic errors.[10]

They found, for example, that predictions were overwhelmingly impacted by vivid anecdotal information, but barely impacted at all by other information of a more statistical nature. Consider the case of "Tom W."

Tom W. is of high intelligence, although lacking in true creativity. Ile has a need for order and clarity, and for neat and tidy systems in which every detail finds its appropriate place. His writing is rather dull and mechanical, occasionally enlivened by somewhat corny puns and by flashes of imagination of the sci-fi type. He has a strong drive for competence. He seems to have little feel and little sympathy for other people and does not enjoy interacting with others. Self-centered, he nonetheless has a deep moral sense.[11]

Undergraduate students at three American universities were told that this assessment was made by a clinical psychologist when Tom was in high school. Asked to predict whether Tom was now a graduate student in computer science, education, or humanities, 95% predicted he was in computer science. Presumably, these students knew there were many more graduate students in education and humanities than in computer science, but they based their predictions not on those known *base rates*, but on the apparent similarities between the description of Tom W. and their (stereotypical) image of a computer geek. In other words, representativeness dominated their predictions and caused them to disregard other, more diagnostic information that should have been easily accessible.

Also in 1973, Kahneman and Tversky introduced a second fundamental heuristic. In "*Availability: A Heuristic for Judging Frequency and Probability*," they showed that representativeness—judging people and predicting outcomes based on similarities to larger categories or processes from which they were derived—was not the only computational shortcut people used to answer difficult questions.

> ***Availability*** **is another simple heuristic based on an equally simple shortcut: things that come to mind quickly or easily are judged to occur more frequently, or with a higher probability, than things that are less mentally available.**

For example, for several letters in the English alphabet, participants were asked to estimate the relative size of two populations: the population of words with the letter in the first position and the population of words with the letter in the third position. The letters chosen by the investigators (K, L, N, R, V) were selected because they were in fact more common in the third position than the first. But because people could much more easily retrieve words from memory based on their first letter, participants significantly overestimated the size of the "first letter" population compared to the "third letter" population. This was the availability heuristic at work:

> *Life-long experience has taught us that instances of large classes are recalled better and faster than instances of less frequent classes, that likely occurrences are easier to imagine than unlikely ones, and that associative connections are strengthened when two events frequently co-occur. Thus, a person could estimate the numerosity of a class, the likelihood of an event, or the frequency of co-occurrences by assessing the ease with which the relevant mental operation of retrieval, construction, or association can be carried out.[12]*

Kahneman and Tversky's next step was to present their findings to a wider audience that extended beyond the readers of specialized psychology journals. For this purpose, they chose the popular and prestigious journal *Science*, where they published "*Judgment under Uncertainty: Heuristics and Biases*" in 1974.[13] This article summarized and provided additional evidence for the representative and availability heuristics. It also introduced a third heuristic, *anchoring*.

Noting that people often make estimates about future or unknown outcomes by starting from an initial value and then adjusting up or down to yield a final answer, Kahneman and Tversky found that the influence of such a starting point was often much greater than expected. Across several experiments, they observed that different starting points for the same estimation problem could yield widely divergent results.

They called this sensitivity to initial values "*anchoring*" because people acted as if they were anchored to the initial value, even when there was no logical reason to do so.

In general, people's adjustments from a given starting point tended to be insufficient. But more problematic for any purely rational account of how people made judgments and choices, Kahneman and Tversky found that even completely irrelevant starting points had a significant anchoring effect on people's estimates.

In one experiment, subjects were randomly assigned a number between 1 and 100 by spinning a wheel of fortune. They then had to answer two questions about the percentage of United Nations members coming from African countries: first, was the actual percentage higher or lower than their randomly assigned number; and second, what would they estimate the correct percentage to be? Even though the wheel-generated numbers had no logical relevance to the second question, they produced significant anchoring effects—subjects who started from 65 on the wheel of fortune, for example, averaged 45% on the second question, while subjects who started from 10 averaged 25%.

After describing the three heuristics and the many biases in thinking they produce, Kahneman and Tversky summarized several conclusions from their research program to date:

- Judgment heuristics produce cognitive biases that are not attributable to motivational effects like wishful thinking or manipulations of incentives.
- The reliance on heuristics and the prevalence of biases are not restricted to statistically-unskilled individuals.
- People are usually not able to detect the biases that influence their judgments of probabilities and likelihoods.
- Judgment heuristics are highly economical in terms of mental effort but lead to systematic and predictable errors that violate basic assumptions of rational choice theory.

Perhaps the most important contribution of this article was its use of the term *heuristics* to express a much more radical notion than Herbert Simon's original concept of *satisficing*. For Kahneman and Tversky, heuristics were not shortcuts to aid computation, but rather fundamental cognitive processes that significantly biased how information (knowledge) was acquired and processed in the first place. Heuristics were the brain's intuitive "first responders" to any situation requiring a judgment or choice.

> Unlike *satisficing*, which Simon saw as a deliberate, conscious strategy for coping with imperfect information, *heuristics* like representativeness, availability, and anchoring were unconscious and uncontrollable processes that inevitably biased judgments in ways that were consistent and therefore predictable.

Although intuitive heuristic responses could be overridden by more effortful deliberation—invoking what Kahneman would later call *System 2* thinking—doing so was neither easy nor natural. In Kahneman and Tversky's formulation, heuristics were basic components of our brains' information processing machinery. They could, with effort, be consciously overridden, but they could not be directly accessed, adjusted, or altered. Kahneman and Tversky's heuristics, unlike Simon's, were not compatible with even a modified form of rational choice or expected utility theory. They were nothing less than an existential threat to the very idea of expected utility.

Prospect Theory

Following the publication of *"Judgment under Uncertainty,"* Kahneman and Tversky shifted their attention from how people make judgments to how they make decisions. In 1979, they published *"Prospect Theory: An Analysis of Decision under Risk"* in the leading economics journal, *Econometrica*.[14] Interestingly, they completed this study in 1975, but it took them four more years to go through a review and editing process before the article was finally accepted for publication.[15] This delay represented, in effect, the extent to which *"Prospect Theory"* challenged a core assumption of neoclassical economic theory—that people made economic decisions among alternative "prospects" (future outcomes) in accordance with the normative rules of rational choice/expected utility theory.

A "decision under risk" is simply a decision for which alternative prospects are known to occur at some probability less than 100%. Technically, it is not the same as a "decision under uncertainty." A "risky" decision is one in which no outcome is certain to occur, but all possible outcomes do occur with known probabilities (for example, a decision to place a bet on "red" or "18" at a roulette wheel). An "uncertain" decision is one in which the probabilities associated with its outcomes, or the possible outcomes themselves, are unknown (for example, a decision whether or not to launch a new product in a new market).

Using hypothetical choice problems similar to those used in their judgment heuristic studies, Kahneman and Tversky showed in *"Prospect Theory"* that when real people make real choices, they regularly violate the assumptions of expected utility theory. And they do so in overwhelming numbers across different countries, education levels, and age groups.

The certainty effect. One violation of expected utility identified in *"Prospect Theory"* was the way in which people responded to certain vs. uncertain outcomes. In multiple examples, people expressed a willingness to accept a lower payoff in exchange for a certain outcome. For example:

Which of the following would you prefer?
A: 4,000 with a probability of .8
B: 3,000 with certainty

Option *A* has an expected value of 3,200 (4,000 x 0.8) and Option *B* has an expected value of 3,000. Expected utility theory says a rational actor should always choose Option *A* over Option *B* because it has a higher expected value. But when Kahneman and Tversky asked this question to college students in Israel, 80% of them chose the certain payoff of *B* to the higher *potential* payoff of *A*. Kahneman and Tversky called this the *certainty effect*.[16]

People consistently overweigh outcomes that are certain, compared to outcomes that are merely probable, even when the latter have an equal or even higher expected value.

The reflection effect. Analyzing responses to a variety of similar choice problems, Kahneman and Tversky identified many more ways that real-world choices violated the principles of rational choice and expected utility theory. For example, they observed what they called a *reflection effect*, in which "the preference between negative prospects is the *mirror image* of the preference between positive prospects."[17] Although expected utility theory states that people should use the same reasoning when choosing between losses or gains, this was found not to be the case. Consider the following pair of questions:

> *Which of the following would you prefer?*
> *A: a 3,000 gain with probability .9*
> *B: a 6,000 gain with probability .45*

> *Which of the following would you prefer?*
> *C: a 3,000 loss with probability .9*
> *D: a 6,000 loss with probability .45*

In both problems, the expected utility of the two options is identical, so people's choices should have divided equally between them. But this is not what happened. In the first problem, 86% of respondents chose Option *A*, demonstrating an "irrational" preference for a smaller gain with a higher probability. In so doing, they ignored the identical expected gain from Option *B*, which offered a larger potential payoff, but at a lower probability.

When choosing between gains, people prefer less riskiness to more, even when the more risky choice offers a larger potential payoff.

Assuming *consistency* with this reasoning, a majority of people should also have chosen Option *C* in the second problem, because it has a higher probability of achieving a smaller loss. But they did not. When choosing between potential losses, 92% chose Option *D*, demonstrating a willingness to risk a greater loss with a higher probability of avoiding the loss altogether.

When choosing between losses, people prefer more riskiness to less, even when the more risky option carries a larger potential loss.

296

The *reflection effect* is one of the most important findings of prospect theory. Contrary to expected utility theory, which assumes people are always risk averse,[18] prospect theory holds that people will be risk-averse only when deciding among prospects that involve gains. When deciding among prospects that involve losses, they are more likely to be risk-seeking.

The isolation effect. Another violation of expected utility theory that emerged from Kahneman and Tversky's hypothetical choice problems was a tendency for most people to discard elements shared by prospects under consideration and base choices exclusively on the distinctive elements in each option. Because elements can be combined or segregated in different ways, this tendency can lead to inconsistent preferences when the same choice is presented in different forms. Kahneman and Tversky provide the following example:

> *Problem 10: Consider the following two-stage game. In the first stage, there is a probability of .75 to end the game without winning anything, and a probability of .25 to move into the second stage. If you reach the second stage you have a choice between:*
> *A: a 4,000 gain with probability .8*
> *B: a 3,000 gain with certainty*

Because the first stage of the problem was shared by both options, respondents tended to ignore it and answer in terms of the second stage only. Accordingly, most people (78%) selected Option *B*, as the *certainly effect* would predict. However, the two stages could also combined into a single choice by multiplying the second-stage prospects by the first-stage probabilities, resulting in a different formulation of the same choice that makes isolation more difficult:

> *C: a 4,000 gain with probability .2*
> *D: a 3,000 gain with a probability of .25*

In this case, a majority of people (65%) chose Option *C*, reversing the stated preferences when the isolation effect was not available to simplify the problem.

The isolation effect can be thought of as a special case of the availability heuristic. People tend to notice and act on information that stands out because it is more available and therefore easier to bring to consciousness.

Gains, losses, and reference points. A final element of expected utility theory that Kahneman and Tversky challenged in *"Prospect Theory"* was the assumption that utility is derived from the *total amount* of an asset held by an individual. According to this logic, if two people each have $100,000 in wealth, they should value that $100,000 equally, regardless of how they acquired it. But suppose Person *A* started with $95,000 in wealth and won $5,000 in a lottery, while Person *B* started with $105,000 in wealth and lost $5,000 in a burglary. Would they *subjectively* value their current total amount of wealth the same? Kahneman and Tversky showed through numerous examples that people do not think that way. Instead, we all seem to think in a way that violates this basic assumption of expected utility theory:

> ... *carriers of value or utility are changes of wealth, rather than final asset-positions that include current wealth.*[19]

To account for these anomalies and provide a coherent framework for understanding and predicting real-world decisions under risk, Kahneman and Tversky introduced prospect theory. Unlike expected utility theory, prospect theory divides the choice process into two phases. In the first phase, called *editing*, people organize and reformulate the available options in order to simplify subsequent evaluation and choice. These operations include both conscious and unconscious processes such as:

- Determining the reference point against which gains and losses will be calculated.
- Combining probabilities associated with the same outcome.
- Segregating risky from riskless components of prospects.
- Discarding components shared by available prospects.
- Simplifying prospects by rounding probabilities of outcomes.

Following the editing phase, decision makers enter the *evaluation* phase, in which they compare the now edited prospects and choose the prospect with the highest calculated value. Evaluation in prospect theory differs from evaluation in expected utility theory in two ways. First, it replaces the concept of "*utility*" with a subjective concept Kahneman and Tversky call "*value*." While *utility* is determined by the total amount of an asset held by an individual, *value* is a function of expected gains and losses from a reference point. *Value* also differs from *utility* in that losses are valued differently than gains. In expected utility theory, positive and negative deviations from a reference point have equal but opposite effects on utility—losing $100 should lower overall utility by the same amount as gaining $100 should increase it. But prospect theory recognizes that people value *avoiding a loss* more than they value *achieving an equivalent gain*. As Kahneman and Tversky put it:

> *The aggravation that one experiences in losing a sum of money appears to be greater than the pleasure associated with gaining the same amount.*[20]

Kahneman and Tversky have illustrated this effect graphically with a "hypothetical value function" like the one shown in Figure 9.[21]

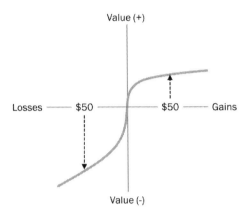

Figure 9. A Hypothetical Value Function

Because losses have greater (negative) value than equivalent gains, the curve is concave in the range of gains and convex in the range of losses. To demonstrate the underlying logic, I've marked a $50 loss and $50 gain on the x-axis. The dotted arrows show the equivalent values as defined by the value curve. Because value decreases more rapidly for losses than it increases for gains, the $50 loss yields a greater negative value than the $50 gain yields a positive value.

The second way prospect theory differs from expected utility theory is in how it treats probabilities attached to outcomes. Expected utility theory assumes that decision makers incorporate probabilities directly and correctly into their evaluations of risky outcomes. In contrast, prospect theory adds "decision weights" to reflect how people actually process probabilities. Decision weights are subjective adjustments people make to objective probabilities. For example, Kahneman and Tversky highlight several decision problems in which people overweight small probabilities and underweight moderate to high probabilities when evaluating alternative choices with different known probabilities.

Taken together, these building blocks of prospect theory add up to a picture of human decision making under risk that differs profoundly from the rational actor/ expected utility model of choice. To readers familiar with Kahneman and Tversky's earlier work on judgment heuristics, this result shouldn't have been surprising. Much of that research revealed how people consistently run into trouble when making judgments and evaluations involving probabilities.

> **"Decision under risk" is basically choosing between prospects with different probabilities (including certainty), so such choices are very likely be influenced by the same cognitive biases that skew logical operations involving probabilities in other contexts.**

Prospect theory adds a number of new considerations to the relatively simple model of rational choice provided by expected utility theory. It paints a more complex, but more descriptively accurate picture of human choice under risk. While expected utility theory simply assumes that decision makers are always risk averse, prospect theory shows how, when, and why that assumption is violated in real-world choices.

In 1981, Kahneman and Tversky returned to the journal *Science* to publish another general report on their work to date. The article, titled *"The Framing of Decisions and the Psychology of Choice"* added an important new element to the lexicon of behavioral economics, the idea of *framing*:

> We use the term "decision frame" to refer to the decision-maker's conception of the acts, outcomes, and contingencies associated with a particular choice. The frame that a decision-maker adopts is controlled partly by the formulation of the problem and partly by the norms, habits, and personal characteristics of the decision-maker.[22]

As this definition emphasizes, a *decision frame* is determined partly by how a decision task is formulated, but also by how that formulation interacts with the full range of traits, predispositions, beliefs, and expectations of the decision maker. While the first part of this definition has been embraced by marketing practitioners, the second part has generally been ignored. This is apparent in how marketing research is commonly conducted today.

> **Many popular market research methods spend considerable time testing alternative presentations of marketing materials, but do so before a general population sample of consumers, as if all consumers are essentially equal in how they respond to marketing messages.**

In contrast, Kahneman and Tversky show that *framing* occurs as much in the minds of consumers as in the configuration of choice opportunities. To illustrate this point, they differentiate between three types of framing that can have significant impacts on how choices are perceived and made.

The framing of acts. Having previously explored the different ways people process gains and losses in choice situations, Kahneman and Tversky investigated how the framing of acts as gains vs. losses could impact people's choices. The effect proved to be significant, as illustrated in the following example:[23]

> *Problem 3: Imagine that you face the following pair of concurrent decisions. First examine both decisions, then indicate the options you prefer.*
>
> *Decision (i). Choose between:*
>   *A. a sure gain of $240*
>   *B. 25% chance to gain $1000, and 75% chance to gain nothing*
>
> *Decision (ii). Choose between:*
>   *C. a sure loss of $750*
>   *D. 75% chance to lose $1000, and 25% chance to lose nothing*

In terms of expected utility, prospect *B* is slightly preferable to prospect *A*, and prospects *C* and *D* are equivalent. But the framing of *Decision (i)* in terms of gains and *Decision (ii)* in terms of losses clearly biased people's choices. In the first case, 84% of respondents chose *A*, "irrationally" sacrificing a slightly more likely gain for the certainty of a "sure thing," as the *certainty effect* would predict. Similarly in the second problem, 87% chose option *D*, "irrationally" accepting a 3-in-4 chance of losing $1,000 in order to avoid the guaranteed loss of $750 in option *C*.

Problem 3 asks respondents to treat these two decisions as a pair. Not surprisingly, 73% of them chose the combination of *A* and *D*. But when the pairs are merged into single prospects, people respond quite differently. The combinations of *A* and *D*, on the one hand, and *B* and *C*, on the other, reduce to these two prospects:

> *Problem 4: Choose between:*
>   *[A+D] 25% chance to win $240, and 75% chance to lose $760.*
>   *[B+C] 25% chance to win $250, and 75% chance to lose $750.*

When framed this way, 100% of respondents chose the second option, reversing the preferences expressed in the first formulation. In addition to showing the power of framing choices as gains vs. losses, these examples provide a good illustration of the *isolation effect*. Few if any people made the cognitive effort to combine the options in *Problem 3*, but when the combination was provided for them in *Problem 4*, they saw the prospects quite differently and chose accordingly.

The framing of contingencies. In Kahneman and Tversky's terminology, contingencies are future events with known (risky) or unknown (uncertain) probabilities of occurring. In prospect theory, people do not process probabilities directly, but rather apply *decision weights* to convert objective probabilities into subjective impressions of contingencies. These adjustments produce predictable biases that alter preferences under different decision frames. One such bias, called the *pseudo-certainty effect*, arises when people perceive an outcome to be certain when it is in fact uncertain.

> **Pseudo-certainty can be induced by framing a risky decision as a two-stage choice in which risk is confined to the first stage (e.g., a 75% chance of reaching the second stage, as in *Problem 10* above) so that the second stage appears to involve certainty.**

When framed as a two-stage decision, pseudo-certainty tends to bias the decision in favor of the erroneously identified certain outcome. This bias disappears when the contingencies are presented in a combined form that reveals the actual degree of risk in each prospect.

The framing of outcomes. People tend to see outcomes as relative gains or losses against some neutral reference point.

> **Changing the reference point through framing can change the perception of an outcome as either a gain or a loss.**

Kahneman and Tversky present several examples in which preferences are reversed when reference points are framed differently. They note that although reference points are fairly easy to determine in simple choice problems, they can be much more complex in real choice situations:

> *A diversity of factors determine the reference outcome in everyday life. The reference outcome is usually a state to which one has adapted; it is sometimes set by social norms and expectations; it sometimes corresponds to a level of aspiration, which may or may not be realistic.*[24]

How different reference points can change the perception of a choice outcome is illustrated by the problem of *sunk costs*. This is a familiar dilemma people face when they must decide whether to hold or sell an investment or asset that is currently worth less than its purchase price. The choice of a reference point in this situation is completely subjective. One can think of the *original purchase price* as the reference point, in which case the sale will be perceived as a loss. Or one can think of one's *current overall asset position* as the reference point, in which case the sale will be perceived as a gain. Expected utility theory says the second way of thinking is the "correct" one, but prospect theory predicts (correctly) that most people find the sunk-cost logic of the first frame difficult to resist, due in part to our demonstrated propensity to prefer avoiding losses over acquiring equivalent gains. In later publications, Kahneman and Tversky give this propensity to avoid losses its own name—*loss aversion.*[25]

Following the publication of "*The Framing of Decisions,*" Kahneman and Tversky continued to publish extensively about both judgment heuristics and prospect theory. However, as Michael Lewis documents in his 2016 biography of the two psychologists, *The Undoing Project*, by the early 1980s they were working largely independently from each other, but still publishing under both names. Influential studies from this period included a major article on loss aversion, written primarily by Tversky,[26] and an article titled "*The Simulation Heuristic*," written mostly be Kahneman.[27] The latter was an exploration of how people construct scenarios, or mental simulations, to estimate the probability of events, imagine the chain of causal connections that might produce them, and anticipate the kinds of emotions they might elicit in response to different outcomes. Like other heuristics, the simulation heuristic is subject to numerous errors and biases, largely due to its dependence on both *availability* and *representativeness* as heuristics for building scenarios to explain past events and predict future outcomes.

Throughout the early 1980s, Kahneman and Tversky began to feel the heat of a "rational backlash" to their work on heuristics and biases. As Tversky told a colleague in 1983: "We started this unknown field. We were shaking trees and challenging the establishment. Now we are the establishment, and people are shaking our tree."[28] Critics[29] objected to the normative implications of their research program, arguing that it painted an exaggerated picture of human fallibility that portrayed humans as incapable of drawing correct inferences or making sound, evidence-based decisions. Some, such as philosopher Max Black, characterized their work as "the psychology of stupid people."[30] These views represented a kind of denial that Kahneman and Tversky found astounding, even irrational, given that their very first experiments on violations of statistical inference had been conducted on professional statisticians.

> **Kahneman and Tversky were discovering that people—often very smart people who should know better—had an irrational need to defend the idea that people must be rational.**

They were also discovering that they had very different personal reactions to their critics, and that those reactions were pulling them apart as collaborators. Kahneman found most criticisms so full of misunderstandings and distortions that he just wanted to ignore them. His default response to criticism was to avoid it. Tversky, in contrast, liked to fight. His preferred reaction, according to Kahneman, was "to crush the opposition." So it was Tversky, not Kahneman, who began working on a paper that he hoped would silence the critics once and for all, by demonstrating just how pervasively judgment heuristics could cause people to violate the most basic principles of logic.[31]

Tversky's paper, to which Kahneman only made minor contributions, examined a statistical principle called the *conjunction rule*. This rule states one of the most self-evident principles of probability—that the probability of two events occurring together can never by higher than the probability of either of them occurring alone. If the probability of prospect *A* is .5 and the probability of prospect *B* is also .5, then the probability of *A* and *B* together must be less than .5. In fact, assuming *A* and *B* are statistically independent of each other, the probability of both occurring can be calculated precisely; it is the product of their individual probabilities, .5 x .5 = .25.

In *"Extensional versus intuitive reasoning: The conjunction fallacy in probability judgment,"* Tversky provided numerous examples of people *not* employing the conjunction principle when reasoning about events.[32] The example that illustrated this most effectively—one of over a dozen in the article—was "the Linda problem:"

> *Linda is 31 years old, single, outspoken and very bright. She majored in philosophy. As a student, she was deeply concerned with issues of discrimination and social justice, and also participated in anti-nuclear demonstrations.*

> *Which of these two alternatives is more probable?*
> *Linda is a bank teller.*
> *Linda is a bank teller and is active in the feminist movement.*

Based on the conjunction rule, the answer is obvious. The probability that Linda is *both* a bank teller and a feminist cannot be greater than the probability that she is a bank teller, because the second alternative is a subset of the first. Whatever the probability that Linda is a bank teller (and the description of Linda is deliberately worded to make that probability seem low), the probability that she is a bank teller and *also* a feminist must be lower. But hundreds of individuals who answered the Linda problem failed to make this logical inference. As Kahneman noted in reviewing the Linda problem and its implications in his 2011 memoir, *Thinking, Fast and Slow*, about 85-90% of undergraduates at several major universities chose the second alternative, in direct violation of the conjunction rule.[33]

Tversky and Kahneman's explanation of the conjunction fallacy focused on how *representativeness* overrides logic when people evaluate the Linda problem and other conjunctive logic tests. Once the *story* of Linda is presented and absorbed by respondents, the logical question at the center of the problem gets elbowed aside by a different goal: to complete the story in the most consistent manner. And the most consistent way to complete the story of Linda is to conclude she is a feminist who just happens to also be a bank teller. Is it more *probable*? No, not recognizing that is a legitimate logical mistake. But is it more *representative* of the picture of Linda sketched by the story? Yes, and that is why great majorities of respondents in multiple experiments ignored logic and opted for the more representative story of Linda, the feminist bank teller.

> **If there is a general lesson here for marketers, it is that people's imaginations are always more easily captured by stories than by logic. Humans are natural story-tellers, if not natural statisticians.**

"The Conjunction Fallacy" did not end the "rational backlash," as Tversky had hoped, but it was widely read and provided additional compelling evidence in favor of the heuristics and biases perspective on human choice.

In 1992, a significant update of prospect theory was published in the *Journal of Risk and Uncertainty* under the title *"Advances in Prospect Theory: Cumulative Representation of Uncertainty."*[34] Written independently by Tversky and graduate student Richard Gonzales, the paper was published under the names of Tversky and Kahneman because, as Gonzales told Michael Lewis, "Amos said that it had always been Kahneman and Tversky and that this had to be Kahneman and Tversky, and that it would be really strange to add a third person to it."[35]

Cumulative prospect theory refined and extended original prospect theory in several ways. It applied to uncertain as well as risky prospects; it extended from two to any number of outcomes; and it allowed different decision weights to be applied to gains vs. losses. It also emphasized two principles to explain the shape of the value and weighting functions that differentiate prospect theory from expected utility theory: *diminishing sensitivity* and *loss aversion*. Tversky defined diminishing sensitivity as the tendency for people to be more sensitive to differences in prospects that are closer to their subjective reference point than more distant. For example, a 10% increase in the probability of winning a prize is more likely to change a person's preference when the probability changes from 90% to 100% than when it changes from 60% to 70% or 30% to 40%. This principle can be seen as a generalization of Kahneman and Tversky's earlier *certainty effect*. Loss aversion, as discussed above, is the principle that losses loom larger than equivalent gains in human decision making.

Tversky summarized cumulative prospect theory's predictions about attitudes toward risk—whether a choice would be risk-averse or risk-seeking—by sketching a *"fourfold pattern"* based on two factors: whether probabilities of outcomes were *low* (less than 10%) vs. *medium to high* (greater than 50%), and whether the options under consideration were seen as *gains* vs. *losses*. Incorporating these factors into a choice equation led to four general predictions about decisions under both risk and uncertainty:

- When choosing between *gains* with *medium to high probabilities*, most people are *risk-averse*. Example: we are more likely to choose a 95% chance to win $10,000 than a 50% chance to win $20,000.
- When choosing between *losses* with *medium to high probabilities*, most people are *risk-seeking*. Example: we are more likely to choose a 50% chance to lose $20,000 than a 95% chance to lose $10,000.
- When choosing between *gains* with *low probabilities*, most people are *risk-seeking*. Example: we are more likely to choose a 1% chance to win $20,000 than a 2% chance to win $10,000.
- When choosing between *losses* with *low probabilities*, most people are *risk-averse*. Example: we are more likely to choose a 2% chance to lose $10,000 than a 1% chance to lose $20,000.

"*Cumulative Prospect Theory*" closed with a direct reply to critics who continued to defend the traditional model of economic rationality as the only way to build a scientific theory for human choice. Prospect theory, Tversky argued, did not make a science of human choice impossible, as some critics claimed. Although human decision making clearly did not follow the logic of expected utility, prospect theory revealed a different kind of logic that led to consistent and predicable behavior, not chaos:

> *Prospect theory departs from the tradition that assumes the rationality of economic agents; it is proposed as a descriptive, not a normative, theory. The idealized assumption of rationality in economic theory is commonly justified on two grounds: the conviction that only rational behavior can survive in a competitive environment, and the fear that any treatment that abandons rationality will be chaotic and intractable. Both arguments are questionable. First, the evidence indicates that people can spend a lifetime in a competitive environment without acquiring a general ability to avoid framing effects or to apply linear decision weights. Second, and perhaps more important, the evidence indicates that human choices are orderly, although not always rational in the traditional sense of this word.[36]*

After Prospect Theory

The immensely consequential collaboration of Kahneman and Tversky came to an abrupt and tragic end in 1996 when 59-year-old Amos Tversky died of a rare form of metastatic melanoma. Kahneman continued to make contributions to the heuristics and biases literature with other co-authors. Particularly influential in the early 2000s was his work with Shane Frederick, a young professor of management at MIT at the time and later Professor of Marketing at Yale School of Management. Kahneman and Frederick's "*Representativeness Revisited: Attribute Substitution in Intuitive Judgment*," published in 2002,[37] was noteworthy as the first Kahneman publication to use the *System 1–System 2* terminology he later popularized in *Thinking, Fast and Slow*.[38] The model provided a useful framework for thinking about three key questions that were emerging as central to the heuristics and biases research program in the new century:

- How do heuristics enter into judgments?
- Why are biases so resistant to detection?
- How and when are errors detected?

Looking at these questions from the perspective of *System 1–System 2* interaction, Kahneman and Frederick proposed for the first time that *System 1* was the intuitive and automatic "first responder" in any judgment situation, while *System 2* was the "monitor" that might or might not detect and correct the results of *System 1* intuitive responses:

> *In the particular dual-process model we assume, System 1 quickly proposes intuitive answers to judgment problems as they arise, and System 2 monitors the quality of these proposals, which it may endorse, correct, or override. The judgments that are eventually expressed are called intuitive if they retain the hypothesized initial proposal without much modification.*[39]

In October 2002, Kahneman learned he had been selected to receive the Nobel Memorial Prize in Economic Sciences. Although the prize was obviously in recognition of his collaborative work with Tversky, Nobel rules dictated that only living recipients could be named as winners, so Kahneman accepted the prize on his own. In his Nobel lecture, published as *"Maps in Bounded Rationality: Psychology for Behavioral Economics*," he generously acknowledged that the work being honored was a joint effort with Tversky, produced "during a long and unusually close collaboration."[40] He also acknowledged other pioneers who had come before him and Tversky, including Herbert Simon, who had incidentally been the first non-economist to win the Nobel Economics Prize in 1978. By referencing *bounded rationality* in the title of his talk, Kahneman connected his and Tversky's work directly to the behavioral choice tradition established by Simon and March in the 1950s.

Kahneman's Nobel Prize was seen by many as the capstone of behavioral economics' rise from fringe rebellion to a core subdiscipline of economics.

The rational choice/expected utility model of economic behavior would never again stand as the pinnacle of economic thought and theory.

Kahneman went on to publish *Thinking, Fast and Slow* in 2011, a summation and popularization of his and Tversky's research on judgement heuristics, choice, happiness, and other topics. The book became a huge success, selling over one million copies in its first year. It has since become perhaps the most influential statement of the behavioral economics perspective, turning concepts like *System 1–System 2*, *judgment heuristics*, and *prospect theory* into a familiar language recognized across the business world, perhaps most prominently—if not always accurately—in the world of marketing theory and practice.

Chapter 16

Ethical Marketing in a Post-Rational World

Behavioral Design, Consumer Well-Being, and Covert Persuasion

"… there is a fine line between using behavioral economics to improve customers' experience and using it to manipulate consumers."
–John Walsh and Valérie Keller-Birrer[1]

Building on the theoretical foundations laid down by Kahneman and Tversky, behavioral economists began exploring the practical implications of heuristics and biases for directly or covertly influencing consumer choice and behavior. Two paths—contradictory in their goals but similar in their methods—have emerged over recent decades. The first, which might be called the *consumer well-being* path, focuses on the idea that behavioral economics can be used to help people make better choices. As summarized by behavioral economist Dan Ariely, the purpose of this approach is to develop "behavioral interventions that help people be happier, healthier, and wealthier."[2] The method of choice, described in detail by Richard Thaler and Cass Sunstein in their 2008 bestseller *Nudge*, is to use *choice architectures* and *behavioral designs* to "nudge" people to overcome various biases that might lead them to make bad decisions:

> *A nudge, as we will use the term, is any aspect of the choice architecture that alters people's behavior in a predictable way without forbidding any options or significantly changing their economic incentives. To count as a mere nudge, the intervention must be easy and cheap to avoid. Nudges are not mandates. Putting the fruit at eye level counts as a nudge. Banning junk food does not.[3]*

The second path, which might be called the *covert persuasion* path, emphasizes how heuristics and biases can be exploited to increase the effectiveness of marketing messages such as online ads and in-store displays. Along this path, the focus has been less on the well-being of the consumer and more on the well-being of the marketer. As noted in Chapter 2, the somewhat reluctant godfather of this approach is Robert Cialdini, whose *Influence: The Psychology of Persuasion*, originally published in 1984, outlined six "weapons of influence" that powered "the pitches of peddlers, fund-raisers, and operators of one sort or another."[4] Although Cialdini's original purpose was to help consumers resist such pitches, his insights were quickly adopted by marketers as techniques for overcoming consumers' resistance to persuasive marketing.

Over time, both marketers and academics have connected many of Cialdini's persuasion techniques with underlying heuristics and biases identified by Kahneman and Tversky. Because those heuristics and biases had been found to operate largely below conscious awareness, using them as tools of persuasion represents a new kind of *covert persuasion*, as opposed to the *overt persuasion* which has dominated marketing and advertising strategies since the birth of the *AIDA* model in the early 20th century (for history and context, see Chapter 1 and Chapter 12).

These two paths differ most significantly in the way they characterize consumer wants, needs, and goals, presenting marketers with a dilemma similar to the ones we observed with regard to *emotional displays* in Chapter 9 and *goal activation* in Chapter 11.

> Marketers can leverage heuristics and biases as a way to help consumers achieve their *intrinsic aspirations* to be happier, healthier, and wealthier, or they can use them as a way to "tip the scales" of consumer choice in favor of their own products or brands.

In the first case they are *compensating for* heuristics and biases that might interfere with consumers' ability to reach their aspirational goals; in the second they are *exploiting* heuristics and biases to shift consumers' goals to the marketer's more immediate and transactional goal—to make a sale. That marketing goal, in turn, may align with the consumer's longer-term aspirations, or it may not.

In order to differentiate their activist and interventionist intentions from those of their theoretical and academic forebears, many advocates and providers of behavioral interventions began calling themselves *behavioral designers*[5] instead of behavioral economists. Behavioral design, whether deployed in the service of consumer well-being or covert persuasion, uses behavioral interventions to achieve the designers objectives. While the two paths differ in the objectives they pursue, they use essentially the same means to get there.

Behavioral Design and Consumer Well-Being

The well-being path is largely aimed at designing *consumer policies* to help people achieve better outcomes when making consumer choices. An early leader in this area was Richard Thaler, a Cornell University and later University of Chicago economist who became interested in both the theory and practice of behavioral economics when he met and worked with Kahneman and Tversky while visiting Stanford University in the late 1970s. Thaler, who had formulated a long list of "anomalies" in human choices and actions that could not be explained by traditional rational choice models, found in Kahneman and Tversky's work not only a theoretical platform that could explain his anomalies, but more importantly, a roadmap that would guide his research interests and output for the rest of his career.[6]

Thaler quickly became one of Kahneman and Tversky's first collaborators and most assertive popularizers within the bastion of economics. Like others who embraced the heuristics and biases perspective, his ideas were at first greeted with skepticism within mainstream economics. But over time, as evidence accumulated and resistance subsided, his persistence paid off. In 2017, Richard Thaler became the third critic of neoclassical rational choice theory to receive the Nobel Memorial Prize in Economic Sciences, following in the footsteps of Herbert Simon in 1978 and Daniel Kahneman in 2002.

Thaler made several independent contributions to the heuristics and biases literature that have had a major impact on the behavioral design and consumer well-being path in behavioral economics. Perhaps most influential was his concept of "mental accounting," introduced in 1985.[7]

> **Thaler recognized that people act differently when they envision financial transactions as belonging to different "bookkeeping buckets."**

His theory of mental accounting applies Kahneman and Tversky's *framing* effect in the domain of money and financial decisions. It highlights the fact that people use and think about financial resources differently when they mentally label them as belonging to different categories or accounts.

Mental accounting is an important aspect of consumer decision making because it has direct implications for behavioral design and consumer well-being. In a 1988 article authored with fellow economist Hersh Shefrin, Thaler showed how people use mental accounts to cope with the perennial problem of consumer *self-control*. In a modern economy in which almost any want or need can be gratified immediately or with minimal delay, short-term gains and benefits often appear as *temptations* that must be resisted in order to achieve longer-term objectives or goals. Classic examples of self-control failures include overspending in the present and undersaving for the future.

Shefrin and Thaler found that people's *marginal propensity to consume (MPC)* could be significantly impacted by the mental account from which money was "drawn." Using a hypothetical choice problem, they asked 122 part-time MBA students how much they would spend over the next year if they received a windfall of $2,400 in three different ways: as $200 per month received over the next year; as a lump sum received today; and as an investment of $2,400 received with interest in five years. The three scenarios were designed to encourage respondents to *frame* the $2,400 windfall as belonging to one of three mental "buckets": *current income, current assets*, or *future assets*. As hypothesized, students' average *MPC* varied substantially across the three mental accounting frames. Respondents estimated they would consume $1,200 from the windfall over the next year when it was assigned to the *current income* account, $785 when it was assigned to the *current assets* account, and $0 when it was assigned to the *future assets* account.[8] This result contrasted quite strikingly with expected utility theory, which assumes that *how money is classified* is irrelevant to *how money is allocated*—in other words, *MPC* should be the same whichever mental account it is placed in.

With regard to self-control and consumer well-being, these results indicate both a behavioral design challenge and a general class of behavioral design solutions. The challenge might be described as follows: Many people do not save enough for retirement; how can they be encouraged to save more? The class of behavioral design solutions might leverage Thaler's finding that some mental accounts (like *current income*) are easier to "invade" than others (like *future assets*) when consumption temptations arise. A behavioral design solution, therefore, might look for ways to make it easier to earmark some percentage of a worker's income as "savings" rather than "discretionary spending." Several such solutions have been proposed and implemented, such as enabling automatic deposits into 401k retirement accounts.

Thaler also discovered and introduced a variant of *loss aversion* he called the *endowment effect*. Based on the observation that people tend to respond to losses differently than they respond to gains, Thaler hypothesized that they would place a higher value on things they already owned than on things they did not yet possess. The hypothesis has been confirmed in numerous experiments and field studies, such as the classic "mug study" in which some participants were asked how much they would pay for a generic coffee mug and others were first given the coffee mug and then asked how much they would accept to give it up. The average *willingness to pay (WTP)* in the first group was around $3, while the average *willingness to accept (WTA)* in the second group was around $7. Simply "owning" the mug increased its value more than twofold, all other factors being held constant.[9]

More recent research has found that physical ownership is not required to invoke an endowment response.

> **Any mental process that connects a product to the self—such as touching it or even imagining owning it—can produce an endowment effect.**[10]

This opens up many implications for consumer behavior and choice, as well as for marketing strategies. We see efforts to leverage endowment effects in many marketing tactics, such as offering free samples, letting consumers handle "demo" products in-store, and presenting expensive products initially without revealing prices or additional fees.

From the point of view of consumer well-being, the endowment effect can often be a hindrance to good decision making. For example, the common practice among investors to "irrationally" refuse to sell a poorly performing stock can be seen, in part, as resulting from the endowment effect of existing ownership. This is also related to another mental accounting "anomaly" identified by Thaler, the *sunk-cost fallacy*, in which people find it difficult to recover from a prior expenditure that failed to meet expectations. Selling that poorly performing stock, for example, means accepting the loss vs. the buying price (the reference point in this case), admitting to an expensive mistake (if only to yourself), and putting the bad decision behind you. As most people have personally experienced, this is often very hard to do.

Although sunk-cost thinking is a powerful motivator, researchers have identified some factors that mitigate its effect. One important moderator is time. The longer the delay between a "bad" acquisition and the act of paying for it, the less likely the acquisition will be seen as a sunk cost.

> **Over time, we come to regret prior decisions less, so they are less likely to influence our current behavior.**

Similarly, "bundling" the payments for multiple transactions—as in a *prix fixe* meal—makes us less likely to treat any individual part of the bundle as a sunk cost. Credit card providers cleverly combine both effects: payment is separated in time from acquisition and acquisitions are bundled together in a single payment. As a consequence, the perceived sunk cost of spending is reduced and consumers tend to spend more when paying with a credit card than when paying with cash.[11]

The sunk-cost fallacy can also be leveraged in the opposite direction to encourage consumer behaviors that may be positive in the long-run but costly in the moment. For example, by adjusting how and when consumers pay for a gym membership, behavioral designers have found they can increase or decrease the vividness of perceived sunk costs and the frequency of visits. When payments are made monthly, rather than annually or semi-annually, people tend to visit the gym more often.[12] In effect, the sunk-cost fallacy is invoked and leveraged to help consumers overcome short-term pain for longer-term gain. From the behavioral designer's perspective, a frequent payment schedule is an intervention that helps consumers overcome short-term laziness to achieve longer-term goals to enhance their overall health and well-being.

If there is a manifesto for the consumer well-being path of behavioral design, it is the book *Nudge*, Thaler's 2008 collaboration with Harvard law professor Cass Sunstein. An expanded version of an earlier article published by Thaler and Sunstein in 2003,[13] *Nudge* makes the case that government-sponsored behavioral interventions are legitimate public policy tools because they enhance the well-being of both individuals and society as a whole. Thaler and Sunstein call the ethical rationale for such interventions *libertarian paternalism*, defined as:

> ... *an approach that preserves freedom of choice but that encourages both private and public institutions to steer people in directions that will promote their own welfare.*[14]

In *Nudge*, they explain further:

> *The libertarian aspect of our strategies lies in the straightforward insistence that, in general, people should be free to do what they like—and to opt out of undesirable arrangements if they want to do so. ...*

> *The paternalistic aspect lies in the claim that it is legitimate for choice architects to try to influence people's behavior in order to make their lives longer, healthier, and better.*[15]

Based on the pathbreaking work of Thaler, Sunstein, and other behavioral economists like Dan Ariely,[16] a formidable movement has emerged that deploys the insights of behavioral economics to design and implement choice architectures in the service of consumer welfare and well-being. These insights have been applied across a wide variety of consumer domains, including but not limited to:

- Consumption and investment decisions
- Retirement savings plans

- Responsible spending and budgeting
- Charitable giving
- Healthy eating
- Physical fitness
- Sustainable energy consumption

As summarized by Lucia Reisch and Min Zhao:

Designing simple heuristics for investment decisions, making it easy and hassle-free to switch energy providers, setting smart defaults for pension schemes, creating useful disclosures of credit card fees and making the healthy or sustainable choice the easy choice by applying smart-choice architecture in restaurants and canteens—these are just a few examples of such policies.[17]

Behavioral Design and Covert Persuasion

A very different mindset informs much of what I've called the *covert persuasion* path of behavioral design. Practitioners of covert persuasion see the purpose of behavioral interventions and choice architectures to be the *control* of consumer buying behavior, not the enhancement of consumer well-being.

> As a marketing strategy, *covert persuasion* uses the heuristics and biases literature as a toolkit of techniques to help marketers achieve the overriding goal of persuasive marketing—to get consumers to do what marketers want them to do.

No doubt enticed by the success of Robert Cialdini's *Influence: The Psychology of Persuasion*, a massive catalog of psychology and marketing books has been published, offering surefire ways to lure others into doing your bidding, whether for the purpose of making a sale, winning a negotiation, or just maintaining an advantage in any interpersonal exchange. Searching for "persuasion methods" in the books section on *Amazon.com*, for example, brings up over 350 books with titles like:

- *Mass persuasion method: activate the 8 psychological switches that make people open their hearts, minds and wallets for you (without knowing why they are doing it)*
- *Banned methods of persuasion: how to covertly convince, influence, persuade, and negotiate with anyone to get them to do what you want*
- *Methods of manipulation: use the psychology of persuasion to analyze & manipulate human behavior*

315

Unfortunately, as these titles hint, this perspective can be accompanied by a somewhat dehumanizing attitude toward the targets of the proposed persuasion techniques. As the author of one "how to" book on persuasion states unambiguously in his introduction:

> *Humans are marionettes. Attached to each of us are sets of strings that, when pulled in a certain direction, guide our behavior without our awareness. If you want to control the strings, then you know how to control behavior. This book teaches you how to control those strings. This book will teach you how to success-fully (and ethically) become a puppeteer in a world full of human marionettes.*[18]

The depiction of humans as marionettes is about as far as one can get from seeing humans as self-motivated agents pursuing their own goals and interests in a complex world. It provides a particularly vivid metaphor for thinking about persuasion as a technique for transferring *control* and *agency* from one person to another. In the marketing domain, that would be from buyer to seller.

Covert persuasive behavioral designs share many features with traditional persuasive marketing, as outlined in Chapter 1. Like traditional persuasion:

- Covert persuasion is transactional rather than relational.
- It assumes we don't want to do what marketers want us to do.
- It uses heuristics and biases to motivate action desired by the marketer.
- It requires replacing any goals currently being pursued by the consumer with a new goal preferred by the behavioral designer.
- It may or may not be in the long-term interest of the consumer.

The two types of persuasion do differ in one important way. Traditional persuasion relies on the *AIDA* model of attention-interest-desire-and-action. Covert persuasion, in contrast, aims directly at producing a motivation to act without necessarily invoking bottom-up attention or logical *if-then* information processing.

Behavioral designs for covert persuasion are most prominent in the world of digital marketing and advertising, but play a large and growing role in real-world, in-store shopping environments as well. The internet is full of articles and blog posts aimed at marketers, promoting "tips and tricks" for pushing consumers toward revenue-generating choices. Many of these articles focus on the process of *conversion*; that is, converting an online viewer or browser into an online buyer. Most of the techniques offered recommend behavioral designs or choice architectures that activate one or more of Cialdini's "weapons of influence." Particularly popular on modern commercial websites are depictions of *scarcity* (e.g., "only one room left at this price" on *Bookings.com*) and *social proof* (e.g., "200 5-star reviews for Tito's Taco Stand" on *Yelp.com*).

These techniques bypass *bottom-up* attention-grabbing because they assume an *aligned-intent motivation* on the part of the site visitor (see Chapter 3). Whether you're reviewing hotel rooms on *Booking.com* or searching for a place to eat lunch on *Yelp.com*, you have voluntarily initiated the choice task, so you are already operating in a state of goal-driven *top-down* attention. Nor does the persuasion effort demand effortful information-processing of the *content* of the item or items you are considering. Rather, your attention is directed by the behavioral design to a *contextual* factor the designer has created for you.

On *Booking.com*, for example, your cognitive miser brain can bypass the difficult task of evaluating and comparing multiple rooms with multiple competing features (location, size, cost, amenities, etc.). Instead, you are offered a much simpler task—pick the room that someone else might grab if you do not grab it first. This is a relatively pure application of two principles from Kahneman and Tversky: replacing a hard question with an easy one, and triggering *loss aversion* to avoid the cognitive pain of losing something you might otherwise gain.

Do these techniques of covert persuasion work? Yes they do. They work because heuristics and biases are ubiquitous, consistent, and accessible in all human brains. They work because we are all susceptible to loss aversion, framing, the endowment effect, and all the other heuristics and biases catalogued by Kahneman and Tversky and the many behavioral economists who have followed them. They work because they take advantage of processes in our brains that *bias* how we think about and respond to choice situations, often in ways that bypass conscious awareness.

But is covert persuasion ethical? That is a more difficult question. The short answer is: it depends.

When Are Behavioral Interventions Ethical?

Richard Thaler got frustrated with how some websites were using his concept of nudging. So in 2015 he wrote an opinion piece in the *New York Times* about what he called "evil nudging."[19] In one example, he recounted his experience with a British newspaper site that had an article he wanted to read, but the article was only available behind a paywall. The paper offered a *one-month-for-£1* subscription, which seemed reasonable, so he decided to subscribe. But then, reading the fine print, he discovered that his credit card would be automatically charged for a "regular" subscription (£26 or $40 per month) at the end of the month if he did not cancel beforehand. Then he read that *to cancel*, he had to do the following: give 15 days' notice; make a telephone call to the newspaper's office in London (he was in Chicago); make that call during British business hours; and accept charges for the call because the number was not toll-free. In essence, the newspaper was "nudging" him into a subscription he did not want, for a product he did not want, in an arrangement from which he would find it very difficult to disentangle himself. Thaler, appropriately, found this nudge unacceptable. He then listed three principles of "nudging for good" that the newspaper's offer violated:

- All nudging should be transparent and never misleading.
- It should be as easy as possible to opt out of the nudge, preferably with as little as one mouse click.
- There should be good reason to believe that the behavior being encouraged will improve the welfare of those being nudged.

While the newspaper's offer may not have been a good example of "nudging for good," it was an excellent example of covert persuasion. It assumed the consumer did not want what it wanted to sell. It focused on a single transaction. It hid the true cost and parameters of its offer behind a veil of "fine print." And its method of persuasion was definitely covert; it nudged the consumer into a "bait and switch" that benefited the newspaper's financial goals at the expense of the consumer's goal to access one article from behind the paper's paywall. Rather than increase the consumer's well-being, the whole episode left the esteemed professor feeling used, manipulated, and angry enough to humiliate the newspaper (by name) in the pages of the *New York Times*. All in all, this was probably not a good outcome for the marketing professional who came up with the subscription scheme in the first place.

Thaler used this article to make a broader point: while *governments* seemed to be scrupulously following his three principles when they applied nudging in public policy contexts, *private companies* were not being so benevolent:

> *As far as I know, the government teams in Britain and the United States that have focused on nudging have followed these guidelines scrupulously. But the private sector is another matter. In this domain, I see much more troubling behavior.*

That behavior, in a nutshell, was this: "Many companies are nudging purely for their own profit and not in customers' best interests."[20] Just as Captain Renault was "shocked ... shocked!" that gambling was going on in Rick's Café in *Casablanca*, so Thaler was shocked that private companies were using the principles of behavioral economics to manipulate consumers into buying things and doing things that they wanted neither to buy nor to do.

Certainly there is nothing wrong with nudging for profit. It's what one should expect from for-profit companies, especially when they are hiring more and more behavioral designers every day. Problems arise when that quest for profits interferes with or diminishes the goals of consumer well-being and welfare. At the societal level—that is, at the level of the marketplace as a whole—that problem is supposed to be addressed by the "guardrails" of national laws and regulations. However, the existence and strength of those guardrails varies from country to country and can even fluctuate from year to year given changes in the ideological orientations of governments. So a certain degree of marketer self-policing and ethical thinking is required.[21]

The question that needs to be asked is not whether covert persuasion makes good business sense, but whether it makes good ethical sense. When is covert persuasion ethically justified and when is it not?

Perhaps not surprisingly, this question has received less attention in both the academic and practical marketing worlds than the far more utilitarian question of how to use behavioral economics and behavioral interventions to get people to do what you want them to do and buy what you want them to buy. But the academic world has not been completely silent on this issue. In 2011, Shlomo Sher, a professor of Humanities and Ethics at the University of Southern California, published a little-read but important piece in the *Journal of Business Ethics* titled "*A framework for assessing immorally manipulative marketing tactics.*"[22]

For Sher, an ethical assessment of marketing tactics revolves around three concepts, *manipulation, deception,* and *moral redemption.* He sees manipulation as a midpoint along a continuum of persuasion tactics that runs from *rational argument* at one end to *coercion* at the other. Rational argument is seen as the gold standard for ethical persuasion because it "respect[s] the interests of the party the marketer is attempting to persuade by not undermining their capacity to make a rational decision through manipulation or deception."[23] At the other endpoint is coercion, a clearly unethical form of persuasion that not only fails to respect a person's capacity to make a rational decision, but presents an "offer" that the recipient must either accept or face consequences so onerous that they virtually guarantee that the offer will be accepted.

Manipulation occupies a wide middle ground between rational argument and coercion that may be judged as ethical or unethical based on certain features of the manipulation attempt. Sher does not embrace the extreme position that rational argument is the only ethical form of persuasion. He argues that manipulation can be ethical in some circumstances, particularly when it is deployed to help people pursue and accomplish their own goals:

> *It seems to me that we can use manipulation benignly to motivate others to pursue the goals they already have.*[24]

319

This position aligns quite closely with the intuitive marketing strategy of *connecting to aspirations and identity*. My argument for that strategy has been largely pragmatic: helping consumers meet their innate aspirational and identity goals can lead to *better outcomes* for both marketers and consumers, because these objectives and strategies enable closer and longer-lasting customer relationships. Sher comes to a similar conclusion, but from an ethical rather than practical starting point. What I call "influence" he calls "benign manipulation," which he sees as an ethical form of manipulation, as do I. What I call "traditional persuasion" is closer to what he calls "manipulation," which by default is *not* benign. Because he is primarily interested in what makes manipulation unethical—or, more broadly, immoral—he offers the following definition of (non-benign) manipulative marketing:

> *A marketing tactic is manipulative if it intends to motivate by undermining what the marketer believes is the audience's normal decision-making process either by deception or by playing on a vulnerability the marketer believes exists in his/her audience's normal decision-making process. Since manipulative action is prima facie wrong, the tactic is immorally manipulative unless it has sufficiently "redemptive" (positive) moral considerations that outweigh what is morally objectionable about the action.*[25]

According to this definition, there are two things that make manipulative marketing unethical: if it is *deceptive* or if it takes advantage of a *vulnerability* in the its audience's normal decision-making process. In turn, there is one thing that can make it ethical in the long run: if it leads to a morally positive outcome that *redeems* the initial use of manipulation. What does this definition tell us about the ethics of covert persuasion via behavioral design?

First, *deception* is not common in behavioral interventions or designs. Sher notes three types of deception: false claims, omitting important facts, and misrepresenting the meaning of facts. None of these are central to the logic of covert persuasion, in part because they all have to do with deceiving the consumer about the *content* of an offering.

Behavioral interventions and designs in general, whether dedicated to enhancing consumer well-being or increasing product sales, are not mechanisms for manipulating *content* claims.

Instead, they are more properly seen as mechanisms for *diverting* consumers' attention from the *content* of an offering to its *form* or *context*. To accomplish this diversion, they exploit consumers' known heuristics and biases with choice architectures and behavioral interventions that contextually nudge consumers toward one behavior or another.

This leads us to consider the second way a marketing manipulation effort can be unethical. Are heuristics and biases *vulnerabilities* in consumers' normal decision making process, or are they simply "normal" aspects of that process? Sher identifies four types of vulnerabilities that, in his view, constitute potential sources of marketing manipulation:[26]

- *Emotional vulnerabilities*, many of them near universal, such as fears of social embarrassments and inadequacies, worries about physical harm, insecurities about physical appearances, and the deep need to feel appreciated and loved.
- *Perceptual vulnerabilities* that distort how we view objects or situations, such as optical illusions that make things seem bigger than they are.
- *Cognitive vulnerabilities* that affect the way we think and remember, such as our use of heuristic generalizations.
- *Ethical failings/character flaws*, such as vanity, greed, and unhealthy obsessions.

Sher's list touches on many of the drivers of consumer choice we have encountered throughout this book. In Chapter 9, we discussed how traditional persuasive marketing can be designed to activate feelings of inadequacy or social embarrassment in order to frame a product as the "solution" to those activated feelings. In Chapter 2, we saw how our built-in *unconscious perceptual guidance system* can have a deep and sometimes misleading impact on the foundational perceptual process of *forming impressions*. In Chapter 10, we examined how *learned needs* can be created through variable-reward systems, sometimes resulting in "unhealthy obsessions" that can have a significant negative impact on personal well-being. Finally, in the series of chapters on learning and memory (Chapter 12), conditioning (Chapter 13), priming and knowledge accessibility (Chapter 14), and behavioral economics (Chapter 15), we identified numerous cognitive processes that could become vulnerabilities if exploited by marketers to meet their own transactional needs at the expense of the longer-term aspirational or identity needs of their consumers.

Here things get tricky. All of these cognitive processes may be "vulnerabilities" as defined by Sher, but they are also *normal* parts of how people think, choose, and act, as revealed by mountains of brain science research.

> **What brain science tells us is that "vulnerabilities" cannot be separated from "normal" decision making processes. All human decisions depend on cognitive processes that may be assets in one context, vulnerabilities in another.**

Take, for example, evaluative conditioning. Is marketing that promotes a product by pairing it with a popular celebrity engaging in unethical manipulation by disrupting its audience's normal decision-making process? We saw in Chapter 13 that conditioning is a *normal* learning process that—importantly—may or may not result in a transfer of liking, based on a number of interacting features of the conditioning process, such as order, familiarity, and awareness. Accordingly, positioning a celebrity next to a bottle of beer in an ad campaign in the hopes of increasing liking for the beer is simply invoking one of the normal ways that people learn associations and change attitudes. I do not believe such a campaign is necessarily unethical, even though it is both *manipulative* and an act of *covert persuasion* designed to automatically and unconsciously manipulate the audience's feelings toward the beer.

Marketing that leverages a specific cognitive process—be it processing fluency, conditioning, priming, a known heuristic or bias, or any other cognitive operation—is not in itself ethical or unethical. The key consideration, as noted earlier, is the purpose with which it is implemented: whether the goals of the seller in deploying this tactic are antithetical to the goals of the buyer. We generally know what the seller's goals are: to sell a product or to get a consumer to engage in some other behavior of benefit to the seller. We also know, at a very high level, what the buyer's goals are: to satisfy wants and needs in a way that strengthens, or at least does not weaken, innate *identity needs* for autonomy, competence, and belonging. With these considerations in mind, we can propose a criterion for determining the ethical or moral status of an act of covert persuasion:

Covert persuasion is unethical if it disrupts, disregards, or attempts to displace a consumer's existing goals with new goals that benefit the seller but do so by damaging the health, wealth, or happiness of the buyer.

In Sher's terminology, an act of covert persuasion with these characteristics is an act of *exploitation* and therefore unethical:

> *What is morally offensive about playing on a vulnerability is the exploitation it is used for.*[27]

The final element in Sher's ethical framework is the question of *redemptive value*. In some cases, he argues, a manipulative act may be unethical on its own terms, but may be *redeemed* if the manipulation enables a greater good to be achieved as a consequence. Such a redemptive value cannot simply be an absence of negative consequences ("it's not illegal!"), but must be the addition of a moral positive:

What, if any, redemptive moral consideration might suffice to make manipulation permissible in a consumer-marketing context? The candidate considerations for redemption are the familiar: those having to do with the beneficial consequences which the act of manipulation is expected to make to the general good, and those pertaining to other, stronger or more numerous, obligations.[28]

Sher suggests four candidate "redemptive values" that might justify an otherwise unethical act of marketing manipulation:

- *The product will benefit the consumer.* This might the justification for automatically enrolling an employee in a 401k plan despite the fact that this lowers their monthly take-home pay.
- *The consumer will not understand why the product is so good without manipulation.* This might be a justification to use manipulation if the seller believes the product has significant benefits for buyers that won't be recognized until after the product is acquired.
- *The marketing tactic (as opposed to the product) will benefit the consumer.* This is essentially the argument in favor of *small emotional rewards* as a source intuitive influence (see Chapter 9).
- *Manipulative marketing can lead to more purchases, which leads to cheaper products, which benefits consumers.* This is a relatively weak justification for marketing manipulation, because the promised benefits are diffuse, in the future, hard to document, and may not reach the individual consumers directly exploited by the manipulation.

Shlomo Sher's analysis of the ethical underpinning of marketing provides a useful framework for assessing the ethics of covert persuasion. Ultimately, the ethical question requires an assessment of both the means and the ends of marketing efforts. The rise of behavioral design as a practical, unobtrusive way to influence consumers brings these issues into sharp relief. Once the myth of the *rational consumer* is dethroned by the reality of the *intuitive consumer*, the idea that nonrational aspects of consumer choice are *vulnerabilities* that interfere with "normal" consumer decision-making becomes problematic as basis for ethical judgment.

Whether or not marketers explicitly target automatic cognitive processes like processing fluency, implicit learning, priming, and the activation of heuristics and biases, those processes are "normal" and deeply embedded in how consumers think and act in the marketplace.

As human beings, we think the way we think. We cannot change the cognitive machinery our evolutionary history has passed down to us. When these processes serve us well, we call them clever decision-making shortcuts. When they sometimes serve us poorly, we call them biases and vulnerabilities. But they are inherently neither. It is the *ends* to which they are put, not the *means* by which they are invoked, that determines their ethical status.

> **In the final analysis, the ethical status of covert persuasion hinges on the marketer's *intent*.**

To the extent it is designed to meet the marketer's goals *at the expense of* the consumer's goals, covert persuasion is exploitative and unethical. Conversely, a behavioral intervention designed to benefit the consumer as well as the marketer may generate enough redemptive value to compensate for the original manipulation.

This formulation is relatively clear and easy to apply. But it does leave us with one last question: Why would a marketer want to implement a marketing tactic that lures customers into behaviors that disrupt, disregard, or displace their deepest needs and aspirations? In Robert Cialdini's memorable language, why would a marketer want to treat consumers as "patsies"? I can imagine two possible reasons.

First, marketers may simply be unaware of any alternative way to think about—or do—marketing. As we have seen, the view of marketing as *nothing more* than transactional persuasion is deeply embedded in how marketing is taught in undergraduate and graduate programs and how it is implemented and *rewarded* in many companies. Despite the numerous obstacles to successful consumer persuasion we have documented throughout this book, many marketers still seem to believe—or at least act like they believe—that persuasion is the only possible purpose of marketing.

The second reason marketers might be drawn to marketing tactics that treat consumers as "patsies" is more sinister. Consider for a moment the "persuasion methods" literature discussed earlier in this chapter. Despite the implicit or explicit messages running through that literature, human beings are not "marionettes." To characterize them as such is to deny them the respect all people deserve as self-motivated actors capable of making their own choices and pursuing their own goals. It is also a bad theory of human behavior.

If human beings were as easily manipulated as the persuasion literature implies, marketing would be the world's easiest profession. But it is not. As we have seen, people do not like being manipulated and they have many means at their disposal for resisting both overt and covert persuasion attempts, from conscious resistance strategies to unconscious reverse priming effects. Consumers are not push-overs, easy marks, or puppets.

An excessive interest in manipulating and controlling consumers says more about those who seek such knowledge than those who are expected to fall under its sway.

It implies a worldview that denies the agency and autonomy of others and extols the idea that people can be treated as means to one's own ends, rather than as autonomous agents who want and need to be treated with respect and dignity. It also renders impossible any hope of building a relationship of trust with consumers. Marketing that maneuvers people into doing things they don't want to do—or buying things they don't want to buy—seldom leads to a second transaction.

If marketing is seen primarily as a way to manipulate and control others, it will appeal as a profession to people who get personal satisfaction from manipulating and controlling others. People with such needs may be attracted to marketing organizations filled with others who think and feel the same way. Such an organization is not difficult to identify. A culture of disrespect for buyers of a company's products is hard to change, bad for business, and ultimately corrosive to the self-esteem of those who work within it. For marketers who find themselves in such an organization, but who reject the idea that consumers as puppets to be manipulated and controlled, there is really only one choice: find a more ethical place to work.

Chapter 17

The Marketer's Dilemma

Rethinking Marketing
with Brain Science in Mind

"Marketing is like cholesterol. There are good kinds and bad kinds."
–Rory Sutherland[1]

In this concluding chapter, we revisit and summarize the main arguments of the book and consider how marketers can rethink some of their most basic assumptions and beliefs—especially about consumers, persuasion, and influence—in light of the brain science insights and findings we have presented.

Modern science confronts marketers with a dilemma. Perhaps ironically, it involves the same novelty-familiarity continuum we introduced in Chapter 5. While brain science suggests that marketers should migrate their consumers from novelty to familiarity as quickly as possible with regard to their products and brands, the findings we have explored in the preceding chapters suggest that marketers need to migrate *themselves* in the opposite direction—from familiarity to novelty—if they want to integrate the lessons of brain science into their own thinking and professional practices. Marketers can either continue the familiar and comfortable practices of persuasive marketing or they can dive into the novel and sometimes counterintuitive practices of intuitive marketing.

This is not an "either-or" dilemma. It is a "when-where-and-how" dilemma.

All marketers—and all theories of marketing—agree that marketing is about influencing consumers to do what marketers want them to do.

Since early in the 20th century, the consensus view among most marketers (with a few notable exceptions) has been that the best way to influence consumers is through *persuasion*, the art of getting them to "change their minds" about products, brands, or categories. Intuitive marketing proposes a different route. It starts from a recognition that people don't like being subjected to external persuasion, unless they are already in a state of mind that makes them receptive to it—such as when they want to make a decision but need more information to make a final choice. In those circumstances, persuasion can be welcomed and effective. But the vast majority of the time, people are exposed to marketing when they are not trying to make an immediate decision; they are just trying to get on with their lives. Intuitive marketing is about how marketers can effectively influence consumers in those circumstances.

Rethinking How Consumers Think

Intuitive marketing is based on a fundamental reassessment of how consumers think. We have seen that this reassessment encompasses a wide variety of cognitive processes, some consciously accessible and some not. Taken together, these processes describe a prototypical individual I have called the *intuitive consumer*. As described in Chapter 1, intuitive consumers seldom follow the rules of *rational choice* that traditional persuasive marketing assumes they do. They don't pay attention, they are suspicious of novelty, they can be fooled by mere exposure and processing fluency, they have weak and fleeting preferences, they experience emotions in complex ways, they pursue goals unconsciously as well as consciously, they are constantly motivated by aspirations and identity needs, they learn without knowing they are learning, and their choices are influenced by features of *form* and *context* as much as by the *content* of marketing messages.

Rethinking Attention

Marketers need to rethink how they use—and abuse—consumers' attention.

Attention is not a spotlight. It is a process and an effort, so our brains use it sparingly and strategically. It is imperfect. it generally aims where we want it to aim, but it also can be redirected by events outside our control, becoming involuntarily attracted to things we would rather ignore. Conversely, when focused elsewhere, it can cause us to miss things we would rather notice.

In Chapter 3, we saw that brain scientists view attention as encompassing three separate but equally important cognitive functions: *orienting*, *vigilance*, and *executive control*. *Orienting* is how our brains "lock in" to a given object of attention. When marketers talk about attention, they are usually talking about orienting. When they talk about "grabbing" attention, "rising above the clutter," or developing a marketing message that has "stopping power," they are talking about orienting a consumer's attention away from whatever else they might have been focused on and redirecting it to the marketer's message.

While orienting is the first step in attention, *vigilance* is the second step that sometimes, but not always, follows. Vigilance the ability to maintain an alert state of self-directed attention for an extended period of time. If orienting is "grabbing" attention, vigilance is "holding" attention. Unlike orienting, vigilance requires the recruitment of conscious *System 2* processing. It is necessary for processing propositional information of the form *if A, then B*. Whenever marketers want to communicate a persuasive argument ("if you care about *A*, then you should buy *B*"), they must activate vigilance for the duration of their message or there is no chance their argument will enter the consumer's long-term memory and be available for later retrieval.

Executive control refers to our ability to concentrate, problem-solve, and evaluate alternatives. It requires aiming attention inward, focusing on our own thoughts and feelings. Executive control allows us to assess any gaps between our current internal state and what we are trying to accomplish at any given moment. It is exclusively a function of *System 2* thinking, operating during the *deliberate and analyze* step in the cognitive timeline. Like vigilance, executive control expends conscious cognitive effort and is therefore something our cognitive miser brains would rather avoid if at all possible.

Attention can be oriented in two very different ways, called *bottom-up* and *top-down* attention. The former is attention that is involuntarily "grabbed" by some external event or object, the latter is internally-directed attention that is voluntarily aimed in the service of goal pursuit. Bottom-up attention is attention that is *demanded*, top-down attention is attention that is *earned*. While traditional persuasive marketing tends to fixate on producing bottom-up attention—the quickest path to orienting consumers' attention—intuitive marketing is more concerned with attracting top-down attention.

Brain scientists have identified three major attractors of attention: *novelty*, *emotional display*, and *reward anticipation*. Novelty draws attention because it produces an *expectancy violation*—our brains are expecting one thing, but something else happens. Emotional displays draw attention because we are highly motivated to identify and interpret the emotions expressed by others, which may signal the onset of potentially beneficial or dangerous circumstances. Reward anticipation draws attention because we are ultimately a species of *reward seekers*. Our brains are especially attentive to rewards that appear irregularly and unpredictably, that provide what is called a *variable reward pattern*.

Getting attention is easier than keeping it. Of the three sources of attention, novelty and emotional display are most commonly found in traditional persuasive advertising. They tend to be effective at orienting bottom-up attention but are less useful for sustaining vigilance or executive control. Reward anticipation is a reliable method for maintaining top-down attentional vigilance, but it is not easily embedded in marketing materials and is more likely to be found in games, puzzles, and other interactive formats.

Aggressively pursuing attention-grabbing in marketing is not without its risks. In fact, there are several ways an over-reliance on acquiring consumer attention can end up being detrimental to marketing goals.

First, marketers may trigger a form of *cognitive backlash* when an effort to attract attention fails. Marketing that demands attention must necessarily wrest that attention from somewhere else. Whether appearing in an ad break on TV or in the margins of a web page, a marketing message starts out as a *distraction* designed to interrupt and disrupt some other attentional focus. Research on *distractor devaluation* has found that when this effort fails, it can negatively impact attitudes toward the product or brand in the message.

Second, there are risks associated with activating other *System 2* cognitive processes when attention is directed toward marketing. When people start *thinking* about marketing, they may start *questioning* marketing. And that can lead to three consequences that marketers generally want to avoid: *persuasion resistance*, *habit disruption*, and *variety seeking*.

A third problem with attention-grabbing is that some consumers, including a large segment of *light buyers* of any product or brand, may simply fail to pay attention to marketing for those products or brands. This is the problem of the *low-attention* or *no-attention* consumer. When Robert Heath first proposed that people could be influenced by advertising without paying attention to it, the marketing world did not react positively. Again, this should not be surprising, because taking attention out of the equation breaks the persuasion model and, not incidentally, challenges the usefulness of several billion-dollar market research methodologies that evaluate marketing and advertising messages precisely on their ability to attract attention and make a persuasive case for the product or brand.

Attention is a scarce resource in our modern world. Marketers need to rethink how and why they deploy attention-grabbing tactics in their messaging. In contrast to traditional persuasive marketing, intuitive marketing starts from the premise that direct attention is optional, not required, to achieve marketing goals. It does not deny that attention and persuasion have their place, but it does ask marketers to weigh the pros and cons of attention before assuming that attracting attention must be the centerpiece of their marketing campaigns or strategies.

Rethinking Novelty and Familiarity

Marketers love novelty. They know—and brain science confirms—that novelty attracts attention. It does so because our brains are *prediction engines* that constantly anticipate and build expectations about what will happen next at any given moment. When we are *surprised* by a violation of our expectations, our *System 2* "lazy controller" is activated and our attention is drawn to the source of the expectancy violation.

Brain scientists have interpreted this automatic reaction in different ways. For a long time, it was believed that we were attracted to novelty because we inherently liked and embraced new things. This belief was supported by the observation that novelty detection tends to trigger the release of *midbrain dopamine*, a chemical neurotransmitter commonly associated with subjective feelings of pleasure. But this interpretation was contradicted by other brain science findings, which showed that most people, in most situations, seemed to have an automatic *aversive* reaction to novelty. And indeed, when we look at the high failure rate for new products and the resistance people express to new ideas, these findings have credibility.

The paradox was resolved when further experimentation revealed that dopamine is not just a "feel good" neurotransmitter. More importantly, it is a *motivation driver*. What is being produced by surges of midbrain dopamine is not pleasure per se, but a chemically-facilitated motivation to learn and act.

Novelty, because it violates expectations, creates an opportunity for learning. Allocating attention and *System 2* processing to novelty allows us to update our expectations and correct our bad predictions. Dopamine release facilitates this process by motivating us to stop and learn from every expectancy violation we encounter. Whether this leads to pleasure or pain depends on *what* we learn. This is why scientists now believe it is not novelty per se that triggers dopamine release and subjective feeling of pleasure, but *anticipation* of a reward that *may* (or may not) result from the novel situation.

The learning that results from experiencing novelty has a natural endpoint—it makes the initially-perplexing experience less novel and more *familiar*. Marketers would do well to rethink the benefits of *familiarity* for marketers, because consumers respond to familiarity very differently than they respond to novelty. While novelty triggers attention, stimulation, conscious deliberation, vigilance, and caution, familiarity has a nearly opposite effect. It can be experienced without much attention; it has a calming rather than stimulating emotional effect; it is processed more automatically than deliberatively; it triggers less conscious vigilance; and it is more strongly associated with approach motivation than withdrawal.

Marketers should think about novelty and familiarity as forming a continuum that consumers move along as they discover and learn about new products, brands, and product categories. At first, novelty draws both attention and some degree of caution (possibly only experienced unconsciously). Over time and through repeated exposures and experiences, what was novel becomes familiar. Figure 6 in Chapter 5 illustrates this *novelty-familiarity continuum* in terms of a sequence of subjective states that consumers might experience over time: *confusion, interest, comfort,* and *boredom.*

Marketers need to keep track of where their products and brands—as well as their competitors' products and brands—are positioned along the novelty-familiarity continuum. This can help diagnose marketing problems and anticipate opportunities as products move through their lifecycles. It is important to recognize that the two "sweet spots" along the continuum, *interesting* and *comforting*, tend to be both unstable and temporary.

Interesting things stop being interesting when they become familiar and comforting things stop being comfortable when they become boring.

Persuasive marketing and intuitive marketing differ in the degree to which they emphasize novelty vs. familiarity. While traditional persuasion regularly uses novel situations and incidents to attract attention and trigger conscious information processing, intuitive marketing focuses more on achieving and maintaining familiarity. This can lead to a very different style of marketing and advertising—a style that is more reflective of Andrew Ehrenberg's view that effective brand advertising should emphasize *publicity* over *persuasion, salience* over *loyalty,* and *distinctiveness* over *differentiation* (see Chapter 12).

Rethinking Mere Exposure and Processing Fluency

Before behavioral economics upset the apple cart of neoclassical economics, marketers embraced the rational choice premise that consumers' decisions and actions were functions of their *preferences*. People bought *Product A* instead of *Product B* because they preferred *A* to *B*. If you wanted to get people to switch from *A* to *B*, you had to get them to change their preference. The default way to do that was a *persuasive argument* or perhaps a *persuasive visual demonstration* that *Product B* was in fact superior in terms of some attribute important to the consumer. The whole process of receiving, processing, and acting on marketing messages was assumed to operate at what we would now call the conscious *System 2* level of cognitive processing.

Robert Zajonc's discovery of the *mere exposure effect* was a seminal moment in the history of brain science. It was also significant for marketing, because it offered the first concrete evidence that there were *shortcuts* to consumer preferences that could bypass the whole messy project of conscious persuasion. Zajonc's discovery went even further, challenging one of the most fundamental premises of persuasive marketing—that preferences were based on *reasons*. Zajonc's experiments said *no*. In his memorable phrase: "preferences need to inferences."

> **The mere exposure effect demonstrates the powerful influence of *repetition* on human cognition.**

People can change their attitudes toward things they don't even recognize (like nonsense symbols in the style of Chinese ideograms) based on repeated exposure alone. Stimuli that are repeated more are liked more, are assumed to represent more positive concepts, and are seen as more aesthetically pleasing. All of these attitudinal changes occur without any prior information processing or *System 2* conscious intervention.

Zajonc attributed the mere exposure effect to a form of *classical conditioning*. Repetition builds a sense of familiarity, which in turn produces feelings of comfort, safety, and a reduced need for vigilance. Zajonc believed this process—*as long as it occurred in the absence of any competing negative stimuli*—conditioned the viewer to judge the repeated item more favorably than other stimuli presented less frequently.

For marketers, the mere exposure effect might sound like a proverbial silver bullet for persuasion: just repeat your marketing message over and over again and you will be automatically rewarded with increased liking and preference for your product or brand. But, as we have seen with most the brain science concepts discussed in this book, things are not quite that simple.

There are three ways the mere exposure effect might not work as expected in a persuasive marketing context. First, it fails to occur in cluttered contexts where multiple stimuli are competing for attention. Specifically, the *distractor devaluation* effect described in Chapter 3 can override the mere exposure effect when the repeating stimulus is neither expected nor desired. Second, like conditioning more generally, mere exposure works best for stimuli that are not already liked or disliked—it is better at creating new preferences than at changing existing ones. And third, the mere exposure effect is diffuse. In perfect conditions it might increase liking for a product or brand, but it can also improve mood in general and increase liking for other items in the immediate vicinity, like a competitor's products or brands. Mere exposure isn't a silver bullet for persuasive marketing. On the contrary, it's not much of a bullet at all. Perhaps it would be better to think of it as a fine spray, like an air freshener that spreads through the room and makes everything smell a little better.

Processing fluency is a second cognitive shortcut that can impact preferences in the absence of persuasion. Like mere exposure, it is relatively well-known in the marketing world, but not well-understood. When our cognitive miser brains find something easy to interpret and understand, we tend to like it. We experience fluency consciously as a subjective feeling of mental ease—what researchers call the "warm glow" of processing fluency. As a result, fluency is easily mistaken for familiarity. Because familiar things can be processed fluently, our uncritical *System 1* may "jump to the conclusion" that fluently processed things must be familiar. This is of course a logical fallacy (*if A-then B* does not imply *if B-then A*), but *System 1* does not do logic, as we learned in Chapter 1.

Experiencing processing fluency is only the first step in a three-stage process that translates a feeling of fluency into an evaluation or buying decision. If marketers want to understand how fluency leads to subsequent judgments and choices, they need to take into account all three stages of the fluency experience: the sources of fluency, the naïve theories people use to interpret the fluency experience, and the judgments that follow from that experience.

Because fluency, once triggered, generates a consciously accessible experience, that experience may be interpreted in different ways by different brains. This process of interpretation is called *meta-cognition* because it is cognition about cognition, thinking about thinking. Brain science researchers have found that fluency experiences, which may derive from many possible sources (in Stage 1), may lead to quite different outcomes and consequences (in Stage 3), depending on how those experiences are interpreted (in Stage 2). And those interpretations, in turn, have been found to depend on the *naïve theories* that consumers bring to mind to determine the meaning and interpretation of the fluency experience.

> **If marketers want to leverage processing fluency successfully in their marketing campaigns and messages, they need to focus not only on making their brands, products, and messages as fluent as possible, but also on whether their consumers are interpreting those fluency cues in the manner intended by the marketing team.**

This requires deeply understanding the naïve theories consumers are applying to the fluent experiences marketers are constructing. Only by taking both aspects of fluency into account—*whether* a fluent experience is occurring and *how* that experience is being interpreted—can marketers accurately trace the causal path from processing fluency to consumers' judgments, choices, and actions.

Two additional points about processing fluency are worth mentioning. First, *unexpected fluency* seems to work better than expected fluency. Researchers have found that processing fluency is more likely to produce conscious feelings of liking or familiarity when it is encountered unexpectedly, rather than when it is expected. Marketers should take note. Looking for ways to build unexpected fluency throughout the *consumer cycle*—from *messaging* to *purchasing* to *delivering* to *consuming* and even to *disposing* of products—can help build positive feeling toward products and brands in new and innovative ways.

A second point about processing fluency has to do with its opposite, processing *disfluency*. While marketers usually don't want their consumers to be thinking too deliberatively about their products and brands, sometimes triggering *System 2* evaluative processing is exactly what they want consumers to do. To that end, making a message or experience harder to process, not easier, can produce the desired effect of waking up *System 2* processing. As we saw in Chapter 5, perceived disfluency is a cue that things are *not* going to be easy and that you'd better "get your head in the game" (to use a well-worn but apt cliché) for whatever's coming next.

Rethinking Preferences

Brain scientists have been chipping away at the idea of preferences as a source of human behavior for decades. Thanks to the legacy of rational choice theory, there is a robust tradition among marketers that resists or is unaware of this work. But as we saw in Chapter 7, preferences do not provide a solid foundation for either explaining or predicting consumer behavior.

Rather than choose what we know we prefer, we humans are much more likely to say we prefer whatever we last chose.

This lesson from brain science requires some serious rethinking from marketers. For years, they have been asking consumers about their preferences. Which would you be more likely to buy, *Product A* or *Product B*? Which features would weigh most heavily in your choice between *A* and *B*? If a new product were introduced in *Category X* with the following features, would you prefer it to the current products in that category? Complex models have been built to predict consumer behavior based on questions like these. The results have been less than spectacular.

Brain science reveals a number of reasons why preferences are poor predictors of behavior in general, and consumer behavior in particular. Rather than preceding and guiding choices, preferences are often *constructed* in real time out of the choice experience itself. They can change radically over time as contexts and goals change. They can be *misattributions* based on unconscious processes like priming, mere exposure, processing fluency, or somatic markers. They can be implicit and inaccessible to conscious awareness. Brain scientists have even found that people can simultaneously hold implicit and explicit preferences that contradict each other—explicitly, I might swear to prefer the cardboard-like "nutritious" snack bar, but implicit measures might reveal my "true" preference for the tasty and tempting *Hershey's* milk chocolate bar.

For all these reasons, consumers' expressed preferences can be a problematic guide to future behavior. This means that marketers and market researchers need to interpret surveys and interviews cautiously. Given the fragility and implicit nature of many consumer preferences, market research is more likely to get generalizable, actionable results by measuring *what consumers do*, not *what they say*, when faced with product or brand choices.

At the end of Chapter 7, I argue that marketing by itself can only build weak and temporary preferences. Lasting preferences come from multiple journeys through the *consumer cycle* in which marketing, shopping, and consuming experiences all mutually reinforce each other and strengthen a reliable product/brand image in the minds of consumers. This is why intuitive marketing doesn't focus on changing preferences. It focuses on building positive mental associations and expectations that anchor and sustain long-term consumer relationships. It focuses on building lasting preferences on a foundation of consistency, reliability, and trust. Preferences are mercurial. Lasting preferences may take years to develop, but one instance of *expectancy violation* can cause them to vanish in a moment.

Rethinking Emotion

Traditional marketers have rebranded *emotion* as an alternative to *information* in the persuasive marketing model. While not abandoning the idea that marketing is about persuasion, they have identified *emotional displays*, rather than arguments, demonstrations, comparisons, or endorsements, as the potential mechanism for delivering persuasion in a marketing message. The underlying belief appears to be: if you can elicit a powerful emotional response during a marketing message, you can attract people's attention and induce them to engage in the main forms of consumer behavior you want them to engage in: buying, consuming, advocating, and repeat buying.

The brain science findings discussed in Chapter 8 and Chapter 9 tell a different story about how emotion interacts with and influences consumer choice and behavior. The first lesson marketers can learn from brain science is that emotion is not a unitary concept. Unconscious and conscious emotions are quite different cognitive phenomenon and play quite different—but interacting—roles in consumer behavior.

Unconscious emotions are not just "feelings" with the volume turned down.

They are more like *echoes* of conscious feelings, inhabiting long-term memory not as full-fledged episodic memories, but as *affective residue* learned automatically and encoded without awareness from direct and observed emotional experiences. What gets encoded is the *valence* of the experience—an answer to the question, "would I want to have that emotion again?" When this affective residue is later retrieved automatically from implicit memory, it does not contain specific information about how to act; it instead provides a *somatic or emotional marker* that represents the extent to which similar experiences in the past have produced overall positive or negative results.

Conscious emotions are "feelings" in the obvious sense that they can be consciously felt. Although there is a long tradition in philosophy that views conscious feelings as direct causes of human behavior, recent research says otherwise. Rather than causing behavior directly, conscious emotions have been found to play a more indirect role, influencing behavior primarily through *learning* and *anticipation*.

Emotion-as-feedback theory provides a useful framework for understanding how conscious and unconscious emotions interact and combine with other cognitive processes to enable decision making and adaptive behavior. It is a theory that aims to answer one question: *how does emotion help humans survive, adapt, and succeed in the world?* Its answer identifies different roles for conscious and unconscious emotions:

Unconscious emotions are for deciding, feelings are for learning.

The *feedback loop* at the heart of this theory operates as follows. We *learn* from a lifetime of experience which emotions tend to follow from the choices we make and the actions we take. Over time we *automatize* some of these lessons as unconscious emotional *markers*. These markers subtly influence our subsequent behavior, usually without conscious awareness. As our repertoire of conscious emotional learnings and unconscious emotional associations grows, we get better at *anticipating* the likely emotional outcomes of new situations in which we find ourselves. In the long run, this feedback system tends to produce adaptive behavior. Conscious and unconscious emotions work together to guide us toward actions that are more likely to achieve the positive emotional states we seek.

What are the implications for marketing? First of all: more work for marketers. It is not enough to focus on the emotions consumers are having *while experiencing* marketing messages. Marketers must also pay attention to what consumers are *learning* from those emotional experiences, as well as how those lessons are impacting what they are *doing* in the marketplace. Once the role of emotion in consumer behavior is properly identified as a feedback system, immediate emotions felt *during* a consumer's exposure to marketing become less important than the emotional *implications* consumers are learning from that exposure, which in turn can significantly impact how and what they *do* in future interactions with the product or brand.

When marketers embrace the idea that emotion in marketing influences consumer behavior largely through learning, they need to take a closer look at the role of memory in the learning process; specifically, how emotional displays in marketing get encoded, consolidated, and retrieved. What brain science tells us about these processes is that they operate in unique ways when strong emotions are present.

Injecting powerful emotional displays into marketing messages can impact consumer memories in ways that diverge from what marketers might expect, or desire.

Emotional displays attract attention. However, memory researchers have found that when our attention is drawn to an emotional episode, we tend to focus more on the central features of the emotional event itself and less on the peripheral details that surround it. This tendency for emotionally-charged experiences to "narrow" memory encoding can create unintended consequences for marketers who want to surround their products and brands with emotionally-saturated narratives. If the product or brand is not deeply embedded in the emotional moment, it may be perceived as peripheral to the central emotion and may not survive the transition from sensory impression to lasting memory.

Recent studies of emotion and memory have found that this narrowing effect is sensitive to *motivational intensity*. It is more likely to occur when people are consciously or unconsciously motivated to pursue a goal than when they are not. While experiencing what might be called *pregoal* (or *goal-activating*) emotions—such as *hope, fear,* or *desire*—our attention automatically narrows to focus on information and aspects of the situation that are relevant to the goals we are pursuing at that moment. It is this goal-directed narrowing of attention that impairs memory encoding for peripheral details, leaving us vulnerable to poor recall, misattribution, and false memories concerning those details. In contrast, *postgoal* emotions that typically follow goal attainment or failure—such as *happiness, sadness,* or *pride*—have been found to actually *broaden* the scope of attention, producing better recall of peripheral details and greater resistance to misattribution, misinformation, and false memories.

This creates an interesting opportunity for marketers. Traditional persuasive marketing is often designed to increase motivational intensity by using emotional displays to activate negative emotions such as *fear, shame, disgust,* or *guilt.* Assuming these emotions have been successfully induced, persuasive marketing then introduces a product or brand as the "hero" that will release viewers from their negative feelings. Using this formula, persuasive marketing deploys negative pregoal emotional displays to make us feel worse about ourselves, in order to motivate us to pursue the marketer's recommended solution, which will presumably bring us back to equilibrium. This is not a formula for using emotion to improve people's lives or anticipate better emotional outcomes in the future.

Intuitive marketing suggests an alternative approach. Marketers can tell stories in their marketing messages that use emotional displays to communicate *postgoal* emotions like *happiness* or *sadness*. These stories are not designed to motivate immediate goal pursuit, but to stimulate longer-term learning to help viewers recognize and achieve better emotional outcomes in the future. Goals are presented as *already* reached, so motivational intensity is low. Released from the memory-narrowing effects of active goal pursuit, emotional displays featuring postgoal emotions can facilitate broader memory encoding and access to a wider range of details and consequences. As a result, more nuanced and contextualized lessons can be communicated, encoded, consolidated, and later retrieved.

From an intuitive marketing perspective, the purpose of emotion in marketing is not to attract attention and increase persuasion, but to build and reinforce automatic emotional associations that can be reactivated reliably at points of sale or points of consumption. Marketing that uses positive postgoal emotional displays is more aligned with the principles of intuitive marketing because it enacts feelings that accompany aspirational success and identity-affirmation, rather than feelings that accompany perceived inadequacy and self-doubt. Simply injecting more and more emotion into ads and other marketing materials does not provide a direct path to consumers' hearts or, more importantly, their pocketbooks.

Rethinking Goals and Motivation

Emotions don't motivate people to act, goals do.

If marketers want to see their marketing and advertising efforts translate into consumer choices and sales, they need to learn how to activate consumer goals and motivations, not just generate consumer emotions. A positive feeling may cause a consumer to answer a survey or interview question in a desired way, but it will not magically turn into a sale unless it also motivates a goal to purchase or consume. This is how emotion and motivation work together in the minds of intuitive consumers.

> **Emotions *accompany* wants and needs. They may *prime* wants and needs. But it is wants and needs that *motivate* goal pursuit. And it is goal pursuit that *produces* choice and behavior.**

Chapter 10 provides a taxonomy of wants and needs. It suggests that marketers should distinguish between different types of motivators that drive human behavior in different ways: *wants*, which are discretionary *desires* or *longings* that can go unfulfilled without serious repercussions; *physiological needs*, which arise from physical signals to regulate and maintain homeostasis and health; *psychological needs*, which arise from innate motivations to maintain and protect feelings of self-worth and accomplishment; and *learned needs*, with derive from recurring and habit-forming episodes of reward-seeking. These different types of motivators operate in different ways to achieve different ends, but they have one thing in common: they impact behavior by activating goals and goal pursuit.

Goals are central to all human behavior, including consumer behavior, because they provide a flexible and adaptive cognitive mechanism for directing actions to satisfy our wants and needs. Goals are *mental constructs* that set us in motion to relieve the persistent tensions created by the motivators that drive us throughout our lives. They can operate consciously, unconsciously, or through combinations of conscious and unconscious activation and pursuit.

Of particular interest to marketers is the phenomenon of *unconscious goal activation*; the process of *priming* a goal with an environmental cue (e.g., a person, place, or thing). Although the prime itself is often—but not always—consciously perceived, its influence on subsequent thoughts and actions (the priming effect) is not. Goal activation is highly contextual: the goals that get activated in different contexts can vary widely from person to person and even for the same person when they encounter primes in different circumstances.

The means and ends of goal pursuit are further explored in Chapter 11, which outlines some of the distinctive features shared by conscious and unconscious goal pursuit: persistence over time, adaptation in the face of obstacles, insensitivity to interruption, and increasing motivational intensity while the goal remains unfulfilled. Equally important are distinctive and observable *consequences* when goal pursuit ends, either successfully or unsuccessfully. These include impacts on mood, self-esteem, and subsequent behavior.

Usually, when a goal is fulfilled, its motivational force dissipates rapidly. This makes sense functionally, because people need to disengage from one goal in order to engage with another. But this effect also raises potential problems for marketers, because goal disengagement is often accompanied by a decrease in positivity toward the goal-object just attained. This also makes sense. Once a goal is accomplished, it often feels less *desirable* than it did during goal pursuit. An example is the subjective feeling of *buyer's remorse.* Having expended time, effort, and money on a product purchase, a consumer might—upon bringing the shiny new object home—find themselves wondering whether the effort was worth it. They might even start second-guessing the purchase. And that postgoal adjustment in their attitudes and expectations might contribute to a less positive feeling toward the product the next time the consumer thinks about it. Such a reevaluation is the last thing marketers want to see, especially for products that depend on repeat buying.

Researchers have found that this decline in positivity toward goal objects is less likely to occur if an immediate, finite goal (such as achieving a high score on a test) is connected to a larger, aspirational goal (such as being seen as a smart, accomplished person). In such situations, the greater goal may continue to be active even after the immediate goal is fulfilled. This presents a challenge for persuasive marketing, because invoking a short-term goal that can be satisfied by a one-time act of purchasing or consuming may not contribute to the long-lasting positivity marketers hope for. But it also presents an opportunity for intuitive marketing, because marketers might be able to establish longer-term, more robust positivity toward their products and brands, as well as more sustainable bonds with their customers, by aligning their offerings with people's more enduring goals and needs—that is, their lifelong pursuits of autonomy, competence, and belonging.

Rethinking Learning and Memory

A major thread in this book has been a reexamination of the central role of *memory* in consumer choice and behavior. Since Andrew Ehrenberg wrote in 1974 that the purpose of advertising is to reinforce memory through repetition, not change attitudes through persuasion, marketers have—with a few notable exceptions—chosen to ignore his findings and conclusions, preferring instead to continue operating under the longstanding view that the purpose of marketing is to persuade. I find Ehrenberg's arguments and the evidence on which they are based to be compelling. The failure of marketers and market researchers to build on

341

Ehrenberg's work over the intervening decades has been a big missed opportunity. In Chapter 12, Chapter 13, and Chapter 14, I attempt to compensate for some of that neglect by tracing the intricate story of how memory actually operates and influences consumer choice and behavior.

Traditional persuasive marketing is built on a partial and outdated view of human memory. It is *partial* in the sense that it assumes marketing messages get committed to memory primarily through conscious processes of intentional learning. It is *outdated* in the sense that, while it does acknowledge that learning can sometimes occur through implicit memory processes (for example, through *evaluative conditioning*), it assumes that what gets encoded through these processes is essentially the same information—semantic and episodic memories of a single object or event—that gets encoded through conscious learning. Neither assumption stands up in light of the latest findings from brain science.

In our tour of human memory systems in Chapter 12, we found that human memory is divided into four generally independent functional areas, delineated by short-term vs. long-term systems along one dimension and consciously accessible vs. inaccessible systems along a second dimension. Short-term *sensory memory* is inaccessible but provides us with moment-to-moment continuity as we experience the world around us. Short-term *working memory* provides us with a temporary and low-capacity "holding area" where we can consciously access and manipulate information drawn from long-term memory. Both these systems interact extensively with long-term memory systems, which provide more or less permanent storage of facts, episodes, beliefs, associations, and expectations. Long-term memory has separate systems devoted to explicit and implicit memories. Explicit memories are *declarative*, in the sense that we can experience them as *recollections*, which we can describe or declare to ourselves or others. Implicit memories are *nondeclarative*, in the opposite sense that we cannot recollect, describe, or declare them. They are hidden from our conscious minds.

> **What marketers need to learn from memory researchers is not just that implicit memories are hidden, but that they are different *in kind* from declarative memories.**

Unlike declarative memories, which can be consciously accessed by short-term working memory, nondeclarative memories cannot be "brought to mind" as recollections of facts or episodes. Rather, they can only be experienced *indirectly* and observed *retrospectively* as invisible influences on mood, preferences, attitudes, habits, choices, and actions.

342

More importantly, implicit memories are not memories of individual facts or events. They are memories of *patterns of association* between multiple facts and events. This is true of all four subsystems of implicit memory. *Procedural memory* records and automatizes a series of steps or motor operations required to learn a skill or develop a habit. *Classical conditioning* identifies and stores co-occurrences between objects and/or events. *Priming* is a memory retrieval system that makes one thought or action more accessible based on its strength of association with a preceding or accompanying thought or action. And *nonassociative learning* is an implicit memory system that enables learning by extracting expectations from repeated or prolonged exposures to a single stimulus.

Implicit learning puts "thoughts in our head" through all these implicit memory systems, with the exception of *priming*, which is a memory retrieval system, not a memory encoding system. Explicit and implicit learning can also occur simultaneously. While explicit learning is helping us encode semantic and episodic information about a single object or event, implicit learning is operating in the background, helping us place that object or event in a broader context.

Explicit learning helps us *remember* an event, implicit learning helps us *classify* it.

Classification is inherently comparative. Implicit learning puts a single event in context in several ways: it allows us to estimate the event's *probability* or *frequency* of occurrence; it updates the event's *emotional valence*; it determines the event's *motivational relevance*; and it allows us to calculate the event's potential *reward value* in light of our immediate and long-term goals. All these learnings occur unconsciously and incrementally over repeated—not single—exposures. They update the *associations* we attach to an object or event, and they alter the *expectations* we bring to bear the next time we encounter a similar object or event.

This is how memory and learning influence consumer choice and behavior. Most marketing reaches our long-term memory through implicit, not explicit, learning. The one exception is *aligned-intent marketing*, which we process explicitly and consciously. Other forms of marketing—messages that are imposed on us, not sought out by us—are generally perceived and encoded implicitly as a statistical flow, with little or no attention allocated to them. We learn from these exposures, despite paying little attention to them, and automatically update our associations and expectations for the promoted products or brands as a result. We carry these mental constructs into subsequent shopping and consuming experiences, where they are further updated through both implicit and explicit learning. As this process repeats over multiple journeys through the full *consumer cycle*, we develop attractions or aversions to different products or brands, usually without ever fully understanding how or why.

Chapter 13 and Chapter 14 examine how implicit learning translates into choices and actions in the marketplace without invoking *System 2* information processing or logical analysis and without absorbing and succumbing to persuasive arguments or emotional displays. The process involves three steps. First, implicit learning systems like *evaluative conditioning* automatically create and strengthen associations between *cognitive representations* or things or events (including products and brands) in long-term memory. These associations get cumulatively stronger or weaker over time, based on ongoing *System 1* monitoring of patterns, co-occurrences, and outcomes in our sensory environment. Second, *priming* makes some of these learned associations more likely to be activated than others. It leverages what we encoded in the past, both implicitly and explicitly, to make some thoughts and actions more accessible in the present. Priming thus biases *knowledge accessibility*. Third, knowledge accessibility leads to *knowledge activation*, the process by which some units of knowledge get transferred into short-term *working memory* as objects of conscious *System 2* attention and deliberation.

Although we tend to believe that we can and do access all relevant knowledge when we face a judgment or choice, brain science tells us our evaluations and decisions are typically based on only a small subset of the knowledge we could apply. Priming is one way that subset of knowledge gets selected, but other cognitive mechanisms can contribute as well, such as familiarity, mere exposure, processing fluency, somatic markers, and mood. Similarly, not all *accessible knowledge* becomes *activated knowledge*. Especially in a busy environment in which multiple primes are present and triggering knowledge accessibility in different ways, additional factors—such as the recency, frequency, and persistence of previously activated knowledge—can further bias and narrow down what eventually "comes to mind" in a judgment or choice situation.

Rethinking Consumer Choice

Making a choice, unlike many of the cognitive processes described in this book, necessarily involves conscious *System 2* thinking. We may not have full conscious awareness of *why* we choose one item over another, but we cannot make a choice without being aware of the choice itself. A choice is an *act* and, as the *cognitive timeline* makes clear, *speaking and acting* are conscious *System 2* operations.

Chapter 15 and Chapter 16 examine consumer choice through the lenses of *behavioral economics* and *behavioral design*, respectively. Chapter 15 begins with a discussion of rationality. According to *rational choice theory*, two fundamental premises define the essence of rationality: first, people know what they want—that is, they have stable and accessible *preferences*—and, second, they know how to get what they want—that is, they can *calculate* or *compute* the best choice alternative that will maximize the *reward value* or *expected utility* they will gain from the choice. The history of behavioral economics is essentially the story of how these premises were slowly but methodically demolished and then replaced by a new, more empirically-grounded theory of human choice.

The demolition of rational choice began with the work of Herbert Simon and James March in the 1950s. Their initial efforts attempted to save at least some of the elements of rationality. Simon's concept of *bounded rationality*, for example, blamed people's failure to follow the rules of expected utility on constraints that were essentially outside their control—constraints that "bounded" their ability to act in accordance with the rules of rational choice due to *incomplete information, limited time*, or *limited capacity* to perform the required calculations. Given these constraints, Simon proposed that we actually choose using a process he called *satisficing*. When we satisfice, we don't search for and compute the optimal choice in a given situation, we only search for alternatives up to the point at which we find a *sufficient* solution. Then we stop searching and make our choice.

It was left to Daniel Kahneman and Amos Tversky to complete the demolition of rational choice theory and begin constructing its replacement, which they called *prospect theory*. Kahneman and Tversky methodically deconstructed human choice to reveal its underlying cognitive foundations. Using answers to carefully-crafted hypothetical choice questions, they found that people made choices on the basis of a completely different kind of "reasoning" than rational choice theorists hypothesized. Rather than expending mental energy trying to "approximate" rational computations, Kahneman and Tversky found that people based their choices on deeper cognitive processes that operate much earlier in the *cognitive timeline*. They called these processes *judgment heuristics*.

Judgment heuristics are elements of *how* we think; they precede and shape *what* we think.

Kahneman and Tversky discovered several important judgment heuristics in their work together. Other researchers have added many more.[2] Heuristics discussed in Chapter 15 and Chapter 16 include the following:

- *Representativeness heuristic.* We are more likely to classify individual events, objects, or persons as members of a group or category the more they *represent* the properties we believe are shared by members of that group or category. Representativeness can cause us to ignore other diagnostic information, such as known *base rates*, when making inferences and judgments.

- *Availability heuristic.* We make judgments about the likelihood or frequency of an event based on how easily we can think of an example or instance of it. Availability is a major determinant of *knowledge accessibility* during a choice task. It is enhanced by recency, frequency, emotional impact, and motivational relevance.

- *Anchoring effect.* We make estimates about future or unknown outcomes by starting from an initial value and then adjusting up or down to yield a final answer. Anchoring influences our estimates even when the anchor is completely arbitrary. It is a function of *priming*.

- *Framing.* How we formulate a choice problem has a big impact on what we end up choosing. Most notably, framing an outcome as a *loss* vs. a *gain* can have a significant biasing effect on a subsequent choice.

- *Loss aversion.* We attach more subjective value to *avoiding a loss* than we do to *achieving an equivalent gain* (see Figure 9). Loss aversion is a key element underlying the predictions of *prospect theory*. It contradicts the expected utility premise that rational decision makers should treat losses and gains equivalently.

- *Simulation heuristic.* We estimate the likelihood of future events by simulating in our minds the processes that might cause them. Our ability to mentally simulate is highly sensitive to both r*epresentativeness* and *availability*.

- *Conjunction fallacy.* The probability of two less-than-certain events occurring together is always less than the probability of either one occurring alone. But if the conjunction of the two events appears to be more *representative* of a narrative or category, we may erroneously judge the conjunction to be more probable than either individual event alone.

- *Mental accounting.* We choose and act differently when we think of financial transactions a belonging to the same or different mental "bookkeeping buckets." For example, we are more willing to spend money we subjectively classify as "bonus income" than money we classify as "retirement savings."

- *Endowment effect.* We place a higher subjective value on things we already own than things we do not yet possess. The endowment effect is a consequence of *loss aversion* and *framing*.

Heuristics are relevant to consumer choice because they *bias* choice outcomes in predictable directions. They are relevant to marketing because they identify ways marketers can align their messages with how consumers actually make decisions, rather than with how they are *supposed to* make decisions, or how they *tell marketers* they make decisions.

Prospect theory incorporates many insights from Kahneman and Tversky's heuristics and biases research to present a theory of human choice in the face of risk and uncertainty that provides many insights into how consumers make choices in the marketplace.

> From a marketer's point of view, the most important insight of prospect theory is the two-part idea that consumers calculate gains and losses in terms of a subjective *reference point* and that *framing* can be used to set that reference point.

If marketers can successfully influence consumers to set a reference point that benefits their products or brands, they can significantly impact how choice options are processed and ultimately decided. Once anchored to a subjective reference point, consumers will identify outcomes as gains or losses relative to that point. By estimating distances from the reference point, they will calculate the *relative sizes* of those gains or losses. Because gains are evaluated differently than losses, and high-probability gains and losses are evaluated differently than low-probability ones, prospect theory can predict outcomes based on consumers' reference points and distance calculations. As described in Chapter 15, these findings can be combined to produce a *"fourfold pattern"* of consumer responses to risky choices: people tend to be *risk-averse* when choosing between high-probability gains or between low-probability losses, but *risk-seeking* when choosing between high-probability losses or between low-probability gains.

Marketers may not be aware of how they use reference points in their messaging, or how different reference points can lead to different choice outcomes. If I want you to buy my product, which reference point is most beneficial to me? Should I present my product as enabling a gain or avoiding a loss? Should I ask you to frame your choice in terms of your past experiences, your present circumstances, or your future possibilities? Do I want you to compare my product to competing products and, if so, do I want you to think of my product as superior to others (enabling a gain), or of other products as inferior to mine (avoiding a loss)? Do I want you to take a chance on something new (seeking risk), or do I want you to embrace the comfort of something familiar (avoiding risk)? All of these are reference point questions.

> All consumer choices are essentially about overcoming risk and minimizing uncertainty.

Consequently, all marketing messages—whether explicit narratives or implicit primes—are about embracing or avoiding risk and/or lowering uncertainty. This is true for both persuasive marketing and intuitive marketing.

Rational choice theory might tell us we should not be "fooled" by availability, representativeness, anchors, mental accounting, or other heuristics or biases, but we can't help it. Kahneman and Tversky compare judgment heuristics to optical illusions. Just as we cannot *unsee* an optical illusion, we cannot "unthink" a judgment heuristic.[3] It is a fundamental part of how our brains perceive and organize the incessant flow of sensory data that pours into our sensory organs every second of every day. We can override heuristics and biases by activating conscious *System 2* deliberative-analytical reasoning, but this is an effortful and burdensome demand on our cognitive miser brains that we tend to use sparingly (see the discussion of *lazy control* in Chapter 5).

There is no question that the pioneers and current practitioners of behavioral economics have provided us with new, deep, and sometimes troubling insights into the mysteries of human choice in general and consumer choice in particular. These insight have found their way into marketing through the discipline of *behavioral design*. As I note in Chapter 1, consumer choice can be influenced by three quite distinct aspects of marketing: the specific *content* of a marketing message, the *form* of the message, and the *context* of the message (see Figure 1). As consumers, we are not always aware of how these influences impact our choices and behavior; specifically, we often mistakenly believe we are responding to the content of a marketing or advertising message when in fact we are responding to the form or the context of the message. Behavioral designs essentially bypass the informational content of a consumer choice opportunity and focuses on the form and context of the experience.

> **Behavioral design manipulates the *form* and *context* of consumer choice experiences to nudge consumers toward one choice rather than another.**

Behavioral designs can and do have significant effects on consumer choice and behavior. In part, they are effective because they operate below consumers' conscious radar—they impact the complex sequence of impressions, interpretations, associations, and assessments that result in a consumer choice in ways that are inaccessible to consumers themselves. In other words, the discipline of behavioral design creates an *information asymmetry* between the designer and the consumer: the marketer/designer knows things the consumer does not.[4]

When sellers know more than buyers, this creates a dilemma for sellers. They can choose to leverage the information asymmetry for their own benefit, at the expense of the buyer's interests, or they can choose to leverage the asymmetry for mutual benefit.

Practitioners of behavioral design have gone down both paths. One approach, led by behavioral economists like Richard Thaler and Dan Ariely, has focused on behavioral designs and "nudges" that promote better choices to improve *consumer well-being*, defined as helping people be "happier, healthier, and wealthier." A second approach, derived somewhat ironically from the work of Robert Cialdini, has focused on *covert persuasion*, emphasizing how heuristics and biases can be exploited to increase marketer's control over consumers' choice processes and outcomes. The first approach shares many goals with intuitive marketing, the second is simply a variation of the traditional persuasive marketing model—one that substitutes the covert persuasion of choice architectures and behavioral interventions for the overt persuasion of the classic *AIDA* model.

Persuasive tactics can be thought of as distributed along a spectrum that runs from *rational argument* at one end to *coercion* at the other. Rational argument is the most ethical form of persuasion, because it only engages a person's reasoning powers and does not depend on hidden information, manipulation, or deception. Unfortunately, if products in a category are essentially identical in terms of features, functions, and price, there may be few convincing rational grounds for choosing one over another. So rational argument may be ethical, but it may not be very persuasive in many marketing contexts. Coercion, at the other end of the spectrum, is clearly unethical, usually illegal, and unlikely to be effective in any market that has at least two sellers competing.

In the middle of this spectrum of persuasive tactics is *manipulation*. All marketing is manipulative to one degree or another. The purpose of marketing—whether persuasive or intuitive—is to get people to do what the marketer wants them to do. According to ethicist Shlomo Sher, manipulation can be *benign*, and therefore ethical, if it is used to "motivate others to pursue the goals they already have."[5] Sher goes on to argue that manipulation is unethical to the extent it involves *deception* or takes advantage of *vulnerabilities* in its audience's normal decision making processes. A difficulty with this characterization is that most of the cognitive processes described in this book, including the heuristics and biases that inform behavioral designs and covert persuasion, are both "normal" aspects of human decision making *and* "vulnerabilities" to the extent they can be exploited by marketers to advance their own transactional goals at the expense of the immediate and longer-term goals of consumers.

This reality—combined with the fact that behavioral designs can influence consumers completely outside their conscious awareness—puts the ethical burden of covert persuasion squarely on the shoulders of marketers, not consumers. It also allows the formulation of a simple rule for determining the ethical status of any covert persuasion attempt:

Covert persuasion is unethical if it disrupts, disregards, or attempts to displace a consumer's existing goals with new goals that benefit the seller but do so by damaging the health, wealth, or happiness of the buyer.

It is the *ends* to which persuasion tactics are put, not the *means* by which they are implemented, that determine their ethical status. Marketers have a responsibility to treat consumers as self-motivated actors capable of making their own choices and pursuing their own ends, however "nonrationally" they may do so. When marketers use behavioral designs to create choice architectures that help consumers advance their immediate goals or pursue their longer-term innate goals of autonomy, competence, and belonging, they are acting ethically. When they treat consumers as "marionettes," they are not. Every marketer needs to decide for themselves which path they wish to take.

Putting Persuasion in Its Proper Place

The noise at the center of traditional marketing—the persistent jabber of persuasion—is often both unnecessary and ineffective, even self-defeating. This is the message from brain science. Although the repetition of persuasive messaging may correlate with sales at a macro level, brain science tells us this effect occurs *despite* the cognitive load imposed by persuasive argumentation, not because of it. People are not so much persuaded by marketing as they are *habituated*. Marketing normally influences us *indirectly* through an extended process of building and reinforcing associations in long-term memory, not directly through immediate emotional or motivational appeals. By highlighting the actual causal mechanisms that connect marketing to sales, brain science provides a powerful rebuttal to the traditional marketing model. In most circumstances, the relationship between persuasion and sales is more accidental than causal. But in some circumstances, it makes both business and ethical sense.

There is a place for persuasion in modern marketing. The key to its use in marketing and advertising is consumer *intention*. As we saw in Chapter 10, humans spend most of their waking hours pursuing goals, sometimes consciously and sometimes unconsciously. As we saw in Chapter 1, persuasion operates exclusively through conscious *System 2* processing because it requires logical reasoning and

350

if-then propositional thinking, both of which are exclusively available as *System 2* functions. Combine these two findings and you get the sweet spot for persuasive marketing: when a consumer is pursuing a conscious goal to satisfy some need or want, driven an active intention, they will be receptive to *information*, including persuasive arguments and/or demonstrations, that they believe will help them fulfill their goal and satisfy their intention. Borrowing a phrase from digital marketer Gordon Hotchkiss, I have called this a state of *aligned intent*.[6]

How can marketers tell if a consumer is in a state of aligned intent? Intentions cannot be measured directly, so marketers must look for cues and clues that indicate a consumer is in a state of mind receptive to persuasive messaging. Walking into a retail establishment is often a good sign, because opportunities for aligned-intent marketing are more likely to appear at the *shopping* and *consuming* stages of the *consumer cycle* than at the *marketing* stage. Messaging on product packaging can often be a good carrier of persuasive messaging in a retail environment. Although it will be ignored by most shoppers, for those who are motivated to choose between similar products or brands, package messaging can be a helpful tie-breaker.

Online and mobile shopping is the domain in which persuasive marketing is most likely to prosper in coming years, because online shopping has become the modern equivalent of the face-to-face shopping experience consumers used to seek out when looking for reasons to choose one product over another. As discussed in Chapter 16, whether one is exploring options on *Bookings.com*, *Yelp.com*, or *shop.nordstrom.com*, one is signaling an intention to buy that implies (but does not guarantee) greater receptivity to persuasive messaging.

It comes down to *permission*—specifically, permission to engage my *top-down attention*. Just as the early 20th century housewife gave the *Fuller Brush Man* permission to pitch his brushes (by not closing the door in his face) so the modern website visitor gives a site permission to make a persuasive pitch if and when their online behavior indicates they are receptive to it.

Marketers must earn the right to engage in persuasion.

If they do not—if they disrupts the consumer's current goals and motivations without implicit or explicit permission—they are likely to trigger any or all of the persuasion resistance responses outlined in Chapter 4: unconscious persuasion correction, counter-arguing, habit disruption, variety seeking.

Persuasion needs to be seen as *one* marketing tactic, useful in some circumstances, counterproductive in others. It is not the purpose of marketing, the guiding light of marketing, or the all-encompassing ideology of marketing. It is one of many marketing tactics that works, when it works, because consumers let it work, based on the wants, needs, and goals they are currently pursuing.

Achieving Influence Without Persuasion

Intuitive marketing is an alternative to persuasive marketing. In Chapter 1, we identified three conspicuous features of intuitive marketing that distinguish it from persuasive marketing: it does not rely on persuasion; it may earn attention, but does not demand it; and it need not make sense. In addition, intuitive marketing has very different purposes than persuasive marketing. Its focus is not on "closing" immediate, discrete, one-time transactional opportunities, but instead on building and maintaining long-term customer relationships spanning multiple journeys through the *consumer cycle* of marketing, shopping, and consumption. Intuitive marketing aims to shape and satisfy consumer wants and needs by leveraging cognitive mechanisms such as unconscious association building, familiarity, trust, conditioning via small emotional rewards, and connecting with consumers' innate aspirations and identity needs.

We have presented *five intuitive marketing strategies* that leverage these cognitive processes in different ways.

Aligned-Intent Marketing

Aligned-intent marketing might be described as "permission-granted" persuasive marketing. It differs from traditional persuasive marketing in that it is based on *earned attention*, not *demanded attention*. It also differs from traditional marketing in that it recognizes the importance of anticipating and responding to a consumer's current mental state and situation. It works by aligning its marketing message with the consumer's existing intentions, motivations, and goals, rather than by trying to interrupt and redirect the consumer to a new goal defined by the marketer—that is, a goal to stop, pay attention to my message, and learn how and why my product should be at the top of your consideration set.

> **Effective aligned-intent marketing can be recognized by the fact that it attracts voluntary *top-down attention*.**

Top-down attention is internally generated and driven by intentions and goals. Once a goal is activated, the process of goal pursuit becomes a powerful determinant of what we notice, what associations we activate in long-term memory, what knowledge we bring to mind, and what actions we take. An aligned-intent marketing message may appear indistinguishable from a traditional persuasive message in terms of its *content*. Its distinctiveness comes from its *placement*, when and where it appears. As noted above with regard to persuasive marketing in general, aligned-intent marketing is likely to find its most promising placement in online and mobile contexts where the consumer's behavior indicates or predicts they are engaged in goal pursuit. Aligning a marketing message with a goal is most likely to generate top-down attention, conscious information-processing, and motivated action. Conversely, it is least likely to generate the various forms of persuasion resistance that can plague persuasive marketing when it interrupts and disrupts a consumer's current goals and intentions.

Aligned-intent is not, strictly speaking, influence without persuasion. But it is persuasion properly placed, avoiding the usual burdens of persuasive marketing: interruption, disruption, distraction, and resistance.

Low-Attention Marketing

Low-attention marketing is the mainstay of intuitive marketing. It acknowledges the fact that marketing usually fails to attract the attention required to reliably deliver a persuasive message to consumers. Given that hard truth, intuitive marketers ask the obvious next question: how can marketing be designed, using principles of brain science, to have a positive influence on consumers even in conditions when attention and persuasion are low or nonexistent?

Much of the brain science examined in this book relates directly to this question of how marketing can influence consumers in the absence of attention and persuasion. To explain how and why this can occur, I have focused on the role of unconscious *System 1* monitoring and how it produces *implicit learning*. The mechanism connecting the two is *associative learning*, a *conditioning* process through which associations between nodes (concepts or representations) in long-term memory are automatically strengthened when *System 1* observes them occurring together frequently. Recognizing co-occurrences necessarily involves multiple exposures to the correlated events, which is why *repetition* is so crucial to low-attention marketing.

What *System 1* commits to implicit memory are not the specific details of an individual event, but patterns of association observed over time. Importantly, *System 1* automatically records and updates these co-occurrences, but does not have the capacity to evaluate them logically. This is why low-attention marketing does not need to make sense. The drumming gorilla in the *Cadbury* commercial described in Chapter 1 has no logical connection to chocolate bars, but *System 1* will dutifully record the association, which it will strengthen every time the ad is viewed.

The final cognitive process that comes into play in low-attention marketing is *priming*. Just as associative learning lets us bypass explicit learning and record conceptual connections in implicit memory, so priming lets us bypass explicit recall and bring those associations to mind at a later point in time. Brain scientists believe priming has survived as a memory retrieval mechanism because it helps us quickly identify and classify things in our immediate environment. It is a source of *knowledge accessibility* and subsequent *knowledge activation* that can bring a product or brand to mind at a point of sale without invoking persuasion, either overt or covert.

> **As a consumer influence strategy, *low-attention marketing* works by creating and reinforcing mental associations with a brand or product through repetitive exposure.**

It builds associations through repetition, conditioning, and implicit learning. It activates those associations and expectations at a point of sale through priming. If the associations and expectations built through low-attention marketing are appropriately positive and motivationally attractive, this sequence of effects can have a significant impact on consumer choice and behavior—with little or no disruption or conscious awareness of how those effects were achieved.

Consistency, Reliability, and Trust

Achieving consumer influence through consistency, reliability, and trust leverages the power of *familiarity*. Novelty and familiarity form a continuum (see Figure 6) through which consumers inevitably pass as they discover, consider, sample, and become familiar with the products and brands they encounter in their regular journeys through the *consumer cycle*. Marketers—creative people at heart—are excited by novel and innovative ideas. Consumers, in contrast, appear to draw more psychological comfort from familiarity. They are attracted to novelty not because it is a direct source of pleasure, but because it offers a chance to learn something new. What starts out as new and different rapidly evolves, through learning, into something that is familiar and comfortable. But consumer learning doesn't stop with familiarity.

The intuitive marketing strategy of *consistency, reliability, and trust* starts from a recognition that consumers seek familiarity. It then asks what marketers can do to build lasting customer relationships on top of that familiarity. The answer involves taking consumers on what might be a lifelong cognitive journey from familiarity to consistency, reliability, and ultimately trust.

If intuitive marketing is going to build positive long-term associations and expectations with regard to a product or brand, it must begin the process by being *consistent.* Consistency, like familiarity, is somewhat underrated by traditional marketing, which emphasizes regular injections of novelty to keep consumers interested and paying attention. This tactic can work, but only if the injection of novelty does not displace any familiarity and consistency already established. We saw with the *Tropicana* packaging example in Chapter 4 how disastrous a violation of familiarity can be for a habitually-bought consumer goods product in a competitive category.

When consistency is rigorously maintained—and this means consistency throughout all three stages of the *consumer cycle*—a product can begin to be seen as *reliable* in the minds of its consumers. Reliability implies future dependability: people no longer simply *associate* the product with past consistency, they have an *expectation* that it will continue to perform consistently in the future. Reliability implies predictability, safety, consistency, and—perhaps most importantly for our cognitive-miser brains—easy mental processing.

Reliability, when experienced consistently over time, leads to *trust.* Trust is a learned attitude toward a product or brand that is built on experience and performance, not persuasion. While the theory behind overt persuasion assumes that people need to be convinced—either through a rational argument or an emotional appeal—to do what marketers want them to do, the theory behind trust as a source of intuitive influence is just the opposite.

> **Familiarity, liking, and fluency, combined with repetition, consistency, and a judgment of reliability lead to a mindset that does not require additional convincing at the moment of choice. Any persuasion required to move someone toward one choice over another is already *built-in* and condensed into the feeling of trust.**

The path from novelty to trust can be long and challenging. There are many opportunities along the way for distraction, diversion, and novelty-for-novelty's-sake. But trust is a goal worth pursuing. The availability of a trustworthy choice at a point of sale has many advantages: it discourages *System 2* deliberation and counter-arguing, decreases uncertainty and risk, inhibits variety seeking and search, increases willingness to try new products presented under a trustworthy brand, and vastly simplifies decision making.

Small Emotional Rewards

Providing small emotional rewards is an intuitive marketing technique that influences consumers indirectly via the cognitive mechanism of *conditioning.*

Most conditioning in marketing and advertising involves two objects presented together, either simultaneously or sequentially. One object is the product or brand (the *conditioned stimulus* or *CS*) and the other is an already-liked person, place, or event (the *unconditioned stimulus* or *US*). Through repeated exposures to this paired presentation, positivity toward the already-liked object gets transferred to the product or brand.

Small emotional rewards works on the same principle, but replaces the already-liked object with the ad or marketing message itself. Small emotional rewards are most often delivered in 30-second TV ads designed to be consumed as short narratives that tell an amusing story. It is the entertainment value of the ad that draws *top-down attention* from the viewer. The short episode of entertainment provides the emotional reward. It also motivates the viewer to pay attention to the ad *again* the next time it appears. Eventually, the entertainment value of the ad either wanes due to over-repetition, or is refreshed with some new variation of the entertaining narrative.

The cognitive processes underlying small emotional rewards are relatively well understood. First comes *top-down attention*, which is earned to the extent the narrative is indeed entertaining. Then comes the *emotional reward* itself, which is recorded by *System 1* along with any and all associations that accompany it, including the promoted product or brand. Repeated viewing of the ad produces automatic *associative learning* that strengthens the originally observed associations in *nondeclarative memory*, making them more likely to be activated by *priming* at a later point of sale, such as during an in-store or online shopping excursion.

The mechanism that transfers the feeling of positivity from the narrative to the product or brand is *evaluative conditioning*. The type of evaluative conditioning produced by small emotional reward marketing is *simultaneous, contingency-aware conditioning*. Viewers experience the entertaining narrative and the product simultaneously, which tends to produce stronger conditioning effects, and they are consciously aware of the pairing of the product with the narrative, which also strengthens conditioning. The result of a successful conditioning process is two-fold: a positive-valence uptick in the *somatic marker* or *affective residue* associated with the product or brand, and an increase in the *salience* of the product or brand in subsequent competitive consumer choice situations.

An important lesson for marketers is that communicating "small emotions" in advertising and marketing can be more effective than communicating "big emotions," as is currently popular in emotional TV advertising.

The unconscious accumulation of small emotional rewards from repeated exposures to seemingly inconsequential but entertaining ads can create and strengthen the implicit memory traces that significantly impact consumers' habits, loyalties, and subsequent choices and actions—all without resorting to overt or covert persuasion.

Connecting with Aspirations and Identity

This is the fifth intuitive marketing strategy introduced in this book. It leverages *motivation* and *goal pursuit* to influence consumers without persuasion. It is based on the idea that all humans share two universal motivations that drive much of their behavior, including their consumer behavior. The first is *aspiration*. We want to be better and to do better tomorrow than today. The second is *identity*. We have a deep need to feel self-esteem, to feel good about ourselves, to believe that we are honorable, likeable, desirable, and appreciated. We are motivated to seek out and pursue goals that help us satisfy these needs. We are also motivated to avoid and defend ourselves against threats to our aspirations and self-esteem.

Connecting to aspirations and identity does not impose motivations on consumers, it focuses on the motivations and goals consumers already have and provides a *narrative* as to how products and brands can help consumers achieve those goals.

Brands are powerful signifiers in our modern consumer-oriented and marketing-saturated world. What they signify has become as important, or perhaps even more important, than what they provide in terms of functionality.[7] Brands and products that signify the aspirations and identities of their consumers can be positive influences in people's lives. Such brands and products seldom resort to the tactics and pressures of persuasive marketing. Instead, they present themselves as partners in consumers' aspirational and identity-affirming goals—goals to improve one's life, to be a better person, to be welcomed and accepted by others, to do something good in the world.

The Limits of Intuitive Marketing

One unfortunate byproduct of persuasive marketing is a tendency to treat consumers as passive recipients of marketing messages, ignoring the deeper motivations and goals they may be pursuing, assuming they are ready and willing to be persuaded to do whatever marketers want them to do. I hope the brain science findings and intuitive marketing strategies presented in this book have succeeded in putting this naïve stereotype to rest.

Consumers are not puppets.

The phrase "tough customer" is appropriate. Consumers are not easy marks. They are not easily won over, they resist persuasion efforts, they are not particularly loyal, and they have real and enduring goals and motivations of their own that may conflict with the goals marketers would like them to embrace. Intuitive marketing takes these realities seriously and recommends a different route to influencing consumers, but it is still marketing. It is not a silver bullet.

No matter how well-crafted and psychologically sophisticated a marketing message might be, marketing alone can never compensate for an unsatisfactory product experience. Being well-positioned in terms of intuitive marketing mechanisms—being reliable and trustworthy, providing small emotionally rewards, relating to consumer aspirations, contributing to peoples' sense of self-worth, etc.—may be a necessary condition for long-term success, but it is not sufficient. If the pizza tastes like cardboard, no amount of marketing, intuitive or persuasive, is going to overcome that fact in the long run. Similarly, if a product's "reasons for buying" cannot withstand the light of conscious attention and appraisal, that product is probably not going to achieve the influential goals of intuitive marketing.

Intuitive techniques can make marketing less annoying, less disruptive, and more useful to both consumers and marketers, but they don't guarantee marketplace success.

Ultimately, conscious *System 2* evaluation and analysis do "wake up" and come into play. If the product or brand does not live up to the promises made by intuitive marketing, it is unlikely to succeed in the marketplace.

In this book, I have developed an alternative theory of marketing called *intuitive marketing* that does not rely on overt or covert persuasion and does not require that consumers be treated as "patsies." Unlike transactional persuasive marketing or covertly persuasive behavioral designs, intuitive marketing focuses on long-term relationship-building through careful monitoring and managing of consumers' expectations as they experience multiple journeys through the *consumer cycle* of marketing, shopping, and consuming. It emphasizes *influence* as an alternative to persuasion and brings together a vast array of findings from brain science research to illustrate both the perils of persuasion as a marketing strategy and the promise of intuitive marketing as a better way to build lasting relationships with customers and consumers.

I am under no illusion that this book will fundamentally change the trajectory of marketing as it is practiced today and has been practiced and taught for over a century. However, I have tried to show that intuitive marketing is a viable, science-based alternative to both overt and covert persuasion. Marketers are not *required* to treat marketing as a zero-sum battle between buyers and sellers. For those who are uncomfortable with either the practical results or the ethical implications of transactional persuasive marketing, intuitive marketing is an alternative worth considering.

–*Tuesday, August 13, 2019, Sunnyvale, CA*

Notes and References

Introduction

[1] Some early speculations regarding causes and consequences of this state of affairs are offered in two posts on my blog, "Can Neuromarketing Get Its Groove Back? Part 1, Part 2". Available online at http://bit.ly/1HpPTgh and http://bit.ly/1NMNQnt.

[2] See "Intuitive Marketing." *Intuitive Consumer Blog*, August 23, 2014 (available online at http://bit.ly/1pTHvLr) and "Intuitive Marketing: Achieving Influence Without Persuasion." *Intuitive Consumer Blog*, October 14, 2014 (available online at http://bit.ly/1rtypkE).

[3] In a 2019 review of the field, "skepticism" about neuromarketing among marketers and marketing organizations is described as "fading," but still high. See "Neuromarketing: What You Need to Know." *Harvard Business Review*, January 23, 2019. Available online at http://bit.ly/2mqQZ81.

Chapter 1. The Promise of Intuitive Marketing

[1] See Jones, Chris, "Emotionally engaged? Maybe you weren't paying attention," *Chicago Tribune*, February 6, 2015. Available online at http://trib.in/2xnMChH. Heath, Robert, "In advertising, emotion is a dish best served on the side—a lesson lost in Super Bowl 2015," *The Conversation*, February 16, 2015. Available online at http://bit.ly/2y9irZx.

[2] See, for example, a Gallup survey of honesty and ethics in professions conducted in December 2014, in which only 10% of respondents rated "advertising people" as high or very high on honesty and ethical standards, barely beating out car salespeople (8%) and that most benighted of professions, members of Congress (7%). Available online at http://bit.ly/1wkoVMf.

[3] For an overview of many forms of "neurobullocks," including a scathing critique of "buy button" language in neuromarketing, see Satel, Sally, and Scott O. Lilienfeld. *Brainwashed: The seductive appeal of mindless neuroscience*. Basic Civitas Books, 2013.

[4] Perhaps the most telling evidence against the "buy button" hypothesis is the discovery of nonconscious processes that appear to get activated to resist persuasive messaging, even in its most subtle and unobtrusive forms. See Laran, Juliano, Amy N. Dalton, and Eduardo B. Andrade. "The Curious Case of Behavioral Backlash: Why Brands Produce Priming Effects and Slogans Produce Reverse Priming Effects." *Journal of Consumer Research* 37.6 (2011): 999-1014. Similar results are described by Roger Dooley in his blog: Dooley, Roger, "'Don't Buy' Button Located in Brain," *Neuromarketing Blog*, August 27, 2007, online at http://bit.ly/bB5PQD, referencing Swaminathan, Nikhil, "Impulse Stopping: When

the Mind Exercises 'Free Won't,'" Scientific American, August 22, 2007, online at http://bit.ly/fBkinr. On "neurobollocks" in general, see the *NeuroBollocks* blog at http://neurobollocks.wordpress.com/.

[5] William, James. *The principles of psychology*. Harvard University Press, Cambridge, MA, (1890). Quotes at pp. 325, 330. An excellent overview of the history of dual process models can be found in Sloman, Steven A. "The empirical case for two systems of reasoning." *Psychological bulletin* 119.1 (1996): 3.

[6] Kahneman, Daniel. *Thinking, fast and slow*. Macmillan, 2011.

[7] See, for example, Barden, Phil. *Decoded: The science behind why we buy*. John Wiley & Sons, 2013; Heath, Robert. *Seducing the subconscious: The psychology of emotional influence in advertising*. John Wiley & Sons, 2012; "Nothing more than feelings: Admen have made a marketing guru of Daniel Kahneman, a prizewinning psychologist," *The Economist*, December 7, 2013, available online at http://econ.st/1kra6kJ.

[8] Rogers, Martha, and Kirk H. Smith. "Public perceptions of subliminal advertising: Why practitioners shouldn't ignore this issue." *Journal of Advertising Research* (1993). See also Nelson, Michelle R. "The hidden persuaders: then and now." *Journal of Advertising* 37.1 (2008): 113-126.

[9] The leading proponent of this view, supported by a substantial body of research, is John Bargh of Yale University. For a general introduction, see Bargh, John A., and Ezequiel Morsella. "Unconscious behavioral guidance systems." *Then a miracle occurs: Focusing on behavior in social psychological theory and research* (2010): 89-118.

[10] After reading about it in Timothy Wilson's great book, *Strangers to Ourselves: Discovering the Adaptive Unconscious*, Harvard University Press, 2002, p. 24. The original calculations were made by Nørretranders, Tor. *The User Illusion: Cutting Consciousness Down to Size*. Trans. Jonathan Sydenham. New York: Viking Penguin (1998).

[11] Schacter, Daniel L., and Donna Rose Addis. "The cognitive neuroscience of constructive memory: remembering the past and imagining the future." *Philosophical Transactions of the Royal Society B: Biological Sciences* 362.1481 (2007): 773-786; Baumeister, Roy F., and E. J. Masicampo. "Conscious thought is for facilitating social and cultural interactions: How mental simulations serve the animal–culture interface." *Psychological review* 117.3 (2010): 945.

[12] Two detailed treatments of the *AIDA* model and its prominence in marketing today are Vakratsas, Demetrios, and Tim Ambler, "How advertising works: what do we really know?" *The Journal of Marketing* (1999): 26-43 and Heath, Robert, *Seducing the subconscious: The psychology of emotional influence in advertising*. John Wiley & Sons, 2012. For a dramatic depiction of the *AIDA* model applied to "boiler room" sales, see Alex Baldwin's impassioned speech, written by the brilliant David Mamet, in the film *Glengarry Glenn Ross*, 1992.

[13] Some will disagree, but this is simply a definitional issue. I prefer to use the term "influence" to describe what others might call unconscious persuasion. Influence is quite different than persuasion in other respects as well.

[14] See Friestad, Marian, and Peter Wright. "The persuasion knowledge model: How people cope with persuasion attempts." *Journal of consumer research* (1994): 1-31; Laran, Juliano, Amy N. Dalton, and Eduardo B. Andrade. "The Curious Case of Behavioral Backlash: Why Brands Produce Priming Effects and Slogans Produce Reverse Priming Effects." *Journal of Consumer Research* 37.6 (2011): 999-1014.

[15] See "IPA Effectiveness Awards 2010: Silver Award - Cadbury Dairy Milk," November 5, 2010, online at http://www.campaignlive.co.uk/news/1040714/.

[16] The idea of "earned" vs. "demanded" attention was originally suggested to me by British digital designer Pete Trainor. Pete's formulation was "reward attention, do not demand it." I gratefully acknowledge stealing, slightly modifying, and then extending his idea into the concept of aligned-intent marketing.

[17] Rory Sutherland in *Forward* to Samson, Alain, ed. *The Behavioral Economics Guide 2014*, p. xv. Available online at http://www.behavioraleconomics.com/.

[18] Binet, Les and Susan Carter, "Mythbusters: The idea that marketing always needs to make sense," *The WARC Blog*, online at http://bit.ly/UWR9jG.

[19] Kay, Gareth. "The post-disruptive advertising era." *Admap Magazine* (October 2014): 15-17. Available online at http://bit.ly/1Moz83Q.

[20] Ibid., p. 17.

Chapter 2. Intuitive Marketing in Perspective

[1] An earlier version of the Cognitive Timeline appeared in Genco et al. *Neuromarketing for Dummies*, p. 26. Modified based on input from readers.

[2] Body sense, called *proprioception* by scientists, is the often-forgotten sixth-sense, and it has nothing to do with seeing dead people. It is the sense of our body's position in space, as well as the position of different parts of our body in relation to each other. It is how we acquire feedback on our own movement in space and keep our balance. We can pay conscious attention to these sensory feelings if we want to, but for the most part our proprioceptive sense operates unconsciously.

[3] Mlodinow, Leonard. *Subliminal: How Your Unconscious Mind Rules Your Behavior.* Random House, Inc. Kindle Edition, p. 50

[4] On the rapidity of impression formation and conceptualization, see Greene, Michelle R., and Aude Oliva. "The briefest of glances. The time course of natural scene understanding." *Psychological Science* 20.4 (2009): 464-472.

[5] Gilbert, Daniel. *Stumbling on happiness.* Vintage Canada, 2009.

[6] An earlier version of Figure 3 was published in Genco et al, *Neuromarketing for Dummies*, p. 250. Modified here to include "activating goals" as part of the cognitive timeline.

[7] These measures are discussed in detail in Genco et al. *Neuromarketing for Dummies*, chapters 16 and 17.

[8] Bargh, John A., and Ezequiel Morsella. "Unconscious behavioral guidance systems." *Then a miracle occurs: Focusing on behavior in social psychological theory and research* (2010): 89-118.

[9] From Bargh, John A., and Ezequiel Morsella. "Unconscious behavioral guidance systems," p. 92. Slightly reformatted for clarity.

[10] Baumeister, Roy F., et al. "How emotion shapes behavior: Feedback, anticipation, and reflection, rather than direct causation." *Personality and Social Psychology Review* 11.2 (2007): 167-203, discussed at length in Chapter 8.

[11] Bargh and Morsella, "Unconscious behavioral guidance systems," p. 101; Lerner, Jennifer S., and Dacher Keltner. "Beyond valence: Toward a model of emotion-specific influences on judgement and choice." *Cognition & Emotion*14.4 (2000): 473-493. For an interesting study of the effects of anger and sadness on responsiveness to vacation ads, see Rucker, Derek D., and Richard E. Petty. "Emotion

specificity and consumer behavior: Anger, sadness, and preference for activity." *Motivation and Emotion* 28.1 (2004): 3-21.

[12] Kahneman, Daniel. "Maps of bounded rationality: Psychology for behavioral economics." *The American economic review* 93.5 (2003): 1449-1475. Fazio, Russell H. "On the automatic activation of associated evaluations: An overview." *Cognition & Emotion* 15.2 (2001): 115-141.

[13] Duckworth, Kimberly L., et al. "The automatic evaluation of novel stimuli." *Psychological science* 13.6 (2002): 513-519.

[14] Chen, Mark, and John A. Bargh. "Consequences of automatic evaluation: Immediate behavioral predispositions to approach or avoid the stimulus." *Personality and Social Psychology Bulletin* 25.2 (1999): 215-224.

[15] See, for example, Cacioppo, John T., Joseph R. Priester, and Gary G. Berntson. "Rudimentary determinants of attitudes: II. Arm flexion and extension have differential effects on attitudes." *Journal of personality and social psychology* 65.1 (1993): 5.

[16] Winkielman, Piotr, et al. "Embodiment of cognition and emotion." *APA handbook of personality and social psychology* 1 (2015): 151-175.

[17] Higgins, E. Tory, John A. Bargh, and Wendy J. Lombardi. "Nature of priming effects on categorization." *Journal of Experimental Psychology: Learning, Memory, and Cognition* 11.1 (1985): 59.

[18] For a summary of the controversy written for non-psychologists, see Meyer, Michelle N. and Christopher Chabris, "Why Psychologists' Food Fight Matters: 'Important findings' haven't been replicated and science may have to change its ways." *Slate.com*, July 31, 2014, online at http://slate.me/1DaBTCI.

[19] An earlier version of the consumer cycle graphic was presented in Genco et al. *Neuromarketing for Dummies*, p. 294.

[20] Binet, Les, and Peter Field. *The Long and the Short of It: Balancing Short and Long-Term Marketing Strategies.* Institute of Practitioners in Advertising. Available online at http://bit.ly/1zvF5nz, p. 53.

[21] Ibid., p. 9.

[22] Frederick, Shane, George Loewenstein, and Ted O'Donoghue. "Time discounting and time preference: A critical review." *Journal of economic literature* (2002): 351-401; McClure, Samuel M., et al. "Separate neural systems value immediate and delayed monetary rewards." *Science* 306.5695 (2004): 503-507.

[23] See, for example, Heath, Robert. *Seducing the subconscious: The psychology of emotional influence in advertising.* John Wiley & Sons, 2012.

[24] These two paragraphs paraphrase Binet and Field, *The Long and the Short of It*, p. 58.

[25] Cialdini, Robert B. *Influence: The psychology of persuasion. Revised edition.* New York, Harper Business (2006). Introduction.

Chapter 3. Understanding Attention

[1] Friestad, Marian, and Peter Wright. "The persuasion knowledge model: How people cope with persuasion attempts." *Journal of consumer research* (1994): 1-31.

[2] See the Federal Communication Commission (FCC) website, "Loud Commercials." Available online at http://fcc.us/1baheE6.

[3] Response to faces is not strictly a visual saliency element, because it requires a prior process of facial recognition before it draws attention. However, once a face is recognized as a face, it very rapidly becomes and object of bottom-up attention, often within 50 milliseconds. See Sugase, Yasuko, et al. "Global and fine information coded by single neurons in the temporal visual cortex." *Nature* 400.6747 (1999): 869-873. An excellent overview of human facial recognition capabilities and limitations is Sinha, Pawan, et al. "Face recognition by humans: Nineteen results all computer vision researchers should know about." *Proceedings of the IEEE* 94.11 (2006): 1948-1962.

[4] See Milosavljevic, Milica, and Moran Cerf. "First attention then intention: Insights from computational neuroscience of vision." *International Journal of Advertising* 27.3 (2008): 381-398.

[5] See, for example, the NeuroVision™ product offered by commercial vendor *Neurons, Inc.* Available online at https://bit.ly/2OSQOeh.

[6] Bar, Moshe, and Maital Neta. "The proactive brain: Using rudimentary information to make predictive judgments." Journal of Consumer Behaviour 7.4-5 (2008): 319- 330; Bar, Moshe. "The proactive brain: memory for predictions." Philosophical Transactions of the Royal Society B: Biological Sciences 364.1521 (2009): 1235-1243; Clark, Andy. "Whatever next? Predictive brains, situated agents, and the future of cognitive science." *Behavioral and Brain Sciences* 36.03 (2013): 181-204.

[7] Kahneman, *Thinking, Fast and Slow*, p. 67.

[8] See, for example, Biederman, Irving, and Edward Vessel. "Perceptual Pleasure and the Brain A novel theory explains why the brain craves information and seeks it through the senses." *American scientist* 94.3 (2006): 247-253.

[9] Poldrack, Russell. "Multitasking: The Brain Seeks Novelty." *Huffington Post*, March 18, 2010. Available online at http://huff.to/1GuuiBj.

[10] For example, negative emotional states tend to narrow the scope of attention, while positive emotions tend to broaden it. See Fredrickson, Barbara L., and Christine Branigan. "Positive emotions broaden the scope of attention and thought-action repertoires." *Cognition & emotion* 19.3 (2005): 313-332.

[11] Codispoti, Maurizio, Margaret M. Bradley, and Peter J. Lang. "Affective reactions to briefly presented pictures." *Psychophysiology* 38.3 (2001): 474-478; Junghöfer, Markus, et al. "Fleeting images: a new look at early emotion discrimination." *Psychophysiology* 38.02 (2001): 175-178.

[12] Baars, Bernard J., Stan Franklin, and Thomas Zoëga Ramsøy. "Global workspace dynamics: cortical 'binding and propagation' enables conscious contents." *Frontiers in psychology* 4 (2013).

[13] Ramsøy, Thomas Zoëga, and Martin Skov. "Brand preference affects the threshold for perceptual awareness." *Journal of Consumer Behaviour* 13.1 (2014): 1-8; Casarotto, Silvia, et al. "Covert brand recognition engages emotion-specific brain networks." *Arch Ital Biol* 150.4 (2012): 259-73.

[14] Baumeister, Roy F., et al. "Bad is stronger than good." *Review of general psychology* 5.4 (2001): 323.

[15] Dutton, Donald G., and Arthur P. Aron. "Some evidence for heightened sexual attraction under conditions of high anxiety." *Journal of personality and social psychology* 30.4 (1974): 510; Schachter, Stanley, and Jerome Singer. "Cognitive, social, and physiological determinants of emotional state." *Psychological review* 69.5 (1962): 379.

[16] These definitions of natural and learned rewards are based on the concepts of intrinsic and extrinsic motivation introduced in Ryan, Richard M., and Edward L. Deci. "Intrinsic and extrinsic

motivations: Classic definitions and new directions." *Contemporary educational psychology*25.1 (2000): 54-67.

[17] Anderson, Brian A., Patryk A. Laurent, and Steven Yantis. "Value-driven attentional capture." *Proceedings of the National Academy of Sciences* 108.25 (2011): 10367-10371.

[18] Bromberg-Martin, Ethan S., Masayuki Matsumoto, and Okihide Hikosaka. "Dopamine in motivational control: rewarding, aversive, and alerting." *Neuron* 68.5 (2010): 815-834; Wittmann, Bianca C., et al. "Anticipation of novelty recruits reward system and hippocampus while promoting recollection." *Neuroimage* 38.1 (2007): 194-202.

[19] Wood, Wendy, and David T. Neal. "The habitual consumer." *Journal of Consumer Psychology* 19.4 (2009): 579-592.

[20] See Lavie, Nilli. "Perceptual load as a necessary condition for selective attention." *Journal of Experimental Psychology: Human Perception and Performance* 21.3 (1995): 451; Lavie, Nilli, et al. "Load theory of selective attention and cognitive control." *Journal of Experimental Psychology: General* 133.3 (2004): 339; Lavie, Nilli. "Distracted and confused?: Selective attention under load." *Trends in cognitive sciences* 9.2 (2005): 75-82.

[21] Posner, Michael I., and Yoav Cohen. "Components of visual orienting." *Attention and performance X: Control of language processes* 32 (1984): 531-556; Klein, Raymond M. "Inhibition of return." *Trends in cognitive sciences* 4.4 (2000): 138-147.

[22] Raymond, Jane E., Mark J. Fenske, and Nader T. Tavassoli. "Selective attention determines emotional responses to novel visual stimuli." *Psychological science* 14.6 (2003): 537-542; Raymond, Jane E., Mark J. Fenske, and Nikki Westoby. "Emotional devaluation of distracting patterns and faces: A consequence of attentional inhibition during visual search?." *Journal of Experimental Psychology: Human Perception and Performance* 31.6 (2005): 1404; Kiss, Monika, et al. "Efficient attentional selection predicts distractor devaluation: Event-related potential evidence for a direct link between attention and emotion." *Journal of cognitive neuroscience* 19.8 (2007): 1316-1322; Duff, Brittany RL, and Ronald J. Faber. "Missing the Mark: Advertising Avoidance and Distractor Devaluation." *Journal of Advertising* 40.2 (2011): 51;

[23] Fang, Xiang, Surendra Singh, and Rohini Ahluwalia. "An examination of different explanations for the mere exposure effect." *Journal of consumer research* 34.1 (2007): 97-103; Matthes, Jörg, Christian Schemer, and Werner Wirth. "More than meets the eye: Investigating the hidden impact of brand placements in television magazines." *International Journal of Advertising* 26.4 (2007): 477-503.

[24] For evidence of distractor devaluation occurring under high perceptual load, see Wang, Zongyuan, and Brittany RL Duff. "All Loads Are Not Equal: Distinct Influences of Perceptual Load and Cognitive Load on Peripheral Ad Processing." *Media Psychology* 19.4 (2016): 589-613.

[25] On the relative roles of bottom-up and top-down attention on product choice, see Milosavljevic, Milica et al. "Relative visual saliency differences induce sizable bias in consumer choice." *Journal of Consumer Psychology* 22.1 (2012). On the financial benefits of good design, see Hertenstein, Julie H., Marjorie B. Platt, and Robert W. Veryzer. "The Impact of Industrial Design Effectiveness on Corporate Financial Performance*." *Journal of Product Innovation Management* 22.1 (2005): 3-21.

[26] Data from "IAB Internet Advertising Revenue Report: 2018 Full Year Results." April 2019, p. 12. Available online at http://bit.ly/2JnB4jQ.

[27] Forrester Research. "Moments that Matter: Intent-Rich Moments Are Critical to Winning Today's Consumer Journey." *A Forrester Consulting Thought Leadership Paper Commissioned by Google*, July 2015. Available online at http://bit.ly/206vJyz.

Chapter 4. Marketing in the Absence of Attention

[1] Jiwa, Bernadette. *Difference: The one-page method for reimagining your business and reinventing your marketing* (Kindle Locations 382-383). The Story Of Telling Press. (2014) Kindle Edition.

[2] Krugman, Herbert E. "The impact of television advertising: Learning without involvement." *Public opinion quarterly* 29.3 (1965): 349-356.

[3] For Heath's study of attention, emotion, and TV viewing, see Heath, Robert G., Agnes C. Nairn, and Paul A. Bottomley. "How effective is creativity? Emotive content in TV advertising does not increase attention." *Journal of Advertising Research* 49.4 (2009): 450-463.

[4] Heath, Robert, David Brandt, and Agnes Nairn. "Brand relationships: Strengthened by emotion, weakened by attention." *Journal of Advertising Research* 46.4 (2006): 410-419, p. 411. References omitted.

[5] Initial exchanges between Robert Heath and Nigel Hollis of Millward Brown were published in *Admap* magazine in 2002, where they can currently be found behind the World Advertising Research Center (WARC) paywall. A subsequent tussle between Hollis and Heath broke out in 2007, revealing that wounds apparently had not healed and minds definitely had not been changed. See Hollis, Nigel. "Will a kick in the teeth get attention?" *Millward Brown* blog. February 13, 2007, available online at http://bit.ly/1LwchXb, and subsequent comments by Heath and Hollis in response to a blog post by Jason Oke, "A defense of pre-testing: let's get ready to rumble." *The Fruits of Imagination* blog, May 19, 2007, available online at http://bit.ly/1GZwON5.

[6] As a sign of how deep some animosities apparently still run, there exists a blog (I will not promote it by providing its URL) written by an anonymous author that is devoted solely to personal and professional attacks on Robert Heath. The author's understanding of Heath's research is quite limited and biased, but the extent to which traditional market research methodologies and providers are "defended" leaves little doubt that this individual is writing on behalf of, if not from within, one of the large ad-testing vendors. Most posts date from 2008, but at least one post was published as recently as 2013.

[7] Binet, Les, and Peter Field. "Empirical generalizations about advertising campaign success." *Journal of Advertising Research* 49.2 (2009): 130-133.

[8] For additional thoughts on Robert Heath's significance for advertising and marketing research, see my blog post: Genco, Stephen. "What if Robert Heath is right? Attention, emotion and advertising," originally published on September 4, 2009, republished on the *Intuitive Consumer Blog* on June 15, 2013. Available online at http://bit.ly/1DCPaG9.

[9] Yoo, Chan Yun. "Unconscious processing of Web advertising: Effects on implicit memory, attitude toward the brand, and consideration set." *Journal of interactive marketing* 22.2 (2008): 2-18.

[10] For example: Janiszewski, Chris. "Preconscious processing effects: The independence of attitude formation and conscious thought." *Journal of consumer research* (1988): 199-209; Janiszewski, Chris. "Preattentive mere exposure effects." *Journal of Consumer Research* (1993): 376-392; Fitzsimons, Gavan J., et al. "Non-conscious influences on consumer choice." *Marketing Letters* 13.3 (2002): 269-279; Labroo, Aparna A., Ravi Dhar, and Norbert Schwarz. "Of frog wines and frowning watches: Semantic priming,

perceptual fluency, and brand evaluation." *Journal of Consumer Research* 34.6 (2008): 819-831; Ferraro, Rosellina, James R. Bettman, and Tanya L. Chartrand. "The power of strangers: The effect of incidental consumer brand encounters on brand choice." *Journal of Consumer Research* 35.5 (2009): 729-741.

[11] Friestad, Marian, and Peter Wright. "The persuasion knowledge model: How people cope with persuasion attempts." *Journal of consumer research* (1994): 1-31.

[12] For an excellent overview, see Heath, Robert. *Seducing the subconscious: The psychology of emotional influence in advertising*. Wiley, 2012, especially Chapter 7, "Problems with Getting Attention."

[13] Campbell, Margaret C., and Amna Kirmani. "Consumers' use of persuasion knowledge: The effects of accessibility and cognitive capacity on perceptions of an influence agent." *Journal of Consumer Research* 27.1 (2000): 69-83.

[14] Laran, Juliano, Amy N. Dalton, and Eduardo B. Andrade. "The curious case of behavioral backlash: Why brands produce priming effects and slogans produce reverse priming effects." *Journal of Consumer Research* 37.6 (2010): 999-1014.

[15] Wood, Wendy, and David T. Neal. "The habitual consumer." *Journal of Consumer Psychology* 19.4 (2009): 579-592.

[16] See Duhigg, Charles. The power of habit: Why we do what we do in life and business. Random House, 2012.

[17] The Tropicana debacle was covered extensively in the press and blogs at the time. See Kiley, David. "*Tropicana Fiasco From Arnell is Gift That Keeps Giving*," April 3, 2009. Available online at http://buswk.co/RfWl. Kirk, Colleen and Karen Berger, "Tropicana: Social Media Teach Marketers a Branding Lesson." Available online at http://bit.ly/1bYJ035. An alternative explanation of why the new packaging failed in provided in Barden, Phil. *Decoded: The Science Behind Why We Buy*. John Wiley & Sons, 2013, pp. 94-96.

[18] Fishbach, Ayelet, Rebecca K. Ratner, and Ying Zhang. "Inherently loyal or easily bored?: Nonconscious activation of consistency versus variety-seeking behavior." *Journal of Consumer Psychology* 21.1 (2011): 38-48.

[19] Ariely, Dan, and Michael I. Norton. "Conceptual consumption." *Annual review of psychology* 60 (2009): 475-499.

[20] Ratner, Rebecca K., Barbara E. Kahn, and Daniel Kahneman. "Choosing less-preferred experiences for the sake of variety." *Journal of Consumer Research* 26.1 (1999): 1-15; Ratner, Rebecca K., and Barbara E. Kahn. "The impact of private versus public consumption on variety-seeking behavior." *Journal of Consumer Research* 29.2 (2002): 246-257.

[21] See Steidl, Peter. *Neurobranding*. CreateSpace, 2012, especially Chapter 9, "Influencing habitual buying," p. 54.

[22] See Sharp, *How Brands Grow*, Chapter 4, "Which Customers Matter Most?"

[23] Ibid., pp. 44-45.

Chapter 5. How We Prefer, What We Prefer

[1] See, for example, the extensive literature review in Evans, Jonathan St BT, and Keith E. Stanovich. "Dual-process theories of higher cognition advancing the debate." *Perspectives on Psychological Science* 8.3 (2013): 223-241.

[2] Kahneman, *Thinking, Fast and Slow*, p. 40.

[3] Wilson, Timothy D., et al. "Just think: the challenges of the disengaged mind." *Science* 345.6192 (2014): 75-77, p. 77.

[4] It is worth noting that the concept of *conflict detection* in this literature is very similar to the concept of *expectancy violation* in the attention and novelty literature. This may be one of those cases where two research streams have not yet intersected to explore whether they might, in fact, be measuring the same mental mechanism in two different contexts.

[5] Pennycook, Gordon, Jonathan A. Fugelsang, and Derek J. Koehler. "What makes us think? A three-stage dual-process model of analytic engagement." *Cognitive psychology* 80 (2015): 34-72.

[6] Pennycook et al. "What makes us think?"; Stanovich, Keith E., and Richard F. West. "On the relative independence of thinking biases and cognitive ability." *Journal of personality and social psychology* 94.4 (2008): 672; Pennycook, Gordon, et al. "Cognitive style and religiosity: The role of conflict detection." *Memory & Cognition* 42.1 (2014): 1-10.

[7] Oppenheimer, Daniel M. "The secret life of fluency." *Trends in cognitive sciences* 12.6 (2008): 237-241; Schwarz, Norbert. "Meta-cognitive experiences in consumer judgment and decision making." *Journal of Consumer Psychology, September* (2004); Novemsky, Nathan, et al. "Preference fluency in choice." *Journal of Marketing Research* 44.3 (2007): 347-356.

[8] This version of the model is slightly modified from the version first presented in Genco et. al, *Neuromarketing for Dummies*, p. 158.

[9] MacLeod, Scott. *The life of Haifisch*. Broken Boulder Press. 1999.

[10] Silvia, Paul J. "Emotional responses to art: From collation and arousal to cognition and emotion." *Review of general psychology* 9.4 (2005): 342. See also Silvia, Paul J. "What is interesting? Exploring the appraisal structure of interest." *Emotion* 5.1 (2005): 89.

[11] Silvia, Paul J. "Interest—The curious emotion." *Current Directions in Psychological Science* 17.1 (2008): 57-60.

[12] As articulated by the mid-20th century philosopher Mick Jagger.

[13] Van Praet, Douglas. *Unconscious branding: How neuroscience can empower (and inspire) marketing*. Macmillan, 2012, Chapter 5, "Step 2: Create Comfort." Kindle location 2275.

[14] Hekkert, Paul, Dirk Snelders, and Piet CW Wieringen. "'Most advanced, yet acceptable': typicality and novelty as joint predictors of aesthetic preference in industrial design." *British Journal of Psychology* 94.1 (2003): 111-124; Wei-Ken, Hung, and Chen Lin-Lin. "Effects of novelty and its dimensions on aesthetic preference in product design." *International Journal of Design* 6.2 (2012).

[15] See the classic treatment of this tradeoff in March, James G. "Exploration and exploitation in organizational learning." *Organization science* 2.1 (1991): 71-87.

Chapter 6. Shortcuts to Consumer Preference

[1] Fox, Margalit. "Robert Zajonc, Who Looked at Mind's Ties to Actions, Is Dead at 85." *New York Times*, December 6, 2008; Gorlick, Adam. "Robert Zajonc, pioneer of social psychology, dies at 85." *Stanford Report*, December 11, 2008.

[2] Zajonc, Robert B. "Attitudinal effects of mere exposure." *Journal of personality and social psychology* 9.2 (1968), p. 15.

[3] For a summary, see Murphy, Sheila T., Jennifer L. Monahan, and Robert B. Zajonc. "Additivity of nonconscious affect: combined effects of priming and exposure." *Journal of personality and social psychology* 69.4 (1995), p. 591.

[4] Rajecki, D. W. "Effects of prenatal exposure to auditory or visual stimulation on postnatal distress vocalizations in chicks." *Behavioral Biology* 11.4 (1974): 525-536. Cited in Zajonc, Robert B. "Mere exposure: A gateway to the subliminal." *Current directions in psychological science* 10.6 (2001): 224-228, at p. 225.

[5] Zajonc, Robert B. "Feeling and thinking: Closing the debate over the independence of affect." (2000). In Forgas, Joseph P. ed., *Feeling and thinking: The role of affect in social cognition.* Cambridge University Press, 2001: 31-58.

[6] Zajonc, Robert B. "Mere exposure: A gateway to the subliminal." *Current directions in psychological science* 10.6 (2001): 224-228.

[7] Monahan, Jennifer L., Sheila T. Murphy, and Robert B. Zajonc. "Subliminal mere exposure: Specific, general, and diffuse effects." *Psychological Science* 11.6 (2000): 462-466.

[8] Zajonc, Robert B. "Feeling and thinking: Preferences need no inferences." *American psychologist* 35.2 (1980): p. 155.

[9] Alter, Adam L., and Daniel M. Oppenheimer. "Uniting the tribes of fluency to form a metacognitive nation." *Personality and social psychology review* (2009).

[10] Palmer, Stephen E. "Goodness, Gestalt, groups, and Garner: Local symmetry subgroups as a theory of figural goodness." In Lockhead, Gregory R., ed., The perception of structure: Essays in honor of Wendell R. Garner. Washington, DC, US: American Psychological Association, 1991.

[11] Reber, Rolf, Norbert Schwarz, and Piotr Winkielman. "Processing fluency and aesthetic pleasure: Is beauty in the perceiver's processing experience?" *Personality and social psychology review* 8.4 (2004): 364-382.

[12] Double Jeopardy is an empirical regularity in marketing in which top brands have both higher market share and higher repeat purchase rates, while lower market share brands have fewer buyers and lower repeat purchase rates among those buyers. See Ehrenberg, Andrew SC. "Towards an integrated theory of consumer behaviour." *Journal of the Market Research Society* 11.4 (1969): 305-337; Sharp, *How Brands Grow*, esp. Ch. 2.

[13] Winkielman, Piotr, et al. "Fluency of consistency: When thoughts fit nicely and flow smoothly." In Gawronski, Bertram, and Fritz Strack, eds. *Cognitive consistency: A fundamental principle in social cognition.* Guilford press, 2012: 89-111.

[14] Whittlesea, Bruce WA, and Lisa D. Williams. "The source of feelings of familiarity: the discrepancy-attribution hypothesis." *Journal of Experimental Psychology: Learning, Memory, and Cognition* 26.3 (2000): 547. See also Whittlesea, Bruce WA, and Lisa D. Williams. "Why do strangers feel familiar, but friends don't? A discrepancy-attribution account of feelings of familiarity." *Acta psychologica* 98.2 (1998): 141-165.

[15] Reber and Winkielman. "Processing fluency and aesthetic pleasure," p. 11.

[16] Try it. It's hard to remember 12 of anything—names, brands, events, experiences, whatever. And it's easy to attribute this difficulty to other sources. This is why the "list 12" task is often used by psychologists to invoke a feeling of processing disfluency in experimental subjects.

[17] Winkielman, Piotr, and Norbert Schwarz. "How pleasant was your childhood? Beliefs about memory shape inferences from experienced difficulty of recall." *Psychological Science* 12.2 (2001): 176-179.

[18] Pocheptsova, Anastasiya, Aparna A. Labroo, and Ravi Dhar. "Making products feel special: When metacognitive difficulty enhances evaluation." *Journal of Marketing Research* 47.6 (2010): 1059-1069.

[19] Schwarz, Norbert. "Meta-cognitive experiences in consumer judgment and decision making." *Journal of Consumer Psychology, September* (2004).

[20] Tversky, Amos, and Daniel Kahneman. "Availability: A heuristic for judging frequency and probability." *Cognitive psychology* 5.2 (1973): 207-232.

[21] Alter and Oppenheimer. "Uniting the tribes of fluency." See also Song, Hyunjin, and Norbert Schwarz. "If it's easy to read, it's easy to do, pretty, good, and true." *Psychologist* 23.2 (2010): 108-111.

[22] Alter, Adam L., and Daniel M. Oppenheimer. "Predicting short-term stock fluctuations by using processing fluency." *Proceedings of the National Academy of Sciences* 103.24 (2006): 9369-9372.

[23] Alter, Adam L., and Daniel M. Oppenheimer. "Easy on the mind, easy on the wallet: The roles of familiarity and processing fluency in valuation judgments." *Psychonomic Bulletin & Review* 15.5 (2008): 985-990.

[24] Song, Hyunjin, and Norbert Schwarz. "If it's difficult to pronounce, it must be risky fluency, familiarity, and risk perception." *Psychological Science* 20.2 (2009): 135-138.

[25] Hertwig, Ralph, et al. "Fluency heuristic: a model of how the mind exploits a by-product of information retrieval." *Journal of Experimental Psychology: Learning, memory, and cognition* 34.5 (2008): 1191.

Chapter 7. Intuitive Marketing and Lasting Consumer Preferences

[1] Tarran, Brian, "Questioning the Nature of Research." Transcript of interview with Rory Sutherland, *Research-Live.com*, August 31, 2011. Available online at http://bit.ly/2mHJUed.

[2] One of the earliest and most influential explorations of this dichotomy between rational economic theory and behavioral treatments of preferences can be found in March, James G. "Bounded rationality, ambiguity, and the engineering of choice." *The Bell Journal of Economics* (1978): 587-608.

[3] Hsee, Chrisopher K., et al. "Preference reversals between joint and separate evaluations of options: A review and theoretical analysis." *Psychological bulletin* 125.5 (1999): 576.

[4] These examples are taken from an excellent overview of the extensive preference construction literature, Warren, Caleb, A. Peter McGraw, and Leaf Van Boven. "Values and preferences: Defining perence construction." *Wiley Interdisciplinary Reviews: Cognitive Science* 2.2 (2011): 193-205.

[5] The case for inherent preferences is made by Simonson, Itamar. "Will I like a "medium" pillow? Another look at constructed and inherent preferences." *Journal of Consumer Psychology* 18.3 (2008): 155-169. Efforts to reconcile the two views include Bettman, James R., Mary Frances Luce, and John W. Payne. "Preference construction and preference stability: Putting the pillow to rest." *Journal of Consumer Psychology* 18.3 (2008): 170-174 and Kivetz, Ran, Oded Netzer, and Rom Schrift. "The synthesis of preference: Bridging behavioral decision research and marketing science." *Journal of Consumer Psychology* 18 (2008): 179-186.

[6] See, for example, Johansson, Petter, et al. "Failure to detect mismatches between intention and outcome in a simple decision task." *Science* 310.5745 (2005): 116-119; Hall, Lars, et al. "Magic at the marketplace: Choice blindness for the taste of jam and the smell of tea." *Cognition* 117.1 (2010): 54-61; Hall, Lars, Petter Johansson, and Thomas Strandberg. "Lifting the veil of morality: Choice blindness and attitude reversals on a self-transforming survey." *PloS one* 7.9 (2012): e45457.

[7] Johansson, Petter, Lars Hall, and Nick Chater. "Preference change through choice." *Neuroscience of preference and choice: Cognitive and neural mechanisms* (2012): 121-138; Johansson, Petter, et al. "Choice blindness and preference change: You will like this paper better if you (believe you) chose to read it!." *Journal of Behavioral Decision Making* 27.3 (2014): 281-289.

[8] March, James G. "Bounded rationality, ambiguity, and the engineering of choice." *The Bell Journal of Economics* (1978): 587-608, p. 593.

[9] See Ariely, Dan, and Michael I. Norton. "How actions create—not just reveal—preferences." *Trends in cognitive sciences* 12.1 (2008): 13-16.

[10] Simon, Dan, et al. "The transience of constructed preferences." *Journal of Behavioral Decision Making* 21.1 (2008): 1-14; Simon, Dan, and Stephen A. Spiller. "The Elasticity of Preferences." *Psychological Science* 27.12 (2016): 1588-1599.

[11] Berger, Jonah, and Gráinne Fitzsimons. "Dogs on the street, pumas on your feet: How cues in the environment influence product evaluation and choice." *Journal of Marketing Research* 45.1 (2008): 1-14.

[12] For example, Ferraro, Rosellina, James R. Bettman, and Tanya L. Chartrand. "The power of strangers: The effect of incidental consumer brand encounters on brand choice." *Journal of Consumer Research* 35.5 (2009): 729-741; Lee, Angela Y., and Aparna A. Labroo. "The effect of conceptual and perceptual fluency on brand evaluation." *Journal of Marketing Research* 41.2 (2004): 151-165; Tanner, Robin J., et al. "Of chameleons and consumption: The impact of mimicry on choice and preferences." *Journal of Consumer Research* 34.6 (2008): 754-766.

[13] Friese, Malte, Michaela Wänke, and Henning Plessner. "Implicit consumer preferences and their influence on product choice." *Psychology & Marketing* 23.9 (2006): 727-740; Friese, Malte, Wilhelm Hofmann, and Michaela Wänke. "When impulses take over: Moderated predictive validity of explicit and implicit attitude measures in predicting food choice and consumption behaviour." *British Journal of Social Psychology* 47.3 (2008): 397-419.

[14] Ajzen, Icek. "From intentions to actions: A theory of planned behavior." *Action control.* Springer Berlin Heidelberg, 1985. 11-39.

[15] Morwitz, Vicki G., Joel H. Steckel, and Alok Gupta. "When do purchase intentions predict sales?." *International Journal of Forecasting* 23.3 (2007): 347-364; Granbois, Donald H., and John O. Summers. "On the predictive accuracy of subjective purchase probabilities." *SV-Proceedings of the Third Annual Conference of the Association for Consumer Research.* 1972.

[16] Chandon, Pierre, Vicki G. Morwitz, and Werner J. Reinartz. "Do intentions really predict behavior? Self-generated validity effects in survey research." *Journal of Marketing* 69.2 (2005): 1-14.

[17] Ibid., pp. 1-2. See also Feldman, Jack M., and John G. Lynch. "Self-generated validity and other effects of measurement on belief, attitude, intention, and behavior." *Journal of applied Psychology* 73.3 (1988): 421; Morwitz, Vicki G., and Gavan J. Fitzsimons. "The mere-measurement effect: Why does measuring intentions change actual behavior?." *Journal of Consumer Psychology* 14.1-2 (2004): 64-74; Zwane, Alix Peterson, et al. "Being surveyed can change later behavior and related parameter estimates." *Proceedings of the National Academy of Sciences* 108.5 (2011): 1821-1826.

[18] Zaller, John, and Stanley Feldman. "A simple theory of the survey response: Answering questions versus revealing preferences." *American journal of political science* (1992): 579-616, pp. 579-580.

[19] See, for example, Kahneman, Daniel, and Shane Frederick. "Representativeness revisited: Attribute substitution in intuitive judgment." In *Heuristics and Biases: The Psychology of Intuitive Judgment*, edited by Thomas Gilovich et al., Cambridge University Press, Cambridge, 2002, pp. 49–81.

[20] This point is made persuasively by Philip Graves in his excellent book, *Consumer.ology*. Graves, Philip. *Consumer.ology, New Edition: The Truth about Consumers and the Psychology of Shopping*. Nicholas Brealey Publishing, 2013.

[21] Winkielman, Piotr, et al. "The hedonic marking of processing fluency: Implications for evaluative judgment." *The psychology of evaluation: Affective processes in cognition and emotion* (2003): 189-217.

[22] Rory Sutherland in Forward to Samson, Alain, ed. *The Behavioral Economics Guide 2014*, p. xiv. Available online at http://www.behavioraleconomics.com/.

[23] Trust is different than loyalty. Trust is expecting the same results every time you use a product. Loyalty is habitually including a product in your consideration set when buying in a category. Trust is an expectation, loyalty is a behavior. Also, loyalty need not imply *exclusive* use of a product. Exclusive loyalty is extremely rare in actual consumer behavior. As we will see in Chapter 12, most consumers engage in *split-loyalty*. They do tend to buy one brand more than others, but they regularly buy other brands as well. See Sharp, *How Brands Grow*, Chapter 12, "Mental and Physical Availability."

[24] For a summary or research on website credibility and trust, see Fogg, B. J., Gregory Cuellar, and David Danielson. "Motivating, influencing, and persuading users: An introduction to captology." *Human Computer Interaction Fundamentals* (2009): 109-122; Casalo, Luis V., Carlos Flavián, and Miguel Guinalíu. "The influence of satisfaction, perceived reputation and trust on a consumer's commitment to a website." *Journal of Marketing Communications* 13.1 (2007): 1-17; Karimov, Farhod P., Malaika Brengman, and Leo Van Hove. "The effect of website design dimensions on initial trust: a synthesis of the empirical literature." *Journal of Electronic Commerce Research* 12.4 (2011): 272.

[25] Sutherland, Rory. "Rory Sutherland knows how to save marketing." *Wired Magazine*, June 3, 2013. Available online at http://bit.ly/2lOJ0gO.

Chapter 8. Emotions in the Marketplace

[1] Damasio, Antonio R. *Descartes' error*. Random House, 2006.

[2] The game is described in detail in Damasio, *Descartes' error*, pp. 211-214.

[3] See Bechara, Antoine, et al. "Insensitivity to future consequences following damage to human prefrontal cortex." *Cognition* 50.1 (1994): 7-15.

[4] The specific brain regions of interest to Damasio and his colleagues were the *ventromedial prefrontal cortices*, commonly abbreviated as the *vmPFC*. As discovered by Damasio and verified by subsequent research, these regions specialize in accessing and interpreting prior emotional experiences as input into decision making. See, e.g., Naqvi, Nasir, Baba Shiv, and Antoine Bechara. "The role of emotion in decision making A cognitive neuroscience perspective." *Current Directions in Psychological Science* 15.5 (2006): 260-264.

[5] Damasio, *Descartes' Error*, p. 53.

[6] Bechara, Antoine, et al. "Deciding advantageously before knowing the advantageous strategy." *Science* 275.5304 (1997): 1293-1295.

[7] *Soma* is the Greek word for body. It often appears in medical terminology, for example in the term *psychosomatic*, which refers to a mental disorder that involves both the mind (*psyche*) and the body (*soma*).

[8] See Shiota, Michelle N., and James W. Kalat. *Emotion*. Wadsworth, 2012, pp. 158-160; Curtis, Val, Robert Aunger, and Tamer Rabie. "Evidence that disgust evolved to protect from risk of disease." *Proceedings of the Royal Society of London B: Biological Sciences* 271.Suppl 4 (2004): S131-S133; Bar, Moshe, and Maital Neta. "Humans prefer curved visual objects." *Psychological science* 17.8 (2006): 645-648.

[9] Janiszewski, Chris, and Robert S. Wyer Jr. "Content and process priming: A review." *Journal of Consumer Psychology*24.1 (2014): 96-118.

[10] Ibid., p. 348.

[11] See, for example, Bechara, Antoine, et al. "Failure to respond autonomically to anticipated future outcomes following damage to prefrontal cortex." *Cerebral cortex* 6.2 (1996): 215-225. At p. 223: *Covertly, somatic markers would (a) help inhibit the normal tendency to approach immediate reward, and (b) enhance and hold the representation of a future negative scenario in working memory, thus counterbalancing the automatic inclination to seek immediate gain. Overtly, the juxtaposition of a somatic marker to the representation of a future negative scenario would operate as an alarm signal by propitiating the inference that an option that causes immediate gain but future loss would be best avoided.*

[12] Martin Lindström is incorrect in his book, *Buy•ology*, when he states that somatic markers are "a shortcut of sorts … that dictates what you just put inside your shopping cart." Lindström, Martin. *Buy•ology: Truth and lies about why we buy*. Crown Business, 2010, p. 130.

[13] Damasio, *Descartes' Error*, p. xi. See also Linquist, Stefan, and Jordan Bartol. "Two myths about somatic markers." *The British Journal for the Philosophy of Science* 64.3 (2013): 455-484; Bechara, Antoine, et al. "The Iowa Gambling Task and the somatic marker hypothesis: some questions and answers." *Trends in cognitive sciences* 9.4 (2005): 159-162.

[14] Damasio, Antonio, and Gil B. Carvalho. "The nature of feelings: evolutionary and neurobiological origins." *Nature Reviews Neuroscience* 14.2 (2013): 143-152; Damasio, A. "Does moral action depend on reasoning? Yes and no." *John Templeton Foundation (Ed.), Big Questions Essay Series: Does moral action depend on reasoning* (2010): 46-49; Damasio, Antonio. *Self comes to mind: Constructing the conscious brain*. Vintage, 2010.

[15] Winkielman, Piotr, Kent C. Berridge, and Julia L. Wilbarger. "Unconscious affective reactions to masked happy versus angry faces influence consumption behavior and judgments of value." *Personality and Social Psychology Bulletin* 31.1 (2005): 121-135.

[16] But we also saw that subliminal priming of *brands* is a bad idea for marketing and advertising, because the effects are relatively short-lived, weak, and imprecise (for example, subliminally priming a particular cereal brand may trigger eating, but not necessarily cereal eating, and probably not cereal eating of the specific primed brand).

[17] Murphy, Sheila T., and Robert B. Zajonc. "Affect, cognition, and awareness: affective priming with optimal and suboptimal stimulus exposures." *Journal of personality and social psychology* 64.5 (1993): 723; Winkielman, Piotr, and Robert B. Zajonc & Norbert Schwarz. "Subliminal affective priming resists attributional interventions." *Cognition & Emotion* 11.4 (1997): 433-465.

[18] Further evidence for this important point is provided by Strahan, Erin J., Steven J. Spencer, and Mark P. Zanna. "Subliminal priming and persuasion: Striking while the iron is hot." *Journal of Experimental Social Psychology* 38.6 (2002): 556-568.

[19] LeDoux, Joseph. "Rethinking the emotional brain." *Neuron* 73.4 (2012): 653-676, p. 653.

[20] Cosmides, Leda, and John Tooby. "Evolutionary psychology and the emotions." *Handbook of emotions* 2 (2000): 91-115.

[21] Baumeister, Roy F., et al. "How emotion shapes behavior: Feedback, anticipation, and reflection, rather than direct causation." *Personality and Social Psychology Review* 11.2 (2007): 167-203.

[22] Ibid., p. 195.

[23] For recent evidence on this point, see the discussion of "survival circuits" in LeDoux, Joseph. "Rethinking the emotional brain." *Neuron* 73.4 (2012): 653-676.

[24] Baumeister et al., p. 168.

[25] Ibid., p. 172: "*This theory depends heavily on the distinction between automatic affect and full-fledged conscious emotion. The two different types of emotional responses are probably interrelated and coordinated, even though they serve different functions within the system.*"

[26] Bargh, John A., and Ezequiel Morsella. "Unconscious behavioral guidance systems." *Then a miracle occurs: Focusing on behavior in social psychological theory and research* (2010): pp. 101-102.

[27] Lang, Peter J., and Margaret M. Bradley. "Emotion and the motivational brain." *Biological psychology* 84.3 (2010): 437-450; Lang, Peter J., and Margaret M. Bradley. "Appetitive and defensive motivation: Goal-directed or goal-determined?" *Emotion Review* 5.3 (2013): 230-234.

[28] See, for example, Harris, Jennifer L., John A. Bargh, and Kelly D. Brownell. "Priming effects of television food advertising on eating behavior." *Health psychology* 28.4 (2009): 404. This study is discussed in detail in Chapter 11.

[29] Lieberman, Matthew D., et al. "Reflexion and reflection: A social cognitive neuroscience approach to attributional inference." *Advances in experimental social psychology* 34 (2002): 199-249.

[30] Baumeister et al., p. 196.

[31] Ibid., p. 175, emphasis in original.

Chapter 9. Emotional Displays in Marketing

[1] Haley, Russell I., and Allan L. Baldinger. "The ARF copy research validity project." *Journal of advertising research* (1991).

[2] Cook, William A., and Theodore F. Dunn. "The Changing Face Of Advertising Research In The Information Age: An ARF Copy Research Council Survey." *Journal of Advertising Research* 36.1 (1996): 55-71.

[3] Bergkvist, Lars, and John R. Rossiter. "The role of ad likability in predicting an ad's campaign performance." *Journal of advertising* 37.2 (2008): 85-98.

[4] Robinson, William S. "Ecological correlations and the behavior of individuals." *International journal of epidemiology* 38.2 (2009): 337-341; Kramer, Gerald H. "The ecological fallacy revisited: Aggregate-versus individual-level findings on economics and elections, and sociotropic voting." *American political science review* 77.1 (1983): 92-111.

⁵ For an overview of these physiological and cognitive responses to emotion, see Sander, David, Didier Grandjean, and Klaus R. Scherer. "A systems approach to appraisal mechanisms in emotion." *Neural networks* 18.4 (2005): 317-352. On the transfer of emotion from an emotional display via the mechanism of "emotional contagion," see Small, Deborah A., and Nicole M. Verrochi. "The face of need: Facial emotion expression on charity advertisements." *Journal of Marketing Research* 46.6 (2009): 777-787

⁶ Kensinger, Elizabeth A. "Remembering the details: Effects of emotion." *Emotion review* 1.2 (2009): 99-113.

⁷ Kensinger, Elizabeth A., Rachel J. Garoff-Eaton, and Daniel L. Schacter. "Memory for specific visual details can be enhanced by negative arousing content." *Journal of Memory and Language* 54.1 (2006): 99-112; Kensinger, Elizabeth A., Rachel J. Garoff-Eaton, and Daniel L. Schacter. "How negative emotion enhances the visual specificity of a memory." *Journal of Cognitive Neuroscience* 19.11 (2007): 1872-1887.

⁸ Brosch, Tobias, et al. "The impact of emotion on perception, attention, memory, and decision-making." *Swiss medical weekly* 143 (2013): w13786.

⁹ Dolcos, Florin, Kevin S. LaBar, and Roberto Cabeza. "Interaction between the amygdala and the medial temporal lobe memory system predicts better memory for emotional events." *Neuron* 42.5 (2004): 855-863.

¹⁰ Payne, Jessica D., et al. "Sleep preferentially enhances memory for emotional components of scenes." *Psychological Science* 19.8 (2008): 781-788; Payne, Jessica D., and Elizabeth A. Kensinger. "Sleep leads to changes in the emotional memory trace: evidence from fMRI." *Journal of Cognitive Neuroscience* 23.6 (2011): 1285-1297.

¹¹ Kensinger, Elizabeth A., and Daniel L. Schacter. "Memory and emotion." *Handbook of emotions* 3 (2008): 601-617.

¹² Kaplan, Robin L., et al. "Emotion and false memory." *Emotion Review* 8.1 (2016): 8-13.

¹³ Engelhardt, Laura. "The problem with eyewitness testimony: Commentary on a talk by George Fisher and Barbara Tversky." *Stan. J. Legal Stud.* 1 (1999): 25-27; Arkowitz, Hal, and Scott O. Lilienfeld. "Why science tells us not to rely on eyewitness accounts." *Scientific American, Jan* 1 (2010). Available online at http://bit.ly/2dJ7LYU. Wells, Gary L., and Elizabeth A. Olson. "Eyewitness testimony." *Annual Review of Psychology* 54.1 (2003): 277-295. See also the *Innocence Project* webpage on "Eyewitness Misidentification." Available online at http://bit.ly/2wivmud.

¹⁴ Mather, Mara. "Emotional arousal and memory binding: An object-based framework." *Perspectives on Psychological Science* 2.1 (2007): 33-52.

¹⁵ Talarico, Jennifer M., and David C. Rubin. "Confidence, not consistency, characterizes flashbulb memories." *Psychological Science* 14.5 (2003): 455-461.

¹⁶ Brosch et al. "The impact of emotion on perception, attention, memory, and decision-making," p. 4.

¹⁷ The first paper to pull these findings together was highlight the role of goals was Levine, Linda J., and Robin S. Edelstein. "Emotion and memory narrowing: A review and goal-relevance approach." *Cognition and Emotion* 23.5 (2009): 833-875, p. 834.

¹⁸ Ibid. See also Kaplan, Robin L., Ilse Van Damme, and Linda J. Levine. "Motivation matters: Differing effects of pre-goal and post-goal emotions on attention and memory." *Frontiers in psychology* 3 (2012).

[19] Harmon-Jones, Eddie, Philip A. Gable, and Tom F. Price. "Does negative affect always narrow and positive affect always broaden the mind? Considering the influence of motivational intensity on cognitive scope." *Current Directions in Psychological Science* 22.4 (2013): 301-307.

[20] Van Damme, Ilse, et al. "Emotion and false memory: How goal-irrelevance can be relevant for what people remember." *Memory* 25.2 (2017): 201-213.

[21] De Houwer, Jan, Sarah Thomas, and Frank Baeyens. "Association learning of likes and dislikes: A review of 25 years of research on human evaluative conditioning." *Psychological bulletin* 127.6 (2001): 853.

[22] Hütter, Mandy, and Steven Sweldens. "Implicit misattribution of evaluative responses: Contingency-unaware evaluative conditioning requires simultaneous stimulus presen-tations." *Journal of Experimental Psychology: General* 142.3 (2013): 638.

[23] Lewis, Richard W. *Absolut Book.: The Absolut Vodka Advertising Story*. Tuttle Publishing, 1996.

[24] In several publications, Robert Heath has discussed the *Andrex* puppy campaign as an example of emotional advertising that works without a strong informational message. See Heath, Robert, *Seducing the subconscious*, "Andrex Case Study," pp. 109-110; Heath, Robert, David Brandt, and Agnes Nairn. "Brand relationships: Strengthened by emotion, weakened by attention." *Journal of advertising research* 46.4 (2006): 410-419. For a review of the brand's success in the marketplace, see "Superbrands case studies: Andrex." Available online at http://bit.ly/2xZNDcu.

Chapter 10. Wants, Needs, and Goals

[1] See, for example, Berridge, Kent C., et al. "The tempted brain eats: pleasure and desire circuits in obesity and eating disorders." *Brain research*1350 (2010): 43-64.

[2] Berridge, Kent C., Terry E. Robinson, and J. Wayne Aldridge. "Dissecting components of reward: 'liking', 'wanting', and learning." *Current opinion in pharmacology* 9.1 (2009): 65-73.

[3] Eyal, Nir. "Hooks: An Intro on How to Manufacture Desire." *Nir & Far Blog*, undated. Available online at http://bit.ly/2xPKNdp.

[4] Hawkins, Kathryn. "5 Marketing Lessons from the Bottled Water Industry," *QuickBooks Resource Center*. Available online at http://intuit.me/2vzMLLe.

[5] Eyal, Nir. *Hooked: How to build habit-forming products*. Penguin, 2014.

[6] Ibid., p. 5.

[7] For an overview of this literature, see Staddon, John ER, and Daniel T. Cerutti. "Operant conditioning." *Annual review of psychology* 54.1 (2003): 115-144. For an overview of variable rewards and other reinforcement schedules, see McLeod, S. A. "BF Skinner: Operant conditioning." *Simply Psychology*, 2007, updated 2015. Available online at http://bit.ly/2ptc7K5.

[8] A point too often passed over by *Hooked* readers is Eyal's distinction between a *habit* and an *addiction*. An application that helps a user form good habits is quite different from an application that produces repetitive, compulsive, addictive behavior. See Eyal, Nir. "The Addictive Products Myth: Who Is the Culprit Here?" *Nir & Far* blog. Available online at http://bit.ly/2mcZx29.

[9] Data from Kemp, Simon. *Digital in 2017: Global Overview*, January 24, 2017. Available online at http://bit.ly/2rvcmGk.

[10] Quoted from Tristan Harris's public *LinkedIn* profile. Available online at http://bit.ly/2y9jgmS.

[11] Harris, Tristan. "What is Time Well Spent (Part I): Design Distinctions." *tristanharris.com* blog, September 30, 2015. Available online at http://bit.ly/2xqRXWL.

[12] Eyal's latest book takes on the issue of distraction directly, in multiple domains of life. Eyal, Nir. *Indistractable: How to Control Your Attention and Choose Your Life.* BenBella Books, 2019.

[13] Eyal, Nir. "Tech Companies are Addicting People! But Should They Stop?" *Nir & Far* blog, May 2017. Available online at http://bit.ly/2yh0KJl.

[14] Eyal, Nir. "Tech companies, if you create addicts, you need to help them." *VentureBeat.com,* May 9, 2017. Available online at http://bit.ly/2pXobRz.

[15] See Alter, Adam. *Irresistible: The rise of addictive technology and the business of keeping us hooked.* Penguin, 2017; Carr, Nicholas. "How Smartphones Hijack Our Minds," *The Wall Street Journal,* October 6, 2017.

[16] Eyal, *Hooked*, p. 111.

[17] Summarized from Harris, Tristan. "What is Time Well Spent (Part I): Design Distinctions." *tristanharris.com* blog, September 30, 2015. Available online at http://bit.ly/2xqRXWL.

[18] Nir Eyal offers a useful way to make this assessment, which he calls the *"Regret Test"*:
"If people knew everything the product designer knows, would they still execute the intended behavior? Are they likely to regret doing this?"
If users would regret taking the action, the technique fails the regret test and shouldn't be built into the product, because it manipulated people into doing something they didn't want to do. Getting people to do something they didn't want to do is no longer persuasion—it's coercion. Eyal, Nir. "Want to Design User Behavior? Pass the 'Regret Test' First." *Nir & Far* blog. Available online at http://bit.ly/2kLy7jG.

[19] See, for example, Frith, Christopher D., Sarah-Jayne Blakemore, and Daniel M. Wolpert. "Abnormalities in the awareness and control of action." *Phil. Trans. R. Soc. Lond. B* 355.1404 (2000): 1771-1788.

[20] Gollwitzer, Peter M., et al. "Flexible tenacity in goal pursuit." *Handbook of motivation science* (2008): 325-341.

[21] Chartrand, Tanya L. "The role of conscious awareness in consumer behavior." *Journal of Consumer Psychology* 15.3 (2005): 203-210.

[22] Bargh, J. A., P. M. Gollwitzer, and G. Oettingen. "Motivation." Chapter 8 in Fiske, Susan T., Daniel T. Gilbert, and Gardner Lindzey, eds. *Handbook of Social Psychology, Volume One.* Vol. 1. John Wiley & Sons, 2010.

[23] Latham, Gary P., and Edwin A. Locke. "Self-regulation through goal setting." *Organizational behavior and human decision processes* 50.2 (1991): 212-247.

[24] Ryan, Richard M., and Edward L. Deci. "Self-determination theory and the facilitation of intrinsic motivation, social development, and well-being." *American psychologist* 55.1 (2000): 68; Ryan, Richard M., and Edward L. Deci. "Intrinsic and extrinsic motivations: Classic definitions and new directions." *Contemporary educational psychology* 25.1 (2000): 54-67.

[25] Bargh, John A. "Auto-motives: Preconscious determinants of social interaction." In Higgins, E., and Richard M. Sorrentino. *Handbook of motivation and cognition: Foundations of social behavior, Vol. 2.* Guilford Press, 1990; Chartrand, Tanya L., and John A. Bargh. "Automatic activation of impression formation and memorization goals: Nonconscious goal priming reproduces effects of explicit task instructions." *Journal of Personality and Social Psychology* 71.3 (1996): 464.

[26] For the importance of situational variables in explaining human behavior, see Bem, Daryl J. "Self-perception theory." *Advances in experimental social psychology* 6 (1972): 1-62. For the origins of dual process models, see Shiffrin, Richard M., and Walter Schneider. "Controlled and automatic human information processing: II. Perceptual learning, automatic attending and a general theory." *Psychological review* 84.2 (1977): 127. For early research on priming of mental representations, see Fazio, Russell H., et al. "On the automatic activation of attitudes." *Journal of personality and social psychology* 50.2 (1986): 229.

[27] Suhler, Christopher L., and Patricia S. Churchland. "Control: conscious and otherwise." *Trends in cognitive sciences* 13.8 (2009): 341-347. Bargh, Gollwitzer, and Oettingen. "Motivation," p. 293.

[28] Mayr, Ernst. "Evolution and the Diversity of Life: Selected Essays, Cambridge, Mass. and London: Belknap." (1976); Dawkins, Richard. *The selfish gene.* Oxford University Press, 1976, revised 1989, 2006.

[29] Ripple, William J., et al. "World Scientists' Warning to Humanity: A Second Notice." *BioScience* (2017).

[30] Diamond, Dan. "Just 8% of People Achieve Their New Year's Resolutions. Here's How They Do It." *Forbes* website, January 1, 2013. Available online at http://bit.ly/2ycRPpn.

[31] Ryan, Richard M., et al. "All goals are not created equal: An organismic perspective on the nature of goals and their regulation." (1996); Hagger, Martin S., Nikos LD Chatzisarantis, and Jemma Harris. "From psychological need satisfaction to intentional behavior: Testing a motivational sequence in two behavioral contexts." *Personality and social psychology bulletin* 32.2 (2006): 131-148.

[32] Markus, Hazel, and Paula Nurius. "Possible selves." *American psychologist* 41.9 (1986): 954.

[33] Bargh, J. A., P. M. Gollwitzer, and G. Oettingen. "Motivation." Chapter 8 in Fiske, Susan T., Daniel T. Gilbert, and Gardner Lindzey, eds. *Handbook of Social Psychology, Volume One.* Vol. 1. John Wiley & Sons, 2010, p. 271.

[34] Bargh, John A. "What have we been priming all these years? On the development, mechanisms, and ecology of nonconscious social behavior." *European journal of social psychology* 36.2 (2006): 147-168.

[35] Fazio, Russell H., et al. "On the automatic activation of attitudes." *Journal of personality and social psychology* 50.2 (1986): 229; Fazio, Russell H. "On the automatic activation of associated evaluations: An overview." *Cognition & Emotion* 15.2 (2001): 115-141.

[36] Banks, R. Richard, Jennifer L. Eberhardt, and Lee Ross. "Race, crime, and antidiscrimination." *Beyond common sense: Psychological science in the courtroom* (2008): 3.

[37] Shah, James. "Automatic for the people: how representations of significant others implicitly affect goal pursuit." *Journal of personality and social psychology* 84.4 (2003): 661.

[38] Harris, Jennifer L., John A. Bargh, and Kelly D. Brownell. "Priming effects of television food advertising on eating behavior." *Health psychology* 28.4 (2009): p. 407.

[39] Ibid., p. 410.

[40] Young, Brian. "Does food advertising make children obese?" *Young consumers* 4.3 (2003): 19-26.

[41] Fitzsimons, Gráinne M., Tanya L. Chartrand, and Gavan J. Fitzsimons. "Automatic effects of brand exposure on motivated behavior: how Apple makes you 'think different'." *Journal of consumer research* 35.1 (2008): 21-35, Experiment 1.

[42] Ibid., Experiment 2.

[43] Ibid., Experiment 3.

[44] Chartrand, Tanya L., et al. "Nonconscious goals and consumer choice." *Journal of Consumer Research* 35.2 (2008): 189-201. Experiment 4.

[45] Ibid., p. 192.

Chapter 11. Consumer Goals in Action

[1] Cesario, Joseph, Jason E. Plaks, and E. Tory Higgins. "Automatic social behavior as motivated preparation to interact." *Journal of personality and social psychology* 90.6 (2006): p. 906

[2] The question of whether conscious and unconscious goal pursuit activate the same brain systems remains open. See Berkman, Elliot T., and Matthew D. Lieberman. "The neuroscience of goal pursuit." *The psychology of goals* (2009): 98-126; Lieberman, Matthew D. "Social cognitive neuroscience: a review of core processes." *Annu. Rev. Psychol.* 58 (2007): 259-289.

[3] These shared features of unconscious and conscious goal pursuit have been documented in many studies. For a summary see Genco et al. *Neuromarketing for Dummies*, Chapter 7, "New Understandings of Consumer Goals and Motivation," pp. 105-118.

[4] Custers, Ruud, et al. "Nonconscious goal pursuit and the surmounting of physical and social obstacles." *European Journal of Social Psychology* 38.6 (2008): 1013-1022.

[5] Bargh, John A., and Julie Y. Huang. "The selfish goal." *The psychology of goals* (2009): 127-150.

[6] Hassin, Ran R., John A. Bargh, and Shira Zimerman. "Automatic and flexible: The case of nonconscious goal pursuit." *Social cognition* 27.1 (2009): 20-36.

[7] Bargh, John A., et al. "The automated will: nonconscious activation and pursuit of behavioral goals." *Journal of personality and social psychology* 81.6 (2001): 1014, Experiment 5.

[8] Chartrand, Tanya L., et al. "Nonconscious goals and consumer choice." *Journal of Consumer Research* 35.2 (2008): 189-201. Experiment 2.

[9] Ibid., Experiment 3.

[10] Ibid., p. 198.

[11] Leander, N. Pontus, Sarah G. Moore, And Tanya L. Chartrand. "Mystery moods: Their origins and consequences." In Moskowitz, Gordon B., and Heidi Grant, eds. *The psychology of goals*. Guilford press, 2009: 480-504.

[12] Chartrand, Tanya L. "Mystery moods and perplexing performance: Consequences of succeeding and failing at a nonconscious goal." *Manuscript submitted for publication* (2001).

[13] Schwarz, Norbert. "Feelings-as-information theory." In Van Lange, Paul AM, Arie W. Kruglanski, and E. Tory Higgins. *Handbook of theories of social psychology: Volume two.* SAGE publications (2011): 289-308.

[14] Baumeister, Roy F. "Yielding to temptation: Self-control failure, impulsive purchasing, and consumer behavior." *Journal of consumer Research* 28.4 (2002): 670-676.

[15] Deci, Edward L., and Richard M. Ryan. "The 'what' and 'why' of goal pursuits: Human needs and the self-determination of behavior." *Psychological inquiry* 11.4 (2000): 227-268.

[16] Bongers, Karin CA, Ap Dijksterhuis, and Russell Spears. "Self-esteem regulation after success and failure to attain unconsciously activated goals." *Journal of Experimental Social Psychology* 45.3 (2009): 468-477.

[17] Ibid., p. 469.

[18] Ferguson, Melissa J. "On becoming ready to pursue a goal you don't know you have: Effects of nonconscious goals on evaluative readiness." *Journal of personality and social psychology* 95.6 (2008): 1268.

[19] Förster, Jens, Nira Liberman, and E. Tory Higgins. "Accessibility from active and fulfilled goals." *Journal of Experimental Social Psychology* 41.3 (2005): 220-239.

[20] Moore, Sarah G., Melissa J. Ferguson, and Tanya L. Chartrand. "Affect in the aftermath: How goal pursuit influences implicit evaluations." *Cognition and Emotion* 25.3 (2011): 453-465, p. 461.

[21] Aarts, Henk, Ruud Custers, and Rob W. Holland. "The nonconscious cessation of goal pursuit: When goals and negative affect are coactivated." *Journal of personality and social psychology* 92.2 (2007): 165.

[22] Ryan, Richard M., and Edward L. Deci. "Self-determination theory and the facilitation of intrinsic motivation, social development, and well-being." *American psychologist* 55.1 (2000): p. 68.

[23] Deci, Edward L., and Richard M. Ryan. "The empirical exploration of intrinsic motivational processes." *Advances in experimental social psychology* 13 (1980): 39-80.

[24] Deci, E. L., and R. M. Ryan. "A motivational approach to self: integration in personality." *Nebraska Symposium on Motivation*. Vol. 38. 1990; Ryan, Richard M., Edward L. Deci, and Wendy S. Grolnick. "Autonomy, relatedness, and the self: Their relation to development and psychopathology." *Ariel* 128.151.189 (1995): 155.

[25] Deci, Edward L., and Richard M. Ryan. "The 'what' and 'why' of goal pursuits: Human needs and the self-determination of behavior," p. 229, emphasis in original.

[26] Deci and Ryan. "A motivational approach to self: integration in personality."

[27] Ryan and Deci. "Self-determination theory and the facilitation of intrinsic motivation." (2000): p. 75. See also Kasser, Tim, and Richard M. Ryan. "A dark side of the American dream: correlates of financial success as a central life aspiration." *Journal of personality and social psychology* 65.2 (1993): 410; Kasser, Tim, and Richard M. Ryan. "Further examining the American dream: Differential correlates of intrinsic and extrinsic goals." *Personality and social psychology bulletin* 22.3 (1996): 280-287; Ryan, Richard M., et al. "The American dream in Russia: Extrinsic aspirations and well-being in two cultures." *Personality and social psychology bulletin* 25.12 (1999): 1509-1524.

[28] Ryan and Deci. "Self-determination theory and the facilitation of intrinsic motivation." (2000): p. 76.

[29] Kasser, Tim, and Richard M. Ryan. "Be careful what you wish for: Optimal functioning and the relative attainment of intrinsic and extrinsic goals." *Life goals and well-being: Towards a positive psychology of human striving* 116-131 (2001).

[30] For example, Doyen, Stéphane, et al. "Behavioral priming: it's all in the mind, but whose mind?" *PLoS one* 7.1 (2012): e29081; Harris, Christine R., et al. "Two failures to replicate high-performance-goal priming effects." *PLoS one* 8.8 (2013): e72467.

[31] With regard to science in general, an often-cited assessment is provided by Ioannidis, John PA. "Why most published research findings are false." *PLoS medicine* 2.8 (2005): e124. A recent update finds little overall improvement. Based on statistical records from 3,801 cognitive neuroscience and psychology papers published between 2011 and 2014, the authors conclude that *"false report probability is likely to exceed 50% for the whole literature."* Szucs, Denes, and John PA Ioannidis. "Empirical assessment of published effect sizes and power in the recent cognitive neuroscience and psychology literature." *PLoS biology* 15.3 (2017): e2000797, p. 1.

[32] See Coe, Robert. "It's the effect size, stupid: What effect size is and why it is important." (2002), available online at http://bit.ly/2EKMNEx:

> *'Effect size' is simply a way of quantifying the size of the difference between two groups. It is easy to calculate, readily understood and can be applied to any measured outcome .... It is particularly valuable for quantifying the effectiveness of a particular intervention, relative to some comparison.*

See also Genco et al., *Neuromarketing for Dummies*, p. 312.

381

[33] Open Science Collaboration. "Estimating the reproducibility of psychological science." *Science* 349.6251 (2015): aac4716.

[34] Ioannidis, John PA. "Contradicted and initially stronger effects in highly cited clinical research." *JAMA* 294.2 (2005): 218-228.

[35] Rosenthal, Robert. "The file drawer problem and tolerance for null results." *Psychological bulletin* 86.3 (1979): 638.

[36] Incorrect interpretations of p-values are common. What *p=.05* means, in strict statistical terms, is that there is only a 5-in-100 chance of finding an effect at least as big as the one found in this sample, *if in fact* there is *no effect* at all (the null hypothesis). A p-value says *nothing* about whether the result is true or false, or how big the effect may actually be. The use of p-values to rate the quality of scientific results has been subjected to withering criticism, but remains a common practice throughout the social sciences. For summaries of problems and solutions, see Cohen, Jacob. "The earth is round (p<.05)." *American psychologist* 49.12 (1994): 997 and Wagenmakers, Eric-Jan. "A practical solution to the pervasive problems of p-values." *Psychonomic bulletin & review* 14.5 (2007): 779-804.

[37] Head, Megan L., et al. "The extent and consequences of p-hacking in science." *PLoS biology* 13.3 (2015): e1002106.

[38] John, Leslie K., George Loewenstein, and Drazen Prelec. "Measuring the prevalence of questionable research practices with incentives for truth telling." *Psychological science* 23.5 (2012): 524-532.

[39] Simmons, Joseph P., Leif D. Nelson, and Uri Simonsohn. "False-positive psychology: Undisclosed flexibility in data collection and analysis allows presenting anything as significant." *Psychological science* 22.11 (2011): 1359-1366.

[40] Zwaan, R. "How to cook up your own social priming article." *Rolf Zwaan blog*, 17 Sept. (2013), available online at http://bit.ly/2onwZl2; Wagenmakers, E. J. "Behavioral priming: Time to nut up or shut up." *Open Science Collaboration website*, 26 Mar. (2014), available online at http://bit.ly/2F0Xx57.

[41] Bargh, John A. "The historical origins of priming as the preparation of behavioral responses: Unconscious carryover and contextual influences of real-world importance." *Social Cognition* 32. Supplement (2014): 209-224.

[42] Weingarten, Evan, et al. "From primed concepts to action: A meta-analysis of the behavioral effects of incidentally presented words." *Psychological Bulletin* 142.5 (2016): 472.

[43] Payne, B. Keith, Jazmin L. Brown-Iannuzzi, and Chris Loersch. "Replicable effects of primes on human behavior." *Journal of Experimental Psychology: General* 145.10 (2016): 1269.

[44] Ibid., p. 1277.

[45] Weingarten et al., pp. 483, 487.

[46] Cesario, Joseph, et al. "The ecology of automaticity: How situational contingencies shape action semantics and social behavior." *Psychological Science* 21.9 (2010): 1311-1317.

[47] Berger, Jonah, Marc Meredith, and S. Christian Wheeler. "Contextual priming: Where people vote affects how they vote." *Proceedings of the National Academy of Sciences* 105.26 (2008): 8846-8849.

[48] Cesario, Joseph. "Priming, replication, and the hardest science." *Perspectives on Psychological Science* 9.1 (2014): 40-48, p. 43.

[49] Eitam, Baruch, and E. Tory Higgins. "Motivation in mental accessibility: Relevance of a representation (ROAR) as a new framework." *Social and personality psychology compass* 4.10 (2010): 951-967; Ferguson, Melissa J. "On becoming ready to pursue a goal you don't know you have: Effects of nonconscious goals on evaluative readiness." *Journal of personality and social psychology* 95.6 (2008): 1268;

Custers, Ruud, and Henk Aarts. "In search of the nonconscious sources of goal pursuit: Accessibility and positive affective valence of the goal state." *Journal of Experimental Social Psychology* 43.2 (2007): 312-318; Custers, Ruud, and Henk Aarts. "Positive affect as implicit motivator: on the nonconscious operation of behavioral goals." *Journal of personality and social psychology* 89.2 (2005): 129.

[50] Higgins, E. Tory, and Baruch Eitam. "Priming… Shmiming: it's about knowing when and why stimulated memory representations become active." *Social Cognition* 32.Supplement (2014): 225-242.

[51] Cesario, "Priming, replication, and the hardest science," p. 44

[52] Gladwell, Malcolm. *Blink: The power of thinking without thinking.* Back Bay Books, 2007.

[53] Shanks, David R., et al. "Priming intelligent behavior: An elusive phenomenon." *PloS one* 8.4 (2013): e56515; Shanks, David R., et al. "Romance, risk, and replication: Can consumer choices and risk-taking be primed by mating motives?." *Journal of Experimental Psychology: General* 144.6 (2015): e142; Johnson, David J., Felix Cheung, and M. Brent Donnellan. "Does cleanliness influence moral judgments? A direct replication of Schnall, Benton, and Harvey (2008)." *Social Psychology* 45.3 (2014): 209; Rohrer, Doug, Harold Pashler, and Christine R. Harris. "Do subtle reminders of money change people's political views?." *Journal of Experimental Psychology: General* 144.4 (2015): e73.

[54] Lakens, Daniël, and Ellen R. K. Evers. "Sailing from the seas of chaos into the corridor of stability: Practical recommendations to increase the informational value of studies." *Perspectives on Psychological Science* 9.3 (2014): 278-292.

[55] Masicampo, E. J., and Daniel R. Lalande. "A peculiar prevalence of p values just below .05." *Quarterly journal of experimental psychology* 65.11 (2012): 2271-2279.

[56] John, Leslie K., George Loewenstein, and Drazen Prelec. "Measuring the prevalence of questionable research practices with incentives for truth telling." *Psychological science* 23.5 (2012): 524-532.

[57] Simmons, Joseph P., Leif D. Nelson, and Uri Simonsohn. "False-positive citations." *SSRN* (2017), p. 4. Available online at http://bit.ly/2DHCsrq.

[58] Vazire, S. "Editorial." *Social Psychological and Personality Science,* 7 (1), 3-7. (2016); Eich, Eric. "Business not as usual." *Psychological Science,* 25 (1), 3-6. (2014).

[59] For example, see the "Reproducibility Initiative" sponsored by the *Laura and John Allen Foundation,* at http://bit.ly/2uaMGRS.

[60] *Berkeley Initiative for Transparency in the Social Sciences,* website at https://www.bitss.org/.

[61] Cumming, Geoff. "The new statistics: Why and how." *Psychological science* 25.1 (2014): 7.

[62] For a detailed discussion and evolutionary rationale for this view of science, see Toulmin, Stephen. *Human Understanding: The Collective Use and Evolution of Concepts.* Princeton University Press, 1975.

Chapter 12. How Consumers Learn Without Trying

[1] Ehrenberg, Andrew, et al. "Brand advertising as creative publicity." *Journal of advertising research* 42.4 (2002): 7-18, p. 7.

[2] Sharp, Byron. "Ehrenberg, Andrew Samuel Christopher." *Oxford Dictionary of National Biography.* 2014. Available online at https://bit.ly/2HUFk6u.

[3] Ambler, Tim. "Persuasion, pride and prejudice: how ads work." *International Journal of Advertising* 19.3 (2000): 299-315, pp. 299-300.

[4] Ehrenberg, Andrew SC. "Repetitive advertising and the consumer." *Journal of Advertising Research* 40.6 (2000): 39-48, pp. 27, 31.

[5] Barnard, N. R., and A. S. C. Ehrenberg. "Advertising and brand attitudes." *South Bank University: R&D I report* (1999), p. 10.

[6] Ehrenberg, "Repetitive advertising and the consumer," p. 32.

[7] The NBD-Dirichlet model was developed by Gerald Goodhardt, Chris Chatfield, and Andrew Ehrenberg in the early 1970s. It was used in private commercial practice for several years before being described publicly in Goodhardt, Gerald Joseph, Andrew SC Ehrenberg, and Christopher Chatfield. "The Dirichlet: A comprehensive model of buying behaviour." *Journal of the Royal Statistical Society. Series A (General)* (1984): 621-655. Thanks to Byron Sharp for this clarification.

[8] Ehrenberg, Andrew SC, Mark D. Uncles, and Gerald J. Goodhardt. "Understanding brand performance measures: using Dirichlet benchmarks." *Journal of Business Research* 57.12 (2004): 1307-1325; Sharp, Byron, et al. "It's a Dirichlet world: Modeling individuals' loyalties reveals how brands compete, grow, and decline." *Journal of Advertising Research* 52.2 (2012): 203-213.

[9] Barnard, Neil, and Andrew Ehrenberg. "Advertising: strongly persuasive or nudging?" *Journal of Advertising Research* 37 (1997): 21-32, p. 27.

[10] Ibid., p. 25

[11] Ibid.

[12] Ehrenberg et al. "Brand advertising as creative publicity."

[13] Ibid., quotes at pp. 8-9.

[14] Ibid., p. 11.

[15] Ibid.

[16] Ibid., p. 8. The idea that salience is not an attitudinal concept, but rather a function of the strength and breadth of brand attributes stored in memory, was first proposed and demonstrated in Romaniuk, Jenni, and Byron Sharp. "Brand salience and customer defection in subscription markets." *Journal of Marketing Management* 19.1-2 (2003): 25-44.

[17] Today, researchers working in the Ehrenberg tradition no longer use the term "salience," preferring the more easily understood term "mental availability." See Sharp, Byron. *How brands grow.* Oxford University Press, 2010; Romaniuk, Jenni, and Byron Sharp. *How Brands Grow. Part 2: Including Emerging Markets, Services and Durables, New Brands and Luxury Brands.* Oxford University Press, 2016.

[18] Ehrenberg et al. "Brand advertising as creative publicity," p. 16.

[19] For further elaboration of Ehrenberg's views on differentiation vs. distinctiveness, along with associated evidence, see Sharp, *How Brands Grow,* Chapter 8, "Differentiation versus Distinctiveness." See also Romaniuk, Jenni, Byron Sharp, and Andrew Ehrenberg. "Evidence concerning the importance of perceived brand differentiation." *Australasian Marketing Journal (AMJ)* 15.2 (2007): 42-54.

[20] Ehrenberg, "Brand advertising as creative publicity," p. 11.

[21] Ibid., p. 16.

[22] See Roberts, Kevin. *Lovemarks: The future beyond brands.* Powerhouse books, 2005.

[23] This multi-memory framework for long-term memory was first introduced by Larry Squire in "Mechanisms of memory." *Science* 232.4758 (1986): 1612-1619. Figure 7 incorporates the terminology recommended in a recent update of this framework by Squire and Adam Dede, "Conscious and unconscious memory systems." *Cold Spring Harbor perspectives in biology* 7.3 (2015): a021667.

[24] Martens, Sander, and Brad Wyble. "The attentional blink: Past, present, and future of a blind spot in perceptual awareness." *Neuroscience & Biobehavioral Reviews* 34.6 (2010): 947-957.

[25] Bahrick, Harry P. "Long-term maintenance of knowledge." *The Oxford handbook of memory* (2000): 347-362.

[26] Squire and Dede. "Conscious and unconscious memory systems," p. 3.

[26] Greenberg, Daniel L., and Mieke Verfaellie. "Interdependence of episodic and semantic memory: evidence from neuropsychology." *Journal of the International Neuropsychological society* 16.5 (2010): 748-753.

[28] Squire and Dede. "Conscious and unconscious memory systems," p. 3.

[29] Ibid., p. 2.

[30] "Habits are learned largely as people pursue goals in daily life, and habits are broken through the strategic deployment of effortful self-control." Wood, Wendy, and David T. Neal. "The habitual consumer." *Journal of Consumer Psychology* 19.4 (2009): 579-592, p. 579.

[31] Reber, Arthur S. "Implicit learning of artificial grammars." *Journal of verbal learning and verbal behavior* 6.6 (1967): 855-863.

[32] A touching account of the most famous of these amnesiac patients, 'H.M.', is found in his *New York Times* obituary. Cary, Benedict. "H.M., an unforgettable amnesiac, dies at 82." December 4, 2008. Available online at https://nyti.ms/2NWbXsu. See also Squire, Larry R. "The legacy of patient HM for neuroscience." *Neuron* 61.1 (2009): 6-9.

[33] Reber, Paul J. "The neural basis of implicit learning and memory: a review of neuropsychological and neuroimaging research." *Neuropsychologia* 51.10 (2013): 2026-2042, p. 2029.

Chapter 13. Can Consumers Be Conditioned?

[1] De Houwer, Jan. "Conditioning as a source of liking: There is nothing simple about it." In Wanke, Michaela. *Social psychology of consumer behavior.* Psychology Press, 2008, pp. 151-166.

[2] Zajonc, Robert B. "Mere exposure: A gateway to the subliminal." *Current directions in psychological science* 10.6 (2001): 224-228, pp. 225-226.

[3] De Houwer, "Conditioning as a source of liking."

[4] Stuart, Elnora W., Terence A. Shimp, and Randall W. Engle. "Classical conditioning of consumer attitudes: Four experiments in an advertising context." *Journal of consumer research* 14.3 (1987): 334-349; Hammerl, Marianne, and Hans-Joachim Grabitz. "Human evaluative conditioning: Order of stimulus presentation." *Integrative Physiological and Behavioral Science* 28.2 (1993): 191-194.

[5] Hofmann, Wilhelm, et al. "Evaluative conditioning in humans: a meta-analysis." *Psychological bulletin* 136.3 (2010): 390-421, p. 405.

[6] Baeyens, Frank, et al. "Human evaluative conditioning: Acquisition trials, presentation schedule, evaluative style and contingency awareness." *Behaviour research and therapy* 30.2 (1992): 133-142. See also Stuart et al. "Classical conditioning of consumer attitudes," Experiment 1, pp. 336-340.

[7] De Houwer, Jan. "The propositional approach to associative learning as an alternative for association formation models." *Learning & Behavior* 37.1 (2009): 1-20.

[8] Hofmann et al., "Evaluative conditioning in humans," p. 406.

[9] Ibid., p. 414.

[10] Hütter, Mandy, et al. "Dissociating contingency awareness and conditioned attitudes: Evidence of contingency-unaware evaluative conditioning." *Journal of Experimental Psychology: General* 141.3 (2012): 539.

[11] Hütter, Mandy, and Steven Sweldens. "Implicit misattribution of evaluative responses: Contingency-unaware evaluative conditioning requires simultaneous stimulus presentations." *Journal of Experimental Psychology: General* 142.3 (2013): 638.

[12] Olson, Michael A., and Russell H. Fazio. "Implicit attitude formation through classical conditioning." *Psychological Science* 12.5 (2001): 413-417.

[13] Jones, Christopher R., Russell H. Fazio, and Michael A. Olson. "Implicit misattribution as a mechanism underlying evaluative conditioning." *Journal of personality and social psychology* 96.5 (2009): 933-948, p. 935.

[14] De Houwer, Jan. "Why a propositional single-process model of associative learning deserves to be defended." *Dual processes in social psychology.* Guilford, 2014. 530-541.

[15] Monahan, Jennifer L., Sheila T. Murphy, and Robert B. Zajonc. "Subliminal mere exposure: Specific, general, and diffuse effects." *Psychological Science* 11.6 (2000): 462-466.

[16] The similarities and differences between evaluative conditioning and the mere exposure effect are discussed in Sweldens, Steven, Olivier Corneille, and Vincent Yzerbyt. "The role of awareness in attitude formation through evaluative conditioning." *Personality and Social Psychology Review* 18.2 (2014): 187-209.

[17] Shimp, Terence A., Elnora W. Stuart, and Randall W. Engle. "A program of classical conditioning experiments testing variations in the conditioned stimulus and context." *Journal of Consumer Research* 18.1 (1991): 1-12, p. 6.

[18] Gibson, Bryan. "Can evaluative conditioning change attitudes toward mature brands? New evidence from the Implicit Association Test." *Journal of Consumer Research* 35.1 (2008): 178-188.

[19] Ibid., p. 186.

[20] Sweldens, Steven, Stijn MJ Van Osselaer, and Chris Janiszewski. "Evaluative conditioning procedures and the resilience of conditioned brand attitudes." *Journal of consumer Research* 37.3 (2010): 473-489.

[21] Ibid., p. 484.

Chapter 14. Priming and Knowledge Accessibility

[1] Weigel, Martin. "Why Being Interesting Might Be More Important Than Being Different." Blog post. March 19, 2012, at https://bit.ly/2E8Q2Xp.

[2] Tulving, Endel, and Daniel L. Schacter. "Priming and human memory systems." *Science* 247.4940 (1990): 301-306, p. 301.

[3] Ibid.

[4] Ibid.

[5] Collins, Allan M., and Elizabeth F. Loftus. "A spreading-activation theory of semantic processing." *Psychological review* 82.6 (1975): 407.

[6] Janiszewski, Chris, and Robert S. Wyer. "Content and process priming: A review." *Journal of Consumer Psychology* 24.1 (2014): 96-118.

[7] Ibid., p. 98.

⁸ See Higgins, E. Tory. "Knowledge activation: Accessibility, applicability, and salience." In Higgins, E. Tory and Arie W. Kruglanski, eds. *Social psychology: Handbook of basic principles.* Guilford Publications, 1st edition, 1996.

⁹ Baror, Shira, and Moshe Bar. "Associative activation and its relation to exploration and exploitation in the brain." *Psychological science* 27.6 (2016): 776-789.

¹⁰ Janiszewski and Wyer. "Content and process priming: A review," p. 97.

¹¹ Laran, Juliano, Amy N. Dalton, and Eduardo B. Andrade. "The curious case of behavioral backlash: Why brands produce priming effects and slogans produce reverse priming effects." *Journal of Consumer Research* 37.6 (2010): 999-1014.

¹² Sela, Aner, and Baba Shiv. "Unraveling priming: When does the same prime activate a goal versus a trait?." *Journal of Consumer Research* 36.3 (2009): 418-433. Higgins, E. Tory, John A. Bargh, and Wendy J. Lombardi. "Nature of priming effects on categorization." *Journal of experimental psychology: Learning, Memory, and Cognition*11.1 (1985): 59.

¹³ Chartrand, Tanya. "Subliminal Suggestion," in *International Encyclopedia of the Social Sciences.* Ed. William A. Darity, Jr.. Vol. 8. 2nd ed. Detroit: Macmillan Reference USA, 2008, pp. 201-202. Available online at http://bit.ly/1kwrfzP.

¹⁴ For a detailed account, see Niedenthal, Paula M. "Emotion concepts." In Lewis, Michael, Jeannette M. Haviland-Jones, and Lisa Feldman Barrett, eds. *Handbook of emotions.* 3rd edition. Guilford Press, 2010.

¹⁵ Chartrand, Tanya L., et al. "Nonconscious goals and consumer choice." *Journal of Consumer Research* 35.2 (2008): 189-201.

¹⁶ Harris, Christine R., et al. "Two failures to replicate high-performance-goal priming effects." *PloS one* 8.8 (2013): e72467; Shanks, David R., et al. "Priming intelligent behavior: An elusive phenomenon." *PloS one* 8.4 (2013): e56515.

¹⁷ Earp, Brian D., et al. "Out, damned spot: Can the "Macbeth Effect" be replicated?" *Basic and Applied Social Psychology* 36.1 (2014): 91-98.

¹⁸ Wegener, Duane T., and Richard E. Petty. "Mood management across affective states: The hedonic contingency hypothesis." *Journal of personality and social psychology* 66.6 (1994): 1034. An extension of these finding that goes beyond priming goals with generic 'good' and 'bad' moods to priming goals with more discreet affective states like 'guilt' and 'sadness' is demonstrated in Zemack-Rugar, Yael, James R. Bettman, and Gavan J. Fitzsimons. "The effects of nonconsciously priming emotion concepts on behavior." *Journal of personality and social psychology* 93.6 (2007): 927.

¹⁹ Chartrand, Tanya L., and John A. Bargh. "The chameleon effect: the perception–behavior link and social interaction." *Journal of personality and social psychology* 76.6 (1999): 893; Lakin, Jessica L., et al. "The chameleon effect as social glue: Evidence for the evolutionary significance of nonconscious mimicry." *Journal of nonverbal behavior* 27.3 (2003): 145-162.

²⁰ Laran, Juliano, Amy N. Dalton, and Eduardo B. Andrade. "The curious case of behavioral backlash: Why brands produce priming effects and slogans produce reverse priming effects." *Journal of Consumer Research* 37.6 (2010): 999-1014.

²¹ Ibid., p. 1009.

²² These studies are reviewed in Higgins, "Knowledge activation: Accessibility, applicability, and salience," pp. 143-145. See also Bless, Herbert, and Norbert Schwarz. "Mental construal and

the emergence of assimilation and contrast effects: The inclusion/exclusion model." *Advances in experimental social psychology.* Vol. 42. Academic Press, 2010. 319-373.

[23] Martin, Leonard L., John J. Seta, and Rick A. Crelia. "Assimilation and contrast as a function of people's willingness and ability to expend effort in forming an impression." *Journal of personality and social psychology* 59.1 (1990): 27; Wegener, Duane T., and Richard E. Petty. "Flexible correction processes in social judgment: the role of naive theories in corrections for perceived bias." *Journal of personality and social psychology* 68.1 (1995): 36.

[24] Herr, Paul M. "Consequences of priming: Judgment and behavior." *Journal of Personality and Social Psychology* 51.6 (1986): 1106.

[25] Wänke, Michaela, Herbert Bless, and Eric R. Igou. "Next to a star: Paling, shining, or both? Turning inter-exemplar contrast into inter-exemplar assimilation." *Personality and Social Psychology Bulletin* 27.1 (2001): 14-29.

[26] Glaser, Jack, and Mahzarin R. Banaji. "When fair is foul and foul is fair: Reverse priming in automatic evaluation." *Journal of personality and social psychology* 77.4 (1999): 669.

[27] Wyer, Robert S. "The role of knowledge accessibility in cognition and behavior." *Handbook of consumer psychology* 4 (2008): 31-76, p. 31.

[28] The definitions and distinctions in the following paragraphs are drawn from Higgins, "Knowledge activation: Accessibility, applicability, and salience," pp. 134-136.

[29] Ibid., p. 135.

[30] Wyer, "The role of knowledge accessibility."

[31] Ibid., p. 32.

[32] Ibid., p. 34.

[33] Ibid., p. 36.

[34] Ibid., p. 37.

[35] Ibid., p. 39.

[36] Ibid.

Chapter 15. The Challenge of Behavioral Economics

[1] Kahneman, *Thinking, Fast and Slow*, p. 373.

[2] For the classic defense of this perspective on choice, see Friedman, Milton. "The methodology of positive economics." In Friedman, Milton, and Marilyn Friedman. *Essays in positive economics.* University of Chicago Press, 1953: 259.

[3] Simon, Herbert A. "A behavioral model of rational choice." *The quarterly journal of economics* 69.1 (1955): 99-118, p. 99.

[4] March, James G. and Herbert Simon, *Organizations.* New York: Wiley, 1958.

[5] For example, Cohen, Michael D., James G. March, and Johan P. Olsen. "A garbage can model of organizational choice." *Administrative science quarterly* 17.1 (1972): 1-25; March, James G. "Bounded rationality, ambiguity, and the engineering of choice." *The Bell Journal of Economics* (1978): 587-608; March, James G. *Decisions and organizations.* Blackwell, 1989; March, James G. "Exploration and exploitation in organizational learning." *Organization science* 2.1 (1991): 71-87.

[6] March, James G. "Model bias in social action." *Review of Educational Research* 42.4 (1972): 413-429, p. 423.

[7] This fateful "collision" of Kahneman and Tversky is described in detail and in context by Michael Lewis in his fascinating history of their partnership: Lewis, Michael. *The Undoing Project: A Friendship That Changed Our Minds*. WW Norton & Company, 2016, pp. 142-152.

[8] For an accessible description and explanation of Bayes Theorem, see the Wikipedia page devoted to it, available online at http://bit.ly/2UMzC12.

[9] Kahneman, Daniel, and Amos Tversky. "Subjective probability: A judgment of representativeness." *Cognitive psychology* 3.3 (1972): 430-454, p. 432.

[10] Kahneman, Daniel, and Amos Tversky. "On the psychology of prediction." *Psychological review* 80.4 (1973): 237-251, p. 237.

[11] Ibid., p. 238.

[12] Tversky, Amos, and Daniel Kahneman. "Availability: A heuristic for judging frequency and probability." *Cognitive psychology* 5.2 (1973): 207-232, p. 208.

[13] Tversky, Amos, and Daniel Kahneman. "Judgment under uncertainty: Heuristics and biases." *Science* 185.4157 (1974): 1124-1131.

[14] Tversky, Amos, and Daniel Kahneman. "Prospect theory: an analysis of decision under risk." *Econometrica* 47.2 (1979): 263-292.

[15] Heukelom, Floris. *Behavioral economics: A history*. Cambridge University Press, 2014. Kindle edition, location 2892.

[16] Tversky and Kahneman. "Prospect theory," p. 266.

[17] Ibid., p. 268. Emphasis added.

[18] Rabin, Matthew. "Risk aversion and expected-utility theory: A calibration theorem." *Handbook of the Fundamentals of Financial Decision Making: Part I*. 2013. 241-252.

[19] Ibid., p. 273.

[20] Ibid., p. 279.

[21] This graphic first appeared in Tversky and Kahneman. "Prospect theory," p. 279.

[22] Tversky, Amos, and Daniel Kahneman. "The framing of decisions and the psychology of choice." *Science* 211.4481 (1981): 453-458, p. 453.

[23] Ibid., p. 454.

[24] Ibid., p. 456.

[25] The term "loss aversion" first appears in Tversky, Amos, and Daniel Kahneman. "Rational choice and the framing of decisions." *Journal of business* 59.4, pt2 (1986): S251-S278, p. S253.

[26] Tversky, Amos, and Daniel Kahneman. "Loss aversion in riskless choice: A reference-dependent model." *The quarterly journal of economics* 106.4 (1991): 1039-1061.

[27] Kahneman, Daniel, and Amos Tversky. "The simulation heuristic." Reprinted in Kahneman, Daniel, et al., eds. *Judgment under uncertainty: Heuristics and biases*. Cambridge university press, 1982.

[28] Quoted in Lewis, *The Undoing Project*, p. 317.

[29] Cohen, L. Jonathan. "Can human irrationality be experimentally demon-strated?" *Behavioral and Brain Sciences* 4.3 (1981): 317-331.

[30] Quoted in Lewis, *The Undoing Project*, p. 317.

[31] This account draws heavily on Lewis, *The Undoing Project*, pp. 317-328.

[32] Tversky, Amos, and Daniel Kahneman. "Extensional versus intuitive reasoning: The conjunction fallacy in probability judgment." *Psychological review* 90.4 (1983): 293.

[33] Kahneman, *Thinking, Fast and Slow*, p. 158.

[34] Tversky, Amos, and Daniel Kahneman. "Advances in prospect theory: Cumulative representation of uncertainty." *Journal of risk and uncertainty* 5.4 (1992): 297-323.

[35] Lewis, *The Undoing Project*, p. 322.

[36] Tversky and Kahneman. "Advances in prospect theory," p. 317.

[37] Kahneman, Daniel, and Shane Frederick. "Representativeness revisited: Attribute substitution in intuitive judgment." In *Heuristics and Biases: The Psychology of Intuitive Judgment*, edited by Thomas Gilovich et al., Cambridge University Press, Cambridge, 2002, pp. 49–81.

[38] As noted in Chapter 5, Kahneman borrowed the concept of dual process cognition from others, as well as the *System 1–System 2* terminology. See Stanovich, Keith E., and Richard F. West. "Individual Differences in Reasoning: Implications for the Rationality Debate?" in Gilovich et al., eds., *Heuristics and Biases*, pp. 421–440.

[39] Kahneman and Frederick, "Representativeness revisited," pp. 51, 52.

[40] Kahneman, Daniel. "Maps of bounded rationality: Psychology for behavioral economics." *American economic review* 93.5 (2003): 1449-1475, p. 1449.

Chapter 16. Ethical Marketing in a Post-Rational World

[1] Walsh, John and Valérie Keller-Birrer. "Using Behavioral Economics in Digital Marketing to Entice Consumers." *Adweek*, April 16, 2019. Available online at http://bit.ly/2HMXJFL.

[2] This is the motto of Ariely's *Center for Advanced Hindsight*, a for-profit consulting business he founded in 2007. Online at http://bit.ly/2WJPmmx.

[3] Thaler, Richard H., and Cass R. Sunstein. *Nudge: Improving decisions about health, wealth, and happiness.* Penguin, 2009, p. 6.

[4] Cialdini, Robert B. *Influence: The psychology of persuasion. Revised edition.* New York, Harper Business (2006). Introduction.

[5] See, for example, Wendel, Stephen. Designing for behavior change: Applying psychology and behavioral economics. O'Reilly Media, Inc., 2013; Leach, Will. *Marketing to Mindstates: The Practical Guide to Applying Behavior Design to Research and Marketing.* Lioncrest Publishing, 2018.

[6] Thaler officially married his "anomalies" research with the heuristics and biases tradition in Kahneman, Daniel, Jack L. Knetsch, and Richard H. Thaler. "Anomalies: The endowment effect, loss aversion, and status quo bias." *Journal of Economic perspectives* 5.1 (1991): 193-206.

[7] Thaler, Richard. "Mental accounting and consumer choice." *Marketing science* 4.3 (1985): 199-214.

[8] Shefrin, Hersh M., and Richard H. Thaler. "The behavioral life-cycle hypothesis." *Economic inquiry* 26.4 (1988): 609-643, p. 619.

[9] Several variants of this famous experiment are reported in Kahneman, Knetsch, and Thaler, "Anomalies" (1991).

[10] See, for example, Brasel, S. Adam, and James Gips. "Tablets, touchscreens, and touchpads: How varying touch interfaces trigger psychological ownership and endowment." *Journal of Consumer Psychology* 24.2 (2014): 226-233; Maddux, William W., et al. "For whom is parting with possessions more painful? Cultural differences in the endowment effect." *Psychological Science* 21.12 (2010): 1910-1917.

[11] Reisch, Lucia A., and Min Zhao. "Behavioural economics, consumer behaviour and consumer policy: state of the art." *Behavioural Public Policy* 1.2 (2017): 190-206; Soman, Dilip. "The mental

accounting of sunk time costs: Why time is not like money." *Journal of Behavioral Decision Making* 14.3 (2001): 169-185.

[12] Gourville, John, and Dilip Soman. "Pricing and the psychology of consumption." *Harvard business review* 80.9 (2002): 90-6.

[13] Sunstein, Cass R., and Richard H. Thaler. "Libertarian paternalism is not an oxymoron." *The University of Chicago Law Review* (2003): 1159-1202.

[14] Ibid., p. 1201.

[15] Thaler and Sunstein. *Nudge*, p. 5.

[16] Ariely, Dan. *The upside of irrationality*. New York: HarperCollins, 2010.

[17] Reisch and Zhao. "Behavioral economics, consumer behavior and consumer policy," p. 200.

[18] Kolenda, Nick. *Methods of Persuasion: How to Use Psychology to Influence Human Behavior*. Kolenda Entertainment, LLC, 2013. The word "ethics" only appears three times in the remainder of the book, and in none of those instances does the book offer guidelines for ethical use of its "methods of persuasion."

[19] Thaler, Richard H. "The power of nudges, for good and bad." *The New York Times* 31 (2015): 2015. Available online at https://nyti.ms/2KCI0eW.

[20] Ibid.

[21] The failure of laws and regulations to solve the problem of profits over welfare in the United States is expertly dissected by two Nobel Prize-winning economists in Akerlof, George A., and Robert J. Shiller. *Phishing for phools: The economics of manipulation and deception*. Princeton University Press, 2015.

[22] Sher, Shlomo. "A framework for assessing immorally manipulative marketing tactics." *Journal of Business Ethics* 102.1 (2011): 97-118.

[23] Ibid., p. 102.

[24] Ibid., p. 99.

[25] Ibid., pp. 99-100.

[26] Ibid., p. 107.

[27] Sher, "A framework for assessing immorally manipulative marketing tactics," p. 110.

[28] Ibid., p. 110.

Chapter 17. The Marketer's Dilemma

[1] From *Forward* to Samson, Alain. "The behavioral economics guide 2014 (with a foreword by George Loewenstein and Rory Sutherland)." (2014), p. x.

[2] An extensive list of "Common Biases and Heuristics" is maintained and updated regularly by behavioral scientist Tim Houlihan on his website. Accessible online at http://bit.ly/2OuWZuf.

[3] Tversky, Amos, and Daniel Kahneman. "Judgment under uncertainty: Heuristics and biases." *Science* 185.4157 (1974): 1124-1131, p. 1124.

[4] The first, and still highly cited, treatment of information asymmetry in economics was Akerlof, George A. "The Market for 'Lemons': Quality Uncertainty and the Market Mechanism." *The Quarterly Journal of Economics* 84.3 (1970): 488-500. Akerlof looked at the used car market as an example of information asymmetry between buyers and sellers. In his case, the information was about the product

itself, that is, the *content* of the offering. Today, behavioral designs and choice architectures expand the scope of information asymmetry from content knowledge to *form* and *context* knowledge.

[5] Sher, Shlomo. "A framework for assessing immorally manipulative marketing tactics." *Journal of Business Ethics* 102.1 (2011): 97-118, p. 99.

[6] See Hotchkiss, Gordon. "Aligned intent: A different ad engagement metric." *Out of My Gord* blog, November 26, 2009. Available online at http://bit.ly/2yHsMgw.

[7] Schmitt, Bernd. "The consumer psychology of brands." *Journal of consumer Psychology* 22.1 (2012): 7-17.

Made in the USA
Columbia, SC
09 December 2020